Digital UNIX System Administrator's Guide

Digital UNIX System Administrator's Guide

Matthew Cheek

Digital Press

Boston Oxford Auckland Johannesburg Melbourne New Delhi

Butterworth–Heinemann supports the efforts of American Forests and the Global ReLeaf program in its campaign for the betterment of trees, forests, and our environment.

Library of Congress Cataloging-in-Publication Data

Cheek, Matthew, 1965–
    Digital UNIX system administrator's guide / Matthew Cheek.
      p.   cm.
    Includes index.
    ISBN 1-55558-199-4 (pbk. : alk. paper)
    1. UNIX (Computer file)   2. Operating systems (Computers)
  I. Title.
  QA76.76.063C4573   1999
  005.4'32—dc21   98-45598
                                    CIP

British Library Cataloguing-in-Publication Data

A catalogue record for this book is available from the British Library.

Contents

Preface

This book, *Digital UNIX System Administrator's Guide*, is the first to address Digital Equipment Corporation's powerful 64-bit UNIX operating system from the viewpoint of a system administrator. Originally released in 1992, Digital UNIX, which runs on high performance Alpha microprocessor systems, has matured into the operating system of choice for a wide variety of applications ranging from Digital's groundbreaking AltaVista Internet Search service to the digital special effects renderings that have appeared in many recent Hollywood blockbuster films. Behind the scenes of these applications is the system administrator responsible for the care and feeding of these complex computer systems. With this book, I hope to meet the needs of the beginning Digital UNIX system administrator, while providing useful tips and resource information to the experienced administrator. If you are responsible for the management of Digital UNIX systems, either directly as a system administrator or indirectly as a manager or team leader, this book may be for you.

This volume is not intended as a replacement for the Digital UNIX product documentation; instead, it is offered as a complementary resource that addresses a broad range of system administration topics in what is hoped to be a more approachable style. In addition, I have tried to share useful, real-world system administration philosophies and techniques that the Digital documentation cannot. As to my success, I respectfully leave that judgment to the reader.

Acknowledgments

Without the contributions of some special folks over the last eighteen months, this book would never have seen the light of day. This support, both technical and moral, kept me going, especially in the last months of the project.

My technical reviewers, especially Colin Walters, have my gratitude. I appreciate their assistance and thank them all for wading through my material. Because of their comments, suggestions, and corrections, this is a better book than I could have done alone. Of course, any errors or omissions remaining are mine and mine alone.

I offer my sincere thanks to Gordon Voss and Bill Kirk of Digital Equipment Corporation for their assistance over the past year. They provided much needed insight into the varying needs of my audience.

I would also like to thank Dave Kastein for his support and encouragement during some very dark days. Your friendship means a great deal to me.

I cannot begin to express my gratitude to Liz McCarthy and Pam Chester, my editors at Digital Press, for taking a chance on me and supporting this project. Thanks for offering encouragement when I needed it and kicking me in the behind when that was warranted too. You two are a great team and do a mean "Good Cop/Bad Cop" routine.

Introduction to Digital UNIX System Administration

1

For all the advances in computing architectures and operating systems, complex computers still require a great deal of care and feeding. No operating system typifies this statement more than UNIX. Now UNIX is a mature operating system that runs on a wide range of systems—from small single-user desktops to the world's fastest supercomputers. The broad spectrum of applications that run on UNIX range from banking and financial applications to telecommunications and manufacturing processes. Simply put, UNIX is everywhere. However, for all its success in the marketplace and all the development work the various UNIX vendors lavish on fancy graphical user interfaces and dynamic this and automatic that, a UNIX system still, almost thirty years after its creation, cannot manage itself. Enter the UNIX System Administrator.

1.1. WHAT IS UNIX SYSTEM ADMINISTRATION?

A UNIX system administrator is the individual whose responsibility it is to manage the complex collection of hardware and software that is a UNIX system. The UNIX operating system comprises a wide variety of services and

1

processes that must be kept running and available and equally distributed among the system's users. A typical day for a UNIX system administrator may include installing systems, creating user accounts, stringing cables, troubleshooting and replacing failed hardware, performing system backups, and any of a hundred other tasks. UNIX system administration is frequently a thankless task. If everything is running smoothly, users and management often forget about the hard work that goes on behind the scenes. However, when a problem occurs and the system is down, it is frequently the system administrator who bears the brunt of user and management unhappiness.

Having said that, UNIX system administration is a booming career field frequently placed in the top-ten lists of the most popular or most needed occupations. UNIX system administrators seem to fall into one of three categories. The first is the individual who was "volunteered" for the job. These folks typically already have a "real" job, but for one reason or another, had the "system administration" role added to their job description. The second type is the professional system administrator who has chosen UNIX system administration as a primary career and has worked and studied to be the very best. This type of system administrator is becoming more common as colleges and universities continue to develop UNIX system administration curriculums and the career field gains respectability. Finally, perhaps the most common type of UNIX system administrator is the one who just accidentally became one. These folks stumbled into it after being programmers or engineers or something completely unrelated to computers, such as musicians. After discovering the ever-changing variety, constant challenges, and deep satisfaction that comes from managing the complex entity that is a UNIX system, they were hooked.

Since you are holding this book, I can safely assume that you are responsible for, or at least interested in, the administration of a Digital UNIX system. Digital UNIX is one of many implementations of the UNIX operating system, and while many aspects of using a UNIX system is similar from one flavor to another, the details of UNIX system administration are all too frequently very much vendor-specific. Because of this, vendor-specific UNIX system administration books will continue to be necessary.

Before outlining the topics covered by this text, it might be helpful to understand the history of Digital UNIX and what versions of the operating system will be addressed in these pages. Following this will be a brief discussion of the Alpha family of systems.

Digital UNIX was originally called "DEC OSF/1" since it was based on the Open Software Foundation's OSF/1 UNIX standard. Version 1.0, the first fully supported OSF/1 version, was released in March of 1992. This version was primarily an internal release and was not shipped to customers. A year later, Digital shipped OSF/1 version 1.2 to customers. This version, the first fully functional release, was also the first that supported the new Alpha-based systems. From this point forward, OSF/1, and later Digital UNIX, would only run on systems with Alpha processors. Throughout the rest of 1993, Digital continued to release minor updates to OSF/1, each adding new functionality or support for new hardware. In March of 1994, Digital released OSF/1 version 2.0. This was a major release that introduced many of the modern operating system features, such as the Advanced File System (AdvFS) and CD-ROM, RAID, and Token Ring support. The next major release of OSF/1 was version 3.0 in August of 1994. This release continued the tradition of enhancement by adding support for Symmetric Multiprocessing (SMP) and loadable drivers. Following in February of 1995 was version 3.2 of OSF/1, which added support for Asynchronous Transfer Protocol (ATM) and the Common Desktop Environment (CDE). Shortly after the release of version 3.2, Digital announced that the name of the operating system would be changed from DEC OSF/1 to Digital UNIX. This was primarily a marketing decision made to better differentiate the product in an increasingly crowded market. Finally, version 4.0 of Digital UNIX was released in March of 1996. This version added a host of new features to improve system management, portability, and performance. At the time of this writing, the most current release of Digital UNIX is version 4.0D. This book will primarily discuss system administration on Digital UNIX version 3.2 and later. Where there are differences between version 3.2 and 4.0, they will be noted.

The future of Digital UNIX looks very bright. The 64-bit operating system combined with the 64-bit architecture of the Alpha processor, positions Digital UNIX in the lead for high-performance UNIX platforms.

Note that Digital Equipment Corporation is now part of Compaq. As of this writing, the name "Digital UNIX" has not changed and it is likely that the name will persist and have market recognition for some time.

1.2. THE ALPHA ARCHITECTURE

Digital Equipment Corporation was a trailblazer in the area of 64-bit RISC microprocessors with its family of Alpha processors. Digital UNIX is currently married to the Alpha processor as it is the only supported computer at the present time. This may change in the future, but for now, if you are running Digital UNIX, you are running it on a system with an Alpha microprocessor.

The Alpha RISC processor was announced by Digital in February of 1992, and its top speed was 200MHz. This was an astonishing feat since the Alpha's contemporaries were running at speeds in the double digits. Digital followed up by announcing the first generation of Alpha-based systems in November of that same year. The first lineup ranged from the DEC 3000 workstation and the DEC 4000 departmental server, all the way to the mainframe class DEC 7000 and 10000 systems. In October 1993, the second-generation Alpha systems were delivered. This strengthened Digital's lead in high-performance systems. Six months later, Digital announced the Alphaserver 2100, which was one of the first of a new breed of Alpha-based multiprocessing midrange servers. The 2100 quickly became a best-seller for Digital. In August of 1995, Digital announced the 300MHz Alpha, and eight months later it delivered the Alphaserver 8400 supporting up to twelve of the new 300MHz processors. The 8400 was truly a mainframe replacement system and broke every performance record in existence. Digital continued pushing the Alpha technology and announced 500MHz parts in July 1996. At the time of this writing, 600MHz Alpha-based systems are being shipped, 750MHz Alpha chips are being announced, and 1GHz processors are being hinted at by Digital.

From the very first Alpha to today's fastest system, the compatibility has been maintained. Digital UNIX runs on the entire range of Alpha-based systems. Digital has ceased supporting the Digital UNIX product on the very earliest Alpha systems, but there is a good possibility that the operating system, or certainly an older revision, will run.

1.3. THE ORGANIZATION OF THIS BOOK

This text is divided into eleven chapters, each covering a different topic or discipline. Note that the book is not intended to replace the Digital UNIX documentation. Rather, it is humbly presented as a supplement. Having said that, I also hope that I was able to present many of the topics in a way that assists you, the Digital UNIX system administrator, in successfully managing your system.

1.3.1. Installation

Before a Digital UNIX system can be administered, it must be installed. The steps necessary to prepare a system for installation and to successfully install Digital UNIX are covered in Chapter 2.

1.3.2. System Configuration

Once a Digital UNIX system is successfully installed, there are many configuration activities that must take place before the system is ready for use. These include planning for and configuring disks and file systems, as well as managing software and licenses, all of which are discussed in Chapter 3.

1.3.3. User Accounts and Security

The most visible of system administration responsibilities is managing users. Chapter 4 covers user account management, and Chapter 5 covers the maintenance of system integrity and security.

1.3.4. Processes, Resources, and Services

A great deal of a system administrator's time and energy is spent managing the myriad UNIX processes, resources, and services. Users learn to depend on the availability of their favorite subsystem, and your job is to make sure that these many services are available and managed correctly. These topics are discussed in Chapters 6 and 7.

1.3.5. Networking

Chapter 8 covers the configuration of the TCP/IP networking subsystem and associated services on a Digital UNIX system. This is an important responsibility as more and more systems are networked to shared resources and distribute loads.

1.3.6. Performance Monitoring and Tuning

Chapter 9 looks at some of the tools and techniques that can be used to identify and resolve performance problems on a Digital UNIX system. UNIX performance tuning is not an exact science, but after reviewing this chapter, a system administrator should be able to understand the variables that affect system performance.

1.3.7. Backups

Safeguarding the user community's data is a sacred trust for a system administrator. Chapter 10 explains the development of a backup strategy and covers the various backup and recovery tools provided on Digital UNIX.

1.3.8. Troubleshooting and Recovery

Finally, what happens when something breaks? Chapter 11 covers system monitoring and error recovery techniques, and introduces several Digital UNIX tools for troubleshooting hardware and software problems.

Installation

2

The initial installation of a Digital UNIX system can be an exciting process. Whether the installation is on a brand-new system or a complete reinstallation of an existing system, the opportunity exists to define many aspects of the final configuration. The key to achieving the desired results is thorough planning. Some of the configuration decisions to be made prior to starting a Digital UNIX installation are disk and file system layouts, the method of installation, and which optional Digital UNIX software to install. In the first part of this chapter I will cover some of these issues that should be considered.

Once you have decided how the system will be configured, it is necessary to ensure that the system is properly prepared for the installation. This means that all components of the system are at the proper firmware revision for the version of Digital UNIX you will be installing. In addition, depending on the method of installation selected, either a local CD-ROM drive must be installed or, if installing from a Remote Installation Server (RIS), the system must be connected to a network. Next, you must have console access to the system. This console can be a serial terminal or a graphics display; Digital UNIX supports installations from either console type. Next, your system needs a suitable boot disk. This requirement may seem obvious, but I mention it because Digital hardware makes it very easy to have multiple versions of Digital UNIX installed on a system. This capability can allow you to evaluate a new version of Digital UNIX by installing the later version on a spare disk rather than upgrading your current version. Simply boot from that new installation and you can determine if the upgrade is right for you. Finally, the procedure for checking and updating system firmware is outlined.

I will then describe the installation process and provide examples of both the character-based install sequence and the graphical installation utility available on Digital UNIX version 4.0 and above. Regardless of which installation interface is used, you will have the ability to select the boot disk, the root, swap, and user partitions and file system types, and the Digital UNIX software subsets to install. After loading the selected subsets, the installation program prompts you to rebuild the kernel. I will provide guidelines for selecting which optional software subsets to install and which kernel options to select.

Once the installation is complete and the system reboots, the remaining system configuration must be done before the system is ready for use. In this chapter I will touch briefly on some of this configuration, but the bulk of the post-installation configuration will be covered in Chapter 3, "System Configuration." Other areas of system configuration, such as user accounts and network management, are dealt with in Chapters 4 and 8, respectively.

An alternative to doing a full installation is an update installation. An update installation updates an existing Digital UNIX system to a later version. For instance, you can do an update installation to update a Digital UNIX 3.2G system to Digital UNIX 4.0A. An update installation preserves existing disk partitioning, file systems, user accounts and files, and the network and printer configuration. The advantage of an update installation over a full installation is that all local customizations remain intact. The details of an update installation are covered; some of the limitations of an update installation are also mentioned.

Finally, Digital's Remote Installation Services (RIS) will be explained. RIS is a facility for installing a Digital UNIX system from a remote server that contains the Digital UNIX distribution. The main advantage of RIS is that multiple systems can be installed without having to have the Digital UNIX distribution CD-ROM in each system. All that is required is copying the Digital UNIX distribution into a remote installation environment on an already installed system that will function as the RIS server. Once this RIS environment is configured and remote clients are registered with the RIS server, remote installations on those remote clients can begin. The special requirements of using RIS will be detailed.

2.1. DIGITAL UNIX PRE-INSTALLATION PLANNING

In order to guarantee a successful Digital UNIX installation, there are several areas that require some consideration and planning. These include:

- Installation Media (Local CD-ROM or RIS Server)
- Installation Method (Default, Custom, or Cloned)
- Selection of Optional Subsets
- Boot Disk Partitioning (Size and Location)
- File System Type
- Swap Areas (Size and Quantity)

2.1.1. Review Digital UNIX Installation Documentation

The very first step is to read the *Digital UNIX Installation Guide* and the *Digital UNIX Release Notes* for the version of Digital UNIX you are planning to install. Both of these documents contain information that will assist you while planning the installation. While a few of these issues can wait to be resolved until after the system installation is complete, most must be decided before the installation can begin.

The *Digital UNIX Installation Guide* is the authority for the installation process. This manual contains specific information for each computer system supported by the version of Digital UNIX covered by the document. This information includes the required console flag settings and instructions on initially booting the system to begin the installation, either from CD-ROM or over a network connection to an RIS server. In addition, the processor-specific section indicates any unique settings or requirements necessary to install Digital UNIX. Finally, the "*Installation Guide*" contains detailed listings of the mandatory and optional software subsets contained in the particular version of Digital UNIX. This information includes subset descriptions and also lists the disk space requirements for each software subset. A separate section in the "*Installation Guide*" contains the default disk partitions for the supported Digital-manufactured disks.

The *Digital UNIX Release Notes* should also be read before beginning an installation. The *Release Notes* document any last-minute changes to either the particular version of the Digital UNIX software or to the installation process itself. Pay close attention to any section in the *Release Notes* that refer to either the type of Digital system being installed or to optional software subsets you have selected. In addition, the *Release Notes* describe features of

the operating system that are new or have changed significantly from previous releases of Digital UNIX.

Both the *Digital UNIX Installation Guide* and the *Digital UNIX Release
Notes* are included in the Digital UNIX Software Distribution Kit, along with
the Digital UNIX CD-ROM media. In addition, the most recent versions of
these two documents are available online via the World Wide Web (WWW)
at Digital's Publications homepage:

> http://www.unix.digital.com/faqs/publications/base_doc/
> DOCUMENTATION/HTML/Digital_UNIX_Bookshelf.html

2.1.2. Selecting Installation Media

The first choice you should make when planning a Digital UNIX installation is whether to install a system from a locally mounted Digital UNIX CD-
ROM or from a Remote Installation Services (RIS) server. Which method
you choose depends mostly on whether an RIS server is available. The special requirements of an RIS server may rule out an RIS installation. However, if an RIS server is available and reachable via the network and has the
correct version of Digital UNIX installed in its repository, RIS can simplify
a client system installation.

Regardless of whether an RIS server is available, installing a system via
a local CD-ROM is always an available option. The only requirements to do
so are the correct version of the Digital UNIX installation CD-ROM and a
CD-ROM drive connected to the target system. At a minimum, the only CD-
ROM that is required for a Digital UNIX installation is the Digital UNIX
base operating system software CD-ROM that is labeled "Digital UNIX Vx.yz
Operating System Volume 1"; here, the "x.yz" stand-in for the major, minor,
and maintenance release number and letter, such as 4.0B.

2.1.3. Selecting the Installation Method

The next decision that should be made concerns the installation type. This
choice assumes that you are conducting a new or overwrite installation;
update installations are discussed later in this chapter. The choices are
Default, Custom, and (new at Digital UNIX version 4.0 and above) Cloned
installations. The following describes these three types of installations.

2.1.3.1. Default Installation

The Digital UNIX Default Installation is the simplest installation type. When doing a default installation, only one decision is necessary: which disk will be the boot disk. No other installation options are presented. A default installation's characteristics are:

- A preselected set of Digital UNIX subsets is installed
- The boot disk is partitioned with the default layout
- The file system type for all file systems is the UNIX File System (UFS)
- The root file system is placed on the a partition
- A single swap area is placed on the b partition
- The /usr file system is placed on the g partition
- The /var file system is contained within the /usr file system
- The kernel is built with a minimal set of options

Once a system has been installed using the Default method and booted, further configuration changes may be made. For instance, optional software subsets may be installed, additional file systems may be created or more swap areas added, or the kernel may be rebuilt with different kernel options. The advantage of the Default installation method is that a system is installed using a predefined system configuration. This results in a quick and consistent system installation due to the lack of installation variables. The main constraint of the Default installation is the lack of control over the boot disk partitioning. However, if the Default installation is adequate for the requirements of the system, this installation type is sufficient. The Default installation is recommended for new system administrators, for it results in an installed Digital UNIX system that is configured with sane defaults for file system layouts, installed software, and kernel options with a minimum amount of user input.

2.1.3.2. Custom Installation

The Custom installation type is the exact opposite of a Default installation. Selecting a Custom installation provides the freedom to customize almost every aspect of the installation. This includes selecting the boot disk; specifying the location of the root, /usr, and, if desired, the /var file system; and specifying the location of the primary and secondary swap areas. When creating the file systems, the option of selecting either the UNIX File System (UFS) or the Advanced File System (AdvFS) is presented. In addition, the

Custom installation allows placing all file systems but the root file system on different physical disks.

Equally important, the opportunity is provided to select any or all optional Digital UNIX software subsets to be installed. The Custom installation option evaluates and resolves any subset dependencies, possibly selecting dependent subsets automatically. The ability to choose which kernel options will be built into the resulting Digital UNIX kernel is also provided.

A Custom installation provides the system administrator with nearly absolute control over the configuration of the resulting Digital UNIX system. Given adequate planning, the Custom installation is the recommended method of manually installing a Digital UNIX system. Of course, without the proper knowledge, selecting a Custom installation could result in a system either poorly configured or completely inoperable. The most important prerequisite to a Custom installation is disk planning. This includes determining the software subsets you wish to install; calculating the space required for the root, /usr, and /var file systems in addition to swap space requirements; being prepared to partition the disk(s) based on these calculations; and choosing the file system types.

2.1.3.3. Cloned Installation

New in Digital UNIX version 4.0 is the Cloned installation type. A Cloned installation is one in which a system is installed based on the contents of a predefined configuration file. This facility provides the ability to install a system with minimal user interaction. For sites with many similarly configured systems, this can result in quick, consistent, and accurate installations. The key to the Cloned installation is the Configuration Description File, or CDF. The CDF contains the following information describing how to install a system:

- Details about the file systems to be created, including name, disk, and partition in which they will reside, and file system type
- Swap area(s) to be created and disk and partitions where they will reside
- Installation Media (CD-ROM or RIS)
- Various system-specific details, such as host name, root password, geographic locations and time zone, and options to use when initially building the kernel
- Software subsets to be installed

See Figure 2.1 for an example of a CDF.

```
install:
      _item=Inst_islinfo
      media_type=CDROM
      server=rz
      _action=create
      srcloc=/ALPHA/BASE


install:
      _item=Inst_disklabel
      name=rz1
      a_size=262144
      a_offset=0
      b_size=262144
      b_offset=262144
      g_size=1090979
      g_offset=524288
      h_size=435593
      h_offset=1615267
      _action=create


install:
      _item=Inst_filesystem
      maj_min_num=8389632
      disk_number=1
      disk_name=rz1
      controller_type=SCSI
      name=root
      partition=a
      controller_number=0
      disk_type=RZ28
      file_system_type=UFS
      _action=create

                                          (continued)
```

Figure 2.1 A Sample Configuration Description File (CDF) from a Digital UNIX V4.0 Installation

```
install:
     _item=Inst_filesystem
     maj_min_num=8389632
     disk_number=1
     disk_name=rz1
     controller_type=SCSI
     name=usr
     partition=g
     controller_number=0
     disk_type=RZ28
     file_system_type=UFS
     _action=create

install:
     _item=Inst_filesystem
     maj_min_num=8389632
     disk_number=1
     disk_name="in /usr"
     controller_type=SCSI
     name=var
     partition=g
     controller_number=0
     disk_type=RZ28
     file_system_type=
     _action=create

install:
     _item=Inst_filesystem
     maj_min_num=8389632
     disk_number=1
     disk_name=rz1
     controller_type=SCSI
     name=swap1
     partition=b
     controller_number=0
```

Figure 2.1   Continued

```
           disk_type=RZ28
           file_system_type=swap
           _action=create

install:
    _item=Inst_subsets
names=OSFBASE410,OSFBIN410,OSFBINCOM410,OSFCDED
T410,OSFCDEMAIL410,OSFCDEMIN410,OSFCLINET410,OS
FCMPLRS410,OSFDPSFONT410,OSFFONT410,OSFHWBASE41
0,OSFHWBIN410,OSFHWBINCOM410,OSFKBDPCXAL410,OSF
MITFONT410,OSFNETCONF410,OSFNETSCAPE410,OSFNFS4
10,OSFNFSCONF410,OSFOLDX11410,OSFPRINT410,OSFSE
R410,OSFSYSMAN410,OSFTCLBASE410,OSFTKBASE410,OS
FX11410,OSFXADMIN410,OSFXPRINT410,OSFXSYSMAN410
    _action=create
    advflag=0

install:
    _item=Inst_cinstall
    timeset=yes
    password=qI/1tJg6egr6E
    locality=GMT
    _action=create
    hostname=saturn
```

Figure 2.1   Continued

When preparing for a Cloned installation, the CDF for a given system may be created from scratch as long as the documented layout and format are followed. Typically, however, a CDF for a new Cloned installation is based on an existing system that has a similar or identical hardware configuration. When Digital UNIX is installed on a system using either the Default or Custom method, a CDF is generated and placed in the /var/adm/smlogs directory and named install.cdf. This generated CDF can then be used as the source for further Cloned installations. For example, given a set of systems with the same or similar hardware configuration, the first system could be installed manually, then the resulting CDF could be used to replicate the remaining systems simply by changing the host name field. As this example shows, a Cloned installation is well-suited for the mass-installation of similar systems. However, with careful modifications to the CDF to describe a system's desired configuration, the Cloned installation can also be used to install individual systems. An example of this could be a site with a large quantity of differently configured systems that must be installed quickly and accurately. By preparing a set of CDFs ahead of time, one for each system, all the systems could be quickly and reliably installed with minimal system administrator involvement.

The CDF of the Cloned installation process only addresses the initial system installation and configuration and cannot, for example, change the default partitioning of the boot disk prior to or add user accounts after the installation. Digital has extended the Cloned installation, starting at version 4.0B, to allow for this type of optional pre- and postinstallation activity. See the Digital UNIX Version 4.0B or greater *Installation Guide*s for details on how to execute user-supplied scripts before or after the installation process.

2.1.4. Selection of Optional Subsets

During a Custom or Cloned installation, the opportunity to select from a set of optional software subsets is presented. This option is not available when doing a Default installation. Regardless of the installation type, however, optional software subsets may be installed after the system has been installed.

When installing Digital UNIX on a system, a mandatory set of subsets is selected for installation. This mandatory set includes a minimal set of software necessary for installation and basic functionality that is always selected. In addition, other mandatory software subsets are selected based on the hardware configuration of the system. For example, if the system has graphic capability, the minimal X-Windows environment subsets are also mandatory. Beyond these mandatory subsets, there are nearly 100 optional subsets that can be selected for installation during the initial system installation. These optional subsets fall into a dozen different categories:

- General Applications
- Mail Applications
- System Administration Tools
- Network Utilities
- Printing Environment

- X-Windows Applications
- X-Windows Environment Support
- Kernel Build Environment
- Kernel Development Environment
- General Software Development Environment
- Reference Pages
- Text Processing Utilities

The *Digital UNIX Installation Guide* contains descriptions of each of the various optional software subsets. Additionally, the *Installation Guide* contains an appendix detailing the disk space requirements for each of the mandatory and optional subsets. Before beginning a system installation, determining which optional subsets will be installed will assist you in disk planning (layout and sizing), which is the next step in installation planning.

Determining which optional subsets to select is best accomplished by first deciding how the system will be used. If, for instance, the system is a graphics workstation that will be used for software development, it is likely that many of the X-Windows and Software Development Environment optional subsets will be installed. Conversely, if a system will be a production server supporting remote clients, the installation of software development utilities or X-Windows applications and fonts would not be appropriate. Finally, if the system will run third-party applications, examine the installation documentation for these products to determine if they specify required Digital UNIX software subsets in order to operate.

One helpful strategy to selecting which optional subsets to install is to determine which subsets should not be installed. Once you have decided what not to install, select the remaining subsets for installation. Keep in mind that the selection or rejection of any particular subset is not permanent. If you determine after the system has been installed that some subsets that were not installed are required, simply install them from the installation media using the setld command. If it becomes apparent that some subsets that were initially installed are not necessary, removing them is equally simple. My recommendation, if you are unsure about whether to install a particular subset, is to select it for installation. Most Digital UNIX optional subsets function satisfactorily well together, and in my experience, selecting all optional subsets will result in a functioning, though not optimally configured, system.

There are some optional subsets that are fairly easy to rule out based on the hardware configuration of your system. For example, there are

separate X-Windows server subsets for specific supported graphics cards.
It is only necessary to load the subset for the graphics card installed in
your system. If a particular system has a PCI bus graphics card, the "X
Servers for PCbus" subset is the only necessary subset of these three:

```
X Servers for PCbus (Windowing Environment)
X Servers for Open3D (Windowing Environment)
X Servers for TurboChannel (Windowing Environment)
```

There is no point in installing the X Servers for Open3D or TurboChannel
when there is not an Open3D or TurboChannel graphics card present.
Likewise, if your system does not have ATM hardware, it is unnecessary to
load the following subsets:

```
ATM Commands (Network-Server/Communications)
ATM Kernel Modules (Kernel Build Environment)
ATM Kernel Header and Common Files (Kernel Build Environment)
ATM Kernel Objects (Kernel Software Development)
```

2.1.5. Boot Disk Partitioning

The Default installation type does not allow modification of the boot disk
layout, and when you are doing a Default installation there is no boot disk
planning necessary. For Custom or Cloned installations, however, the default
layout of the boot disk is likely to be inadequate, depending on the selection of optional software subsets. Once you have decided which optional
software subsets will be installed, the next step is to calculate the amount of
disk space required given that set of software. The *Digital UNIX Installation
Guide* lists the disk space requirements for each mandatory and optional
software subset. The sizes are listed as the number of 512-byte blocks required
in the root, /usr, and /var file systems. Simply consult the table in the *Installation Guide* and sum the values of each selected subset for each file system.
This will result in the minimum size of the root, /usr, and /var file system.
If /var will reside in the /usr file system, which is an option of the Digital
UNIX installation, add the /var size to the /usr file system size. Since the
Installation Guide lists subset sizes in 512-byte blocks, divide this value by
2048 to convert the size to megabytes. These resulting minimum values for
the root, /usr, and /var file systems, however, are just the base for calculating
the layout of the system disk. Other variables that influence disk layout are:

- The size and number of swap areas
- Crash dump space requirements
- The location of user home directories
- The file system type (UFS or AdvFS)

2.1.5.1. Swap Space Requirements

The Digital UNIX installation procedure requires that a primary swap space be allocated; it also provides the option to create a secondary swap space during the installation. By default, the primary swap space is placed on partition b of the system boot disk. This default location is by convention only, and the primary swap area can be located in any boot disk partition except partition a, which is required to be the root file system. Alternately, the primary swap area can be located on a disk other than the boot disk.

Unless special configuration requirements dictate otherwise, the recommended boot disk layout is to place the primary swap area on the boot disk in partition b. This will keep the boot partition and the primary swap partition together on the same disk and ensure that the system has, on a single disk, the necessary partitions to start up. Given this configuration, the optimal size of the primary swap partition depends on whether the system will have additional secondary swap partition(s). This decision is based primarily on the physical memory size of the system, as well as the size and number of disks in the system. If, for example, the system is a desktop AlphaStation with 64-megabytes of memory and two 2-gigabyte disks, a single 128-megabyte swap area on partition b of the boot disk is likely to be sufficient. A larger system, such as an AlphaServer with 512-megabytes or more of memory and many disks, may benefit from a primary 256-megabyte swap area on partition b of the boot disk plus two additional 512-megabyte secondary swap areas on other disks. These two examples illustrate the strategy of placing a relatively small primary swap area on the boot disk and, if necessary, placing secondary swap area(s) on other disks. Ideally, the size of the primary swap area should be 25% or less of the total size of the boot disk.

2.1.5.2. Crash Dump Space Requirements

When a Digital UNIX system crashes, by default the resulting crash dump is copied into /var/adm/crash by the savecore(8) utility. This crash dump is composed of a partial or full memory image at the time of the crash and a copy of the /vmunix kernel. The file system that contains the directory

/var/adm/crash must be large enough or, more accurately, have sufficient free space to contain at least one crash dump. The size of a system's crash dump is determined by two factors—the amount of physical memory and whether partial or full dumps are selected. On systems configured for full crash dumps, the /var/adm/crash area should be at least as large as the size of the system's physical memory, and on systems configured for partial dumps, can be somewhat smaller. I mention these crash dump requirements here only to let you be aware that initially this destination is contained in the /var file system, or in the /usr file system if a separate /var file system is not selected. Ensure that enough space is allocated for at least one crash dump in the file system where the /var/adm/crash directory will be.

One recommendation is to create a separate file system solely to contain crash dumps. Mount this file system either at /var/adm/crash, or select a different mount point and configure the system to save crash dumps to this new location. Following this strategy means that no space need be allocated in either the root, /usr, or /var file systems for crash dumps. See Chapter 11, "Troubleshooting and Recovery," for guidelines on configuring and managing crash dumps.

2.1.5.3. User Home Directory Location

The Digital UNIX user creation utilities, adduser, XsysAdmin, and the CDE Account Manager, all default to creating user account home directories in the /usr/users directory. Depending on the number of user accounts a system will support, this may be an unwise choice. A better alternative is to create a separate file system after the installation is complete to contain user account home directories. Placing user account home directories in a file system other then /usr, or for that matter the root or /var file system, prevents users from impacting system operation by filling any of these three important system file systems. If, however, the decision is made to place user account home directories in the root, /usr, or /var file system, a rule of thumb to follow is to allocate approximately 100-megabytes for each user account. This will provide some amount of buffer space to reduce the possibility of a particular user filling the system file system containing the home directories. Of course, decrease or increase this per-user disk space preallocation if you have an accurate understanding of the amount of disk space any particular user may need.

2.1.5.4. File System Overhead

After calculating the minimum size of the boot disk file systems based on the mandatory Digital UNIX subsets, plus any optional subsets, and taking into consideration the issues described above, the final variable in the boot disk partitioning equation is related to the choice of file system type for a particular file system. A certain percentage, depending on the file system type, of the total space allocated is unavailable for use. This percentage is approximated to be:

- UNIX File System (UFS): 4%
- Advanced File System (AdvFS): 5%

This means that when you are planning the size for a particular file system, this percentage should be added to the calculated value to arrive at a final partition size. This percentage is used by the operating system for file-system housekeeping. In addition, UFS file systems are created with an additional percentage of space marked as unavailable to non-root users. The root user or root-owned processes can make use of this reserved space. The percentage held back, by default 10%, can be changed by specifying a different value for the minfree parameter of the newfs(8) and tunefs(8) commands. See Chapter 3, "System Configuration," for details on adjusting this minfree value.

2.2. SYSTEM PREPARATION

Once the pre-installation planning has been completed, the next step prior to actually beginning the installation is ensuring that the system itself is suitably prepared. This means surveying the system to see that its configuration is compatible with a Digital UNIX installation. This is especially important for older systems, which may need to be updated to support the version of Digital UNIX being installed. The following are the system prerequisites of a Digital UNIX system installation:

- Any existing data is backed up
- Installation media is available
- A system console is in place
- A suitable boot disk is available
- The system's firmware is at the required version

2.2.1. Backup Existing Data

If the installation is to be onto a Digital system currently running an instance of either Digital UNIX or another operating system such as Open-VMS or Windows NT, take the time to back up any important data before proceeding to install Digital UNIX. This is not so much a requirement as a recommendation. Even if the system was being backed up regularly, make two copies of data deemed important and ideally make two full backups. This step is inexpensive insurance and could save you or your organization a great deal of pain.

2.2.2. Available Installation Media

This requirement simply means that the Digital system must have access to the installation media. If you will be installing Digital UNIX from the distribution CD-ROM, a CD-ROM drive must be installed on the target system and the selected version of the Digital UNIX distribution installation CD-ROM must be available. The only supported method of installing a stand-alone Digital UNIX system is by booting from the distribution CD-ROM and installing from that locally mounted media.

If, however, you plan on installing the system from an RIS (Remote Installation Services) server, the target system must be connected to a network via Ethernet, Token Ring, or FDDI. The RIS server must be reachable by the target system across the network, and, unless special requirements are met, both the target system and the RIS server must be on the same network segment or subnet in order to allow remote booting. In addition, the target system must be registered as a client with an RIS server that is serving the desired version of Digital UNIX. This registration procedure and the details of configuring an RIS server are covered in the RIS section of this chapter.

2.2.3. System Console

In order to install Digital UNIX, the target system must have a system console. The system console is the display/keyboard from which many important system administration activities, including installation, must occur. There are two types of supported system consoles for Digital systems:

- A graphical display, keyboard, and mouse, such as those commonly found on a desktop workstation
- A character-based display and keyboard, such as a serial terminal connected to the system's console or serial port

An additional supported console interface is a modem connected to the console port, but this feature is only available on Digital AlphaServers that support Remote System Management. This allows a remote system to be installed over a dial-up connection. Consult the system documentation to determine if this remote console is an option for your system.

If you are installing Digital UNIX version 3.2G or earlier, a character-based installation utility is presented regardless of whether the system's console has graphics capabilities or not. If, however, Digital UNIX version 4.0 or greater is being installed on a system with a graphical display and 32-megabytes or more of memory, a graphical point-and-click Installation Setup application is displayed. The two installation procedures, text-based and graphical, provide equivalent flexibility when installing a Digital UNIX system.

2.2.4. System Disk

Before beginning a Digital UNIX installation, the disk that will be the system disk must be selected. The system disk, or more accurately the disk that will contain the root file system, will be the disk from which the installed operating system will boot from. There are two requirements for this disk:

- The selected disk must be one of the supported disks specified in the Digital UNIX Software Product Description (SPD). It may be possible to successfully install Digital UNIX on a disk not listed, but Digital may or may not provide support in the event of problems. Since most Digital systems are delivered with at least a single disk, I strongly recommend that the system disk be one of the supported types.
- The selected disk must have partition a available. The Digital UNIX root file system must be located on partition a, and this partition must start at block 0 and be, at a minimum, at least 48 megabytes in size. Digital recommends that the root partition actually be 64 megabytes or greater.

A complete Digital UNIX operating system installation can reside on a single, sufficiently large disk. Such an installation would mean the root and /usr file system, plus a swap partition are contained on one disk. This is a perfectly acceptable configuration, especially for a small desktop or server system. However, only the root file system must reside on the system disk. Other file systems and swap partitions can be placed on additional disks. For instance, the custom installation allows the selection and creation of a root file system, a /usr file system, a /var file system, and two swap partitions. By placing each of these on distinct disks, a custom Digital UNIX installation could be placed on five disks.

2.2.5. System Firmware

Before beginning a Digital UNIX installation, you must check that the version(s) of firmware on the target system are at a minimum level for the version of Digital UNIX to be installed. Firmware is software that is stored in programmable read-only memory (PROM) on a Digital Alpha system that is responsible for certain hardware behavior. The most important firmware on an Alpha system running Digital UNIX is the System Reference Manual, or SRM Console firmware. This firmware is commonly referred to as simply the Console Firmware, and its main role is to load the Digital UNIX operating system from disk or from a network and then pass control to it. The SRM is also where a Digital UNIX installation is begun from.

Other firmware to be aware of includes:

- Advanced RISC Computing (ARC) Console
- EISA Configuration Utility (ECU) Firmware
- I/O Adapter Firmware

The ARC console is an alternate console firmware that supports Windows NT. If you choose to run Windows NT on a Digital Alpha system, you must switch from the SRM console to the ARC console. For Alpha systems running either Digital UNIX or OpenVMS, the ARC console is rarely used. The main exception is the requirement to switch to the ARC console in order to run certain configuration utilities.

The ECU Firmware is used on Digital Alpha systems with an Extended Integrated System Architecture (EISA) bus. While most newer Digital Alpha systems use the PCI bus for expansion cards, many Digital Alpha systems also support the EISA bus. Before installing Digital UNIX on a system with an EISA bus, you must run the EISA Configuration Utility to configure any installed EISA boards. The ECU is typically included on a separate floppy disk. Refer to the system owner's guide for information on running the ECU.

Many Digital I/O boards also have their own firmware that define their functionality. Some examples of these boards include SCSI adapters, RAID controllers, and I/O modules. The firmware level on any such components in a system must be verified to be at a minimum level for the version of Digital UNIX being installed.

2.2.6. Determining Firmware Requirements and Current Version

Before installing Digital UNIX, make sure that your system has the correct Console Firmware version. To determine the minimum firmware revision, consult the *Digital UNIX Installation Guide* for the version of Digital UNIX being installed. This manual contains a table titled "Minimum Firmware Revision Levels for Alpha Systems." Simply find the Alpha system model being installed in the table to determine the minimum Console firmware level for that version of the operating system. For instance, using Table 2.1, if Digital UNIX version 4.0B is to be installed on an AlphaServer 1000, the Console firmware must be at version 4.7 or higher.

Alpha System	Minimum Firmware Level
AlphaPC64 SBC	Version 4.5
AlphaPC164 SBC	Version 4.5
AlphaServer 300	System ships with correct firmware
AlphaServer 400	Version 6.3
AlphaServer 1000	Version 4.7
	(continued)

Table 2.1 Minimum Firmware Revision Levels for Alpha Systems—Digital UNIX V4.0B

AlphaServer 1000A	Version 4.7
AlphaServer 2000	Version 4.7
AlphaServer 2100	Version 4.7
AlphaServer 2100A	Version 4.7
AlphaServer 4000/4100	Version 3.0
AlphaServer 8200	Version 4.1
AlphaServer 8400	Version 4.1
AlphaStation 200	Version 6.3
AlphaStation 250	Version 6.3
AlphaStation 255	Version 6.3
AlphaStation 400	Version 6.3
AlphaStation 500	Version 6.3
AlphaStation 600	Version 6.3
Alpha VME 4/224	Version 1.0
Alpha VME 4/288	Version 1.0
Alpha VME 5/nnn	Version 1.0
AXPvme 64	Version 16.0
AXPvme 100	Version 16.0
AXPvme 160	Version 16.0
AXPvme 166	Version 15.0
AXPvme 230	Version 15.0
AXPpci	X4.7
DEC 2000	Version 2.2
DEC 3000	Version 6.9

Table 2.1 Continued

DEC 4000	Version 3.9
DEC 7000	Version 4.9
DEC 10000	Version 4.9
Digital Alpha VME 2100	Version 4.3
Digital 21064A PICMG Alpha CPU	X4.7
Digital 21164A PICMG Alpha CPU	X4.7
EB64+ SBC	Version 4.5
EB66+ SBC	Version 4.5
EB164 SBC	Version 4.5

Table 2.1 Continued

Once the minimum Console firmware level has been determined, display the target system's current Console firmware level by getting to the system's SRM Console prompt (>>>) and issuing the following command:

```
>>> show version
version   V4.0-4, 15-AUG-1996 15:02:37
```

In this example, the Console firmware version is 4.0-4. Again, referring to Table 2.1, the minimum required Console firmware level for Digital UNIX version 4.0B must be 4.7, this system's Console firmware must be updated prior to installing the operating system.

If the system is already up and running Digital UNIX, you can quickly determine the current Console firmware version by running the following command and searching for the "Firmware revision" entry in the output:

```
# /usr/sbin/uerf -R -r 300 | more
                        uerf version 4.2-011 (122)


********************* ENTRY 1. *********************


---- EVENT INFORMATION ----

EVENT CLASS       OPERATIONAL EVENT
OS EVENT TYPE     300.   SYSTEM STARTUP
```

```
SEQUENCE NUMBER        0.
OPERATING SYSTEM          DEC OSF/1
OCCURRED/LOGGED ON         Wed Aug 13 14:53:23 1997
OCCURRED ON SYSTEM        saturn
SYSTEM ID   x00060011
SYSTYPE    x00000000
MESSAGE          Alpha boot: available memory from
                 _0x76e000 to 0x3fee000
                 Digital UNIX V3.2G (Rev. 62); Wed Jun
                 _11 10:07:10 MST 1997
                 physical memory = 64.00 megabytes.
                 available memory = 56.64 megabytes.
                 using 238 buffers containing 1.85
                 _megabytes of memory
                 AlphaServer 1000 4/266
                 Firmware revision: 4.0
                 PALcode: OSF version 1.45
```

Note that new Digital Alpha systems may have a higher firmware revision than the firmware level specified in the latest version of Digital UNIX. A higher firmware revision usually indicates changes to support the operating system version that shipped with the system. Digital recommends that Alpha systems should not be loaded with earlier versions of firmware than is currently installed. An exception to this recommendation might be if a firmware upgrade caused system problems and it became necessary to back-out the firmware upgrade to the previous version.

2.2.7. Upgrading Firmware

If it is determined that the Console firmware needs to be upgraded before a Digital UNIX installation can begin, the procedure for updating a system's firmware follows. Updating the Console firmware is a fairly quick procedure, and there are three main update methods supported by Digital:

- A Digital Alpha Systems Firmware Update CD-ROM
- A bootable floppy disk
- Over a network using the BOOTP protocol

Each of these three methods are basically different ways to load and run the firmware update utility on the target system. Once this update utility is running, the procedure to actually update the firmware is identical regardless of the delivery method (CD-ROM, floppy, or BOOTP).

Below are details on using each of these delivery methods followed by the generic instructions for the actual firmware update utility. In each of the following sections, the particular boot device (CD-ROM, floppy, or the network for BOOTP) is referenced. Enter the following command from the SRM Console prompt (>>>) to determine this boot device on your system:

```
>>> show device
```

A device information table similar to the following is displayed:

```
dka0.0.0.6.0          DKA0          RZ26N 0568
dka100.0.0.6.0        DKA100        RZ26N 0568
dka300.3.0.6.0        DKA300        RRD45 0436
dva0.0.0.1000.0       DVA0
ewa0.0.0.11.0         EWA0          00-00-F8-01-42-5F
pka0.7.0.6.0          PKA0          SCSI Bus ID 7
```

The second column displays the boot device name for each device in the table. For network interfaces, the hardware address (MAC address) is shown in the third column. For instance, using the above table:

- DKA300 is the CD-ROM drive
- DVA0 is the floppy disk
- EWA0 is the Ethernet network interface (See Table 2.2 for other network interfaces types)
- 00-00-F8-01-42-5F is the network interface hardware address

2.2.7.1. Firmware Update CD-ROM

The simplest method of loading the firmware update utility is via a Digital Alpha Systems Firmware Update CD-ROM. This CD-ROM is usually included with the Digital UNIX Software Distribution Kit, but is occasionally shipped separately from Digital as the CD-ROM is updated on a quarterly basis. This CD-ROM is "versioned" and contains the latest version of the Console firmware for each Digital Alpha system. The Firmware Update CD-ROM also contains one previous version of each system's Console firmware so that the firmware can be downgraded in the event a problem arises after updating a system to the latest version. In addition, system-specific *Release Notes* on the CD-ROM provide information about the Console firmware

Network Interface Type	Boot Device
Ethernet (TULIP chip, DECchip 21040)	ewa0
Ethernet (LANCE chip, DEC 4220)	era0
Ethernet (ISA LeMAC)	ena0
EISA (Extended Integrated System Architecture) FDDI	fra0
PCI (Peripheral Component Interconnect) FDDI	fwa0
Turbochannel FDDI	"#/ez0"
XMI (Extended Memory Interface) FDDI	fxa0

Table 2.2 Network Interface Boot Devices

version. See Table 2.3 for the minimum acceptable Digital Alpha Systems Firmware Update CD version for recent versions of Digital UNIX.

2.2.7.2. Booting from the Firmware Update CD-ROM

To boot from the Firmware Update CD-ROM, simply insert the CD into the CD-ROM drive and from the SRM Console prompt (>>>), issue the following command:

```
>>> boot <CD-ROM drive Device Name>
```

Substitute the previously determined CD-ROM device name in the boot command. Using the previous example, the command would be:

```
>>> boot DKA300
```

The system will then proceed to boot from the Firmware Update CD-ROM, and after several minutes of boot activity, the first screen of system-specific "README-First" information announcements will be displayed. This README information may include details of firmware changes or enhancements, known problems, and the directory location on the CD of the firmware *Release Notes*. Simply press the <Return> key to scroll through the information or press <CTRL/C> to skip the remainder of the screens. I recommend that this information be scanned for issues that may impact your system.

DU Version	Minimum Acceptable Firmware CD Version
V3.0	V2.9
V3.0B	V3.0
V3.2	V3.1
V3.2A	V3.1
V3.2B	V3.2
V3.2C	V3.3
V3.2D	V3.4
V3.2E	V3.5
V4.0	V3.5
V3.2F	V3.6
V3.2G	V3.6
V4.0A	V3.7
V4.0B	V3.8
V4.0C	V3.9
V4.0D	V5.0

Table 2.3 Minimum Acceptable Firmware CD-ROM Version for Recent Digital UNIX Versions

After the final screen of README information, the default firmware update utility "bootfilename" will be displayed, followed by the prompt "Bootfile:". At this point, simply press <Return> to load the default (latest) version of the update utility, or type a specific firmware update utility bootfilename to load an alternate, usually older version. For example:

```
The default bootfile for this platform is
        [ALPHA1000]AS1000_E4_V4_8.EXE
Hit <RETURN> at the prompt to use the default bootfile.
Bootfile:
```

After either selecting the default or an alternate firmware update utility boot-filename, the system will proceed to load that version and present the main menu of the firmware update utility. Continue to section 2.2.10., "Firmware Update Utility," later in this chapter to proceed with the firmware update.

2.2.8. Bootable Firmware Update Floppy Disk

While the Alpha Systems Firmware Update CD-ROM is the most convenient method of updating a system's firmware, there may be times when using the CD-ROM is not possible. Perhaps the correct CD-ROM is simply unavailable, or Digital has released an interim firmware release between the regularly scheduled releases of the Firmware Update CD-ROM, which is upgraded quarterly. For these situations, Digital has provided a second method of updating an AlphaSystem's firmware: a bootable floppy disk. Updating a system via a bootable floppy is not as convenient as a CD-ROM since you must download the necessary firmware image from Digital and copy this image to a floppy disk. The advantage, of course, is that if you need the very latest firmware update, you do not have to wait for the next release of the Firmware Update CD-ROM.

Digital provides a Website specifically for the distribution of firmware updates. This page provides the contents of the most recent Firmware Update CD-ROM for those without access to a local copy. In addition, any interim firmware updates that have not yet been released on a Firmware Update CD-ROM are also available for download. The firmware updates are listed by supported Alpha systems. The URL for this Firmware Update page is:

> http://ftp.digital.com/pub/DEC/Alpha/firmware

Additionally, the firmware updates are also available via anonymous FTP from:

> ftp://ftp.digital.com/pub/DEC/Alpha/firmware

Each system has its own directory containing the appropriate firmware updates. The /pub/DEC/Alpha/firmware/vX.Y/doc/ directory (where X.Y is the version of the Firmware Update CD-ROM) contains the *Release Notes* for each system, as well as the necessary information for updating the firmware with from the images. The /pub/DEC/Alpha/firmware/readmes/ directory contains HTML and text files for each system, which describe the methods for updating the firmware from files downloaded from this FTP area. This "readmes" directory, in conjunction with the *Release Notes* for a given Alpha system, should provide the necessary information for updating a particular system's firmware. Any individual Alpha system firmware releases that occur between Firmware CD-ROM releases will be located in the /pub/Digital/Alpha/firmware/interim directory.

2.2.8.1. Creating a Bootable Firmware Update Diskette

The first step in updating an Alpha system's firmware via floppy disk is to create a bootable firmware floppy disk. Several prerequisites are necessary in order to create such a bootable diskette:

- The appropriate firmware update image for the system to be updated
- A 3.5-inch floppy diskette
- An Alpha system running Digital UNIX with a 3.5-inch floppy diskette drive

The third item is a requirement for both the system that will be used to actually create the bootable floppy disk and for the system whose firmware is to be updated via the resulting bootable floppy disk. Obviously, the system that creates the bootable floppy disk can be the same system being updated. Certain Digital Alpha systems (e.g., the AlphaServer 8200 and 8400) do not have floppy drives and, as such, cannot be updated via the bootable floppy disk. For the same reason, such Alpha systems cannot be used to create bootable floppy disk either.

2.2.8.2. Download the Firmware Image

Digital provides bootable firmware update images that fit on a single 3.5-inch floppy disk. Due to the limited capacity of a floppy disk, however, Digital prepares an individual image for each type of Alpha system, and the appropriate image must be downloaded for transfer to a floppy disk. Using either the Digital Alpha Systems Firmware Update Web page or Digital anonymous FTP server, download the appropriate image to a Digital UNIX system. The Firmware Update Web page makes it simple to download the correct file for a particular system; simply click on the link for the desired system, then scroll down to the "Boot Floppy (Digital UNIX systems)" section and select the link for the correct firmware update image.

In the event the Website is unavailable or inaccessible, firmware update images may also be downloaded from Digital's anonymous FTP server.

Unfortunately, you will have to know which file to download. Each individual system type's firmware update image is located in a directory named for the type of system. The naming convention of the firmware update image itself varies from system type to system type, but typically the file name contains the system type, optional architecture, version, and ends with a ".exe". For example, consider these two examples:

```
Digital Alpha System Model        Firmware Update
                                    Image File
AlphaStation 255 Model 4/xxx      as255_v7_7.exe
AlphaServer 1000 Model 4/xxx      as1000_e4_v5_0.exe
```

The following is an example session of downloading a firmware update image for an AlphaServer 1000 Model 4/xxx:

```
# ftp ftp.digital.com
Connected to ftp.digital.com.
220 gatekeeper.dec.com FTP server (Version 5.181 Fri Jun 16
  12:01:35 PDT 1995) ready.
Name (ftp.digital.com:root): anonymous
331 Guest login ok, send ident as password.
Password:
230 Guest login ok, access restrictions apply.
Remote system type is UNIX.
Using binary mode to transfer files.
ftp> cd /pub/DEC/Alpha/firmware/v5.0/alpha1000
250 CWD command successful.
ftp> get as1000_e4_v5_0.exe
200 PORT command successful.
150 Opening BINARY mode data connection for as1000_e4_v5_0.exe
  (1216512 bytes).
226 Transfer complete.
1216512 bytes received in 3.5 seconds (3.4e+02 Kbytes/s)
ftp> bye
221 Goodbye.
#
```

Once the appropriate firmware update image has been downloaded, rename the resulting file to fwupdate.exe. This is a requirement of the bootable floppy creation process.

2.2.8.3. Download the Bootable Floppy Creation Utility

Digital provides a utility, mkbootfirm, that is used to convert the down-loaded firmware update image to the appropriate format for copying to a low-level formatted floppy disk. This utility is available from the same Web page or FTP site as the firmware update images. The URL for this utility is:

> ftp://ftp.digital.com/pub/DEC/Alpha/firmware/utilities/
>   mkbootfirm.tar

Download this file to a convenient place on your Alpha system and unpack it with the following command:

```
# tar -xvf mkbootfirm.tar
```

This will result in a directory named mkbootfirm in the current directory that contains the mkbootfirm utility itself and a README file.

2.2.8.4. Create the Bootable Floppy

Once you have downloaded the firmware update image and the mkboot-firm utility, the next step is to create a bootable firmware update floppy. Insert a blank or scratch 3.5-inch floppy disk into the floppy drive and low-level format the diskette with the following command. Note that this command is for a floppy in the first floppy drive. If the diskette is in a second floppy drive, substitute "rfd1a" for "rfd0a":

```
# fddisk -f -fmt /dev/rfd0a
```

After low-level formatting the floppy, transfer the firmware update image to the diskette with the following command:

```
# mkbootfirm fwupdate.exe | dd of=/dev/rfd0c bs=64k
```

This command assumes that the firmware update image has been renamed "fwupdate.exe" and that the floppy disk is in the first floppy drive.

2.2.8.5. The I/O Options Firmware Update Floppy Disk

The limited capacity of a 3.5-inch floppy disk prevents Digital from includ-ing any firmware images other than for the SRM and ARC consoles. Since some I/O options, such as SCSI adapters, network interface controllers, and I/O modules, also have upgradable firmware, Digital distributes firmware updates for these options also. If you wish to update these I/O options firmware when using the bootable floppy method, you must create a second floppy that contains these firmware updates. Creating an I/O options firmware update floppy disk is entirely optional—you will be prompted for it during the process of booting the console firmware update floppy disk. If you have elected not to create the I/O options firmware update diskette, simply press <Return> at that prompt.

These I/O option firmware updates are available as a single image from the same Web page or FTP site as the system firmware update images. The URL for this image is:

    ftp://ftp.digital.com/pub/DEC/Alpha/firmware/vX.Y/options/
    vZ_options.dd

where X.Y is the version of the Firmware Update CD-ROM and Z is the version of the I/O options firmware update image.

Once you have downloaded the I/O options firmware update image, the next step is to copy this image to a floppy disk. Insert a blank or scratch 3.5-inch floppy disk into the floppy drive and low-level format the diskette with the following command:

    # fddisk -f -fmt /dev/rfd0a

After low-level formatting the floppy, transfer the I/O options firmware update image to the diskette with the following command:

    # dd if=v39_options.dd of=/dev/rfd0c bs=64k

This command assumes that the I/O options firmware update image is named "v39_options.dd" and that the floppy disk is in the first floppy drive.

2.2.8.6. Booting from the Firmware Update Floppy Disk

To boot from a Firmware Update floppy disk, insert the floppy into the floppy drive and from the SRM Console prompt (>>>), issue the following command:

    >>> boot <floppy drive Device Name>

Substitute the previously determined floppy drive device name in the boot command. Using the previous example, the command would be:

    >>> boot DVA0

The system will then proceed to boot from the Firmware Update floppy disk, and after several minutes of boot activity, you will be prompted to insert a floppy containing option firmware. If an I/O Options Firmware Update diskette was previously created, remove the Firmware Update floppy and insert the I/O Options Firmware diskette and hit the <Return> key, otherwise simply hit the <Return> to continue. After this prompt, the load will proceed and finally present the main menu of the firmware update utility. Continue to section 2.2.10., "Firmware Update Utility," later in this chapter to proceed with the firmware update.

2.2.9. Updating Firmware Across the Network via BOOTP

Digital provides the ability to update an Alpha system's console firmware by booting a firmware update image located on another system across the network using BOOTP (Boot Protocol). This can be a useful alternative to either the Firmware Update CD-ROM or a bootable Firmware Update floppy disk, especially when there are many systems to be updated. Simply copy the appropriate firmware update image(s) to a suitable system and configure the BOOTP server on that system for each client system to be updated. Once these steps are completed, each target system can be booted from the BOOTP server and the firmware update can proceed. Note that as of version 5.0 of the Alpha Systems Firmware Update, there is no BOOTP support for updating the I/O options firmware—only the SRM and ARC firmware can be updated via BOOTP.

When selecting a system to be a BOOTP server for firmware updates, there are several requirements to consider. To be a BOOTP server, a system must be on the same network segment as the systems to be updated, and the systems must be able to communicate with each other. Check connectivity with the ping(8) command. See Chapter 8, "Networking," for details on Digital UNIX network configuration. In addition, the optional "Additional Networking Services" subset containing the BOOTP daemon must be loaded. This subset is named OSFINETxxx, where the "xxx" specifies the version of the subset. To determine if this subset is loaded, execute the following command, searching for the correct subset:

```
# /usr/sbin/setld -i | grep -i osfinet
OSFINET410   installed    Additional Networking
   Services (Network-Server/Communications)
```

Based on this output, the subset is installed. If you do not receive any output, or if the "installed" keyword in the second column is absent, you must install the subset from the master Digital UNIX operating system installation media using the setld command. For assistance in installing optional Digital UNIX subsets, see Chapter 3, "System Configuration."

2.2.9.1. Copy the Firmware Update Images to the Server

After determining that the chosen system meets the requirements of a BOOTP server, the next step is to copy the firmware update image(s) to a directory on the BOOTP server. The images can be copied from the Firmware Update CD-ROM or downloaded from Digital's Alpha Systems Firmware Update Website or FTP server. See earlier section 2.2.8.1., "Creating a Bootable Firmware Update Diskette," for details on downloading the appropriate firmware update image from Digital's Website or FTP server.

Place the resulting firmware update image(s) in a directory on the BOOTP server. A suggested directory is /usr/firmware, but the location is completely arbitrary. The following is an example session of mounting the Firmware Update CD-ROM and copying the firmware update image for an AlphaServer 1000 into a directory on the BOOTP server:

```
# mkdir /usr/firmware
# mount -rt cdfs -o noversion /dev/rz3c /mnt
# cp /mnt/alpha1000/as1000_e4_v5_0.exe /usr/firmware
```

2.2.9.2. Modify or Create the Client Entry in the /etc/bootptab File

The BOOTP daemon's configuration file is /etc/bootptab, and this configuration file is read when the daemon receives a boot request packet. This configuration file defines information for remote clients. Edit the /etc/bootptab file and add or modify an entry for each system whose firmware will be updated. The format of an /etc/bootptab client entry is:

```
<host_name>:ht=<hw_type>:ha=<hw_address>:bf=
    <filename>:ip=<ip_address>
```

where:

- host_name is the client's system name as specified in /etc/hosts.
- hw_type is the network interface type. Ethernet and FDDI are ht=1 and Regular token-ring (IEEE 802) is ht=6.

- hw_address is the network interface hardware address (MAC address): use the console command show device.
- filename is the full pathname of the bootable firmware update image
- ip_address is the corresponding Internet protocol address of the system name in /etc/hosts.

The following is an example of a bootptab file:

```
saturn:ht=1:ha=00-00-F8-01-42-5F:bf=/usr/firmware/
  as1000_e4_v5_0.exe:ip=10.0.0.5
```

2.2.9.3. Invoke BOOTP and tftpd daemons

In order to activate the BOOTP process, two system daemons must be enabled. The name of the BOOTP daemon itself depends on the version of Digital UNIX installed—on Digital UNIX version 3.2G and earlier, the daemon is named bootpd, while on version 4.0 systems, the BOOTP daemon is joind. The second necessary daemon is tftpd, the Trivial File Transfer Protocal Daemon. This daemon actually does the work of transferring the bootable firmware update image across the network to the client.

Both of these daemons are controlled by entries in the /etc/inetd.conf configuration file. Simply edit this file and modify or create the entries for the BOOTP and tftpd daemons. Ensure that the entries in /etc/inetd.conf for these daemons do not have a "#" character at the beginning of the line. For the BOOTP daemon, modify or create the correct entry (bootpd or joind), depending on the version of Digital UNIX installed. In addition, modify the tftpd entry to reflect the directory where the bootable firmware update image is by appending the directory name to the end of the line. The entries should be similar to the following examples:

```
tftp  dgram udp wait root /usr/sbin/tftpd tftpd
  /tmp /usr/firmware
```

For Digital UNIX version 3.2G and earlier:

```
bootps dgram udp wait root /usr/sbin/bootpd
  bootpd
```

For Digital UNIX version 4.0 and later:

```
bootps dgram udp wait root /usr/sbin/joind  joind
```

After creating or modifying the entries in the /etc/inetd.conf file, signal the inetd process to reread this configuration file by sending the process a hang-up signal. This enables the BOOTP process and causes future boot requests received by inetd to be forwarded to the BOOTP daemon. To force inetd to reread /etc/inetd.conf, issue the following command:

```
# kill -HUP `cat /var/run/inetd.pid`
```

2.2.9.4. Boot the Client

Once the appropriate bootable firmware update image is copied to the BOOTP server and the BOOTP and tftpd daemons are configured and enabled, the next step is to begin the firmware update from the client's console. From the client's SRM Console prompt (>>>), issue the following command:

```
>>> boot -protocol bootp <network interface Device Name>
```

Substitute the previously determined network interface device name in the boot command. Note that the "-protocol" option is used to specify the boot protocol—in this case BOOTP. Using the previous example, the command would be:

```
>>> boot -protocol bootp EWA0
```

The client system will then broadcast a BOOTP request packet and, if the BOOTP server is available and configured correctly, proceed to boot the firmware update image served by the BOOTP server. The following is an example session of booting a client with BOOTP:

```
>>>boot -protocol bootp EWA0
(boot ewa0.0.0.11.0 -flags A)
FRU table creation disabled

Trying BOOTP boot.

Broadcasting BOOTP Request...
Received BOOTP Packet File Name is:
  /usr/firmware/as1000_e4_v5_0.exe
local inet address: 10.0.0.5
remote inet address: 10.0.0.3
TFTP Read File Name:
  /usr/firmware/as1000_e4_v5_0.exe
```

```
netmask = 255.255.255.0
Server is on same subnet as client.
(The boot proceeds...)
```

After several minutes of boot activity, you will be prompted to hit the <Return> key. After this prompt, the load will proceed and finally present the main menu of the firmware update utility. Continue to the section 2.2.10., "Firmware Update Utility," below to proceed with the firmware update.

2.2.10. The Firmware Update Utility

Regardless of the method used to load the firmware update utility (CD-ROM, bootable floppy disk, or across the network via BOOTP), the process of actually updating a system's firmware is the same. Once the load process is complete, the main menu of the Firmware Update Utility is displayed:

```
***** Loadable Firmware Update Utility *****
_____

Function   Description
_____


Display  Displays the system's configuration table.
Exit  Done exit LFU (reset).
List  Lists the device, revision, firmware name, and
        update revision.
Readme  Lists important release information.
Update  Replaces current firmware with loadable data
        image.
Verify  Compares loadable and hardware images.
? or Help  Scrolls this function table.
_____

UPD>
```

The Firmware Update Utility's prompt is "UPD>" and the various functions are selected by entering the function name followed by <Return>. From this prompt, it is actually only necessary to enter the first letter of each of the functions. The first step is to issue the "List" command, which displays all firmware options available for update, their current revision, and the revision they would be updated to. For example:

```
UPD> list

Device    Current Revision    Filename    Update Revision
ARC       v4.52               arc_fw      v4.54
SRM       v4.8-65             srm_fw      v5.0-92
kzpsa0    A10                 kzpsa_fw    A11
kzpsa1    A10                 kzpsa_fw    A11
```

After listing the components available for firmware update, the next step is to actually do the firmware update. Simply issue the "Update" command to update all the devices to the firmware version displayed in the fourth column of the list output. If only a single device is to be updated, specify that device's name after the "Update" function. For instance, to update just the SRM, issue the following command:

```
UPD> update SRM
```

After entering the Update command, you will be prompted to confirm the update and, after entering a "Y", the update will begin. Once the firmware update has begun, it is important not to interrupt the update as one or more devices could be left in an inoperative state. Do not reset or remove power from the Alpha system being updated. An example update sequence:

```
UPD> update
Confirm update on:
ARC
SRM
kzpsa0
kzpsa1
[Y/(N)]y
WARNING: updates may take several minutes to complete
  for each device.
    DO NOT ABORT!

ARC  Updating to v4.54... Verifying v4.54... PASSED.
SRM  Updating to v5.0-92... Verifying v5.0-92...
  PASSED.
kzpsa0  Updating to vA11... Verifying vA11... PASSED.
kzpsa1  Updating to vA11... Verifying vA11... PASSED.
UPD>
```

Once the update is complete, the "Verify" function can be used as confirmation that the update was successful:

```
UPD> verify

ARC      Verifying v4.54... PASSED.
SRM      Verifying v5.0-92... PASSED.
kzpsa0   Verifying vA11... PASSED.
kzpsa1   Verifying vA11... PASSED.
```

Finally, issue the "Exit" command to exit from the Firmware Update Utility. This will reinitialize the system, and the value of the "auto_ation" console environmental variable will determine the system's next action. If "auto_action" is set to "BOOT" or "RESTART", the system will attempt to boot; if "auto_action" is set to "HALT", the system will return to the console prompt (>>>).

Note that the Firmware Update Utility may appear slightly different on different Alpha platforms. These differences are typically minor menu formatting changes or command output alterations. Read the firmware update *Release Notes* and readmes for the particular model and version being updated so as not to miss any new or changed features of both the Firmware Update Utility and the firmware upgrade itself.

2.3. DIGITAL UNIX INSTALLATION

After completing the necessary pre-installation planning and ensuring that the system itself is suitably prepared, you are ready to begin the actual installation of Digital UNIX on your system. In this section I will detail the actual installation process. I will also compare both the character and graphical installation utility interfaces. Note that the installation to be detailed here is a Full installation, where the Alpha system is booted from the installation media—either a local CD-ROM or across the network from an RIS server. An Update installation, which is detailed later in this chapter (see section 2.4.1., "Update Installation Steps"), is performed with the Alpha system running the version of Digital UNIX to be updated from single-user mode.

2.3.1. Full Installation Steps

    0. Complete pre-installation planning and preparation.
    1. Take the System to the Console Prompt (>>>). Power up the system. After the Power On Self-Test (POST) and other startup and

diagnostic messages, the console prompt should be displayed. If the system begins to boot, halt the system by pressing the Halt button. If the system is already running a version of Digital UNIX or another operating system, shutdown and halt the system with a command similar to the following:

```
# shutdown -h +1 "Shutting down for full installation"
```

2. Set the Necessary Console Flags. Refer to the "Processor-Specific Boot Instructions for Full Installations" chapter in the *Digital UNIX Installation Guide* for system-specific console variable settings. The following flags are typically specified on all Alpha systems prior to beginning a full installation:

   • This command clears the boot_osflags variable to ensure the kernel takes the correct action upon bootup:

   ```
   >>> set boot_osflags ""
   ```

   • This command sets the auto_action variable to halt, which causes the system to return to the console prompt after the system is powered up or initialized:

   ```
   >>> set auto_action halt
   ```

   • Typically, after the installation is complete, the auto_action variable is reset to "boot" or "restart" so the system will automatically boot upon power-up.

   This command sets the os_type variable to UNIX, which specifies that the SRM Console firmware will be booted when the system is powered on:

   ```
   >>> set os_type unix
   ```

3. Initialize the System. Whenever certain SRM environment variables are changed, it is necessary to reinitialize the system in order to activate the new variable values. Issue the following command from the SRM Console prompt (>>>) to reinitialize the system:

   ```
   >>> init
   ```

4. Identify Boot Device. Once the system has been reinitialized and the SRM Console prompt (>>>) is presented, enter the following command from the prompt to determine the boot device of either the CD-ROM or the network interface on your system:

```
>>> show device
```

A device information table similar to the following is displayed:

```
dka0.0.0.6.0          DKA0        RZ26N 0568
dka100.0.0.6.0        DKA100      RZ26N 0568
dka300.3.0.6.0        DKA300      RRD45 0436
dva0.0.0.1000.0       DVA0
ewa0.0.0.11.0         EWA0        00-00-F8-01-42-5F
pka0.7.0.6.0          PKA0        SCSI Bus ID 7
```

The second column displays the boot device name for each device in the table. For instance, using the above table:

- DKA300 is the CD-ROM drive—Use this boot device when installing from CD-ROM media
- EWA0 is the Ethernet network interface—Use this boot device when installing from an RIS server

(See Table 2.2 for other network interfaces types)

5. Boot from Installation Media. Boot the system and begin the installation by issuing the following boot command:

```
>>> boot <Device Name>
```

If you are installing from CD-ROM, substitute the previously determined CD-ROM device name in the boot command. Using the previous example, the command would be:

```
>>> boot DKA300
```

Output similar to the following will be displayed as the system boots from the CD-ROM:

```
(boot dka300.3.0.6.0 -flags a)
block 0 of dka300.3.0.6.0 is a valid boot block
reading 16 blocks from dka300.3.0.6.0
bootstrap code read in
Building FRU table
base = 1be000, image_start = 0, image_bytes = 2000
initializing HWRPB at 2000
initializing page table at 3ff0000
initializing machine state
setting affinity to the primary CPU
jumping to bootstrap code
```

```
Digital UNIX boot - Fri Nov 15 21:24:46 EST 1996
```

If the installation will be from an RIS server, boot from the network interface and specify the protocol as BOOTP. For example:

```
>>> boot -protocol bootp EWA0
```

Output similar to the following will be displayed as the system boots from the RIS server:

```
(boot fwa0.0.0.12.0 -flags a)
FRU table creation disabled

Trying BOOTP boot.

Broadcasting BOOTP Request...
Received BOOTP Packet File Name is: /var/adm/ris/ris0.alpha/hvmunix
local inet address: 10.0.0.5
remote inet address: 10.0.0.3
TFTP Read File Name: /var/adm/ris/ris0.alpha/hvmunix
netmask = 255.255.255.0
Server is on same subnet as client.
...................................
...................................
.................
bootstrap code read in
base = 1cc000, image_start = 0, image_bytes = 9d67a0
initializing HWRPB at 2000
initializing page table at 3ff0000
initializing machine state
setting affinity to the primary CPU
jumping to bootstrap code

Secondary boot program - Thu Jul 18 17:50:38 EDT 1996
```

6. Begin the Actual Installation. Once the system completes the boot process, what you see next depends on the version of Digital UNIX being installed and the system's hardware configuration. If you are installing Digital UNIX version 4.0 or greater and the system has a graphics console and 32 megabytes or more of memory, refer to section 2.3.2. If the system being installed has a serial console, less than 32 megabytes of memory, or a version of Digital UNIX prior to 4.0 that is being installed, refer to section 2.3.6.

7. Reboot the System. After the installation of the system is complete, the system is halted and a message is displayed on the screen instructing the installer to set several console variables and boot. For instance:

```
Issue the following console commands to set
your default bootpath variable and to boot your
system disk to multiuser:
>>> set boot_osflags A
>>> set bootdef_dev DKA0
>>> boot
```

Issuing these commands will boot the newly installed system to multiuser mode and continue the installation.

8. Initial System Configuration. After the newly installed system boots, the process of configuring the system begins. First, the mandatory and any optional software subsets are configured for the newly installed system. This software configuration occurs automatically with no user input necessary. The name of each software subset is displayed as it is configured. This process is fairly quick; depending on the number of installed subsets, the configuration should take no more than five minutes to complete. The output is similar to the following:

```
*** SYSTEM CONFIGURATION ***

Configuring "Base System " (OSFBASE410)
Configuring "Base System - Hardware Support " (OSFHWBASE410)
Configuring "Compiler Back End " (OSFCMPLRS410)
Configuring "Ref Pages: CDE Development " (OSFCDEMANOP410)
Configuring "Ref Pages: CDE Admin/User " (OSFCDEMANOS410)
Configuring "XIE Version 5 Online Documentation " (OSFXIEDOC410)
```

In addition, this initial system configuration is when the system's personality (host name, date and time, root password) are actually configured. If any of these parameters were not specified at the time of installation, you will be prompted to enter them at this point.

9. Kernel Build. Immediately after the initial system configuration, the system kernel is built for the first time. If a Default installation was performed, the kernel is built automatically with the mandatory kernel parameters for that system's configuration. For a Custom

installation, however, the installer is presented with a menu of available kernel options similar to the following:

```
*** KERNEL CONFIGURATION AND BUILD PROCEDURE ***

*** KERNEL OPTION SELECTION ***

 Selection   Kernel Option
_____

   1 System V Devices
   2 Logical Volume Manager (LVM)
   3 NTP V3 Kernel Phase Lock Loop (NTP_TIME)
   4 Kernel Breakpoint Debugger (KDEBUG)
   5 Packetfilter driver (PACKETFILTER)
   6 Point-to-Point Protocol (PPP)
   7 STREAMS pckt module (PCKT)
   8 X/Open Transport Interface (XTISO, TIMOD, TIRDWR)
   9 File on File File System (FFM)
  10 ISO 9660 Compact Disc File System (CDFS)
  11 Audit Subsystem
  12 ACL Subsystem
  13 Logical Storage Manager (LSM)
  14 LAN Emulation over ATM (LANE)
  15 Classical IP over ATM (ATMIP)
  16 ATM UNI 3.0/3.1 Signaling for SVCs
  17 Asynchronous Transfer Mode (ATM)
  18 All of the above
  19 None of the above
  20 Help
  21 Display all options again
_____

Enter the selection number for each kernel option you
  want.
For example, 1 3 [19]:
```

Select the desired kernel options that will be built into the resulting system kernel. In order for a functionality in this list to be available, that option must be installed into the kernel. Select only those kernel options necessary and appropriate for the system being installed. See the "Building the Kernel" section of the *Digital UNIX Installation Guide* for descriptions of each available option.

For instance, to use the Logical Storage Manager (LSM) on the system, the LSM kernel option must be selected. Note that an exception to this is the ISO 9660 Compact Disc File System (CDFS) option. Starting at Digital UNIX version 4.0D, this option is dynamically loaded by the kernel when a CDFS file system is mounted. This option may still be statically loaded into the kernel, but it is unnecessary and the resulting kernel will be larger, thereby consuming a small amount of memory at all times.

After selecting the desired kernel options, confirm your choices at a prompt similar to the following:

```
You selected the following kernel options:
     Point-to-Point Protocol (PPP)
     Logical Storage Manager (LSM)

Is that correct? (y/n) [y]:
```

At this point the following prompt will allow for manual editing of the configuration file of the kernel being built:

```
Do you want to edit the configuration file? (y/n) [n]: n
```

This configuration file might be edited to add or modify a kernel parameter whose value is then hardcoded into the resulting kernel. Typically the answer to this question is no, as Digital UNIX provides a system configuration file, /etc/sysconfigtab, that is read each time the system boots. This sysconfigtab file is a better place to add or modify such kernel variables, since all that is required to change them is to update their value in the file and reboot. There is no advantage to putting these variables in the kernel configuration file.

At this point, the system builds this initial kernel and then reboots. This completes the actual installation of Digital UNIX.

10. Login as Root to Continue System Configuration. After the system reboots, login as root using the previously specified root password to continue the system configuration. Refer to Chapter 3, "System Configuration," for details on configuring additional disks and file systems, terminals and modems, license management, and other important subsystems.

2.3.2. The Digital UNIX Graphics Installation Utility

When installing Digital UNIX version 4.0 or greater on a system that supports a graphic installation, an X-Windows server is started after booting from the install media and the Digital UNIX Installation Setup utility is displayed (Figure 2.2). This graphical Installation Setup utility supports both Default and Custom installations. In addition, the Installation utility allows individual disks to be custom partitioned by providing access to the Configure Partitions utility (Figure 2.3). The selection of which optional software subsets are to be installed is done from the Software Selection window (Figure 2.4). Finally, the UNIX Shell button on the main Installation Setup window permits file or disk maintenance while the system is in single-user mode. The UNIX shell option allows experienced system administrators to perform tasks before starting the installation.

The Installation Setup utility is an X-Windows application with a series of fields, buttons, and drop-down menus for entering system characteristic parameters. When the Installation Setup utility first starts, a Default Installation Type is automatically selected. As mentioned earlier, a Default installation is only appropriate for the most simple installations. As a result, several functions are disabled or unavailable when doing a Default installation. To perform a Custom installation, click on the Install Type button and switch from Default to Custom. This will enable the software selection and custom disk partitioning buttons, as well as allowing specification of the /usr and /var partions and file systems and swap partions.

2.3.2.1. Default Graphical Installation

When performing a Default installation, it is not necessary to enter any information; simply clicking the Setup Down button will cause the install to proceed. Certain parameters, such as the software subsets to be loaded, will default to preset values, and others, such as the date and time information and the root password, will be prompted for during the installation. However, unless there is a particular reason not to enter any parameters, I recommend entering the following parameters prior to starting a Default installation:

- Host name
- Root Password
- Date

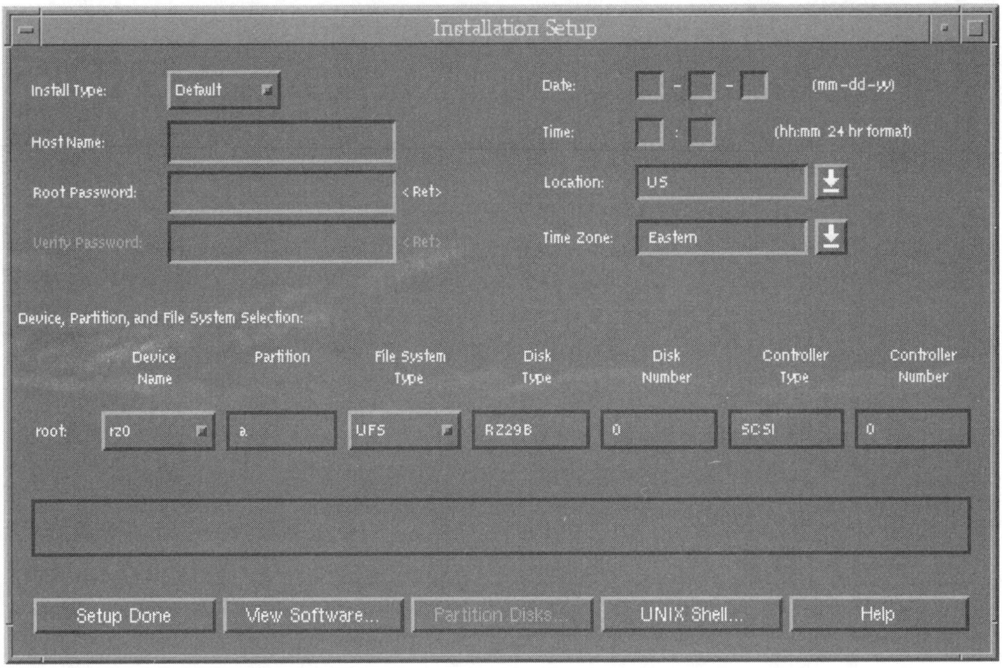

Figure 2.2 The Digital UNIX V4.0 Installation Setup Utility

- Time
- Location
- Time Zone

Simply click in each field and enter the desired value. The Installation Setup utility does perform validity checking on the information entered as it is entered. For instance, a system host name must begin with an alphabetic character, and if a nonalphabetic character is entered as the first character in the Host name field, a dialog box will be displayed indicating entry of an invalid host name. If such a warning box is displayed, click on the OK button to dismiss it. The parameters can be entered in any order with the exception of the Root Password entry, which must be followed by the Verify Password field, and the Location field, the selection of which may be required before choosing a Time Zone.

The installer may choose to review the mandatory software subsets for the Default installation by clicking on the View Software button. This will

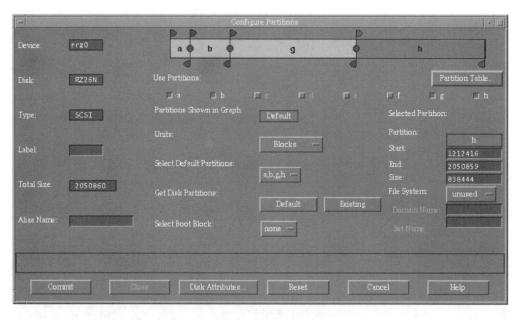

Figure 2.3 The Digital UNIX V4.0 Configure Partitions Window

display the Software Selection window (Figure 2.4) with the software subsets that will be installed displayed in the Selected Software pane. Note that only mandatory software subsets will be loaded when doing a Default installation; to add or remove software subsets, either switch to a Custom installation or add/remove subsets manually upon completion of the installation.

Once the installer is satisfied with the parameters presented by the Installation Setup utility, click the Setup Done button to continue the installation. A dialog box is presented to inform the user that the installation is ready to proceed. Once the OK button is clicked, the graphical screen will be replaced by a character mode output displaying the status of the continuing installation. This will include the file system creation process of the root and /usr file systems, followed by a status notification (e.g., Loading 1 of X subset(s) . . .) as each mandatory software subset is loaded. The software load of a Default installation will take approximately 30 to 120 minutes, depending on the number of mandatory subsets being loaded, the distribution media, and the type of Alpha system being installed.

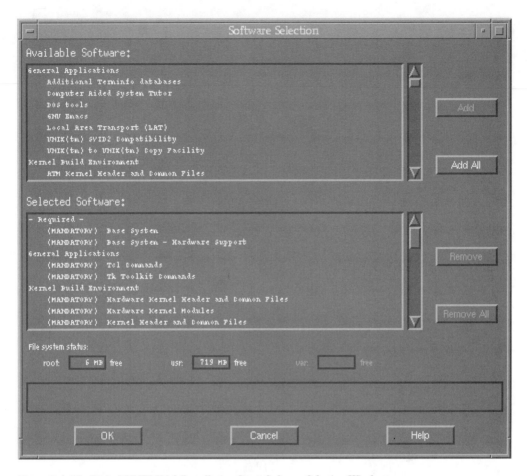

Figure 2.4 The Digital UNIX V4.0 Installation Setup Software Selection Window

2.3.2.2. Custom Graphical Installation

Performing a Custom Installation with the Installation Setup utility is required when installing a system needing custom disk partitioning, software subsets, or specific kernel options. Select a Custom installation by clicking on the Install Type button and switch from Default to Custom. See Figure 2.5 for the Custom Window of the Installation Setup utility. The most striking distinction between the Installation Setup utility's Default

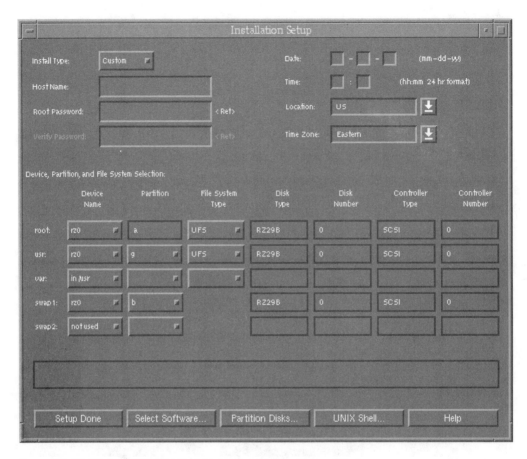

Figure 2.5 The Digital UNIX V4.0 Installation Setup Utility Custom Window

mode and Custom mode is that the "Device, Partition, and File System Selection" section is much expanded in Custom mode to allow for the selection of disk, partition, and file system type for each of the root, /usr, and /var file systems. In addition, up to two swap areas may be configured. Less obvious is that the "Partition Disks... " button is enabled and that the Default mode's "View Software... " button is now labeled "Select Software...."

As in a Default installation, very little user input is required to commence a Custom installation. However, if the installation parameters are not customized, the resulting installation will simply resemble a Default installation. The point of a Custom installation, of course, is to customize the installation. The top half of the window is identical to the Default installation window and permits specification of the host name, root password, date, time, and geographical location. If desired, enter some or all of these parameters before starting the installation, otherwise you will be prompted for their values during the installation configuration phase.

2.3.3. Device, Partition, and File System Selection

A Custom installation allows the selection of the physical disk(s), the disk partition(s), and the file system type(s) for the installation. Below the basic parameter entry fields are five rows of buttons and informational fields. These five rows correspond to the five disk partitions (root, /usr, /var, swap1, and swap2) that may be customized (See Figure 2.5). Only the columns Device Name, Partition, and File System Type are changeable and only for certain rows. For instance, since the root file system is required to be partition a, the Partition field for this row is preset to a. Assuming that the pre-installation planning has been completed, the installer simply selects the desired disk, partition, and file system for each row.

2.3.3.1. Device Name

To select the Device Name, left click on the button and a window will be displayed listing all the available devices. In addition, for each device, the disk type and number and the controller type and number are displayed to facilitate selecting the correct device. A device must be selected for the root, /usr, and swap1 partitions. For the /var partition, an additional selection in the pop-up device window is "in /usr" to specify that a separate /var file system is not desired. Also, the swap2 partition is optional, and an additional option in its pop-up device window is "not used." The default device values for /var and swap2 are "in /usr" and "not used," respectively. Note that the disk and controller type and number are displayed if appropriate in read-only fields for reference.

2.3.3.2 Partition

The second adjustable field in this section of the Installation Setup window is Partition. This allows specifying which physical partition a file system or swap area will occupy on the selected device. The allowable values for this parameter are the letters a through h and a dash (-), which signifies no partition selected. Left click on a row's Partition button to modify its value and a pop-up window will be displayed that contains a table of all the partitions on the selected device. This table shows the starting and ending block numbers, the size in blocks, and any partitions that are overlapped for each partition. Available partitions are highlighted. If a partition is dimmed in the window, it is not available for selection either because it has already been selected for another file system or because it overlaps with a previously selected partition. Click on the desired partition to select it, or click on "none" to unselect a partition. It may be necessary to change a partition to "none" on one row in order to make other partitions available.

Note that this table shows the current partition layout of the selected device. If the device is repartitioned later in the Installation process, either with the Disk Configuration tool or manually with the disklabel(8) command from the UNIX Shell, the partition size and overlap values may change. If you plan to repartition disks, it is recommended that they be partitioned as desired before selecting partitions for the file systems and swap areas.

2.3.3.3. File System Type

The final adjustable field in this section is File System Type, and the allowable values are UFS (UNIX File System) and AdvFS (Advanced File System). Since swap areas in Digital UNIX must be block (or raw) partitions and do not have file systems, the file system type fields are not displayed for the two swap areas. Simply left click on the file system type button for a particular partition and a pop-up window showing the two options is displayed. Select the desired file system type for the partition by clicking on the name.

2.3.4. Partition Disks...

Digital has defined default partition layouts for all the Digital UNIX supported disks. These partition layouts, while sufficient for a Default installation that loads just the mandatory software subsets, are frequently inadequate for a Custom installation. Because of this, Digital provides the ability to repartition one or more disks from within the Installation Setup utility. By clicking on the Partition Disks... button at the bottom of the window, the installer can invoke the Configure Partitions window. This window (Figure 2.3), is the same window available from the Disk Configuration application on the installed system with a few minor limitations. The Configuration Partitions windows is basically a graphical version of the disklabel(8) utility, allowing the installer to view and modify the partition layout of a disk.

After clicking on the Partition Disks... button, a dialog box is displayed listing the available disks. The disks are listed by name and disk and controller type and number. Select the disk to be partitioned by clicking on the desired disk entry and pressing the OK button. This will display the Configure Partitions windows for the selected disk. Along the top of this window is a graphical representation of the disk with individual rectangles representing the partitions. Using the mouse, the sizes of each partition may be adjusted by dragging the rectangles into larger or smaller sizes. Sizing the partitions in this manner is not very exact, but may be sufficient for rough adjustments. For absolute control, click on a partition to be adjusted and modify the Start, End, and/or Size fields directly. By default, these fields display their values in blocks. Click on the Units button to change the display unit to either Megabytes or Bytes. In addition, the default disk partition layout for that type of disk may be selected by clicking on the Default button. After adjusting the partition size to the desired layout, click the Commit button to apply the changes to the disk and return to the Installation Setup window.

The Configure Partitions window has two buttons that do not apply when doing an installation. These buttons are the Select Boot Block button and the File System type button. If either of these buttons are clicked, the installer is shown an informational dialog box explaining why it is unnecessary to select these items. Simply click the OK button to dismiss these dialog boxes.

2.3.5. Select Software...

After customizing the disk and file system layout, the next aspect of a Custom installation to complete is selecting the software subsets to load. A mandatory set of subsets is automatically selected and loaded, but this set is the bare minimum to install a system. There are always some additional, optional subsets that are needed or wanted for an optimally configured system. Click on the Select Software... button to display the Software Selection window (Figure 2.4). This window has three regions: the Available Software pane, the Select Software pane, and File System Status fields. When the Software Selection window is opened, the installation determines the list of

mandatory software subsets for the system being installed. This set of
mandatory subsets is based on the hardware configuration of the computer
(e.g., whether the system has graphics capability or an Asynchronous Mode
Transfer—ATM—adapter), and whether AdvFS is chosen as one or more
file system types. The resulting list of mandatory software subsets are then
displayed in the Selected Software pane and, since these subsets are mandatory, they cannot be unselected.

In addition to the mandatory software subsets, there are many optional
subsets. These subsets include reference pages, development tools, system
administration tools, network utilities, and X Windows servers and environment support utilities. The recommended strategy is to select and load only
those optional subsets that are needed for the system being installed. Having said that, it may be difficult to say with certainty whether a given subset
is truly needed or not. The downside of loading an unnecessary subset is
that the subset takes up disk space and possibly other resources, depending
on the nature of the subset. The Software Selection window does provide an
Add All button that simplifies the selection by selecting all optional subsets.
This is a valid choice and will result in a functioning Digital UNIX system,
assuming sufficient disk space to load all the subsets. In some cases, it may
be simpler to just load all the optional subsets, but I encourage you to give
some thought to this software selection process.

Use the Add/Add All and Remove/Remove All buttons to move subsets to and from the Selected Software pane. Monitor the File System Status
fields as subsets are added for installation to ensure that there is sufficient
free space in the root, /usr, and /var file systems. If one or more file systems
are inadequately sized to contain all the desired subsets, click Cancel to
return to the main Installation Setup window and either choose larger par-
titons or repartition the disk to allocate more space for the deficient file sys-
tem(s). Once you are satisfied with the subsets in the Selected Software
pane, click the OK button to return to the Software Installation window to
continue the installation.

Once the installer is satisfied with the parameters presented by the
Installation Setup utility and the desired software subsets are selected, click
the Setup Done button to continue the installation. A dialog box is presented to inform the user that the installation is ready to proceed. Once the
OK button is clicked, the graphical screen will be replaced by a character
mode output status of the continuing installation. This will include the file
system creation of the root, /usr, and possibly /var file systems followed by
a status (Loading 1 of X subset(s) . . .) as each mandatory and optional soft-

ware subset is loaded. The software load of a Custom installation will take approximately 30 to 120 minutes, depending on the number of mandatory and optional subsets being loaded, the distribution media, and the type of Alpha system being installed.

2.3.6. The Digital UNIX Character Installation Utility

When installing a version of Digital UNIX prior to 4.0, or when working on systems with a serial console less than 32 megabytes of memory, the installation interface is a character-cell menu-driven application. This application provides almost all of the same functionality of the Graphical Installation Utility. The only exception is access to an easy disk-partitioning utility such as the Configure Partitions window available when doing a Graphics installation. If it becomes necessary to customize the partitions of disks, the disklabel(8) command must be used manually from the UNIX Shell mode. See Chapter 3, "System Configuration," for details on use of the disklabel command.

   After the initial boot from the installation media, the following information is displayed, followed by the three-option installation menu:

```
Welcome to the Digital UNIX Installation Procedure

This procedure installs Digital UNIX onto your system. You will
  be asked a series of system configuration questions. Until you
  answer all questions, your system is not changed in any way.

During the question and answer session, you can go back to any
  previous question and change your answer by entering: history
You can get more information about a question by entering: help
There are two types of installations:
```

   • The Default installation installs a mandatory set
     of software subsets on a predetermined file sys-
     tem layout.
   • The Custom installation installs a mandatory set
     of software subsets plus optional software sub-
     sets that you select. You can customize the file
     system layout.

   The UNIX Shell option puts your system in single-
user mode with superuser privileges. This option is
provided for experienced UNIX system administrators who

want to perform file system or disk maintenance tasks
before the installation.

The *Installation Guide* contains more information
about installing Digital UNIX.

```
1. Default Installation
2. Custom Installation
3. UNIX Shell
```

Enter your choice.

This character-cell Installation utility supports both Default and Custom installations, and the UNIX Shell menu choice permits file or disk maintenance to the system in single-user mode as root. The UNIX shell option allows experienced system administrators to perform tasks such as partitioning disks and creating file systems before starting the installation.

Both the Default and the Custom installation options initiate a series of questions that must be answered before the installation begins. The answers to these questions define the various configuration parameters. These parameters include the boot disk, the root password, and the date, time, and location information in installing from CD-ROM. In addition, if doing a Custom installation, the location of the swap area, the location and type of the /usr and /var file systems, and the optional software subsets to be loaded are prompted for. The system is not changed in any way until all these questions are answered and the installer is prompted to actually begin the installation.

Refer to the sample character-based installation sessions in the appendix of the *Digital UNIX Installation Guide* for examples of both a Default and a Custom installation. Review these examples before beginning a character-based installation to familiarize yourself with the type and order of configuration questions. Also, these sample installation sessions are useful as a guide to follow when doing an installation.

2.4. UPGRADING DIGITAL UNIX

The process of upgrading an existing installed version of Digital UNIX to a later version of Digital UNIX is an Update installation. An Update installation is performed on an existing system and results in an upgraded system while preserving disk and file system configuration, user accounts, printer and network configurations, and any other custom configurations that existed prior to the upgrade. An Update installation is similar to a Full installation in two important ways:

- Many of the pre-installation tasks are the same. These include backing up the system prior to beginning, updating the system firmware if necessary, and planning disk space.
- Updates can be done from CD-ROM or across the network from a Remote Installation Services (RIS) server

The Update installation process is different from a Full installation primarily in the way the update is begun. While a Full installation is started from the console prompt (>>>), an Update installation is begun while the system is running and in single-user mode.

In addition, Digital has provided only certain update paths. For instance, to upgrade to version 4.0D of Digital UNIX, the system must already be at version 4.0A, 4.0B, or 4.0C. Unfortunately some system upgrades may take two or more updates to get the system to the desired target version. As an example, consider a Digital UNIX version 3.2G system. In order to upgrade this system to V4.0D, the supported path is:

1. Update from version 3.2G to version 4.0A, followed by an:
2. Update from version 4.0A to version 4.0D

See the Performing an Update Installation chapter in the appropriate *Digital UNIX Installation Guide* for details on the supported update paths.

A Digital UNIX Update installation requires as much, if not more, pre-installation planning as a Full installation. This is so because the system being upgraded is likely an existing system that is depended upon by users. A successful Update installation is very nearly transparent to the users, and adequate planning is the first step in achieving this goal.

2.4.1. Update Installation Steps

Complete all pre-installation planning and preparation. Planning for an Update is similar to a normal Full installation and includes:

- Backing up the system prior to beginning the update
- Ensuring there is sufficient disk space for the upgraded and new software subsets
- Upgrading the system's firmware if necessary

Additionally, there are two prerequisite tasks specific to an Update installation that may apply:

- Remove any saved configuration files resulting from a previous Update installation. These files are saved versions of customized configuration files and are managed by the Update Administration Utility, that is, updadmin(8). If the system had been previously updated, there may be .PreMRG, .PreUPD, and other obsolete files residing on the system. These files could possibly conflict with the update process, and they should be removed prior to starting the update. Additionally, removing such files also frees disk space. If the system has never been updated, this step is unnecessary.
- Delete certain software subsets if installed. Some Digital UNIX software subsets must be removed prior to beginning an Update installation. These software products are of a nature such that if they are installed, the Update installation will halt. Simply delete any of these products that are installed with the setld(8) command. Once the Update installation is complete, reinstall the version of each product that is compatible with the resulting version of Digital UNIX. As an example, the following products must be removed before beginning an upgrade to Digital UNIX version 4.0D:

  - DEC Open3D
  - DECnet/OSI
  - DECsafe Available Server Environment (ASE)
  - Distributed Computing Environment/Distributed File System (DCE/DFS)
  - Kubota Workstation Software (KWS)
  - Multimedia Services (MME)
  - System V Environment (SVE)
  - Worldwide Language Support

Refer to the "Performing an Update Installation" chapter in the specific *Digital UNIX Installation Guide* for the appropriate list of incompatible products that must be removed.

1. Start the Update Installation. An Update installation can be run from either CD-ROM media inserted into the system's local CD-ROM drive or from an RIS server across the network. In either

case, the procedure to start the Update is the same except for the distribution argument passed to the installupdate(8) utility.

- Shutdown or boot to single-user mode. An Update installation must be done from the console of the system due to the requirement that the system be in single-user mode.

  If the system is running Digital UNIX as root, issue a command similar to the following:

```
# shutdown +1 "Shutting down for update installation"
```

This example will shutdown the system to single-user mode in one minute, displaying the message "Shutting down for update installation" to all logged-in users.

If the system is halted at the console prompt (>>>), boot to single-user mode by issuing the following command:

```
>>> boot -flag s
```

This command assumes that the bootdef_dev console variable contains the value of the system disk.

- Start the Logical Storage Manager (LSM) if appropriate. If LSM is used on the system to be updated, start LSM by issuing the following command:

```
# /sbin/lsmbstartup
```

- Mount the local file systems by entering the following command:

```
# /sbin/bcheckrc
```

- Ensure that either the correct Digital UNIX CD-ROM is inserted into the CD-ROM drive or that the RIS server is up and running. The RIS server must have the correct version of Digital UNIX in the RIS environment, and the system to be updated must be registered with the RIS server.
- Run the installupdate utility to start the update. The installupdate utility expects an argument that specifies the Digital UNIX distribution source. This distribution source is either the CD-ROM special device file or mount point for a CD-ROM update, or a host name for an RIS server update. For example, for a CD-ROM

update, the following example updates a system from a CD-ROM whose special device is /dev/rz4c:

```
# /sbin/installupdate /dev/rz4c
```

Optionally, if the CD-ROM is automatically mounted because of an entry in the /etc/fstab file, specify the mount point instead of the CD-ROM's special device file. For example, if the CD-ROM is mounted on /cdrom, the following command would begin the update also:

```
# /sbin/installupdate /cdrom
```

For an update from an RIS server, simply specify the RIS server's host name appended with a colon (:) to initiate the update. For example, if the RIS server's host name is pluto, issue the following command:

```
# /sbin/installupdate pluto:
```

The installupdate utility has an optional flag, -i, that tells installupdate to invoke an interactive kernel build at the conclusion of the update. This allows the selection of kernel options and also provides the opportunity to manually edit the kernel configuration file. If the –i flag is not specified, the system's kernel will be built containing only the mandatory kernel options for the install software subsets. This is an example of running installupdate with this flag:

```
# /sbin/installupdate –i /dev/rz4c
```

2. Monitor the Update installation and Respond to prompts. There are nine phases of an Update installation:
   a) Verifying the system state
   b) Checking for layered products that may halt the update installation
   c) Checking the system status
   d) Checking for file type conflicts
   e) Checking file space requirement
   f) Detecting unprotected customized files
   g) Loading and merging software subsets
   h) Configuring and merging software subsets
   i) Building the kernel

Each of these steps must be completed successfully before the process will move onto the next step. All but a few of the steps may require interaction from the user; however, the response is typically a simple yes or no. Because of the version variances, I will refer the reader to the appropriate version of the *Digital UNIX Installation Guide* for details on these update phases. See the section entitled "What Happens During the Update Installation Process" in the "Performing an Update Installation" chapter for information on what to expect as the update progresses and also how to recover from problems that may occur during the update.

3. Complete Post-Update tasks. After the system reboots upon successful completion of the update, log in as root to complete these post-installaton tasks:

   - Review the Update installation log files. The Update process logs status and error information in a series of log files for review after the update completes:
     - The main Update installation log file is /var/adm/smlogs/ update.log
     - Software subset and kernel configuration information is contained in /var/adm/smlogs/it.log
     - Any system files rendered obsolete by the update are listed in /var/adm/smlogs/upd_obsolete_files
     - Any system configuration files customized during the update are listed in /var/adm/smlogs/upd_custom_files
     - Any failed merges of system configuration files are listed in /var/adm/smlogs/upd_mergefail_files

   - Examine these log files to ensure that the update completed successfully and that there were no errors in merging system configuration files.
   - Manually review, merge, and delete custom system and configuration files not automatically merged by the Update process. Only certain configuration files are automatically merged during the update. If a particular configuration file is either not automatically merged, or the merge fails, it may be necessary to manually merge the pre-update information into the newly updated configuration file. This is an important final step that ensures that the newly updated system configuration is as identical as possible to the previous system configuration.

There are three types of manual updates that may need to be completed. These are:

- Unprotected system files—These are files that are not automatically merged by the Update process, but were identified as having been customized since they were originally installed. The Update process lists any such files in the /var/adm/smlogs/ upd_custom_files log file. Review this log file and, if necessary, manually edit the new version to include the customizations. For example, consider the following entry in /var/adm/smlogs/ upd_custom_files after an update:

```
./usr/dt/config/Xservers.con.PreUPD OSFCDEDT410
```

This indicates that the file Xservers.con, which is a component of the OSFCDEDT410 software subset, was found to have been modified. During the Update process this customized version was renamed to /usr/dt/config/Xservers.con.PreUPD and the new, updated version of this file was installed. After the update, compare the saved .PreUPD version of this file with the newer version and manually update the new one to reflect the customizations. For instance:

```
# diff /usr/dt/config/Xservers.con.PreUPD
  /usr/dt/config/Xservers.con
71c71
<   :0 Local local@console /usr/bin/X11/X :0 -screen 800
—

>   :0 Local local@console /usr/bin/X11/X :0
```

This indicates that there is only one difference. Simply edit the /usr/dt/config/Xservers.con file and add the option "-screen 800" to that line. Once this customization has been completed, the .PreUPD file is no longer needed and may be deleted to save disk space.

- Failed merges of system files—These are files that the Update process attempted to merge automatically but was unsuccessful. A list of failed merges are in /var/adm/smlogs/upd_merge-fail_files. Review this file and manually merge any list files. The process of manually merging files is the same as for merging Unprotected System Files (see above), with the exception of the name of the saved original file. The Update process renames the original of failed merges with a .PreMRG suffix. For example, /etc/sysconfigtab.PreMRG.

- The kernel configuration file—The Update process saves the kernel configuration file prior to the kernel build phase of the update. Compare the new, updated config file (/sys/conf/ UPPERCASE_HOSTNAME) with the original (/sys/conf/ UPPERCASE_HOSTNAME.bak), manually add any customizations into the new configuration file, rebuild the kernel, and reboot. For example, if the system host name is saturn:

```
# diff /sys/conf/SATURN.bck /sys/conf/SATURN
71c71
< maxusers    256
—
> maxusers    32
```

edit /sys/conf/SATURN and change the value of maxusers from 32 to 256, rebuild the kernel with the doconfig(8) utility, copy the new kernel into place, and reboot.

Digital provides a utility, the Update Administration Utility, to list, save, and delete these pre-update configuration files. Refer to the "Performing an Update Installation" of the appropriate *Digital UNIX Installation Guide* for details on using this utility to manage the unprotected customized, failed merge, and obsolete files.

Once these post-update tasks are complete, the system is ready for use.

System Configuration

3

The configuration of a Digital UNIX system is a broad topic that touches every possible system and user subsystem and service, both hardware and software. Rather than attempt to cover each subsystem in exhaustive detail, I will address certain areas that are of interest to all Digital UNIX system administrators. If a topic is not covered, refer to the appropriate Digital UNIX documentation for configuration details.

This chapter will discuss the following aspects of Digital UNIX system configuration:

- Disk Management
- UFS File System Configuration
- Advanced File System (AdvFS) Configuration
- Digital UNIX Software Subset Management
- The Digital UNIX License Management Facility

3.1. DISK MANAGEMENT

The subject of disk management is an important topic for a Digital UNIX system administrator. Almost every Digital UNIX system has one or more physical disk drives that are the primary online storage media for the operating system itself as well as user applications and data. Before proceeding further, it is necessary to define which disks will be discussed and also describe several important characteristics of a disk drive that will be helpful to understand when partitioning disks. In this section, the term "disk" will be used to refer to rotating magnetic media. Disks are also commonly called disk drives, hard drives, or fixed storage. This last term refers to the fact that disk drives are normally "fixed" in place, as opposed to media such as floppy diskettes and optical disk subsystems, including CD-ROMs in which the media is removable from the drive mechanism. See Chapter 7, "Services," for information on managing and using both floppy diskettes and CD-ROMs on Digital UNIX.

In addition, a reference to a "disk" will mean a single disk drive of a specific capacity. This may be an individual disk or two or more disks grouped together for increased capacity, availability, or performance that appear to Digital UNIX as a single disk. From an operating system viewpoint, the management of disks and their space is typically the same regardless of what type of disk or disks are in use.

A disk is composed of a stack of platters spaced along a central hub. This entire assembly rotates at a very high speed, ranging from 3600 rotations per minute (rpm) up to 10000 rpm and higher. Both sides of the individual platters are coated with a magnetic material. Each platter surface is serviced by an electromagnetic read/write head that is mounted on a movable arm. The simplest analogy to a disk's platter and head is a phonograph needle on a record. The read/write heads on a disk, however, hover two to three thousandths of an inch over the surface of the platter, either sensing or changing the magnetic polarity of magnetic particles formatted in concentric circles, or tracks, on the platter. A typical disk may have many thousands of tracks on its recording surfaces. The group of tracks located at a given head position across all platters is called a cylinder. Finally, each track is divided into individual logical units called sectors. A sector is the smallest contiguous part of a track that can be accessed with a single head read. There are 512 bytes in a sector.

3.1.1. Disk Types

Digital UNIX supports two type of disks:

- Small Computer System Interface (SCSI)
- Digital Storage Architecture (DSA)

SCSI, commonly pronounced "Scuzzy," has quickly become the most common type of disk available on a Digital UNIX system, making the DSA disk almost obsolete. In fact, DSA disks are currently only supported on the DEC 7000 and DEC 10000 systems. Because of this, DSA disks will only be discussed briefly.

3.1.2. SCSI

The term SCSI actually refers to the disk interface or disk controller. SCSI supports multiple disks on an individual controller. Currently, the practical limit on the number of disks on a SCSI controller is about a half dozen. This limit is based both on performance concerns and physical cable length. Placing a lot of very active drives on a single SCSI bus will result in performance degradation as the bus becomes saturated. Each drive connected to a system's SCSI controller must have a unique identifier called the SCSI ID, which is typically in the range of 0-7.

To add a SCSI disk to a system, shutdown the system, if possible, and connect the new disk to the SCSI bus, either by plugging the unit into the SCSI interface via a cable or, in the case of Digital's Storageworks product, by plugging a disk module into a Storageworks shelf. When cabling external disks, ensure that the SCSI ID for the new disk does not conflict with any existing disks. In addition, avoid SCSI ID 7, which is almost always the SCSI ID of the disk controller itself. For Storageworks disk modules, the SCSI ID of a disk is determined and set automatically, based on the module's location within the Storageworks shelf.

3.1.3. Disk Device Names

Once disks are properly connected to the system and powered up, turn the system on and bring the system to the console prompt (>>>). This will occur automatically if the console variable "auto_action" is set to the value "HALT." If the system begins to boot, simply press the Halt button on the front panel of the computer or, if you are working on systems without a Halt button, press Ctrl-P at the console. From the console prompt, issue the following command to display all attached devices:

```
>>> show device
dka0.0.0.6.0      DKA0      RZ26N 0568
dka100.1.0.6.0    DKA100    RZ26N 0568
```

```
dka400.4.0.6.0      DKA400      RRD43 1084
dva0.0.0.1000.0     DVA0
ewa0.0.0.13.0       EWA0        00-00-F8-01-42-5F
pka0.7.0.6.0        PKA0        SCSI Bus ID 7
```

In this example, the second column indicates the unit identifiers that are assigned to each device on the system. For disks, the nomenclature of these unit identifiers is:

- The letters DK refer to a SCSI disk (Including CD-ROMs)
- The third letter (A, B, C, D, or E) refers to the SCSI bus number
- The number refers to the SCSI ID

These identifiers are significant only in console mode and are used primarily to instruct the console from which device the system should boot. However, using this method to display the devices is a good practice, especially after connecting new disks for the first time. If a new disk is not listed from the console, it is unlikely that Digital UNIX will see the disk either.

The third column of the "show device" output is usually a model name or other identifier. The information displayed in this field is often helpful in identifying which disk is which. For Digital disks, the model number followed by the firmware revision of the disk is displayed.

3.1.4. Disk Device Files

While from the console, disks (and other devices) are described by a unit identifier as discussed in the previous section, the Digital UNIX operating system uses a different naming method to refer to and communicate with disks. Since Digital UNIX (and all other UNIX flavors) is a file-based operating system, all physical devices, including disks, are accessed through special files called Device Files. These special device files normally reside in the /dev subdirectory on a system, and each file's name indicates its purpose. It is important for a system administrator to be familiar with the Digital UNIX special device files for disks in order to be able to perform disk management tasks.

Each disk is represented by at least sixteen special devices files. The names of each of these individual disk device files are significant and indicate several pieces of information about how that disk is accessed. The key for disk special device naming is straightforward:

- The first letter "r" indicates the device is a disk
- The second letter specifies the type of disk:
  "z" — SCSI Disk
  "e" — SWXCR RAID Array Controller[1] Disk
  "a" — DSA Disk
- A decimal number indicates the disk unit number
- A final letter ("a" through "h") specifies the disk partition

Using this legend, the special device file "rz0c" refers to partition C of a SCSI disk at unit 0.

In addition, a disk can be accessed using either a block special device file or a character special device file. A block special device file accesses the disk through the operating system's buffer process. This is the method used by the Digital UNIX file systems and imposes a certain amount of overhead on disk reads and writes. However, the buffering that occurs allows disk reads and writes to be any size.

The character special device file is a direct interface to the disk. A single disk read or write to the character device file results in exactly one disk I/O operation. The character device file interface is frequently called the "raw" interface, since no buffering or "cooking" of the reads and writes occurs. The names of character special device files for a disk are prefaced with an additional "r" to indicate the device is raw.

For instance, the following is a list of the device files for a single SCSI disk:

/dev/rz0a	/dev/rrz0a
/dev/rz0b	/dev/rrz0b
/dev/rz0c	/dev/rrz0c
/dev/rz0d	/dev/rrz0d
/dev/rz0e	/dev/rrz0e
/dev/rz0f	/dev/rrz0f
/dev/rz0g	/dev/rrz0g
/dev/rz0h	/dev/rrz0h

The first column is the block special device files, one for each of the eight partitions on the disk. The second column is the character (raw) special devices files for the disk.

---

[1] A SWXCR RAID Array Controller is a special Digital SCSI controller that can do disk mirroring and striping independently of the operating system.

These special disk device files are used to refer to specific disks and partitions. Some Digital UNIX utilities require that the block special device be specified. For instance, when using the mount(8) command to mount a file systems, the block device must be used. Other commands require the character special device when referring to disks. Most such utilities are disk management tools that communicate directly with the disk without the operating system buffering mechanism. Some examples include the newfs(8) command, which is used to create UNIX File Systems (UFS), and the disklabel(8) command, which is used to partition disks.

3.1.5. Creating Disk Device Files

The installation of Digital UNIX on a system automatically creates all the necessary disk device files in the /dev subdirectory for all available disks at install time. When new disks are added later, it is sometimes necessary to manually create the disk device files before the disks can be accesses. Digital provides a utility, MAKEDEV(8), that will create all the required device files. Simply change to the /dev subdirectory and execute the MAKEDEV program, specifying the desired disk device on the command line. For example, to create the special device files for the disk rz3, use the following commands:

```
# cd /dev
# ./MAKEDEV rz3
MAKEDEV: special file(s) for rz3:
rz3a rrz3a rz3b rrz3b rz3c rrz3c rz3d rrz3d rz3e
  rrz3e rz3f rrz3f rz3g rrz3g rz3h rrz3h
```

3.1.5.1. Identifying Disk Types

Occasionally, it is desirable to be able identity the model or manufacturer of a disk represented by a special device file. Certainly one could shut the system down to the console prompt (>>>) and execute the "show device" command. However, one of the goals of a system administrator is to keep the Digital UNIX system up and running. For this, simply use the file(1) command to display device-specific information, specifying the character special device file of the disk in question. For example:

```
# file /dev/rrz0a
/dev/rrz0a:   character special (8/0) SCSI #0 RZ26N
disk #0 (SCSI ID #0) (SCSI LUN #0)
```

3.1.6. Disk Partitioning

A characteristic of UNIX disk management is the concept of disk partition-ing. Disk partitioning is logically dividing a disk into separate areas of vary-ing sizes. The system administrator uses disk partitions to subdivide a disk into manageable pieces for containing the operating system, paging areas, and user applications and data. As the capacity of individual disks increases, par-titioning allows more efficient use of disk space. In addition, segregating dif-ferent types of data prevents system problems. For instance, placing user home directories on a different disk partition than the partition in which the /usr file system resides, prevents user activity from affecting the operating system.

As mentioned earlier, there are eight partitions on a Digital UNIX disk and the partitions are labeled with the letters "a" through "h." The sizes and uses of each of the partitions on a disk are user-definable, and the sys-tem administrator is responsible for defining the partition layout. In Digital UNIX, only two partitions (a and c) have any particular significance. On a boot disk, the root file system must reside in partition a, while partition c normally refers to the entire disk.

Determining how to partition a disk is often a matter of personal pref-erence. UNIX disk partitioning philosophies range from the practice of not partitioning at all and simply using an entire disk as one large partition, to the other extreme of partitioning each disk into the maximum possible number of partitions. Each strategy has pros and cons and, as with most sit-uations, the best solution is probably somewhere between the two extremes. The main advantage of a single, large partition is that all processes and users have access to the entire disk and are not limited to a single partition that may be a subset of the total disk space. This, however, is also a disadvantage in that any process or user has the ability to fill the entire disk and possibly impact all other processing. The other end of the disk partitioning spec-trum is to create many, small partitions. Depending on the disk's intended purpose, this may be exactly what is needed for the most efficient use of the disk space. If, however, in the future, one or more of the partitions needs to be resized, the system administrator may find it difficult and time-consuming to manage the disk repartitioning. The best recommendation regarding disk partitioning is to create only enough partitions on a disk to sufficiently isolate different types of users and processes to prevent each from impacting others in the event of an unexpected or inadvertent disk usage increase. For example, in addition to separating partitions for the Digital UNIX operating system (the root, /usr, and possibly the /var file systems and the swap partitions), create a partition for user home directories.

A default disk partition table is provided by Digital, but it is up to the system administrator to decide whether to use this default layout or customize the partition sizes and locations. Most default layouts are similar to that described in Figure 3.1. Using this example, it should be clear that it would be impossible to use all eight of these partitions at the same time, since there would be overlap, which is not permitted. Assuming that the partition sizes were not changed, the following are the possible partition combinations:

- c
- a, b, d, e, and f
- a, b, g, and h
- a, b, d, and h
- a, b, f, and g

The first three combinations would use the entire disk, while the fourth and fifth would leave some of the disk unallocated. Fortunately, Digital UNIX allows partition sizes to be adjusted to suit the system requirements. The tool for adjusting the partition layout of a disk is disklabel(8).

3.1.6.1. The disklabel(8) Command

The disklabel(8) command is used to display, install, and modify a disk's partition layout, or disk label, as Digital UNIX terms it. The disk label is physically located on the disk on one of the first sectors of each disk (usually block 0). In addition to the partition layout, the disk label also contains detailed information about the characteristics of the disk.

3.1.7. Writing a Default Disklabel

The first step when working with a disk, especially a new disk, is to write a default disklabel to a disk. Prior to doing this, a disk is unlabeled and, until

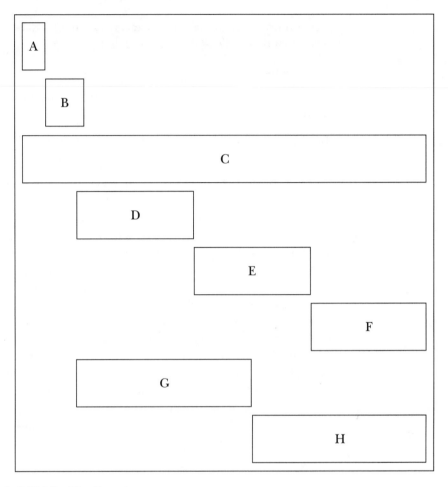

Figure 3.1 Default Disk Partition Layout

a label is installed, Digital UNIX cannot make use of the disk. Writing this default disklabel prepares the disk for use, either using the default partition layout or when planning to configure a custom partition layout. Writing a default disklabel is not reserved for new disks. Occasionally, it becomes necessary to repartition an existing disk; if the entire disk will be redone, it is recommended to rewrite a default disklabel onto the disk and repartition it.

Before writing a new default disklabel to a disk, one recommended step is to remove any existing label. This is not entirely necessary, but it is a simple step that will avoid the possible situation where certain existing partitions may persist onto the new label. To clear any existing disklabel, use the following command, specifying the appropriate disk:

```
# disklabel -z rz1
```

If the following harmless message is returned, the disk was already unlabeled:

```
Disk is unlabeled or, /dev/rrz1a does not start at
  block 0 of the disk
```

Note that while the simple disk name (rz1) is specified as the disklabel argument, the disklabel command actually translated that into a full pathname to the character special device file (/dev/rrz1a). It is perfectly legal to specify the fully qualified character special device file, but using just the simple disk name is a convenient shorthand. If a particular partition is not specified, the disklabel command uses the first partition that starts at block zero on the disk. Typically, this is the a or c partition.

Once any existing disklabel is removed from a disk, use the disklabel command to write a new default disklabel. The syntax for writing a new disklabel varies, depending on whether the disk to be labeled will be a non-bootable data disk or a bootable system disk. The most common will be for non-bootable disks, but the ability to disklabel a bootable disk is equally important, especially in a recovery situation when the system disk must be relabeled prior to restoring its contents from a backup.

To label a normal (non-bootable) disk, use a command similar to the following:

```
# disklabel -r -w rz1 RZ26N
```

The "-r" flag instructs the disklabel command to write the new label directly to the disk rather than to an in-memory cache. The "-w" flag simply means to write a default disklabel to the disk, in this case, rz1. The final parameter is the disk type or model number. If known, specify the correct value. In this example, the disk being labeled is a Digital RZ26N. In the event the disk type is unknown, using a value of "UNKNOWN" will cause the disklabel command to query the disk driver for the disk's geometry. For example:

```
# disklabel -r -w rz2 UNKNOWN
```

To label the disk and configure it as a bootable system disk, an additional command line argument must be specified. This argument, "-t", is used to indicate to disklabel(8) the type of root file system. The disklabel command will write the appropriate bootstrap programs to the boot blocks on the disk. For example, to write a standard disklabel to a disk that will contain an Advanced File System (AdvFS) root file system, use the following command:

```
# disklabel -r -w -t advfs rz1 RZ26N
```

For a disk with a UNIX File System (UFS) root file system, specify "ufs" as the type rather than "advfs."

3.1.7.1. Displaying a Disklabel

Executing the disklabel command with only a disk argument will display the disklabel written on that disk. To ensure that the information displayed is the most current, always use the "-r" flag to instruct the disklabel command to read the label directly from the disk rather than from the in-memory copy of the disklabel. The format of this disklabel output is fairly standard regardless of disk type or size. An example of using the disklabel command to display a disk's label follows:

```
# disklabel -r rz1
# /dev/rrz1a:
type: SCSI
disk: RZ26N
label:
flags:
bytes/sector: 512
sectors/track: 57
tracks/cylinder: 14
sectors/cylinder: 798
cylinders: 2570
sectors/unit: 2050860
rpm: 5400
interleave: 1
trackskew: 40
cylinderskew: 43
headswitch: 0        # milliseconds
track-to-track seek: 0 # milliseconds
drivedata: 0
```

```
8 partitions:
#    size       offset    fstype   [fsize   bsize   cpg]
a:   131072     0         unused   0        0       #  (Cyl.  0-164*)
b:   262144     131072    unused   0        0       #  (Cyl.  164*-492*)
c:   2050860    0         unused   0        0       #  (Cyl.  0-2569)
d:   552548     393216    unused   0        0       #  (Cyl.  492*-1185*)
e:   552548     945764    unused   0        0       #  (Cyl.  1185*-1877*)
f:   552548     1498312   unused   0        0       #  (Cyl.  1877*-2569)
g:   819200     393216    unused   0        0       #  (Cyl.  492*-1519*)
h:   838444     1212416   unused   0        0       #  (Cyl.  1519*-2569)
```

The first part of the disklabel output presents some useful disk characteristic information, and the final eight lines show the partition layout of the disk. Probably the most useful piece of disk geometry information displayed is the number of bytes per disk sector. Since the partition size and offset values are displayed in sectors, the bytes per sector value allows conversion of the partition size and conversion of the offset to the more useful bytes, megabytes, or gigabytes.

3.1.7.2. Editing the Disklabel

After writing a default disklabel on a new disk, typically the next operation is to customize that label, adjusting the partitions to meet the requirements. The disklabel program allows easy editing of a disk's label using the "-e" flag. As with displaying a disk's label, always specify the "-r" flag to instruct the disklabel command to edit a copy of the label directly from the disk rather than from the in-memory copy of the disklabel. The following command takes a copy of the disklabel and invokes an editor specified by the EDITOR environment variable:

```
# disklabel -e -r rz1
```

If no editor is specified, the vi(1) editor is used, and if vi is not available, the ed(1) editor is used. While in the editor session, only a copy of the disk's label is being modified.

The purpose of editing a disk's label is to modify the partition layout and, as such, to only modify the last eight lines of the disklabel. The size and offset values for each of the eight partitions are in sectors, which can be converted to megabytes by dividing the sector value by 2048. For example, consider the following disk label fragment:

```
#   size      offset    fstype  [fsize  bsize  cpg]
a:  131072    0         unused  0       0      #  (Cyl.  0-164*)
b:  262144    131072    unused  0       0      #  (Cyl.  164*-492*)
c:  2050860   0         unused  0       0      #  (Cyl.  0-2569)
d:  552548    393216    unused  0       0      #  (Cyl.  492*-1185*)
e:  552548    945764    unused  0       0      #  (Cyl.  1185*-1877*)
f:  552548    1498312   unused  0       0      #  (Cyl.  1877*-2569)
g:  819200    393216    unused  0       0      #  (Cyl.  492*-1519*)
h:  838444    1212416   unused  0       0      #  (Cyl.  1519*-2569)
```

In this example, partition a starts at the beginning of the disk (sector 0) and is 64 megabytes (131072/2048) in size. Partition b starts immediately after partition a (sector 131072) and is 128 megabytes (262144/2048) in size, and so on. After determining the number of partitions desired and their size, convert the sizes to sectors and calculate the appropriate offset values and update the disk label in the editor. Normally all that is necessary is to change the size and offset values for the desired partitions. The other fields in each of the partition rows are automatically updated, either by the disklabel program itself or by other utilities when the partitions are used.

Once the desired partition updates are completed, quit the editor, saving the file. The following prompt will be displayed:

```
write new label? [y]:
```

If the changes were satisfactory, simply press the <Return> key to write the updated label to the disk. Otherwise, enter an "n" to discard the changes, and you will be given the opportunity to re-edit the disk label. Note that if the ed(1) editor is used and there is an unexpected error during the editing session, the following message will be displayed:

```
Warning, edit session exited abnormally!
```

If this occurs, do not write the label to the disk. Re-edit the label to ensure that the modifications are made correctly.

As an example, suppose a system administrator has installed a new 1-gigabyte RZ26 disk and wishes to create a 300- and a 500-megabyte partition on this disk using partitions a and b, respectively. These partition sizes result in the first partition starting at sector zero and being 614400 sectors in size, and the second partition starting at sector 614400 and being 1025430 sectors in size. The sizes of the partitions in sectors are calculated by multiplying the number of megabytes desired by 2048.

The following demonstrates this example by clearing any existing disk label, writing a new default label, and then editing the label to change partitions a and b:

```
# disklabel -z rz3
# disklabel -r -w rz3 RZ26
# disklabel -e -r rz3
```

In the editor, the following two lines:

```
a:   131072    0          unused  0  0   # (Cyl. 0-164*)
b:   262144    131072     unused  0  0   # (Cyl. 164*-492*)
```

are changed to:

```
a:   614400    0          unused  0  0   # (Cyl. 0-164*)
b:   1025430   614400     unused  0  0   # (Cyl. 164*-492*)
```

3.1.8. The diskconfig(8X) Utility

Starting at Digital UNIX version 4.0, Digital added a new graphical Disk Configuration tool for partitioning disks. This tool, diskconfig(8X), provides all the functionality of the disklabel(8) command along with a graphical representation of partitions allowing dynamic sizing of individual partitions. The Disk Configuration tool is invoked through the CDE Application Manager, which is opened by selecting the Application Manager icon from the CDE Front Panel, followed by selecting the System_Admin application group icon, then the Configuration application group icon, and finally the Disk Configuration Manager icon. Once you double-click on the Disk Configuration Manager icon, if you are not logged in as root, you will be prompted via a Get Password dialog box for the root password. The Disk Configuration utility may also be run from the command line:

```
# /usr/sbin/diskconfig
```

3.2. DIGITAL UNIX FILESYSTEMS

Once a disk has been partitioned, it is ready for the creation of file systems, which are the most common use of disk space on a Digital UNIX system. A file system is a structure built on a disk partition that allows the partition to contain files and directories in a hierarchical format. The file system is the primary environment of files and directories that most users see when logging onto the system. Digital UNIX supports the following types of disk-based file systems:

- UNIX File System (UFS)
- Advanced File System (AdvFS)
- Compact Disk File System (CDFS)

These three file system types make up the majority of all file systems in use on Digital UNIX systems, and system administrators should be familiar with their management. The UFS and AdvFS file systems will be discussed in this chapter; information on the CDFS file system can be found in Chapter 7, "Services," in the section on managing CD-ROMs.

In addition, the following file system types are also supported by Digital UNIX:

- Memory File System (MFS)
- Process File System (PROCFS)
- File-on-File Mounting File System (FFM)
- File Descriptor File System (FDFS)

The Memory File System and the Process File System are both memory-based file systems that appear to the users of a system as disk-based but are not built on disk partitions. The File-on-File Mounting File System and File Descriptor File System are specialized file systems that are not commonly used. Refer to the Digital UNIX Technical Overview manual for information on these four file system types.

3.2.1. UFS

The Digital UNIX UFS file system is Digital's implementation of the Berkeley Software Distribution (BSD) version 4.3 Fast File System. UFS is the default file system type on a Digital UNIX system and is commonly used for both system and user file systems. The maximum file system size for a UFS file system is 128 gigabytes for Digital UNIX version 3.2G and below, and 512 gigabytes for version 4.0 and above. UFS was the first file system type on Digital UNIX and, because of it's heritage, does not have features such as disk spanning and fast recovery, which exist in more modern file systems such as the Advanced File System (AdvFS). Nevertheless, UFS is considered by some to be a more robust file system, and it continues to enjoy great popularity.

3.2.2. UFS File System Layout

A UFS file system is made up of disk blocks, each 8K in size. Each disk block in a UFS file system is one of four possible types:

- Boot Block—The first block (block 0) of every UFS file system is reserved for an initialization, or boot, program. Typically, only a root file system contains such a boot program, but any UFS file system may have such a boot program.
- Superblocks—The second block (block 1) of every UFS file system contains information that describes the configuration of the file system. This information is called the Superblock and is critical to the proper operation of the file system. A UFS superblock contains:

  - The total size of the filesystem
  - Number of inodes
  - List of Free inodes
  - The beginning of the free-block list
  - Date of the last superblock update

  The superblock is so important that when the file system is created, redundant copies of the superblock are distributed across the disk in a pattern that reduces the chances that a single track, cylinder, or platter failure would not destroy all copies of the superblock.

- Inode Blocks—The UNIX File System uses a structure called an inode, or Index Node, to allow random access and multiple file allocations (links). Inodes are simply pointers to a file's data blocks. Inodes are statically allocated when the file system is created, and there is a one-to-one correspondence between an inode and a file.
- Data Blocks—Finally, the majority of disk blocks in a UFS file system are dedicated to the storage of user file and directory data.

3.2.3. Creating UFS File Systems

The creation of a UFS file system is the process of formatting a disk partition and building the disk structures to support a hierarchy of directories and files. This task is accomplished with the newfs(8) command, specifying the disk partition as the only required command line argument. For instance, to create a UFS file system on the first partition of the rz1 disk, use the following syntax:

```
# newfs rz1a
Warning: 400 sector(s) in last cylinder unallocated
/dev/rrz1a: 131072 sectors in 198 cylinders of 8 tracks, 83 sectors
  64.0MB in 13 cyl groups (16 c/g, 5.19MB/g, 1280 i/g)
super-block backups (for fsck -b #) at:
32, 10752, 21472, 32192, 42912, 53632, 64352, 75072,
85024, 95744, 106464, 117184, 127904,
```

This example demonstrates the default use of newfs(8). Unless additional file system option arguments are specified, the newfs command uses default values along with the geometry values specified in the disk's label to construct the new file system. While the newfs command actually uses the character disk device file when creating the file system, a simple disk name and partition may be specified in addition to either the full character or block disk device name. The newfs command translates any of these disk specifications into the full character (raw) disk device.

There are a group of optional newfs command options that override the default method of creating UFS file systems. Most of the default newfs values are normally sufficient for most situations, and these command options are infrequently used. Refer to the newfs(8) man page for information on the UFS file system options.

One of the newfs options specifies how many inodes are created in the new file system. This is a particularly important parameter since the number of inodes determines the number of files the new file system may contain regardless of disk space. The default is to create one inode for each 4K (4096 bytes) of disk space. This value makes the assumption that the average file size in a new file system will be approximately 4K. If, for instance, the average file size were actually 1K, it would be possible that the file system could run out of inodes before running out of disk space. In this case, the file system should be created with more inodes than default. On the other hand, if a file system were going to contain fewer, larger files, the recommendation would be to create the file system with less inodes. Since each inode takes up a small amount of disk space itself (approximately 100 bytes), fewer inodes leaves more disk space for user data. The newfs command provides a command line option (-i) to specify a "bytes per inode" value. Simply put, estimate the projected average file size in bytes and create the file system with that value. For example, if a file system will contain relatively large files, averaging approximately 500K, the following newfs command will create that file system specifying 512000 bytes (500 * 1024) per inode:

```
# newfs -i 512000 /dev/rrz2c
```

Specifying a value larger than the default of 4096 bytes results in fewer inodes; to create more inodes in the file system, a smaller number should be given. To display the number of inodes configured in a file system, use the df(8) command with the "-i" switch:

```
# df -i /home
Filesystem 512-blocks Used Available Capacity Iused
  Ifree %Iused Mounted on
/dev/rz1a   126462 476   113338   1%   36 16637   0% /home
```

In this example, the file system has a total of 16,637 inodes with 36 in use.

Finally, newfs(8) has a special parameter that permits the system administrator to execute a newfs command without actually creating the file system. This parameter, "-N", displays the file system creation parameters that would be used if the file system were actually created. This can be useful for displaying the default file system creation parameters or for trying different options without touching the disk. For example:

```
# newfs -N -i 12288 /dev/rrz3b
/dev/rrz3b: 262144 sectors in 395 cylinders of 8 tracks, 83 sectors
128.0MB in 25 cyl groups (16 c/g, 5.19MB/g, 448 i/g)
super-block backups (for fsck -b #) at:
32, 10752, 21472, 32192, 42912, 53632, 64352, 75072,
85024, 95744, 106464, 117184, 127904, 138624, 149344, 160064,
170016, 180736, 191456, 202176, 212896, 223616, 234336, 245056,
255008,
```

3.2.4. Mounting File Systems

After creating a file system, the next operation is to "mount" the file system onto the existing hierarchy. The mount(8) command is used to mount all types of file systems and make them available for use. Only the root user may mount and unmount file systems. Refer to the mount(8) man page for details on the various file system mount options. The following example will mount the UFS file system on partition a of the disk rz1 onto the /home mount point:

```
# mount /dev/rz1a /home
```

The mount point parameter of the mount command is simply a directory that must exist. This directory may be empty but does not have to be. Be aware that any contents of a mount point directory will be unavailable while a file system is mounted on that point. Mount points are often created at the base of the root file system (/), but this is not a requirement. The only issue to be aware of when mounting a file system on a mount point in a non-root file system is that the base file system should be mounted before attempting to mount the secondary file system. For example, if a file system is mounted on /home, and a second file system is mounted on /home/tools, then ensure that /home is mounted first before attempting to mount /home/tools. Also, if a file system is manually mounted with the mount command and a file system is not listed in the /etc/fstab file, the mount will be temporary and will not persist after a system reboot.

3.2.4.1. The /etc/fstab File

Permanent file systems are ones that should be automatically mounted when the system is started. The mechanism for doing this is the /etc/fstab file. File systems listed in this file are mounted when the system boots and, as the file is read from top to bottom, also enforce any necessary mount sequence. During a Digital UNIX installation, any file systems created as part of the installation are added to the fstab file. This includes the root, /usr, and, if created, the /var file systems. In addition, the fstab file contains a record for each swap partition on the system and is consulted when activating the system's swap files. Following is a sample /etc/fstab file:

```
/dev/rz0a      /             ufs    rw 1 1
/dev/rz1g      /usr          ufs    rw 1 2
/dev/rz2g      /var          ufs    rw 1 2
/dev/rz0b      swap1         ufs    sw 0 2
tools#utils    /tools/utils  advfs  rw,userquota,groupquota 0 2
```

The format of the /etc/fstab file specifies that each file system be on a separate line and that each field be delimited by space or tab characters. Blank lines or lines that begin with a hash sign (#) are ignored. Each file system line should contain the name of the file system to be mounted, the mount point, the file system type, any special mount options, whether the file system should be backed up with the dump(8) command, and the sequence in which the file system should be checked with the fsck(8) command. The format of the first parameter depends on the file system type. For UFS file systems, the block special device file name should be used, while for AdvFS file systems, the parameter should be in the form filedomain#fileset.

Once a file system is properly listed in the /etc/fstab file, the file system can be mounted by issuing the mount command and specifying simply the mount point. For example, assuming the following entry in the /etc/fstab file:

```
/dev/rz4c   /home   ufs   rw 1 2
```

this file system could be mounted with this command:

```
# mount /home
```

rather than the more verbose:

```
# mount /dev/rz4c /mnt
```

3.2.5. Unmounting File Systems

The opposite of the mount(8) command is the umount(8) command, which is used to unmount a file system. Unmounting a file system flushes any uncommitted writes to the disk and then disconnects the file system, making it unavailable for use. Only the root user may unmount file systems with the umount command. Simply specify the mount point as an argument to the umount command to unmount that file system. For example:

```
# umount /home
```

If any user process is active in a file system, that file system cannot be unmounted and the umount command returns the following error message:

```
<mount point>: Device busy
```

This can occur even if only a single user has changed directories into the file system. If the file system must be unmounted, determine which user or process is using the file system and either shut the process down or, in the case of an interactive user session, have that user cd(1) to another directory outside of the target file system. Digital UNIX version 4.0 and greater provides a utility, fuser(8), to quickly identify the processes and/or users that are occupying a file system. Run the fuser command specifying the mount point of the file system in question. For instance:

```
# fuser /home
/home: 608c      879c
```

This output indicates that two processes (PID 608 and 879) are running. Search the process table listing with the ps(1) command to identify the processes. A useful fuser option is "-u," which indicates the user name associated with the process Ids:

```
# fuser -u /home
/home: 608c(jsmith)     879c(jsmith)
```

3.2.6. Checking UFS File Systems

The UFS file system, not having the write-ahead logging feature of AdvFS, is somewhat vulnerable to improper system shutdowns or unexpected system failures. Since the UFS file system provides buffering of disk writes, if a file system is not properly unmounted and the buffers flushed to disk, there exists the possibility of corrupting the file system. This is the primary reason a Digital UNIX system should be shutdown gracefully. However, hardware or power problems or system errors resulting in kernel panics can and do occur, and for these situations a file system check utility is provided. The fsck(8) program checks UFS file systems and can correct file system inconsistencies, such as incorrect inode or free block count, unreferenced inodes, or orphan data blocks. When using fsck to check a UFS file system, the file system must be unmounted and the character disk device name should be specified on the fsck command line. The fsck command then proceeds to check the file system in five passes. If inconsistencies are found, the fsck program prompts before each correction is attempted. This allows the system administrator to answer yes or no. Typically, the answer should always be yes to the questions. For instance:

```
# fsck /dev/rrz1c
/sbin/ufs_fsck /dev/rrz1c
** /dev/rrz1c
** Last Mounted on /home
** Phase 1 - Check Blocks and Sizes
INCORRECT BLOCK COUNT I=48862 (288 should be 208)
CORRECT? [yn] y
```

```
INCORRECT BLOCK COUNT I=48892 (560 should be 208)
  CORRECT? [yn] y

** Phase 2 - Check Pathnames
DIRECTORY /bin: LENGTH 6676 NOT MULTIPLE OF 512
ADJUST? [yn]
** Phase 3 - Check Connectivity
** Phase 4 - Check Reference Counts
** Phase 5 - Check Cyl groups
FREE BLK COUNT(S) WRONG IN SUPERBLK
SALVAGE? [yn] y

BLK(S) MISSING IN BIT MAPS
SALVAGE? [yn] y

SUMMARY INFORMATION BAD
SALVAGE? [yn] y

724 files, 51002 used, 940226 free (258 frags,
  117496 blocks, 0.0% fragmentation)

***** FILE SYSTEM WAS MODIFIED *****
```

In this example, several corrections were successful made and the file system is now ready to be mounted.

The fsck command is automatically run in a noninteractive mode when the system boots to check all UFS file systems listed in the /etc/fstab file. For file systems unmounted cleanly, no checking is necessary. However, if a file system was not unmounted properly, fsck silently checks the file system. Any inconsistencies that are discovered are repaired if the correction can be completed safely without risk of data loss. If a severe inconsistency is encountered, the fsck program exits, leaving the system in single-user mode with a recommendation to run fsck manually.

3.3. THE ADVANCED FILE SYSTEM (ADVFS)

The Advanced File System (AdvFS) is a file system option on Digital UNIX that is quickly replacing UFS as the file system of choice. AdvFS provides many modern file system features, such as write-ahead logging for fast file system recovery, disk spanning, and file striping. The architecture of the

AdvFS allows managing the file systems while they are mounted and online. This includes dynamically resizing file systems, defragmenting to make files more contiguous on the disk, and cloning of file systems for backup purposes.

The base AdvFS functionality is a licensed part of the Digital UNIX operating system and can completely replace UFS on a Digital UNIX system, including the root, /usr, and /var file systems. The Digital UNIX advanced installation option allows the installer to select AdvFS as a file system for the system partitions. (See Chapter 2, "Installation," for details on performing an advanced installation.) In addition, an optional set of utilities provides additional capabilities to the AdvFS file system. This optional product, the Advanced File System Advanced Utilities (AdvFS Utilities), is available as a separately licensed subset from Digital. The AdvFS Utilities provide such features as file undelete capability, online file migration, and a graphical user interface (GUI).

From a system administration standpoint, a AdvFS file system differs significantly from a UFS file system, both in terms of initial creation and ongoing management. Some of the concepts are similar, but it is necessary for a Digital UNIX system administrator to understand the unique characteristics of AdvFS to fully utilize its capabilities. This section covers the components of an AdvFS configuration and details setting up an AdvFS file system. Two new concepts that characterize the Advanced File System are File Domains and Filesets.

3.3.1. AdvFS File Domains

A file domain is a grouping of one or more volumes into a shared pool of disk storage. In this context, a volume is any physical or logical object that can be referenced as a Digital UNIX block special device, for example:

- An entire physical disk
- An individual disk partition
- A logical volume configured with the Logical Storage Manager (LSM)

When creating an AdvFS file domain, the domain initially consists of exactly one volume. If the AdvFS Utilities are installed and licensed, additional volumes may be added to a domain, up to 250 volumes. Volumes may be added to an AdvFS domain immediately after initial file domain creation, or one can wait until the domain requires additional space. Without the AdvFS utilities, however, one is limited to single-volume domains. There is no limit to the total number of AdvFS file domains per system; however, there may only be 100 active file domains at any one time. A file domain is considered active if at least one of its filesets is mounted.

The AdvFS file system automatically creates and updates the /etc/fdmns directory structure, which is used by the various AdvFS utilities to ensures access to file domains. The /etc/fdmns directory will contain a subdirectory for each file domain on the system. Within each subdirectory is a symbolic link to block special device files for every volume in the file domain. This directory is crucial to the healthy operation of the AdvFS file system. Do not edit or remove the /etc/fdmns directory or its subdirectories without fully understanding the implications of the action.

When planning the layout of file domains, the best performance can be achieved by dedicating entire disks to individual file domains. Though splitting a disk's partitions between multiple file domains is permitted, the performance of such a configuration might suffer significantly due to head contention within that disk. In addition, since a single volume failure within a file domain means that the entire file domain fails, avoid large numbers of volumes in single file domains. Digital has recommended that there should be no more than three volumes in a file domain to reduce the risk of file domain failure.

3.3.2. AdvFS Filesets

The second important component of the AdvFS file system are Filesets. A fileset is an object that contains files and directories that can be mounted for use identically, as in a UFS file system. A fileset differs from a regular file system in one important manner: while a UFS file system resides on a single disk partition, an AdvFS fileset is created inside a file domain, which can be one or more volumes. This means that a fileset can be larger than a single disk partition and is able to span multiple disks. In addition, there can be many filesets within a single file domain. The concept of filesets provides much of the flexibility of the AdvFS file system.

Digital UNIX permits an unlimited number of filesets per system; however, the total allowable number of actively mounted filesets is limited to 512 minus the number of active AdvFS file domains. When planning fileset layout, keep in mind that the design philosophy of the Advanced File

System encourages multiple filesets per file domain. Since filesets are managed independently, regardless of which file domain they reside in, there is no penalty for large numbers of filesets. The most flexible configuration is fewer file domains and more filesets. This allows the system administrator to worry less about disk space since it is collected into pools larger than individual disks.

3.3.3. Creating an AdvFS File Domain

The first step in setting up an AdvFS file system is to create a file domain using the mkfdmn(8) command. The mkfdmn command requires two arguments: the block special device file and the file domain name. A file domain name must be unique, may be up to 31 characters in length, and cannot contain white space characters (space, tab, etc.) or certain special characters (/ # : * ?). An example of creating a new file domain follows:

```
# mkfdmn /dev/rz3c tools
```

This command creates a new AdvFS file domain named "tools." This file domain is composed of the entire rz3 disk (partition c). As a result of this file domain creation, a subdirectory with the same name as the new file domain was added to the /etc/fdmns directory:

```
# ls -l /etc/fdmns
total 8
drwxr-xr-x   2 root    system     8192 Feb 14 12:13 tools
# ls -l /etc/fdmns/tools
total 0
lrwxr-xr-x   1 root    system     9 Feb 14 12:13 rz3c -> /dev/rz3c
```

The mkfdmn command has several optional command line arguments to modify how AdvFS file domains are created. Refer to the mkfdmn(8) man page for more information on these options.

3.3.4. Creating an AdvFS Fileset

Once an AdvFS file domain has been created, the next step is to create one or more filesets within that domain. For this, use the mkfset(8) command, specifying the file domain name and the name of the fileset to be created.

For instance, to create two filesets within the tools file domain, use the following commands:

```
# mkfset tools project1
# mkfset tools project2
```

Each fileset within a file domain must have a unique name no longer than 31 characters. The space character and the / # : * ? characters are invalid for fileset names. A common convention is to name a fileset with its intended mount point. This is not required, but is a helpful organizational practice.

3.3.4. Mounting AdvFS Filesets

After creating a file domain and one or more filesets, the fileset(s) must be mounted before they are available for use. As with UFS file systems, the mount(8) and umount(8) commands are used to mount and unmount AdvFS filesets. The main difference is that rather than specifying the full pathname to the block special device file for a UFS file system, an AdvFS fileset is referred to using the "filedomain#fileset" descriptor. For instance, the following commands will create two mount points, then mount our example filesets:

```
# mkdir /tools/project1
# mkdir /tools/project2
# mount -t advfs tools#project1 /tools/project1
# mount -t advfs tools#project2 /tools/project2
```

The hash sign (#) between the file domain name and the fileset is required as part of the syntax representing an AdvFS fileset. Also, the mount command's "-t" flag specifies the file system type. If newly created and mounted AdvFS filesets are to be a permanent configuration, add an entry to the /etc/fstab file for each fileset. This will cause the filesets to be automatically mounted when the system reboots.

3.3.5. AdvFS Fileset Quotas

When using multiple AdvFS filesets within a single AdvFS file domain, it is important to understand the concept of AdvFS fileset quotas. Fileset quotas are a management tool available to the system administrator to limit the amount of disk space and the number of files consumed by a fileset. This is important since, by default, all the filesets within a file domain have equal access to the domain's disk space. This means that a single fileset could consume all available disk space in a file domain. For example, the following two newly created filesets are in the same file domain:

```
# df -k /tools/project1 /tools/project2
Filesystem      1024-blocks  Used  Available  Capacity  Mounted on
tools#project1  1025424       16    1020952    1%        /tools/
                                                         project1
tools#project2  1025424       16    1020952    1%        /tools/
                                                         project2
```

This df(1) output can be somewhat misleading in that it appears that both the tools#project1 fileset and the tools#project2 fileset each have almost 1000 megabytes of space available. This is not really the case, however, as the file domain is a fixed pool of disk space. Since there are no fileset quotas set on either of these two filesets, each has access to the entire amount of disk space in the file domain.

By setting a fileset quota on one or both of these filesets, each is limited to the amount specified by the quota limit. For instance, suppose that it is decided to set the quota limit on the first filset (tools#project1) to 400 megabytes and the second fileset (tools#project2) to 600 megabytes. The following chfset(8) commands will implement these quotas:

```
# chfsets -b 409600 tools project1
project1
  Id    : 3584af2e.000e8160.1.8001
  Block H Limit: 0 -> 409600
# chfsets -b 611328 tools project2
project2
  Id    : 3584af2e.000e8160.2.8001
  Block H Limit: 0 -> 611328
```

Now, after setting these fileset quota limits, the df(1) output of the two filesets is more understandable:

```
# df -k /tools/project1 /tools/project2
Filesystem      1024-blocks  Used  Available  Capacity  Mounted on
tools#project1  409600        16    409584     1%        /tools/
                                                         project1
tools#project2  611328        16    611312     1%        /tools/
                                                         project2
```

The AdvFS fileset quotas are a valuable tool for managing AdvFS filesets. Suppose that a fileset had become full or, more accurately, had reached the configured fileset quota limit. If the file domain where the file set resided still had available disk space, it would be a simple matter to increase the fileset quota limit on the full fileset. This will allow data to be added to the fileset, effectively increasing the size of the fileset. Refer to the chfsets(8) man page for more information on managing AdvFS fileset quotas.

3.3.6. Logical Storage Manager (LSM)

Digital UNIX supports the Logical Storage Manager (LSM), a robust logical storage manager based on the VERITAS Volume Manager from VERITAS Software. LSM supports all of the following:

- Disk spanning—Disk spanning allows you to concatenate entire disks or parts (regions) of multiple disks together to use as one, logical volume. For example, you could "combine" two RZ28s and have them contain the /usr file system.
- Mirroring—Mirroring allows you to write simultaneously to two or more disk drives to protect against data loss in the event of an individual disk failure.
- Striping—Striping improves performance by breaking data into segments that are written to several different physical disks in a "stripe set."
- Disk management—LSM supports disk management utilities that, among other things, change the disk configuration without disrupting users while the system is up and running.

The mirroring, striping, and graphical interface require a separate, optional license PAK (Product Authorization Key).

For each logical volume defined in the system, the LSM volume device driver maps logical volume I/O to physical disk I/O. In addition, LSM uses a user-level volume configuration daemon (vold) that controls changes to the configuration of logical volumes. The root user can administer LSM either through a series of command-line utilities or via an X-Windows graphical interface (dxlsm).

To help users transform their existing UFS or AdvFS file systems onto LSM logical volumes, Digital has developed a utility that will transform each partition in use by UFS or AdvFS into a nonstriped, nonmirrored LSM volume. After the transformation is complete, the system administrator can mirror the volumes if desired.

Note that LSM volumes can be used in conjunction with AdvFS, as components of AdvFS file domains. For more information on LSM, refer to the *Digital UNIX Logical Storage Manager* guide.

3.4. SOFTWARE SUBSET MANAGEMENT

A system running Digital UNIX is actually composed of a collection of individual software pieces, each providing a different type of functionality. These software pieces, called Software Subsets, are packaged to provide ease of installation, removal, inventory, and validation. A software subset is composed of data and script files and is basically an installation kit for an individual software product or service. All Digital UNIX software, both the base operating system products and optional, layered products, produced by Digital is packaged in this software subset format. In addition, some third-party software vendors also deliver their software products in this subset format. Finally, all regular Digital UNIX operating system patches are also provided in this format. This broad acceptance of the software subset facility means that a Digital UNIX system administrator must be familiar with the process of managing software subsets in Digital UNIX. The key to the software subset facility is the setld(8) command.

3.4.1. The setld(8) Utility

Digital UNIX provides the setld(8) command for managing software subsets on a Digital UNIX system. The common pronunciation of the setld command is "Set-L-D." The system administrator uses this tool to:

- Display Installed Software Subsets
- Load Software Subsets
- Delete Installed Software Subsets
- Verify Installed Software Subsets
- Configure an Installed Software Subsets
- Extract Software Subsets

Each of these functions are executed by running the setld command with the necessary argument(s). Invoking setld with no arguments displays a usage message showing the syntax of each of the functions. Each of the setld functions either require or can optionally accept one or more software subset names as arguments. The software subset names are displayed with all letters in the name capitalized, but the setld command is case insensitive and will accept subset names in all lower, all upper, or mixed case. All but the display function of setld requires root access to execute.

3.4.2. Subset Inventory

Probably the most common use of the setld(8) command is to display an inventory of all software subsets loaded on a Digital UNIX system. To perform this function, simply execute the following command:

```
# setld -i

Subset          Status         Description
____            ____           _____

OSFACCT425      installed      System Accounting Utilities (System
Administration)
OSFADVFS425     installed      POLYCTR advfs (System
Administration)
OSFADVFSBIN425  installed      POLYCTR advfs Kernel Modules
(Kernel Build Environment)
OSFADVFSBINOBJECT425           POLYCTR advfs Kernel Objects
(Kernel Software Development)
OSFBASE425      installed      Base System (- Required -)
OSFBIN425       installed      Standard Kernel Modules (Kernel
Build Environment)
OSFBINCOM425    installed      Kernel Header and Common Files
(Kernel Build Environment)
OSFBINOBJECT425                Standard Kernel Objects (Kernel
Software Development)
OSFCLINET425    installed      Basic Networking Services (Network-
Server/Communications)
  .
```

Typical Digital UNIX installations have many software subsets installed, and this inventory output may run on for hundreds of lines. Note that the setld command displays three pieces of information for each software subset: Subset Name, Status, and Description. The Subset Name has a length of seven or more characters, is normally a combination of capital letter and numbers, is usually an abbreviation of the subset name, and contains some version number information. The Status field displays the current status of the subset. The Status will always be one of four possible values:

1. installed—The "installed" status indicates the subset is correctly loaded and installed
2. incomplete—A value of "incomplete" indicates that at the time this subset was loaded, the subset kit was incorrect or incomplete
3. corrupt—A "corrupt" subset means that the installation of the subset failed
4. <null>—No value in the Status field indicates that either the subset was installed in the past but has been deleted, or the subset installation was canceled

The Description field is normally the software product's name as described in the Software Product Description (SPD) issued with the product.

In addition to displaying the entire software subset inventory, the setld command can display a listing of all the files in a particular software subset. Specify one or more software subsets after the "-i" flag for the subset inventory:

```
# setld -i OSFBASE425
./.new...cshrc
./.new...login
./.new...profile
./.new..DXsession
./bin
./dev
./dev/SYSV_PTY
./etc
./etc/.new..TIMEZONE
./etc/.new..autopush.conf
.
```

Individual software subsets can have from only a few component files to many hundreds of files. Note that the files in an inventory listing are displayed relative to the root path, which, by default, is /. The inventory for a software subset may be displayed regardless of the status of the subset, that is, if the subset is listed in the master inventory.

3.4.3. Subset Installation

The most important role of the setld(8) command is as a software subset installer. Every Digital UNIX and third-party software product that is packaged as a software subset is installed via the setld utility. The process of installing a software subset is much more than just copying software onto a system. The setld utility does the following during a software load operation:

- Validate dependencies and prerequisites
- Execute pre-installation procedures, if any
- Copy subset components into place
- Register the product in the system software subset inventory
- Execute post-installation procedures, if any

In addition, the setld utility can load software subsets from three possible sources: a disk distribution, directly from a tape or floppy disk, or from a Remote Installation Server (RIS) across the network.

The most common software subset distribution media is probably CD-ROM. Most Digital software, especially the Digital UNIX operating system and layered products, is shipped on CD-ROM. After inserting a software distribution CD-ROM into a system's local CD-ROM drive and mounting the CD-ROM, issue the setld command to commence the load operation. For example, the following session demonstrates mounting the Digital UNIX Associated Products distribution CD-ROM and running the setld command to display a menu of available software subsets, in this case, the Advanced File System Advanced Utilities:

```
# mount -d -r /dev/rz4c /mnt
# setld -l /mnt
```

```
The subsets listed below are optional:
 There may be more optional subsets than can be presented on a
 single screen. If this is the case, you can choose subsets
 screen by screen or all at once on the last screen. All of the
 choices you make will be collected for your confirmation before
 any subsets are installed.
```

```
- General Applications:
1) Advanced File System Advanced Utilities Reference Pages,
v4.0d, r425
2) Advanced File System Advanced Utilities, v4.0d, r425
3) Advanced File System Daemon, v4.0d, r425
4) Advanced File System Graphical User Interface, v4.0d, r425

Or you may choose one of the following options:
5) ALL of the above
6) CANCEL selections and redisplay menus
7) EXIT without installing any subsets

Enter your choices or press RETURN to redisplay menus.
Choices (for example, 1 2 4-6):
```

This menu of software subsets is a feature of the setld utility and is displayed whenever specific subsets to be loaded are not specified on the setld command line. Only subsets not currently installed are listed as menu choices. Also, individual subsets are designated as either mandatory or optional by the software subset producer. This distinction is used to ensure that certain required subsets are loaded, and the setld menu enforces this by requiring the user to load mandatory subsets. Alternatively, the software load may be aborted by selecting the EXIT menu choice.

Select the desired software subsets for installation by entering the menu choice(s). Either enter individual menu choices separated by a space (e.g., 1 2 3) or select a range of menu choices (e.g., 1-3). Also, the menu contains a menu choice for "ALL of the above." Select this to install all listed subsets. After choosing the software subsets to load, a prompt similar to the following is displayed as a final confirmation:

```
You are installing the following optional subsets:
- General Applications:
 Advanced File System Advanced Utilities Reference Pages, v4.0d,
 r425
 Advanced File System Advanced Utilities, v4.0d, r425
 Advanced File System Daemon, v4.0d, r425
 Advanced File System Graphical User Interface, v4.0d, r425

Is this correct? (y/n):
```

Simply enter a "y" if the list is correct to proceed with the subset installation.

While the setld menu interface provides an interactive interface to the installation of software subsets, it is occasionally desirable to quickly load individual software subsets in a noninteractive fashion. An example of this would be to load a single subset from a disk distribution without scrolling through a menu containing possibly hundreds of unnecessary subsets. To load one or more individual subsets, simply specify the subset name(s) on the command line. For multiple subsets, separate the subset names with spaces. The following example demonstrates this method using tape as the install media:

```
# setld -l /dev/rmt0h AFAADVANCED425
    AFAADVDAEMON425 AFAADVGUI425 AFAADVMAN425
```

This noninteractive setld subset load does not prompt for confirmation and immediately begins the installation.

3.4.4. Subset Deletion

The opposite of software subset installation is subset deletion, and the setld command can quickly remove individual subsets from a Digital UNIX system. In order to remove a subset, the subset must be installed and the user must know the subset's name. Use setld's inventory flag (-i) to determine a particular subset's name. Once this is known, run the setld command to remove the subset:

```
# setld -d OSFLEARN425
Deleting "Computer Aided System Tutor " (OSFLEARN425).
```

Be aware that no confirmation is requested and the subset is immediately deleted from the system. If a subset is inadvertently removed, simply reinstall it from the distribution media.

3.4.5. setld(8) Activity Logging

The setld utility conveniently logs all operations (installs, deletes, inventories, etc.) along with a time/date stamp in a log file for future reference. This log file is:

```
/var/adm/smlogs/setld.log
```

Refer to this log file for information on a past setld transaction.

3.5 LICENSE MANAGEMENT

The Digital UNIX operating system and many of the Digital UNIX layered products are licensed to the end user rather than sold. This means that the vendor, Digital Equipment Corporation in this case, has sold only an authorization to use a particular software product. The license agreement between the software vendor and the end user specifies the terms of the license. These license terms typically specify each party's responsibilities with regarding the use of the software product. A system administrator should be aware of the licensing terms to ensure that the organization honors the terms of the license. If that was all there were to licensing, a system administrator's responsibility would be minimal and consist mostly of just administrative paperwork. However, certain software products produced by Digital have special licensing characteristics and requirements.

3.5.1. Types of Licensing

There are two types of software licenses issued by Digital, and a software product might be licensed only one way or the other, or optionally both ways, depending on the product itself. A product's licensing type is indicated on the license information provided with the software media and documentation.

3.5.2. Availability Licensing

A software application might be licensed to allow unlimited use of the product, but only on certain specific models of processors. This type of license is called an availability license or, occasionally, a traditional license. An availability license is purchased based on the model and size of the Alpha system on which the software product will be run. For example, an availability license sized for a small server such as an Alphaserver 1200 could not be run on a large Alphaserver 8400. However, an availability license purchased for the Alphaserver 8400 would run fine on the Alphaserver 1200. Since the price of the license is proportional to the price of the computer, a license for an 8400 is usually significantly more than the same license for a 1200. While it would be foolish to purchase more licenses than necessary, the ability to move a "larger" license to a "smaller" system may be useful when planning for a "backup" system. In the event that a main server is unavailable, it is possible to move a software product and its license to a smaller (and less expensive) system so the product is still available to its users.

3.5.3. Activity Licensing

Other products may be licensed to allow only a certain number of users to run the product simultaneously. This type of license is called an activity license, or a per-user or concurrent use license. For example, consider a software development software product such as a compiler that is used by many users, but not on a constant basis. Analyzing the usage of the compiler may indicate that no more than five users are ever actively compiling at any one time. An availability license providing unlimited use for such a product may be prohibitively expensive and unnecessary, but an activity license for five concurrent users would be very economical and would likely be sufficient. If, in this example, the number of developers were increased and the new concurrent use average was eight users, all that would be necessary would be to purchase three additional per-user licenses to increase the size of the activity license.

While all software products are licensed, only certain software licenses are enforced, that is, the product will only run with proof of a license. Since software is usually a source of revenue for a company such as Digital Equipment Corporation, the vendor must take measures to protect that software development investment and prevent illegal use of software licenses. For this purpose, Digital created the License Management Facility for Digital UNIX.

3.5.4. The License Management Facility

Digital developed the License Management Facility (LMF) for Digital UNIX as a way for software products to validate licensing information. The LMF maintains a list of licensed software products on a particular system in a database. The system administrator is responsible for managing this license database to ensure that all LMF licensed products are registered. Every Digital UNIX system will have at least two, and probably more, LMF licenses as the operating system itself is a licensed product. Licensed software products will call license-checking functions to check that a valid license is registered with the LMF before making the product available for use. In addition to meeting the legal responsibility of licensing, properly administering the license database ensures that users are able to log in to the system and run the software products necessary to doing their job.

In addition to the License Management Facility, there are other types of license managers available that run on Digital UNIX. Most of these license managers are third-party products that independent software developers have used for license management with their applications. These other license managers, FLEXlm by GLOBEtrotter Software is an example, typically ship with the particular software product and are not part of Digital UNIX. This section will only concern itself with Digital's LMF and the software products that support LMF. If it becomes necessary to install and manage a third-party license manager, consult the documentation that came with the product for assistance. Regardless, any such third-party license manager will run in conjunction with Digital's LMF and understanding the operation of LMF is still a requirement.

If a software product's licensing information is in the form of a Product Authorization Key (PAK), the software product supports the LMF, and the PAK must be registered with the LMF in order for the software to be used. A Digital PAK is a special document incorporating security printing that makes it difficult to forge or copy and, as formal proof of purchase of software license, should be retained indefinitely in a secure place. See Figure 3.2 for description of the fields on a license PAK. In addition to these fields, a Digital PAK usually provides the following one or more of the following useful pieces of information, none of which are entered into LMF:

- Customer P.O.—This field may contain the purchase order number used to purchase this license.
- License Issue Date—This is the date the PAK was actually produced by Digital.
- Descriptive Product Name—Since the PAK PRODUCT NAME field is limited in length, this field usually contains a more readable description of the licensed software product.
- License Type—This field indicates whether the license is a Traditional (Availability) or Concurrent (Activity) license type.

Finally, a PAK has a box labeled "For Customer Use," which contains two fields that the system administrator may want to complete in pencil after registering the PAK:

- CPU Serial No
- Node Id

Issuer:[1]   DEC
Authorization Number:[2]   ALS-MT-1998JAN31-2
Product Name:[3]   OSF-BASE
Producer:[4]   DEC
Number of units:[5]   15
Version:[6]
Product Release Date:[7]
Key Termination Date:[8]
Availability Table Code:[9]   A
Activity Table Code:[10]
Key Options:[11]   MOD_UNITS,ALPHA
Product Token:[12]
Hardware-Id:[13]
Checksum:[14]   2-DKSK-OEKS-ORGP-DKNU

1. The Issuer is the vendor licensing the software product. For Digital Equipment Corporation products, this is typically the string "DEC".

2. The Authorization Number is a unique string that the PAK issuer assigns to a specific PAK. The combination of the Issuer and the Authorization Number uniquely identifies a PAK.

3. The name used by the LMF to distinguish among different software products.

4. The name of the company that produced the licensed software. This is typically DEC.

5. The Number of Units indicates how many license units are supplied by the PAK. If this field is zero (0), the PAK provides unlimited use of the product on any type of processor.

6. The Version field is used if the PAK applies only to certain versions of the software product. If a version is specified, the PAK will work with that version and earlier of the software. If this field on the PAK is empty, the PAK is not restricted to a specific version of the software.

Figure 3.2 Example of License PAK Fields

7. The Product Release Date is used if the PAK is restricted to only versions of the software product released before the specified date. If this field on the PAK is empty, the PAK is not restricted to a specific release date of the software.

8. The Key Termination Date is the date when the PAK expires. Once this date passes, LMF no longer allows users to invoke the software product. If this field on the PAK is empty, the PAK will function indefinitely.

9. The Availability Table Code represents the number of units required to give unlimited use of a product on a particular hardware system model.

    A letter represents a value from the License Unit Requirement Table (LURT) which specifies the number of units necessary for the product to run on a specific hardware model. The LURT is internal to LMF and cannot be displayed or modified.

    If the field specifies "CONSTANT=integer", the integer value indicates the number of units necessary to run the software product, regardless of the hardware model in use.

10. The Activity Table Code represents the number of units required for each concurrent user of the product. This field may either be a single letter or the string "CONSTANT=integer".

    A letter represents a value from the License Unit Requirement Table (LURT) which specifies the number of units necessary for each concurrent user to run the product on a specific hardware model. The LURT is internal to LMF and cannot be displayed or modified.

    If the field specifies "CONSTANT=integer", the integer value indicates the number of units necessary for each concurrent user to run the software product, regardless of the hardware model in use.

(continued)

Figure 3.2 Continued

11. The Key Options field may contain one or more of the following options delimited by commas:

• MOD_UNITS – This option indicates that the system administrator is able to modify the value specified in the NUMBER OF UNITS field. See the lmf(8) modify command for more information.
• ALPHA – This option indicates that the PAK is valid only on the Alpha family of computers.
• NO_SHARE – This option indicates that the license cannot be combined with another license for the same software product on the same computer.

12. The Product Token field is not currently used by LMF. However, if a PAK contains data in this field, you must enter the specified string when registering the PAK.

13. The Hardware-Id is not currently used by LMF. However, if a PAK contains data in this field, you must enter the specified string when registering the PAK.

14. The Checksum is a string generated from a sum of the values of the other PAK fields. This string is used to verify the accuracy and integrity of the entered PAK data.

Figure 3.2 Continued

3.5.4.1. PAK Units

The LMF concept of license units is the key to the operation of LMF. A license unit is the basic unit of measurement that Digital uses to specify how much product use a license provides. The producer of a software product determines the number of units that are required to run the application on a particular system. This value is tied to the License Unit Requirement Table (LURT), which is a part of the Digital UNIX operating system. The LURT specifies a series of license unit requirements, essentially performance ratings, for each model of processor. Processors that provide more performance (more or faster CPUs, for instance) have greater license unit requirements. The LURT is internal to the LMF and cannot be displayed or modified. Suffice it to say that larger and more powerful server systems have higher license unit requirements than smaller workstations and servers.

3.5.4.2. LMF Database Files

The LMF database files are located, by default, in /var/adm/lmf and consist of two files:

- ldb—The actual LMF database file
- ldb_history—The license management history file, which is a record of all LMF maintenance commands that have been issued on the system

The LMF database files are binary files and should not be edited or modified except via the utilities provided by the LMF. However, the database files can be safely copied using cp(1) as long as no LMF activities are occurring. Once the LMF database is populated with a system's licenses, the database files are normally only accessed at the system startup to copy the license information into the system's license cache. This cache, not the database files on disk, is what is accessed by a software product when verifying that a valid license is registered. To maintain license database consistency, always copy both files (ldb and ldb_history) together when backing them up, whether to tape or to another directory.

3.5.4.3. lmf(8) Utility

The principal tool provided by Digital UNIX to manage and manipulate the license database is the lmf(8) command. The lmf command is used to register new licenses, delete existing licenses, list registered licenses, update the system's license cache, and other license maintenance tasks. The ldb command is, by default, executable by all users. However, the LMF database files are normally only readable and writable by the root user. The effective result of this is that the lmf command is only usable by root, as probably should be the case. Do not change the ownership of the LMF database files.

The lmf command has two modes: command line arguments and an interactive environment. Both modes provide identical functionality, and the use of one mode over the other is normally a matter of personal preference. The exception to this is if you wish to place lmf commands into a script. In this case, use the lmf command line arguments for the desired functionality. Actually, the lmf commands themselves are identical, and the mode only differs in the invocation. To run an lmf command from the command line, simply execute the lmf utility followed by the desired command. For example:

```
# lmf command
```

This will execute the command, then return to the shell prompt.

The interactive mode of the lmf utility is entered by simply typing lmf followed by a return. This will present an lmf> prompt where lmf commands may be executed by entering just the command (without prefacing "lmf"). To exit from interactive mode, enter exit or type a Ctrl-D. For example:

```
# lmf
lmf> command
```

In the following examples, the command line mode of the lmf command will be used for brevity.

Additionally, there is a command line flag that can be specified regardless of the execution mode. This flag, -d, allows an alternative location for the LMF database files to be specified. By default, the database files are located in the /var/adm/lmf directory, and lmf(8) will use this directory if another directory is not specified. The –d flag is useful when experimenting with the LMF configuration on a system. By copying the LMF database files (ldb and ldb_history) to another directory, then specifying that alternate directory, one can manipulate a backup copy of the database without affecting the primary copy.

3.5.4.4. Listing Licenses

The most basic LMF command is "list". This command provides the ability to query and display either the LMF database files, the kernel license cache, or both. At its simplest, list without any modifiers displays a one-line summary of the PAK data for each product in the license database:

```
# lmf list
Product             Status            Users: Total  Active

OSF-USR             active            10            0
OSF-USR             active, multiple  10            0
OSF-BASE            active            unlimited
NET-APP-SUP-200     active            unlimited
LSM-OA              active            unlimited
```

```
DMQ-RTO            active              unlimited
ADVFS-UTILITIES    active              unlimited
ACAS-RT            active              unlimited
```

The list command also has modifiers to provide more complete information on individual PAKs, and allows listing only specific PAKs based on product name and producer. These options provide a fair amount of flexibility when listing a system's PAKs. To display all PAK fields except for the checksum, plus several additional fields related to the current status of the PAK, use the following list command:

```
# lmf list full
```

To list just a specific product's PAK, use the following syntax:

```
# lmf list full for OSF-BASE
Product Name: OSF-BASE
      Producer: DEC
      Issuer: DEC
  Authorization Number: ALS-MT-1998JAN31-2
   Number of units: 400
      Version:
  Product Release Date:
  Key Termination Date:
Availability Table Code: A
  Activity Table Code:
    Key Options: MOD_UNITS, ALPHA
    Product Token:
    Hardware-Id:
    License status: active
  Cancellation Date:
  Revision Number: 0
   Comment:
Cache Total Units: 400
   Activity Charge: 0
```

3.5.4.5. Registering Licenses

One of the first tasks after installing the Digital UNIX operating system is to register the operating system PAKs (OSF-USR and possibly OSF-BASE). Registering a PAK is the process of copying the PAK data into the LMF for use by the product licensed by the PAK. Since the fields containing license data varies from PAK to PAK, the registration process prompts for all possible fields. When registering a PAK, only enter data into a field when the corresponding field on the PAK has data. Simply hit <Return> to skip unnecessary fields. Also, entry of data from a PAK is case-insensitive. Usually the characters on a PAK are all uppercase, however it is not necessary to enter the characters in uppercase—lowercase or mixed case is fine.

The simplest way to register a PAK is to use the lmfsetup(8) command. This command is actually a shell script that prompts the user for each PAK field, then registers the PAK after all the fields have been entered. The following is an example lmfsetup session:

```
        # /usr/sbin/lmfsetup
Register PAK (type q or quit to exit) [template]
      Issuer : DEC
 Authorization Number : ARS-MT-1998JAN31-249
  Product Name : OSF-USR
    Producer : DEC
 Number of units : 1050
    Version :
 Product Release Date :
 Key Termination Date :
 Availability Table Code : H
  Activity Table Code :
   Key Options : MOD_UNITS,ALPHA
   Product Token :
   Hardware-Id :
    Checksum : 2-ROLE-ADPY-DDSM-AAOQ
PAK registered for template successfully
      Register PAK (type q or quit to exit) [template]
  quit
```

Alternatively, a PAK can be registered by issuing the following lmf command:

```
  # lmf register
```

This will open an editor containing an empty PAK template allowing the license data to be added to the appropriate fields. The lmf utility runs the editor specified by the EDITOR environment variable, or if the environment variable is undefined, the vi editor is run. After completing the template, simply exit the editor and the completed PAK will be validated by the LMF. If the PAK does not validate, the user is given the opportunity to reenter the editor to correct any mistakes. Once all the PAK fields are correctly entered into the template, the PAK is successfully registered into the LMF.

Occasionally, a PAK may be supplied in electronic format, such as in an E-mail message or as a text file. Rather than typing in the data to register the PAK, the lmf command provides a simple method of registering such PAKs. To register a PAK from a file that contains valid license data, issue the following command:

```
# lmf register - < PAK.txt
```

The dash (-) instructs the lmf command to take registration data from standard input, which is redirected in from the PAK.txt file via the less than symbol (<).

3.5.4.6. Updating the Kernel License Cache

Once a PAK is registered in the LMF database file, the next step is typically to enable that newly entered license. Until the PAK data is copied to the system's kernel license cache, the license is unavailable to users. To update the system's license cache, simply issue the following command:

```
# lmf reset
```

This reset can be done at any time without disturbing active users or processes. Note that an "lmf reset" is executed as part of the system startup to initially copy the license data from the LMF database file to the active license cache.

3.5.4.7. Transferring Licenses

Occasionally it may be desirable to move a software product from one system to another. This may be because the original system is going to be taken down for maintenance, or perhaps an organization is upgrading or downgrading to a newer system. Whatever the reason, such a move would also require moving the license information in addition to the software product itself. Obviously, the system administrator could simply reregister the PAK(s), but Digital has provided a way to remove a license from a system and produce a file containing the removed PAK data in one step. This process is called issuing a PAK and is done with the following syntax:

```
# lmf issue <file> <product> [ <producer>
[ <authorization number> ] ]
```

Replace <file> with a filename to contain the reconstructed PAK data and specify the product name in place of <product>. If there is more than one PAK with the same product name, it is necessary to specify the producer and authorization number to identify which specific PAK is to be issued. For example, the following command will issue a specific OSF-USR PAK to the file /tmp/OSF-USRPAK.txt:

```
# lmf issue /tmp/OSF-USRPAK.txt OSF-USR DEC
ARS-MT-1998JAN31-249
```

To load this issued PAK on another system, transfer the PAK.txt file to that system and issue the following register command:

```
# lmf register - < OSF-USRPAK.txt
```

Note that using the "lmf issue" command to illegally copy license PAKs is against the terms of the license agreement and is forbidden. Refer to the license terms on the back of the license PAK for more information.

User Accounts

4

4.1. USER ACCOUNT MANAGEMENT

User account management is, if not the most important job of a system administrator, certainly one of the most visible. An individual's log-in account defines the overall system to the user. When the system administrator configures the log-in environment appropriately by determining the PATH, setting an informative shell prompt, defining helpful aliases and any necessary environment variables, and assigning group membership, the user can immediately become productive.

Actually, creating user accounts and the subsequent removal or retirement of user accounts is just the beginning, and end, of user account management. In between is the ongoing day-to-day support of your user community. This includes account modifications, such as resetting passwords and adjusting group memberships, ensuring that users are aware of upcoming system changes or outages, and managing security to allow the users to get their work done while protecting the system from accidental or intentional harm. Behind the scenes, the administrator should define and assign user and group IDs (UIDs and GIDs) to avoid collisions, create appropriate default account "dot" files, create and monitor home directory file system(s), and a variety of other mundane and not so mundane tasks that are necessary for the smooth operation of a Digital UNIX system.

This chapter covers the details of adding and removing user accounts and addresses other aspects of user account management. In addition, some administrative strategies to be aware of are presented.

4.2. BASE SECURITY VS. ENHANCED SECURITY

Before moving onto the particulars of user account management in Digital UNIX, the two levels of security provided by Digital UNIX must be explained, since which security level is in effect on a given system impacts certain operations. The two levels are:

- Base Security
- Enhanced Security (or C2 Security)

Base Security is the default security level when installing Digital UNIX and is distinguished by traditional UNIX passwords. Base Security is often sufficient for single-user workstations or less critical systems.

Enhanced Security provides a rich set of Password and Log-in controls, plus extensive Auditing features. The Password controls include shadow passwords, configurable password length (both minimum and maximum) and password usage history. The Log-in controls provide per-terminal settings for delays between consecutive successful or failed log-in attempts, the ability to retire or lock accounts, and logging of the last successful log-in and unsuccessful log-in attempt. The Audit features include per-user audit profiles, extensive site-definable event auditing, and the ability to send audit logs to a remote host. Enhanced Security is the recommended security level for Digital UNIX systems deemed sensitive due to the type of data they contain, and especially for any systems connected to the Internet.

The command to determine the security level is:

```
# /usr/sbin/rcmgr get SECURITY
```

If the string "BASE" or a null string is returned, you are running Base Security. If, however, the string "ENHANCED" is returned, Enhanced Security is enabled on your system.

See Chapter 5, "Security," for instructions on enabling Enhanced Security on your system.

4.3. USER ACCOUNT CREATION

There are several methods of creating user accounts:

- Manually, by modifying system files
- With the adduser program
- With the CDE Account Manager (version 4.0 and above)
- With the XSysAdmin program (version 4.0 and earlier running Enhanced Security)

4.3.1. Manually Adding Accounts

Of these four methods, the least desirable is Manually. This method entails adding an entry to the /etc/passwd file and possibly the /etc/group file, creating the user's home directory, and copying in default "dot" files (.profile, .exrc, etc). In addition, if you have Enhanced Security enabled, you must create an appropriate protected password authentication database file, which, among other things, contains the actual encrypted password. This method is discouraged unless you have a thorough understanding of all the details of the security database files.

4.3.2. adduser

The adduser program, which is actually a Korn shell script, provides a character cell method of adding user accounts. It is sufficient if you are running the Base Security level. If you have Enhanced Security enabled, adduser is Enhanced Security-aware. Regardless of the Security level that is enabled, adduser does create a protected password authentication database file. In addition, since adduser is a shell script, it is easily modifiable to extend its functionality.

The following is an example of adding a user account with the adduser utility:

```
# adduser
Enter a login name for the new user (for example, john): jsmith
Enter a UID for (jsmith) [101]: <RETURN>
Enter a full name for (jsmith): John Smith
Enter a login group for (jsmith) [users]: <RETURN>

Enter another group that (jsmith) should be a member of.
```

```
(<Return> only if none): <RETURN>
Enter a parent directory for (jsmith) [/usr/users]: <RETURN>
The shells are:

/usr/bin/sh     /usr/bin/ksh     /bin/sh        /bin/ksh
/usr/bin/csh    /usr/bin/posix/sh/bin/csh
Enter a login shell for (jsmith) [/bin/sh]: /bin/ksh

Adding new user...
Rebuilding the password database...
20 password entries (longest entry is 105 bytes long)
jsmith
Do you wish to edit the auth file entry for this user (y/[n])? n
Creating home directory...

You must enter a new password for (jsmith).
Last successful password change for jsmith: UNKNOWN
Last unsuccessful password change for jsmith: NEVER

New password:
Re-enter new password:
Finished adding user account for (jsmith).
#
```

4.3.3. Account Manager

The Digital UNIX Common Desktop Environment (CDE) Account Manager, dxaccounts(8X), is the recommended utility for managing user accounts on Digital UNIX 4.x and greater systems. Account Manager is an X-Windows/ Motif application that can be used to add and delete users from your system, and is also used to modify both individual and global security parameters such as password aging and quality. The CDE Account Manager is invoked through the CDE Application Manager, which is opened by selecting the Application Manager icon from the CDE Front Panel, followed by selecting System_Management_Utilities, then DailyAdmin, and finally Account Manager. Once you double-click on the Account Manager icon, you will be prompted via a Get Password dialog box for the root password (Figure 4.1), if not already logged in as root.

The initial Account Manager window is shown in Figure 4.2.

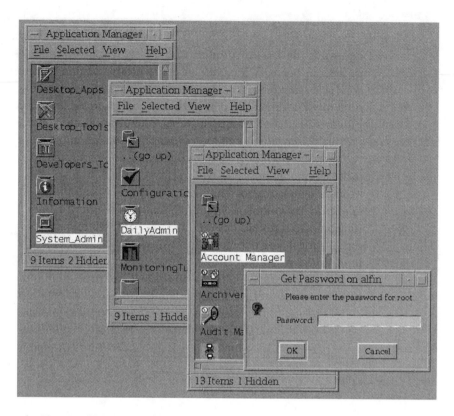

Figure 4.1 Example of Starting CDE Account Manager from Application Manager

Optionally, you can start the Account Manager from the command line:

```
# /usr/bin/X11/dxaccounts
```

When adding a user account, the Account Manager performs these tasks for you:

- Ensures that the new user name and user ID do not already exist
- Adds user to specified secondary groups
- Updates /etc/passwd and protected password authentication databases
- Creates the home directory (optional)
- Copies default configuration files from a skeleton directory (optional)

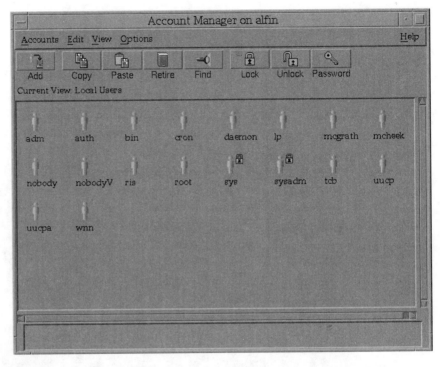

Figure 4.2 Main CDE Account Manager Window

- Configures password aging and quality parameters (optional)
- Sets parameters to limit system resource usage (optional)
- Forces a password change at initial log-in (optional)

To add an account from the main Account Manager window (Figure 4.2), click the Add icon or use the Accounts pull-down menu to select Add New User. The Create/Modify User window will be displayed (Figure 4.3).

The Account Manager will insert default values into certain fields. If these defaults are acceptable for the user being added, the only actions necessary to create a new account are to enter an account user name and specify a password, and select either Apply or OK.

Optionally, you may enter comments for the account, such as the user's full name, phone number, or location. This information can be most helpful in identifying users via the finger command, especially on systems with more than a few accounts. In addition, this information can show up as the "From:" information in outgoing mail.

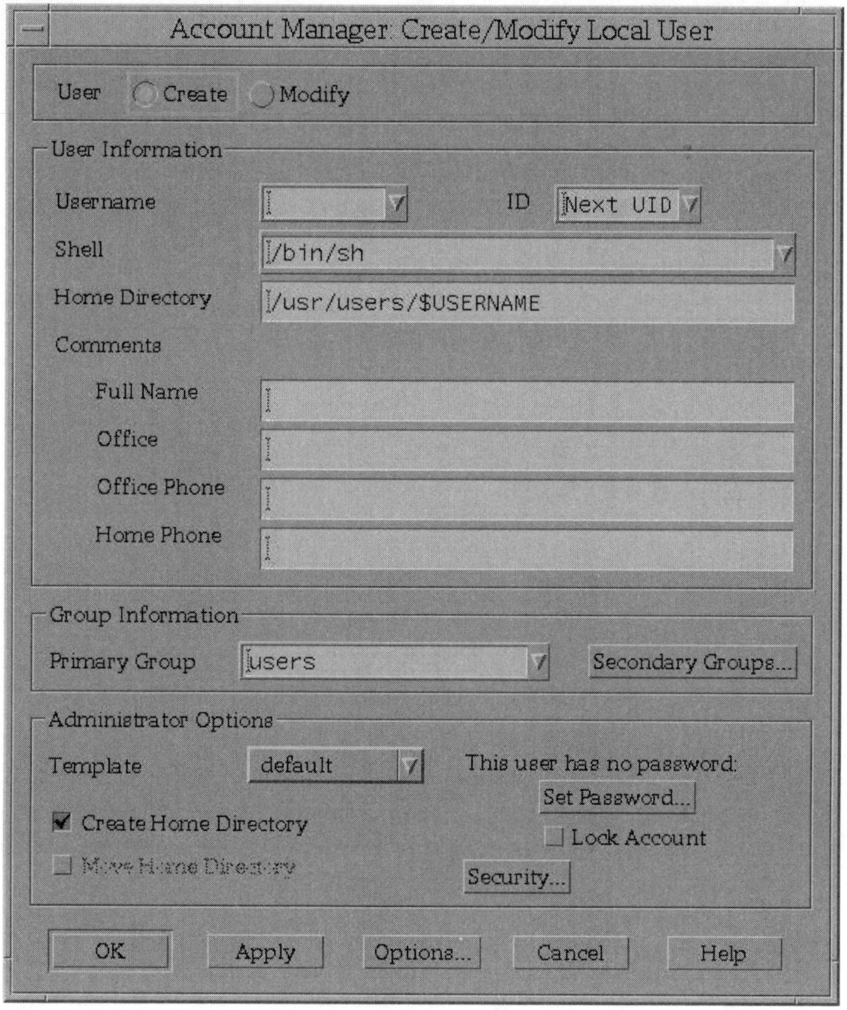

Figure 4.3 CDE Account Manager Create/Modify User Window

If you find yourself changing the Account Manager defaults (such as default shell, primary group, or Home Directory) each time you create an account, it is easy to permanently change the defaults that the Account Manager displays. To do so, select the Save Options choice from the Options drop-down menu from the initial Account Manager window. This will save a configuration file in a subdirectory of your home directory ($HOME/sysman) named Account_defaults. Simply edit this file and change the defaults you wish to modify, and restart Account Manager to cause the new defaults to take effect.

For example, this Account_defaults file specifies a default base directory for new users as /usr/users:

```
max_uid 65535
min_uid 12
next_uid 200
max_gid 65535
min_gid 22
next_gid 200
dup_uid 0
dup_gid 0
max_groups_per_user 32
base_dir /usr/users
distributed 0
local 1
lock 0
local_first 0
primary_group users
skel_dir /usr/skel
shell /bin/sh
```

To change the default base directory as displayed by Account Manager for new accounts to /home, replace the string "/usr/users" with "/home" in $HOME/.sysman/Account_defaults and restart Account Manager.

4.3.4. XSysAdmin

A predecessor to the CDE Account Manager is XsysAdmin(8). XSysAdmin is used to create accounts on Digital UNIX systems prior to version 4.0 running Enhanced Security. If you are using version 4.0 or higher, I recommend using the Account Manager rather than XSysAdmin as the latter is obsolete and will be discontinued after the version 4.0 release. XSysAdmin is started from the command line:

```
# /usr/tcb/bin/XSysAdmin
```

XSysAdmin is similar to the CDE Account Manager in its account creation functionality. The Create User Account window of XSysAdmin is shown in Figure 4.4.

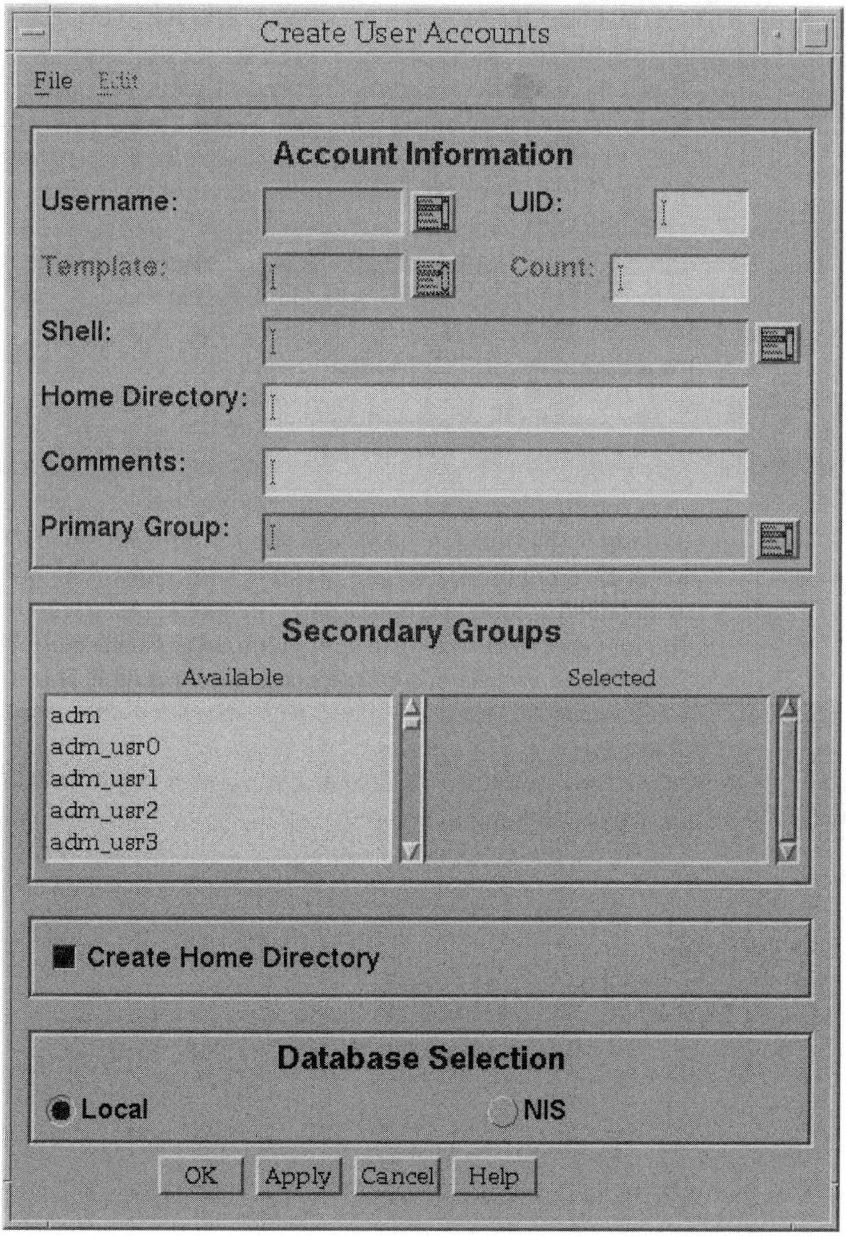

Figure 4.4 XIsso Create/Modify User Window

4.4. USER ACCOUNT REMOVAL OR RETIREMENT

When the time comes to remove a user account, such as when a user leaves the organization or simply no longer needs access to the system, you have two options: either completely remove the account from the system, including the home directory and all files owned by that account, or retire the account. Retiring an account permanently locks the account, preventing reuse of that account's user ID and name, avoiding user ID collisions in the future. Once an account is retired on a system that is running Enhanced Security, that account can not be re-enabled. Whether to remove or retire an account depends on two factors:

- The local security policy
- The current security mode (Base or Enhanced)

Often a locally defined security policy specifies the procedure to follow when an account is no longer needed. This may include disabling the account but not removing any of the account's files for a specific period of time before final removal, or archiving the files owned by an account prior to removing the account. In addition, if your organization is running Enhanced Security and is required to conform to the more stringent C2[1] account requirements, you may have to retire accounts rather than remove them.

As in Account Creation, there are several methods of removing or retiring an account:

- Manually
- With the removeuser program
- With the CDE Account Manager (version 4.0 and above)
- With the XSysAdmin program (version 4.0 and earlier running Enhanced Security)

4.4.1. Manually Removing Accounts

Manually removing an account from your system entails deleting the account's entries from the /etc/passwd and /etc/group files, deleting the

---

[1]C2 is a security classification, as defined by the Trusted Computer System Evaluation Criteria (TCSEC, also called the Orange Book).

protected password entry and removing all files owned by the account. This method of removing accounts is also strongly discouraged unless you have a thorough understanding of the security database files. It would be very easy to miss one or more account references and create system inconsistencies that could lead to account issues.

4.4.2. Disabling Accounts

There are also several methods of manually retiring an account or disabling log-in access for an account. These include prepending the /etc/passwd entry of the account with a character that is invalid, inserting an asterisk (*) in front of the encrypted password entry of the account, and replacing the login shell with an invalid program, such as /bin/false. For example, these accounts are disabled:

```
-jsmith:qk5fPbrx2djcc:101:15:John Smith:/usr/users/jsmith:/bin/ksh
styler:*xCd99zWvR4YGo:102:15:Sally Tyler:/usr/users/styler:/bin/ksh
tlee:1o2A5Adx3oXXm:103:15:Theresa Lee:/usr/users/tlee:/bin/false
```

Disabling accounts in this manner provides a way to lock an account quickly and supports unlocking by not disturbing the existing account password. However, as these are unsupported methods, I strongly encourage you to properly lock any accounts so disabled using either the Account Manager or XIsso at a later time.

4.4.3. removeuser

The removeuser(8) program, which complements the adduser program, is, like adduser, a Korn shell script. The removeuser script will remove all traces of a user account from a system. This optionally includes the user account's home directory and incoming mailbox. Also, since removeuser is a Korn shell script, you can examine it to understand how it works and modify it if desired to extend it functionality.

You should not use removeuser if you have Enhanced Security enabled and are required to retire accounts rather than delete them. However, if you are running Enhanced Security and wish to remove an account completely, you will have to use removeuser, for the Account Manager will only allow accounts to be retired.

```
# removeuser
Enter a login name to be removed or <Return> to exit: jsmith
This is the entry for (jsmith) in the /etc/passwd file:

jsmith:dK451pE2iUd1a:101:15:John
  Smith:/usr/users/jsmith:/bin/ksh

Is this the entry you want to delete (y/n)? y <RETURN>
Working ...Rebuilding the password database...19 password
  entries(longest entry is 105 bytes long)

Entry for (jsmith) removed.
Searching relevant directories and files for user (jsmith) ...
None found.

Do you want to remove the home directory, all subdirectories,
files and mail for (jsmith) (y/n)? y <RETURN>
The files for (jsmith) will be lost if not backed up.
Are you sure you want to remove these files (y/n)? y <RETURN>

Removing /home/jsmith

Removing /usr/spool/mail/jsmith

Finished removing user account for (jsmith)
#
```

Note that if removeuser is used to delete user accounts on a Digital UNIX version 4.0 or greater system that is running Enhanced Security, a second step must be completed to remove the deleted user account's information from the protected password database. In this case, the edauth(8) command should be run shortly after running removeuser. Continuing the above example:

```
# edauth -r jsmith
```

4.4.4. Account Manager

The CDE Account Manager can also remove or retire accounts and is the recommended tool if you are running Digital UNIX version 4.0 and greater. Depending on the Security level enabled (Base or Enhanced), the Account Manager allows you to either delete an account (Base Security) or retire an account (Enhanced Security). The menu choice and icon label reflects whether you have the option of deleting or retiring accounts.

Regardless of whether you can delete or retire an account, the process is the same in the Account Manager. Select a user account icon to be deleted/retired and then either select the Edit drop-down menu and choose Delete or click the trash can icon. A dialog box is presented, giving you the option to remove the user's files also.

When an account is retired, the icon for that user remains in the user account view of the Account Manager, but it is marked as retired with a distinctive symbol. You are still able to select a retired account icon and view the account information, but are unable to modify any of the fields.

4.4.5. XSysAdmin

The XSysAdmin program, a predecessor to the CDE Account Manager, is only applicable on Digital UNIX systems prior to version 4.0 running Enhanced Security. As such, it can only be used to retire accounts and functions similarly to the Account Manager in this regard. Accounts are marked as disabled and no further changes may be made, including reenabling.

4.5. USER ACCOUNT MODIFICATION

Modifying user accounts is an ongoing task that occupies a considerable amount of a System Administrator's time and includes resetting forgotten passwords, adjusting group memberships, changing personal information in the /etc/passwd file, and so on. There are several ways of accomplishing these types of account modifications, including, in certain cases, letting the users manage the change themselves; these include:

- Manually
- With the CDE Account Manager (version 4.0 and above)
- With the XIsso program (version 4.0 and earlier running Enhanced Security)

4.5.1. Manual Account Modifications

Manual modifications are typically done from the command line and can involve editing a system configuration file such as /etc/passwd or /etc/

group, or executing a system utility such as /usr/bin/passwd or /usr/bin/chfn.

4.5.2. Account Manager Modifications

The CDE Account Manager provides a complete solution to user account modifications. Nearly everything a System Administrator would do to change an account can be done from the Account Manager. These changes can be as simple as resetting the password, modifying the user's personal information, or adjusting group membership, or as complex as changing the user ID (UID) or moving the user's home directory.

To modify a particular user account in the Account Manager, simply click on the desired account icon and select Modify... from the Edit pull-down menu. This will open the familiar Create/Modify User window. Select and change the desired field(s) and click the OK or Apply button to complete the edit.

4.5.3. XIsso

The XIsso program, a predecessor to the CDE Account Manager, is only applicable on Digital UNIX systems prior to version 4.0 running Enhanced Security. It is used to modify existing user accounts and functions analogously to the Account Manager in this regard with a similar interface. Select Modify User Accounts from the Accounts pull-down menu and a XIsso Modify User Accounts window will open. Enter a user name of an account you wish to modify or view into the Username field and press return. The window will then be populated with the current information for that account. Select and change the desired field(s) and click the OK or Apply button to commit the changes. Click the Cancel button to discard any changes made to this window.

4.6. MANAGING USER ACCOUNT RESOURCES

There are several types of resources a system administrator should consider and plan for when managing user accounts:

- Account Names
- User ID (UID) Space
- Groups
- User Disk Space

These resources are finite and a system administrator must ensure that they are shared. On a system with few accounts, these resources probably do not need to be tended as closely as on a system with hundreds or thousands of users. Frequently user accounts are created shortly after the initial system installation with little thought given to the long-term management of these resources. Some strategic planning prior to turning your users loose on the system will pay handsome dividends later, either by reducing your day-to-day fire fighting or by eliminating massive, and painful, future system reorganizations. Of course, you must know something about your user's workload patterns and disk space requirements, both now and in the future, to make adequate plans. This is sometimes impossible or unrealistic, and oftentimes will force you to take a guess. Experience will have to guide you in these situations.

4.6.1. Account Names

User account names only have a few format restrictions:

- One to eight characters in length
- Cannot begin with a hyphen (-)
- Cannot contain a colon (:)

In addition, it is recommended that user account names be unique and not contain either capital letters or dots (.). Beyond this, there is no universal standard or convention. User account names are, by their very nature, often a personal choice, and on system(s) with just a handful of users, this is probably fine. However, as the number of user accounts and/or the number of systems increases, the necessity of defining a local convention (or two) becomes obvious. For example, if the local convention is the user's first initial, followed by up to seven characters of the last name, the likelihood of more than one jsmith is proportional to the size of the organization. A less than desirable solution to this is to select a naming convention based on semi-random strings. While this could guarantee uniqueness, the drawback to this approach is obvious:

```
$ who
mcheek      ttyp1      Jun  4 09:35
p5mpc7      ttyp2      Jun  4 15:19
```

(Matt Cheek is logged on, but who is p5mpc7?)

The administrator should select a reasonable standard and expect to make exceptions either for name conflicts (for instance, the second and subsequent jsmith's would use their first and second initials plus last name) or individual user resistance, as longtime UNIX users occasionally get very possessive of their chosen account name. The name of the game with user account names is consistency, both on one system and across multiple systems that users share.

4.6.2. UID Space

The User ID (UID) is a unique number between 0 and 65535 that the system uses to identify a user and determine access permissions to files. The UID should be unique across a system or a group of like systems to avoid UID collisions. This uniqueness across multiple systems becomes crucial if you are using the Network File System (NFS) to share file systems. File ownership problems can arise if, for instance, two different users on two different systems have the same UID. In this example, each user would then have access via NFS to the other users files depending on how the file systems are mounted.

While there is nothing preventing you from having multiple user accounts with account names and/or UIDs, it is almost always a bad idea. System calls that return account names or UIDs will usually only return one, and there is no guarantee which one that will be.

The root or superuser account is always UID zero (0). If other accounts are created with a UID of zero, those accounts will have the same privileges as root and, in effect, also be superuser accounts.

By convention, UIDs from 0-100 are considered "system" UIDs, and you should avoid creating accounts with UIDs in this range. One important reason to not use these system UIDs is to avoid UID conflicts if future releases of Digital UNIX create new system-required accounts. Simply create your accounts with UIDs greater than 100 and you will have no problems. If you wish to be cautious, start at 1000 instead.

One final recommendation regarding UIDs is to select "ranges" of UIDs for different types of user's. For instance, you could place all the system administrators/operators in the range 101-999, all your developers in the range 1000-1999, all the application testers in the range 2000-2999, and so on. Obviously this is just an example, but categorizing your users and placing them in appropriately sized UID ranges is just another way to organize your user community.

4.6.3. Groups

Along with UIDs, you should plan your Groups and Group IDs (GIDs). Groups are a mechanism to allow users with similar needs or responsibilities to share resources based on group membership(s). A user account must belong to at least one group, which is specified by Group ID in the GID field of the /etc/passwd file. This group is called the account's primary group and is only significant if the account does not belong to any secondary groups, which are specified in the /etc/group file. A Digital UNIX account may belong to up to thirty-two groups.

Group IDs (GIDs) are unique numbers between 0 and 65535 that the system uses to identify a specific group. Like UIDs, GIDs should be unique across a system or a group of like systems to avoid GID collisions. If you are using the Network File System (NFS) to share file systems across the network, this GID uniqueness is doubly important to avoid security issues. For example, if System A has some accounts that belong to a group named payroll with a GID of 2001 that can access the accounting system containing the company's salary data, and System B has several accounts belonging to a group named clerks also with a GID of 2001, the clerk accounts will have group access to any NFS file systems from System A mounted on System B. Depending on the file system(s) mounted and the data contained on those file systems, this could be a disaster as a clerk possibly could read, or worse, change or delete, company salary information. This is an extreme example, but the potential for this type of exposure is significantly reduced by ensuring unique GIDs.

Only members of group 0 (system group) are permitted to assume the role of root using the su(1) command. It is especially important to add those individuals who need the ability to become the superuser to group 0 if remote root log-ins are disabled.

Groups are used by the system administrator to provide shared access to files and directories on the system to users with similar responsibilities or jobs. For instance, all the developers who need access to the source code for an ongoing development project would likely be placed in the same group, and the source files would be group-owned with the group permission set to provide group-read, and, possibly, group-write and -access. This would allow all members of the group to read or write the files, regardless of who created or currently owns the files. Determining the number and membership of groups on your system requires some level of knowledge about your user community and the work they are required to do. Group management is frequently an ongoing task that, if planned and set up intelligently early on, can be a minor responsibility.

4.6.4. User Home Directories and Other Disk Space

Management of disk storage space can involve considerable effort. Disk space is a system resource that is always in high demand, no matter how many gigabytes you have at your disposal. By having an idea of your users' needs and requirements, you are a step closer to having the ability to successfully manage the limited disk resources at your disposal.

The first place to concentrate on is the user's home directory. The file system(s) containing home directories are often the most active and are probably where you will spend the most time and energy fighting disk space shortages. Small systems and/or systems with small user communities usually have only one file system for user's home directories. Some common names for the user's file system are /home, /users, and /u. The important thing to note about these common names are that they should be separate file systems and not simply directories off either the root file system (/) or /usr. The Digital UNIX account creation tools (adduser, Account Manager, and XSysAdmin) all default to a home directory for new accounts of /usr/users/$HOME. I strongly recommend against creating your user home directories in /usr/users, either as a separate file system mounted on /usr or, worse, actually in a subdirectory of the /usr file system. There is nothing technically wrong with mounting a separate file system on the /usr/users mount point, but, just from an aesthetics point of view, it is ugly. Even worse is actually putting your user's home directories in the /usr file system. The first time your system grinds to a halt because the /usr file system is full because of an active user, you will quickly understand that the best strategy is to isolate the users on their own file system to prevent such collateral impact.

That leads to the idea of segregating your users onto different file systems in order to isolate an active user group from a quiet, or less active, group of users. For example, if you have a team of developers actively compiling, linking, and debugging on a large development effort, and another group of users who simply run a canned accounting package and rarely if ever even see a shell prompt, it might be prudent to place the developer's home directories on one large file system all by themselves and the accounting staff on a separate file system sized appropriately for their needs. Then if one or two busy developers fill up their own home file system, neither the accounting staff nor the rest of the system will not be impacted.

A tip to help manage multiple user file systems is to create a directory, such as /u, that contains symbolic links to the user's true home directories, which could reside on different file systems. This then allows you to specify any user's home directory as /u/<user name>. Specify this symbolic link in the home directory field of the /etc/passwd file, and you will be able to relocate user home directories transparently to the users by simply changing the link after physically moving the directory. By educating your users to use either this symbolic link or the $HOME environment variable in their scripts and aliases, you will be able to reorganize your file systems when required without much user impact.

4.7. MANAGING USER ACCOUNT ENVIRONMENT

Configuring new and existing user accounts with appropriate environments is an important task for system administrators. Accounts should have certain environment variables set with suitable default values, and there may be site-specific commands or programs that every user should run during the log-in process. Experienced users will reset environment variables to their requirements and even change their personal log-in files, but you, as the system administrator, can ensure that every user at least has the minimum necessary environment.

There are two primary ways to ensure that your user accounts are properly "provisioned" before a user even logs on for the first time:

- A Skeleton Account
- Global Default Shell Login-In Files

4.7.1. Skeleton Account Setup

A skeleton account is simply a directory that serves as a template for new account home directories. By default, on Digital UNIX, this skeleton directory is /usr/skel and contains files named .profile, .cshrc, and .login, plus a bin directory. During account creation, whether with adduser, the Account Manager, or XSysAdmin, the contents of the skeleton account is copied to the new account's home directory. If you construct a default .profile or .cshrc/.login pair containing site-specific environment variables or aliases, they will be placed in every new user account's home directory. In addition, you can place directories and links in the skeleton directory, they will be copied into newly created user home directories, and the ownership will be set to the new user. Note that symbolic links should be avoided. Symbolic links are simply recreated as new symbolic links in the new home directory. If the source pathname of the symbolic link is absolute, there should be no problems. However, if the source pathname is relative from the skeleton directory, the resulting link may or may not point to the source file. In the case of hard links, the source file itself will simply be copies of the newly created user home directory. Unless there is a really good reason to use links, either symbolic or hard, in your skeleton directory, it is probably best to avoid links.

In addition to the typical shell initialization files, or "dot" files such as .profile and .cshrc, the skeleton directory is also the place for any type of user default or configuration files. For example, the vi editor initialization file (.exrc), an E-mail auto forwarding file (.forward), or a .hushlogin file that will suppress the display of the Message of the Day (/etc/motd). Any file or directory that you would manually have to copy into newly created user home directories and will initially be the same for all users is a good candidate for the skeleton directory.

If you are using the Account Manager to create user accounts, you can have several different skeleton directories for different type of users. Account Manager makes it easy to select different skeleton directories to use when creating a particular user account. Click on the Options... button at the bottom of the Create/Modify User window to open a dialog box where you can specify, or even browse for, the desired skeleton directory.

As your users' needs evolve and your experience and knowledge increases, you will probably add new files/directories to and modify existing files in your skeleton directory. Changes to your skeleton directory will, of course, take effect for subsequent new user accounts, but will not automatically be applied to existing user accounts. If you wish to update your existing accounts to reflect any skeleton directory changes, you will have to manually make the updates yourself. At first glance, this is a straightforward task, especially when you have a small user community. However, as both the size and proficiency of your users increases, you may run into resistance trying to standardize the user account environment configuration. For this reason, I recommend keeping the shell initialization files (.profile, .cshrc, .login) stored in your skeleton directory reasonably generic and using the Global Default Shell Login-In files for most of your shell environment standardization.

4.7.2. Global Default Shell Login-In Files

As part of the log-in sequence, all the shells read a global default initialization file that contains environment variables and commands before running the user account private shell initialization file, which is usually located in the user's home directory. For example, the Bourne shell (/bin/sh), the Korn shell (/bin/ksh), and the BASH shell all read the /etc/profile initialization file at log-in before running the user's local $HOME/.profile. In the case of the C shell (/bin/csh) and the TCSH shell, the /etc/csh.login initialization file is read at log-in before running the user's $HOME/.cshrc and $HOME/.login files. This shell behavior means that you as the system administrator can force your users to have certain desired environment variables and aliases. Of course, a user can override any variable or alias in his or her local initialization file, but the purpose of defining global defaults is not to interfere with your knowledgeable users, but to provide a default environment for the majority of users who never concern themselves with customizing their personal environment.

By placing the desired default configuration into a single global file that only root can change, you avoid having to edit each user's local shell initialization files when you need to add a new environment variable or change an alias.

Since these global default shell login-in files are read by several different shells (e.g., /etc/profile is read by sh, ksh, and bash), ensure that any commands you add are generic enough for all the shells that will read the particular global default file. For example, to set an environment variable in /etc/profile, use the following syntax:

```
MANPATH=/usr/man:/usr/local/man; export MANPATH
```

rather than:

```
export MANPATH=/usr/man:/usr/local/man
```

In the Korn shell (/bin/ksh) and the BASH shell, both formats produce the same result. However, since the latter is not a valid command in the Bourne shell (/bin/sh), setting and exporting environment variables in one statement will cause an error at log-in and, more importantly, not achieve the desired result of the MANPATH environment variable being set. See Table 4.1 for a list of common environment variables.

4.8. USER COMMUNICATION

A system administrator frequently needs to communicate important information to both the user community at large or sometimes to just an individual user. Digital UNIX provides several mechanisms for you to communicate to your users.

- The message of the day (/etc/motd)
- The system identification file (/etc/issue)
- System news
- talk
- write
- wall (Write ALL)

4.8.1. /etc/motd

When you have something to tell your users that is not too urgent, such as when the next scheduled reboot will occur, the message of the day might be the way. Simply edit (or create) the file /etc/motd with a text editor such as vi, and enter the text you wish your users to see. This file is displayed when each user logs on. The main drawback to using the message of the day as a communication channel is that a user can suppress the display of the /etc/motd file simply by placing a .hushlogin file in his home directory:

```
$ touch $HOME/.hushlogin
```

Because the message of the day does not change too frequently, users become accustomed to its contents and will ignore or miss important information. Because of this, I usually only place reasonably static information in

DISPLAY	The default display for X-Windows programs
EDITOR	Default editor
HOME	Home directory
LOGNAME	User name
MAIL	Primary incoming mailbox (/usr/spool/mail/<username> by default)
MAILCHECK	How often (in seconds) the shell checks for new mail
MANPATH	A list of directories that the man command searches for man pages
MAILPATH	A list of file names separated by colons that the shell monitors for new mail
PAGER	The default file viewer (e.g., more(1), pg(1))
PATH	A list of directories to search for commands
PS1	The primary shell prompt ($ by default)
PS2	The secondary shell prompt (> by default)
SHELL	The pathname of the shell
TERM	The terminal type
TIMEOUT	The Bourne shell idle time (in minutes)
TMOUT	The Korn shell idle time (in seconds)
TZ	Time Zone
USER	User name
VISUAL	Default visual (full screen) editor

Table 4.1 Common Environment Variables

the /etc/motd file: the Digital UNIX version, the system host name and IP address, and the standard legalese disclaimer required by local policy. This way, experienced users can safely ignore the message of the day, but the information is there for new users.

4.8.2. /etc/issue

While the contents of the message of the day file (/etc/motd) are displayed after a user successfully logs on, Digital UNIX version 4.0 and greater provides a mechanism to identify the system before the log-in prompt is presented. Simply edit (or create) the file /etc/issue with a text editor, and insert the text you wish to be displayed immediately prior to the login prompt. If this file is present, the getty(8) command writes the contents of the /etc/issue file to the screen prior to starting the log-in dialog. Typically, a system administrator would want to display identification information, such as host name, location, or contact instructions. Other sites may be required to present a standard disclaimer to warn against unauthorized system access.

The /etc/issue file is primarily for serial terminal connections, including a serial console. Digital provides a second file, /etc/issue.net, which works identically to /etc/issue, except that the contents of the /etc/issue.net file are displayed by the telnetd(8) daemon over a new telnet connection prior to starting the log-in dialog. If the /etc/issue file exists and the /etc/issue.net file does not exist, the telnetd daemon displays the contents of the /etc/issue file instead.

4.8.3. System News

News, not to be confused with USENET News, is a little-used mechanism that is ideal for presenting information to your users. News consists of two pieces: the news program itself (/usr/bin/news), and the news directory (/usr/news). To set up news on your system, add the following command to your global default shell login-in files:

```
/usr/bin/news
```

This addition will have no effect until you create one or more news items. A news item is a text file placed in the /usr/news directory. For example:

```
This system will be unavailable for two hours on
    Friday, June 13, starting at 01:00 for the
    installation of a new disk array. A full system
    backup will be taken immediately prior to the
    shutdown. Your friendly system administrator
```

The next time a user logs in, the following will be display immediately after the message of the day:

```
root (root) Mon Jun 2 18:39:36 1997
```

```
This system will be unavailable for two hours on
   Friday, June 13, starting at 01:00 for the
   installation of a new disk array. A full system
   backup will be taken immediately prior to the
   shutdown. Your friendly system administrator
```

One nice feature of news is that this particular news item will not be displayed on the subsequent log-ins of each user. The news program keeps track of which news items have been seen by placing a file in each user's home directory ($HOME/.news_time) that is used as a time-stamp to determine if a particular news item has been seen or not.

A user can see all the news items at any time regardless of whether they have been seen or not by issuing this command:

```
$ news -a
```

Finally, news is not just for the system administrator. To allow non-root users to place news items in the news directory, change the permissions of the news directory to allow world writable access:

```
# chmod 1666 /usr/news
```

This also sets the sticky bit on the /usr/news directory, which is recommended for any world writable directory, and prevents users from deleting other user's news items.

4.8.4. talk, write, and wall

Both the /etc/motd and news are passive communication mechanisms, that is, you as the superuser create the message(s) to be seen at a later time when and as users log in. The opposite type of communication often required is more immediate. You are logged on and want or need to talk to or with other logged-on users. There are three commands that provide this instant communication.

Talk is for when you wish to have a two-way conversation with an individual user. In its simplest form, the command is

```
# talk username
```

where username is the account name of the user you wish to talk to. If the target user is also logged on, the screen of the user who initiated the talk session will display a split-screen talk interface with the following status line:

```
[Waiting for your party to respond]
```

and the target user will see the following invitation:

```
Message from Talk_Daemon@pluto at 19:17 ...
talk: connection requested by root@pluto.
talk: respond with: talk root@pluto
```

If the target user chooses to accept the invitation and join the talk session, all he needs to do is respond with the suggested command:

```
$ talk root@pluto
```

At this point, the target user's screen also displays the same split-screen talk interface and the two users are now connected. Whatever each user types (including typos and backspacing) in the top half of this display is simultaneously displayed on the bottom half of the other user's screen. If either user's screen gets disrupted, say by additional talk invitations, pressing Control-L will refresh the screen. Finally, either user can cancel the talk session by pressing either the Interrupt key sequence, which is usually Control-C, or the End-of-File key sequence, typically Control-D.

If the target user is logged on more than once, there is an additional command line argument to talk, tty-name, to specify which tty the initiating user would like to send the talk invitation to. To determine which tty you wish, simply issue the who command, and the second column of the output specifies the tty for each log-in session. For example:

```
# who
root      console   Jun 6 09:34
mcheek    ttyp4     Jun 6 15:45 <- This session is the most recent
mcheek    ttyp3     Jun 3 09:35
mcheek    ttyp1     Jun 3 09:35
# talk mcheek ttyp4
```

Write is similar to talk in that it is directed to only one active user account. The difference is that write is only one-way. The syntax of write is similar to talk:

```
# write mcheek [tty-name]
```

After issuing the write command, any text you type is immediately displayed on the target user's screen, one line at a time, preceded with an identifying header, regardless of what they are doing or which application they are currently in. Since each line is not sent until a carriage return, keep lines short if a multiline message is being sent. This avoids frustrating the target user with long delays between each line of the communication. The sending continues until the user doing the writing issues an End-of-File key sequence, usually with Control-D.

I encourage you to use write sparingly, as user's will get annoyed if uninvited messages or talk invitations are constantly appearing on their screen, possibly disrupting their task at hand. UNIX even provides a command that regular users can use to block incoming talks or writes: the mesg(1) command. The mesg command acts like a toggle. By default, incoming talks and writes are enabled. But by issuing this command, incoming communications are blocked:

```
$ mesg -no
```

When a user has blocked messages in this manner, other users attempting to talk or write to that user receive the following error message:

```
[Your party is refusing messages]
```

Running mesg with the "-yes" command line switch enables incoming talks and writes, and issuing the mesg command with no arguments reports the current terminal message permission setting. Finally, the superuser account (root) and members of the sysadmin group can issue talk invitations and send write messages to any terminal regardless of the mesg setting.

Wall is nearly identical to write, with one important exception: the text is sent to ALL logged-in users. Running wall with no command line arguments behaves like write in that any text you type, including carriage returns, is immediately display on all logged-in users' screens, preceded with a broadcast header, regardless of what they are doing or which application they are currently in. Wall also has the ability to read from a prepared file, which can be useful for broadcasting prepared statements for periodic events such system reboots. For example, to broadcast the contents of a file, issue the following command:

```
# wall /tmp/shutdown.txt
```

All logged in users will see the following on their screen:

```
Broadcast Message from root@pluto (console) at 19:50 ...
```

```
The system will be shutdown in 10 minutes to perform a cold
  backup. Please save your work and log off. The system will be
  available in approx. 1 hour.
Operations Staff
```

4.9. SUMMARY

User accounts administration on a Digital UNIX system requires you, as the system administrator, to determine your user's wants and needs in order to successfully manage the user's environment, disk space, and communication.

Security

5

5.1. DIGITAL UNIX SECURITY

This chapter describes several important aspects of Digital UNIX system security. As a system administrator, you are responsible for the overall security of the system, which includes both physical system security and Digital UNIX operating system security. By default, Digital UNIX is installed with a minimal security configuration, which may be sufficient for a noncritical, single-user workstation. For a Digital UNIX system that supports a mission-critical application or is connected to the Internet, however, this default minimal security configuration may be inadequate. The purpose of this chapter is to address these enhancements with the goal of a more secure Digital UNIX system. The following topics will be covered:

- Physical Security
- Resetting Passwords
- Log-in Controls
- The Trusted Host facility
- Enhanced Security

Prior to beginning our discussions, it is important to understand the history and implications of implementing security on a UNIX system. UNIX was originally developed in a research environment with little thought given to security. The scientists at Bell Labs created UNIX for their own use, and such facilities as passwords and file permissions were avoided. This was the origin of the belief that UNIX is an inherently insecure operating system. UNIX can be configured to be completely insecure, of course, but so can any other computer operating system. Conversely, most modern implementations of UNIX, Digital UNIX included, provide facilities and tools to secure the system as tightly as necessary.

5.2. PHYSICAL SECURITY

The issue of physical security should be covered before moving onto operating system security. The reason for this is that, given physical access to a Digital UNIX system, it is very easy to circumvent operating system security measures, such as passwords and permissions. The physical security of a Digital UNIX system simply means restricting physical access to the system itself, usually by placing the computer in a secure, locked room or area. This is especially important for mission-critical systems containing important data and programs. Note that the console or console port of a system should also be secured. This, of course, precludes connecting a modem to the console port and allowing unrestricted dial-in access to the console. A secure computer room or data center with secure power feeds and climate controls is ideal, but a locked office or closet is perfectly adequate.

The two vulnerabilities with a physically insecure Digital UNIX system are:

- The ability to simply turn the system off, preventing use
- The ability to break into the system as the root user

5.2.1. Unauthorized Power Removal

The first vulnerability is a denial-of-service type of attack. If someone turns the system off, either accidentally or intentionally, the system obviously becomes unavailable for use. Some Digital UNIX systems also have halt buttons on the front panel that cause the operating system to halt and leave the system at the console prompt. In addition, the Control-P key sequence on a Digital UNIX system console will also halt the system. Halting a system is as bad as removing power, for the system is no longer running Digital UNIX.

5.2.2. Unauthenticated Root Access

The second vulnerability of a physically unsecured Digital UNIX system is the ability to halt and reboot the system in single-user mode, which provides a root log-in on the system console without prompting for the root password. As this point, the system is compromised and the intruder can view any file, change passwords, create new accounts, or simply destroy files or data. Digital UNIX provides this ability to allow resetting of the root password in the event that this important password is forgotten or lost; Digital assumed that the physical security requirement would be followed.

Physically securing a Digital UNIX system should be the first step a system administrator addresses when developing a system security strategy. The environment, the criticality of the system, and the available physical resources are all important factors when deciding where and how to physically secure a system. Obviously, an individual desktop workstation is not very useful locked in a computer room and probably belongs on a user's desk. But in a cubical environment, such a workstation may be impossible to secure. In this situation, the best strategy may be to ensure that all critical or confidential data is not stored locally on the workstation's disks, but is located on a remote file server that is physically secured in the computer room. This reduces the vulnerability of having an individually unsecured workstation.

5.3. RESETTING PASSWORDS

A frequent request of a system administrator is to reset user's forgotten passwords. Since Digital UNIX stores user account passwords in a one-way encrypted format, it is not possible to determine what an existing password is. The only option is to reset the password to a new value. This is a simple operation that requires the root user. First, either become the root user via the su(1) command or log-in as root. Then issue the passwd(1) command for the account you are resetting. For example, to reset the password for jsmith:

```
$ su -
Password:
# passwd jsmith
Changing password for jsmith.

New password:
Retype new password:
#
```

To change the root password, specify "root" on the passwd command line. Note that only the root user can change the root user account password.

If, however, the root password is forgotten or lost, the only recourse is to "break into" the system and reset the root password. This requires access to the console of the system and the ability to halt and reboot the system. It is necessary to halt the system since only root can gracefully shutdown the system and, in this situation, the root account is inaccessible.

The procedure is as follows:

1. Halt the system either by pressing the HALT button or typing the Control-P (^P) key combination from the console; this should bring the system to the boot prompt (>>>).

2. Examine the auto_action console variable, and if auto_action is not HALT, set it to HALT:

```
>>> show auto_action
auto_action  BOOT
>>> set auto_action halt
```

3. Initialize the system:

```
>>> init
```

4. Boot the system to single-user mode:

```
>>> boot -fl s
```

5. When the system reaches SINGLE-USER MODE, start LSM (if applicable) and mount the filesystems:

```
# lsmbstartup (to start LSM)
```

```
# bcheckrc
```

6. Change the root password:

```
# passwd root
Changing password for root.

New password:
Retype new password:
#
```

7. Resume booting the system to multi-user mode by typing the Control-D (^D) key combination
8. Log in as root using the newly changed password to verify success.

5.4. LOG-IN CONTROLS

Digital UNIX provides a variety of mechanisms to control log-in access and restrict the abilities of user accounts once they are successfully logged in. These log-in and account controls include the following:

- Restricting root log-in to the system console
- Restricting File Transfer Protocol (FTP) access
- Specifying approved shells or command interpreters
- Restricting the ability to su(1) to root
- A restricted shell to provide an environment with limited capabilities

5.4.1. Restricting Root Log-In

The root account on a Digital UNIX system is, by its very nature, a shared log-in account. In other words, the account is typically used by multiple people. Because the root account is all powerful, access and use of the root account should be restricted to only those individuals who are trained, knowledgeable, and, most importantly, authorized. The root account should normally be accessed by logging onto the system using the user's individual user account, then using the su(1) command to "switch" to the root account. By default, Digital UNIX restricts direct root log-in to the console, or the primary display on a system with a graphics console.

The mechanism to control direct root log-in is the file /etc/securettys. This file specifies the locations from where root is permitted to log-in. The default /etc/securettys file contains the following lines:

```
/dev/console
local:0
:0
```

In order to allow direct root log-in from across the network, via telnet, for example, add a line to /etc/securettys containing the string "ptys". If you have a terminal or modem connected to a serial port on the system and wish to allow direct root log-in from that port, add a line containing the serial port's device name, for example, "/dev/tty00".

Unless there is a special requirement for nonconsole direct root log-ins, I recommend restricting root log-ins to the console. The root account is obviously a prime target for remote attacks, and by preventing network and nonconsole terminal root log-ins, you effectively block such attacks.

5.4.2. Restricting File Transfer Protocol (FTP) Access

Digital UNIX provides the ability to block incoming FTP connections on a per-account basis. This functionality is, by default, used to prevent remote users from "logging" into a system via ftp(1)as either root or the uucp account, but any system or user account can be blocked. The FTP server ftpd(8) consults the /etc/ftpusers file when authenticating inbound FTP connections. If a user account is specified in this file, that inbound connection is rejected, as the following example illustrates:

```
$ ftp jupiter
Connected to jupiter.
220 jupiter FTP server (Digital UNIX Version 5.60) ready.
Name (jupiter:mcheek): root
530 User root access denied.
Log-in failed.
ftp>
```

Accounts to be restricted are listed one to a line in the /etc/ftpusers file. The ftpusers file can have no white space, and accounts must match exactly the user account name in the /etc/passwd file. If this syntax is not adhered to, the FTP server may incorrectly parse this ftpd(8) security file and possibly allow undesired FTP access. If the /etc/ftpusers file does not exist, no FTP security checks are done. A representative /etc/ftpusers file is:

```
root
daemon
bin
uucp
cron
adm
jsmith
```

In this example, the six listed system accounts and the regular user account jsmith are all prevented from logging in via FTP.

I strongly recommended that all system accounts listed in /etc/passwd be added to the /etc/ftpusers file. These accounts are rarely used interactively and should never be permitted to be FTP'ed into. A common break-in strategy is to attempt to FTP into a system using a known system account, and listing accounts in /etc/ftpusers effectively removes this vulnerability.

5.4.3. Specifying Approved Shells

The Digital UNIX FTP server (ftpd) also validates inbound FTP connections by checking if the shell of the account being logged into is approved. The shell, or command interpreter, is specified in the seventh field of the /etc/passwd file entry for each system account and is typically the Korn shell or C shell for interactive users. The FTP server determines if a shell is valid by consulting the /etc/shells file, which is simply a listing of the acceptable shells on the system. If an account's shell is not found in the /etc/shells file, the FTP log-in session is rejected.

The /etc/shells file should be maintained by the system administrator and should contain, in addition to the standard system shells, any additional shells or command interpreters. For example, this /etc/shells file also lists two common public domain shells:

```
/usr/bin/sh
/usr/bin/csh
/usr/bin/ksh
```

```
/bin/sh
/bin/csh
/bin/ksh
/usr/local/bin/bash
/usr/local/bin/tcsh
```

Note that each entry is the full path name of the shell executable, and that all possible paths for a given shell are listed. Blank lines and all characters after a pound sign (#) are ignored. When troubleshooting FTP access-denied issues, ensure that the /etc/shells file exists and that it contains all appropriate shells.

5.4.4. Restricting the Ability to su to Root

The su(1) command demands the password of the account being specified and, upon providing that account's password, changes to that user and invokes that user's shell. There is no restriction, other then having to provide the password, to becoming non-root users with the su command. However, su does restrict the ability to become the root user. Only users who belong to group number 0, the system group, can issue the su command to become root, even while possessing the root password.

To allow a user account to become root via the su command, simply add that user to the system group. To do so, either specify the system group as one of an account's groups when initially creating the account, or add an existing account to the system group in the /etc/group file. For example, given the following /etc/group file, only jsmith and styler are permitted to su to root:

```
# head /etc/group
system:*:0:root,jsmith,styler
daemon:*:1:daemon
uucp:*:2:uucp
mem:*:3:
kmem:*:3:root
bin:*:4:bin,adm
sec:*:5:
mail:*:6:mail
terminal:*:7:
tty:*:7:root
```

5.4.5. The Restricted Shell

The designers of UNIX recognized the need to occasionally create user accounts whose abilities are more controlled than those running standard shells. For just this purpose, the Restricted Shell was created. The Restricted Shell, Rsh, is a derivative of the standard Bourne shell, sh, and has all the capabilities of the Bourne shell except for the following, which are not allowed:

- Changing directories with the cd command
- Setting the value of PATH or SHELL
- Specifying pathnames or command names containing /
- Redirecting output (with > and >>)

The Restricted Shell is invoked for an account by specifying /usr/bin/Rsh as the log-in shell when creating the account, or by placing /usr/bin/Rsh in the seventh field of the /etc/passwd file entry for an existing account. Upon logging into an account running Rsh, the $HOME/.profile for that account is executed before the above restrictions are enforced. For this reason, the creator of a restricted account's $HOME/.profile has complete control over what commands are executed, what environment variables are set, and which directory the restricted user is left in after the log-in. Ideally, the final directory should not be the log-in directory, but rather a directory not owned by the restricted user.

Rsh is ideal for novice or risky users, for you, as the system administrator, can enforce their PATH and prevent them from running undesirable commands. Rsh is not a complete security solution, especially for technically savvy users, but for certain, low-risk situations it is a useful tool to restrict user's activities on the system.

5.5. THE TRUSTED HOST FACILITY

UNIX has a set of commands typically referred to as the "R-commands," due to the fact that the name of each begins with the letter "R" for "Remote." These commands are rlogin(1), rsh(1), and rcp(1), and are used to log-in to, execute commands on, and copy files to remote hosts. For example, the following command will log-in to the host pluto:

```
$ rlogin pluto
```

The rsh command is usually used to execute a command on a remote system. For instance, this example will return the process status of the remote system:

```
$ rsh pluto ps -ef
```

Finally, this command will copy a file from the local system to a remote system:

```
$ rcp /tmp/file.txt pluto:/tmp/file.txt
```

One issue I have omitted about these commands is that the preceding three examples will fail unless the remote host specified in each command is configured to permit these operations. This configuration, in which one system allows a second system to connect via the r-commands, is known as trust—the first system trusts the second system. This trust relationship must be managed carefully by the system administrator, especially if two systems in such a relationship are not managed by the same department, organization, or company. Depending on the level of trust granted, a user on one system could, either inadvertently or maliciously, compromise or damage another system that that user may not normally have access to.

There are two mechanisms to specify trust relationships on a Digital UNIX system:

- $HOME/.rhosts file(s)
- /etc/hosts.equiv file

5.5.1. The .rhosts File

The .rhosts file, a user-specific file that can be located in a user's home directory, contains a list of remote hosts, and, optionally, accounts on those remote hosts, that are not challenged for a password when they execute the rcp, rlogin, or rsh commands. The permissions of an .rhosts file must be set to 600 (read and write by the owner only), and the file must be owned by the owner of the home directory it is located in or by the root user.

The format of the .rhosts file is:

```
host [user]
```

where host is the name of the remote system. If the remote system is in a different domain than the local system, the full domain name must be specified.

The second field, user, is the log-in name of the remote user. This field is optional. If this field is not specified, any user on the specified remote system is exempt from providing a password, and is assumed to have the same account name on both the local and remote systems. Entries in the .rhosts file are either positive or negative. A positive entry allows access, while a negative entry denies access. Negative entries are specified by prefacing either a host name or a user name with a minus sign. Positive entries are the default and have no special indicator. In addition, a plus sign (+) can be used in place of either a host name or a user name in a .rhosts entry. In place of the host name, it means any remote host, and in place of the user name, it means any user on the specified host.

For example, the following entries in the /home/styler/.rhosts file on a system named jupiter allows the user jsmith on remote host pluto to log on the host jupiter as styler without providing a password, prevents the user tlee on pluto from logging onto jupiter as styler, and allows any user on remote hosts saturn to log on to jupiter as styler:

```
pluto jsmith
pluto -tlee
saturn +
```

Obviously, as the last entry shows, the .rhosts file can potentially be a large vulnerability. The worst entry a user can have in his .rhosts file, of course, is a single plus sign (+). This allows any user from any remote system to log-in as that user without being challenged with a password. If the root user has such a .rhosts file, it is only a matter of time before this vulnerability is discovered and exploited. A system administrator responsible for systems connected to the network, and especially the Internet at large, must be diligent in examining any user-created .rhosts for such entries.

5.5.2. The /etc/hosts.equiv File

The second configuration file that defines trust of remote systems is /etc/hosts.equiv, which is similar to individual user's .rhosts file, except that /etc/hosts.equiv specifies trust relationships for the entire system. In addition, the /etc/hosts.equiv file is checked first before the local .rhosts file, and if a match is found in the hosts.equiv file, the validation ends. The syntax of the hosts.equiv file is identical to the .rhosts file with one notable addition. By specifying the keyword "NO_PLUS" in /etc/hosts.equiv, the use of the plus character (+) to match any host or user is disallowed on a systemwide basis. Because of the security implications of users specifying a plus sign in local .rhosts files, it is strongly recommended that the NO_PLUS entry be added to the /etc/hosts.equiv file to close the vulnerability made possible by the plus sign.

In addition, when an r-command is run against the root account on a remote system, only that root account's personal .rhosts file, if it exists, is checked for permission. The /etc/hosts.equiv does not apply when validating remote access to the root account.

Similarly to the .rhosts command, the contents of the /etc/hosts.equiv file are critical for ensuring system security. An incorrectly placed plus sign could open a system up to unauthorized access. Carefully manage the individual entries in both the /etc/hosts.equiv file and any individual user's .rhosts files.

5.6. ENHANCED SECURITY

There are two levels of security on Digital UNIX:

- Base Security
- Enhanced Security (or C2 Security)

Base Security is the default security level when installing Digital UNIX and is distinguished by traditional UNIX passwords. Enhanced Security provides a rich set of Password and Log-in control, plus extensive Auditing features. The Password controls include the previously mentioned shadow passwords feature, configurable password length, both minimum and maximum, and password usage history. The Log-in controls provide per-terminal settings for delays between consecutive successful or failed log-in attempts, the ability to retire or lock accounts, and logging of the last successful log-in and unsuccessful log-in attempt. The Audit features include per-user audit profiles, extensive site-definable event auditing, and the ability to send audit logs to a remote host.

Digital UNIX systems typically have been Base Security enabled due to the perceived complexity and limited understanding of the features of Enhanced Security, as well as the fact that Base Security is the default level on a newly installed system. Running Enhanced Security is certainly more complex than Base Security from a system administration viewpoint, but Enhanced Security provides so many useful facilities that the additional effort necessary is worthwhile.

5.6.1. Enabling Enhanced Security

The very first step to successfully implementing Enhanced Security is deciding on the global defaults for the password and log-in control pieces of Enhanced Security. These systemwide global defaults reside in /etc/auth/system/default and provide values for users and devices. Determine and record the settings that make the most sense for your environment. (See Figure 5.1 for field definitions of the System Default Database and suggested values.)

The global configuration file for Enhanced Security on Digital UNIX is /etc/auth/system/default and defines values for users at a system-wide level. An administrator planning to implement Enhanced Security must be familiar with the values specified in this file in order to configure Enhanced Security appropriately for his or her system. The following is a default file I will use as an example of a relaxed security configuration. To avoid frustration in the initial implementation, I recommend Enhanced Security be enabled with most options either loose or disabled altogether. Once you are more familiar with Enhanced Security, tighten down the option that make the most sense for your environment.

```
default:\
:d_name=default:\
:d_secclass=c2:\
:d_boot_authenticate@:\
:d_pw_expire_warning#864000:\
:d_pw_site_callout=/tcb/bin/pwpolicy:\
:u_minchg#0:u_minlen#8:u_maxlen#12:u_exp#0:\
:u_life#0:u_pickpw:u_genpwd@:u_restrict:\
:u_pwdepth#0:u_nullpw@:u_genchars@:u_genletters@:\
:u_maxtries#0:u_lock@:\
:t_logdelay#2:t_maxtries#10:\
:chkent:
```

(continued)

Figure 5.1 System Default Database File Format

The default file consists of options in a single, continuous entry that can be broken into multiple lines with a backslash ("\"). Each option is preceded and followed by a colon (":"). If the entry is broken into multiple lines, a colon and a backslash are required at the end of each line and each continuation line must begin with a colon and continuation lines are indented by a tab. Options can have numeric, Boolean, or string values. Numeric options have the format "name#num". Boolean options have the format "name" or "name@", where the first form indicates the option is True and the second form indicates the option is False. String options have the format "name=string" where string is zero or more characters.

At the end of the entry is the chkent field which indicates that the entry is complete. This field is used as an integrity check on the entry by the programs that read the file.

The example options have the following meanings:

default: This first option is simply the header which specifies the name of file for this security database and is required.

d_name: This option specifies the name of this security database and should not be changed from the string "default".

d_secclass: This is an informational identifier of the security classes supported by the system and should be be set to "c2".

d_boot_authenticate: This option is not currently used by Enhanced Security.

d_pw_expire_warning: This option specifies, in seconds, is used to determine whether a password expiration warning is given at login time. If the password expiration for a user falls within this time interval, a warning is given.

Figure 5.1 Continued

d_pw_site_callout: This is the full path name of the script to call for site specific security policy conformance decisions. The /tcb/bin/pwpolicy by default does nothing but exit with a positive return code. See the "DEC OSF/1 Security" manual for more information on this option.

u_minchg#0: This is the minimum time between password changes in seconds. If the value assigned is zero (0), there is no minimum time enforced.

u_minlen#8: This is the minimum password length.

u_maxlen#12: This is the maximum password length.

u_exp#0: This is the number of seconds after a successful password change that the account password will expire. If the values specified is zero (0), passwords will not expire.

u_life#0: This is the lifetime of a password in seconds. If this time interval is reached, the account is locked and can only be unlocked by the superuser. Specifying zero (0) indicates an unlimited password lifetime.

u_pickpw: This Boolean option specifies whether a user can pick his own password (True) or will have a password generated by the system (False).

u_genpwd@: This Boolean option is the reverse of u_pickpw; i.e. a True value indicates that the system will generate passwords for a user and a False value specifies that a user can select his own password.

u_restrict: This Boolean option specifies whether password triviality checks are performed on a user-selected password. A u_restrict entry indicates that triviality checks including verifying that the password is not a login or group name, a palindrome, or a dictionary word; a u_restrict@ entry indicates that these checks are not performed.

(*continued*)

Figure 5.1 Continued

u_pwdepth#0: This is the number of old encrypted passwords to save to prevent reuse of previously used passwords. A value of zero (0) indicates that passwords can be reused.

u_nullpw@: This Boolean option controls the ability of a user to choose a null password. A u_nullpw entry indicates a null password can be chosen; a u_nullpw@ indicates that it cannot.

u_genchars@: This Boolean option controls the ability of a user to generate random characters for a password. A u_genchars entry indicates that the user can generate passwords made up of random characters and a u_genchars@ entry indicates that he cannot.

u_genletters@: This Boolean option controls the ability of a user to generate random letters for a password. A u_genletters entry indicates that the user can generate passwords made up of random letters and a u_genletters@ entry indicates that he cannot.

u_maxtries#0: This is the maximum number of consecutive unsuccessful login attempts to an account before the account is locked. Setting this option to zero (0) disables the locking of accounts due to unsuccessful login attempts.

u_lock@: This Boolean option is used to administratively lock an account. A u_lock entry indicates that the account is locked; a u_lock@ entry indicates that it is not. The presence of the u_lock@ entry in the Default Database File is to globally indicate that all accounts are unlocked unless locked in the individual Protected Password Database Files.

t_logdelay#2: This is the number of seconds between unsuccessful login attempts. This field is designed to slow the rate at which penetration attempts on a terminal device can occur.

Figure 5.1 Continued

> t_maxtries#10: This field specifies the maximum number of
> consecutive unsuccessful login attempts permitted using the
> terminal before the terminal is locked. Once the terminal is locked,
> it must be unlocked by an authorized administrator.
>
> For additional information, set the manpage for default(4).

Figure 5.1 Continued

Once reasonable values have been selected for the system defaults, the process of enabling Enhanced Security can begin. The steps are:

1. Log in as root.
2. Install the Enhanced Security subsets if not already installed.
3. Run the secsetup utility and select the ENHANCED security level.
4. Reboot the system.
5. Adjust System Default Database file to reflect desired global default.
6. Remove hashed passwords from /etc/passwd file.
7. Test your application(s).

Obviously, in order to enable Enhanced Security, you must have the ability and opportunity to reboot your system(s). Coordinate a time that is convenient with your users so as not to disrupt their work.

The subsections that follow present detailed instructions for enabling Enhanced Security.

5.6.1.1. Log-in as Root

This process can be done from either the system console logged in directly as root, or logged in from a terminal or across the network as a regular, non-privileged user who has become the root user via the su(1) command. Before proceeding, ensure that Enhanced Security is not already enabled with the following command:

```
# /usr/sbin/rcmgr get SECURITY
```

If the string "BASE" is returned, you are running Base Security and can proceed to enable Enhanced Security. If, however, the string "ENHANCED" is returned, Enhanced Security is already enabled on this system and you should move to step 5 to adjust the global defaults.

5.6.1.2. Install the Enhanced Security Subsets

Before you can enable Enhanced Security, two Enhanced Security Software Subsets must be loaded. These subsets are named OSFC2SECxxx and OSFXC2SECxxx (the "xxx" specifies the version of the subset.) To determine if these subsets are loaded, you can check as follows:

```
# /usr/sbin/setld -i | grep -i c2sec
OSFC2SEC350    installed    C2-Security (System Administration)
OSFXC2SEC350   installed    C2-Security GUI (System Administration)
```

In this example, both subsets are installed. If you do not receive any output, or if the "installed" keyword in the second column is absent, you must install both subsets from the master operating system install media using the setld command. For assistance in installed Digital UNIX subsets, see Chapter 3, "System Configuration."

5.6.1.3. Run the secsetup Utility

The secsetup(8) utility is an interactive program with toggles between Base and Enhanced Security on Digital UNIX systems. You must be prepared to answer the following two questions in addition to selecting which System Security Level you desire:

- Do you wish to disable segment sharing?
- Do you wish to run the audit setup utility at this time?

Typically, the answer to both of these questions is "no," unless you have special requirements. See the *Digital UNIX Security* manual for information on these options.

The following dispalys an example secsetup session showing the security level being changed from Base to Enhanced:

```
# /usr/sbin/secsetup
Enter system security level(BASE ENHANCED ?)[ENHANCED]: <RETURN>
ENHANCED security level will take effect on the next system reboot.

Do you wish to disable segment sharing(yes no ?)[no]: <RETURN>
```

```
Do you wish to run the audit setup utility at this time(yes
no ?)[no]: <RETURN>

Press return to continue: <RETURN>
#
```

Notice how the default answers to each prompt are in square brackets and can be selected by simply pressing the Return key.

5.6.1.4. Reboot the System to Enable Enhanced Security

Before the new security level change takes effect, the system must be rebooted. The simplest way to accomplish this is:

```
# /sbin/shutdown -r +2 "System being rebooted to
   enable Enhanced Security."
```

This shuts down and reboots the system with two minutes grace time and displays an informative message to any logged-in users.

5.6.1.5. Adjust System Default Database File

Once the system has successfully rebooted, log-in as root and make the previously recorded adjustments to the System Default Database File:

```
# cd /etc/auth/system
# cp default default.orig
# vi default (and apply desired changes)
```

5.6.1.6. Remove Encrypted Password Strings from /etc/ passwd File

The secsetup utility has copied the encrypted passwords from the password field of /etc/passwd into the individual user security databases under the /tcb/files/auth hierarchy. However, secsetup does not replace the encrypted passwords from /etc/passwd. When Enhanced Security is installed on your system, the password field should contain an asterisk (*) as the encrypted password is no longer stored in /etc/passwd. See Figure 5.2 for a Korn shell script to safely remove the encrypted password string from the password field of /etc/passwd and replace it with an asterisk. Note that this is only necessary at V3.2g and earlier.

```
#!/bin/ksh
# Script to replace the encrypted password
# strings in /etc/passwd with an asterisk (*)

if test ! -w /etc/passwd
then
      print 'Please su to root first.'
      exit 1
fi

trap 'rm -rf /etc/ptmp ; exit 1' 1 2

if [[ `rcmgr get SECURITY BASE` = BASE ]]
then
      print 'Security Level is not ENHANCED.'
      exit 1
fi

if mkdir /etc/ptmp
then
      :
else
      print 'The /etc/passwd file is busy. Try again later.'
      exit 1
fi

awk 'FS=":", OFS=":" {print $1,"*",$3,$4,$5,$6,$7}'
  /etc/passwd > \
      /etc/ptmp/passwd.modified

cp /etc/ptmp/passwd.modified /etc/passwd

if [ -f /etc/passwd.pag -o -f /etc/passwd.dir ]
then
      print 'Rebuilding the password database...'
      ( cd /etc ; mkpasswd passwd )
else
      print 'The hashed password database does not exist.'
      print -n 'Do you want to create it ([y]/n)? '
      if read Y
```

Figure 5.2 remove_passwd.ksh

```
      then
            case "${Y}"
            in [yY]*|'') print 'Rebuilding the password
              data base...'( cd /etc ; mkpasswd passwd ) ;;
            esac
      fi
fi

rm -rf /etc/ptmp
print 'Successfully replaced encrypted passwords with
asterisks'
exit 0
```

Figure 5.2 Continued

5.6.1.7. Test Your Application(s)

At this point, your system is running Enhanced Security, and you should con-
duct whatever testing of your applications is deemed appropriate before
declaring success. In addition, there is an issue related to passwords on newly
enabled Enhanced Security systems that bears mentioning. If any user's password prior to enabling Enhanced Security was longer than eight characters,
only the first eight characters will be accepted as the valid password. For
example, if a password was "toogood2be", the user must enter only "too-
good2" (the first eight characters) to successfully log-in. This anomaly is only
an issue until the user changes her password under Enhanced Security, at
which point the global, or user defaults if different, dictate the password
length. Ensure that your users are aware of this password issue prior to logging into the newly Enhanced Security-enabled system.

5.6.2. Disabling Enhanced Security

In the hopefully unlikely event that you find it necessary to disable Enhanced
Security and return to Base Security, the steps are:

1. Log-in as root.
2. Run the secsetup utility and select the BASE security level.
3. Reboot the system.

This will quickly revert the system back to Base Security and copy the encrypted passwords from the /tcb/files/auth hierarchy into the /etc/passwd file. Rebooting the system completes the process. This will leave all the Enhanced Security files (/etc/auth/* and /tcb/files/*) in place if you decide to re-enable Enhanced Security at a future date.

5.6.3. Account Management

One of the primary responsibilities of a UNIX system administrator is user account management. This includes account creation, account modification, and account removal. Once Enhanced Security is enabled on a Digital UNIX system, new utilities are provided and should be used whenever possible to manage user accounts. The primary tools are XsysAdmin/XIsso and the CDE Account Manager, dxaccounts, which are all X-Windows applications. Unfortunately, Digital has not provided a character cell interface to accomplish the same functionality. However, as you will see, account management can also be performed without running these GUIs, which is occasionally necessary when logged in remotely, when X applications cannot be easily run. See Chapter 4, "User Accounts," for details on account creation, deletion, and modification using the Digital UNIX account management tools while running both Base and Enhanced Security.

Account creation can also still be accomplished with the Base Security command, adduser(8). This command is mostly Enhanced Security-aware, with the only exception being that instead of an asterisk (*) being placed in the password field of the /etc/passwd file, the string "Nolog-in" is inserted in the password field. This in no way prevents the user account from being used, since the password field of the /etc/passwd file is completely ignored when the security level is Enhanced. However, this inconsistency may be confusing, and you may manually edit the /etc/passwd file—via the vipw(8) command—to correct it. You could also run the remove_passwd script (Figure 5.2) again after adding accounts with adduser to clean up this minor wrinkle.

I strongly recommend that account creation on Digital UNIX systems be done with either the XSysAdmin program, the CDE Account Manager, or the adduser command, unless you have a thorough understanding of all the details of the security database files.

Creation of new groups is accomplished by specifying the group name and group ID in the XSysAdmin or CDE Account Manager New Group dialog box. Optionally, either the Base Security command, addgroup(8), can be used to create new groups, or the /etc/group file can be manually edited by the superuser to add a new group.

XsysAdmin or the CDE Account Manager is also used to edit the new user account template, which specifies the default account parameters used when a new account is created. These parameters include password length, account expiration date, time of day restrictions, and so on. These parameters are only the defaults and can be overridden on a per account basis.

The parameters are actually stored in the System Default Database File, /etc/auth/system/default, and can be manually edited by the superuser.

Finally, the XSysAdmin program or the CDE Account Manager is used to retire user accounts. Retiring a user account, rather than simply deleting the account, is a requirement of C2 Security, which Digital UNIX with Enhanced Security conforms to. Retiring an account permanently locks the account, preventing reuse of that account's user ID. Once an account is retired, that account can not be re-enabled.

The Base Security command, removeuser(8), however, will completely remove all traces of an account. If the stringent account retirement requirements of C2 Security are not necessary, the removeuser command can continue to be used to remove user accounts.

Existing account security characteristics can be viewed and changed via the Modify User Accounts dialog box of the XIsso program or the CDE Account Manager. You can specify the groups the account belongs to, the log-in control parameters, and the password quality and aging parameters. These parameters are stored in the protected password database files, which reside under /tcb/files. The format of the protected password database and the method of manually manipulating it are different depending on the version of Digital UNIX.

For versions of Digital UNIX prior to 4.0, the protected password database files are located in the /tcb/files/auth directory. Contained within this directory are subdirectories with single letter names, each of which represents initial letters of account names. Inside of each of these twenty-six subdirectories is a file containing a protected password entry for a single-user account, in which the file names are the same as the user account names. For example, the protected password file for root is /tcb/files/auth/r/root. These files can be manually edited by the superuser. See Figure 5.3 for format and field definitions.

In Digital UNIX version 4.0 and later, the protected password database is located in the /tcb/files/auth.db file, which is a single binary database file

An authentication file is maintained for each user account on an Enhanced Security-enabled system. These files are located under /tcb/files/auth, which is accessible only to the superuser. The encrypted password string, among other things, is stored in this file. Options specified in an individual account Protected Password file override any Global settings specified in the System Default file. The following is the Protected Password file for my account on a system running Enhanced Security:

```
mcheek:u_name=mcheek:u_id#247:u_oldcrypt#0:\
:u_pwd=1o2A5Adx3oXXm:\
:u_succhg#828919424:u_unsucchg#829276329:\
:u_suclog#839193127:u_suctty=ttyp1:\
:u_unsuclog#838691522:u_unsuctty=ttyp1:u_lock@:\
:chkent:
```

The format for this file is identical to the format for the System Default file (See sidebar "System Default Database File Format".) The example options have the following meaning:

mcheek: This first option is simply the header which specifies the name of file for this security database and is required.

u_name=mcheek: This is the user name for the account and must match the user name in a corresponding /etc/password entry.

u_id#247: This is the user ID for the account and must match the user ID in a corresponding /etc/password entry.

u_oldcrypt#0: This is the algorithm number used to encrypt the current password.

u_pwd=1o2A5Adx3oXXm: This is the encrypted password string for the account. (This is not an actual password)

Figure 5.3 Protected Password Authentication Database File Format

u_succhg#828919424: This option specifies the time of the last successful password change. The time is specified as the number of seconds since the Epoch, 00:00:00 GMT 1 Jan 1970. Obviously, this time value is not immediately useful and in fact, this field should only be set by programs (such as passwd(1)) that can be used to change the account password.

u_unsucchg#829276329: This option specifies the time of the last unsuccessful password change. This field should not be manually edited.

u_suclog#839193127: This option specifies the time of the last successful login. This field should not be manually edited.

u_suctty=ttyp1: This is the name of the terminal associated with the last successful login to the account.

u_unsuclog#838691522: This option specifies the time of the last unsuccessful login. This field should not be manually edited.

u_unsuctty=ttyp1: This is the name of the terminal associated with the last unsuccessful login to the account.

u_lock@: This Boolean option is used to administratively lock an account. A u_lock entry indicates that the account is locked; a u_lock@ entry indicates that it is not.

For additional information, set the manpage for prpasswd(4).

Figure 5.3 Continued

that contains the protected password entries for all the accounts on the system. The auth.db file is manipulated manually via the edauth(8) program. The individual protected password entry for an account can be viewed, edited, or removed from the auth.db file using the edauth command. For example, the following command displays the protected password entry for the root account:

```
# edauth -g root
```

To edit the entry for the root account:

```
# edauth root
```

This second command invokes the editor specified by the EDITOR environment variable, or /usr/bin/ex by default, with the protected password entry for the specified account. See Figure 5.3, for format and field definitions.

Xisso and the CDE Account Manager also allow the system administrator to set the global system parameters of Inactivity Timeout and Account Expiration Warning. The Inactivity Timeout is the number of minutes that a logged-in account can remain idle before the session is closed. If a value of zero minutes is specified, no inactivity timeout is enabled and account sessions will not be terminated. The Account Expiration Warning parameter specifies how many days prior to an account's scheduled expiration date that warning messages will be shown to the user upon log-in. These parameters are universal and cannot be set on a per-user basis. Both of these parameters (d_inactivity_timeout and d_pw_expire_warning) are stored in the System Default Database File, /etc/auth/system/default, and can be manually added/edited by the superuser.

5.6.4. Enhanced Security Logging

One unique feature of Digital UNIX is a consolidated security authentication mechanism called the Security Integration Architecture (SIA). This SIA layer isolates the security-related commands such as log-in, su, and passwd from the specific security mechanisms, which include, in addition to Base and Enhanced Security, optional products such as the Distributed Computing Environment (DCE). You do not need to be concerned with this SIA layer except to take advantage of the centralized logging that the SIA provides via the sialog file. This log will record all security events, including the success and failure results of log-in, password changes, and su. To enable the sialog, simply create the log file

```
# touch /var/adm/sialog
```

and the log will begin to be written to by the SIA. The recommended permissions for the sialog are 600. Typically, you would want to prevent non-privileged users from viewing the contents of security logs such as sialog, for there is the possibility of passwords appearing in the log. An excerpt from the sialog shows the types of events recorded:

```
SIA:EVENT Wed Jun 5 05:22:08 1997
Successful session authentication for mcheek on :0
SIA:EVENT Wed Jun 5 05:22:08 1997
Successful establishment of session
SIA:ERROR Wed Jun 5 05:24:11 1997
Failure on authentication for su from mcheek to root
SIA:EVENT Wed Jun 5 05:24:40 1997
Successful authentication for su from root to mcheek
SIA:EVENT Wed Jun 5 05:25:46 1997
Successful password change for mcheek
```

As this log will continue to grow without bounds, it must be manually truncated periodically. To stop logging of SIA events, remove the logfile. Since the SIA is part of the Digital UNIX operating system, the sialog can be used whether the security level is Base or Enhanced.

5.6.5. Application Issues

As the system administrator, you will usually be responsible for installation and configuration of Commercial Off The Shelf (COTS) software. Prior to enabling Enhanced Security, you must ensure that any applications currently installed are Enhanced Security-aware. If an application that relied on the system for user authentication, such as a database or security tool, were not aware of Enhanced Security, user authentication into the application would most likely fail. In the event that the application vendor does not know if enabling Enhanced Security will affect its product, proceed slowly with implementing Enhanced Security, and test the application as much as possible prior to going to production.

An additional responsibility you may have is to support software development efforts, both in-house and commercial applications. Coordinate the implementation of Enhanced Security with any software developers you support on your system(s). The Digital *DEC OSF/1 Security* manual provides a "Programmer's Guide to Security" section that details programming techniques and provides coding examples that would be invaluable to your development staff.

As you can see, successfully implementing Enhanced Security requires a thorough knowledge of your environment and requirements, careful planning, and a significant amount of ongoing administrative responsibility, both in account management and general system maintenance. However, the benefits of Enhanced Security, such as comprehensive auditing of security events and more robust identification and authentication features, far outweigh the disadvantages of the Enhanced Security system.

Processes and Resources

6

6.1. PROCESS MANAGEMENT

Digital UNIX provides a rich environment to users due to its multiprocessing and multi-user nature. The ability for multiple users to each run multiple jobs simultaneously is a blessing for end users. Of course, this ability is not limited to Digital UNIX, nor even just to UNIX itself, but exists in a variety of computing environments, such as large mainframe environments, vendor proprietary systems such as DEC's OpenVMS, and Microsoft's Windows NT. UNIX, however, and Digital UNIX in particular, has gained a reputation since the early 1970s as the operating system of choice for supporting software development efforts, especially large team projects, and multi-user database applications, such as those based on Oracle, Informix, and Sybase.

A Digital UNIX System Administrator comes to this environment needing the skills to understand and manage this multiprocessing capability. In UNIX, a single job, whether it has a system function, such as authenticating user log-ins or receiving and handling print requests, or is a user activity, such as compiling a C++ program or querying a database, is called a Process. Managing these processes, which can be as few as a couple dozen processes on a small, lightly used workstation, or many thousands of processes on a large database or Web server, is an important part of a system administrator's responsibility.

In this chapter I will cover the various attributes of a process, how these attributes interrelate, and which attributes can actually be adjusted to change the behavior of the process. In addition, the Parent/Child relationship will be covered. This relationship is important in understanding how processes start and finish. Controlling processes includes the various ways to start a process, changing the state of a process by sending signals to that process, and the concept of foreground and background processes. Digital UNIX also provides several methods of scheduling processes to be run at a future date. This capability is used extensively by the system administrator to schedule periodic maintenance processes, such as system backups, to be run without user-intervention.

6.2. PROCESS OVERVIEW

A process is composed of executing code and its address space. Note that a program and a process are not necessarily one and the same. A single program can be made up of many processes, since UNIX has a fork() system call, and there are performance benefits to breaking large or complex programs into multiple processes on a UNIX system. Each individual active process has an entry in the system process table, which is managed by the system scheduler. Processes are the mechanism by which all work, whether system or user, gets done on a Digital UNIX system.

The process table is a memory structure that contains information for each running process. This information includes the process identification number, or PID, the current state of the process such as RUNNING or SLEEPING, accounting data such as amount of CPU time used, and the actual command or program associated with the process. The process table is used by the system scheduler to assign CPU usage to individual processes based on their priority. The system scheduler is the first "process" per se and has a process identification number, or PID, of zero (0). The second process, init, is always PID 1 and is the ultimate parent from which all subsequent processes are spawned.

There is a maximum number of processes that can be running simultaneously on a Digital UNIX system. This value, called the task_max keyword, is a calculated number and is based on the maxusers parameter located in the kernel configuration file, /sys/conf/HOSTNAME. The formula for calculating task_max is:

```
1 + (20 + (8 * maxusers))
```

For example, if maxusers is set to 32, task_max is calculated to be 277, or $1 + (20 + (8 * 32)) = 277$. This value is used to determine the size of a data structure that controls the number of user processes that can run simultaneously. Increasing the value of task_max allows more user processes to be active at the same time. Decreasing this value limits the number of user processes.

The system displays the following message in the /var/adm/messages file and in the kernel event-logging file if it reaches the task_max limit:

```
pid: table is full
```

To resolve this situation, simply increase the maxusers value in the kernel configuration file, rebuild the kernel with the doconfig(8) command, place the new kernel into place and reboot.

6.3. PROCESS ATTRIBUTES

Digital UNIX stores a variety of attributes about each active process in a kernel memory data structure. This structure, proc, is defined in the /usr/include/sys/proc.h header file. Following are some of the more interesting attributes:

- Process Identifier Number (PID)
- Parent Process Identifier Number (PPID)
- Process Group Identifier Number (PGID)
- Process Owner's Real and Effective User Identifier Number (UID/EUID)
- Process Owner's Real and Effective Group Identifier Number (GID/EGID)
- Process Priority
- Resource Utilization
- Controlling Terminal (if any)
- Process State

6.3.1. Displaying Process Attributes

The attributes of active processes can be displayed using the ps (process status) utility. Running ps with no command line arguments prints information about processes associated with the controlling terminal:

```
$ ps
PID TTY    S       TIME COMMAND
21281 ttyp0  S   0:00.08 -ksh (ksh)
```

This default output format displays the process ID (PID), the controlling terminal (TTY), the state (S), the CPU time used by the process including both user and system time (TIME), and the command that is running (COMMAND). A system administrator is more interested in seeing the attributes of either system processes (daemons) or user processes or both. The Digital UNIX ps utility has a variety of command line switches that specify which attributes to display and their display format. The ps utility has two distinct command line sets, SYSV and BSD, each with it's own distinct features. The SYSV command line set is used when the arguments are preceded with a dash "-", otherwise the arguments are considered to be BSD format. For example:

SYSV process display output
```
# ps -ef
UID     PID   PPID  C    STIME     TTY      TIME       CMD
Root    0     0     0.0  Jun 03    ??       15:20.91   [kernel idle]
root    1     0     0.0  Jun 03    ??       0:35.07    /sbin/init -a
root    3     1     0.0  Jun 03    ??       1:30.53    /sbin/kloadsrv
root    22    1     0.0  Jun 03    ??       12:15.65   /sbin/update
root    95    1     0.0  Jun 03    ??       0:16.80    /usr/sbin/syslogd
root    97    1     0.0  Jun 03    ??       0:00.04    /usr/sbin/binlogd
root    349   1     0.0  Jun 03    ??       0:20.21    -accepting
connections  (sendmail)
root    401   1     0.0  Jun 03    ??       0:25.62    /usr/sbin/os_mibs
root    403   1     0.0  Jun 03    ??       3:47.75    /usr/sbin/snmpd
root    420   1     0.0  Jun 03    ??       0:00.58    /usr/sbin/inetd
root    453   1     0.0  Jun 03    ??       0:01.02    /usr/sbin/cron
root    469   1     0.0  Jun 03    ??       0:00.02    /usr/lbin/lpd
root    536   1     0.0  Jun 03    console  0:00.42    /usr/sbin/getty
console console vt100
mcheek 28727 28801 0.3  17:13:51  ttyp0    0:00.90    -ksh (ksh)
root    6959  28727 0.0  18:47:47  ttyp0    0:00.19    ps -ef
```

BSD process display output

```
# ps auxw
USER     PID   %CPU   %MEM   VSZ   RSS      TTY  S        STARTED  TIME
COMMAND
root     0     0.0 7.5 76.0M 4.6M  ??       R <  Jun 03   15:20.91 [kernel
idle]
root     1     0.0 0.1 440K  40K   ??       I    Jun 03   0:35.07
/sbin/init -a
root     3     0.0 0.0 904K  0K    ??       IW   Jun 03   1:30.53
/sbin/kloadsrv
root     22    0.0 0.1 1.55M 56K   ??       S    Jun 03   12:15.65
/sbin/update
root     95    0.0 0.2 1.61M 120K  ??       S    Jun 03   0:16.80
/usr/sbin/syslogd
root     97    0.0 0.0 1.59M 0K    ??       IW   Jun 03   0:00.04
/usr/sbin/binlogd
root     349   0.0 0.1 1.86M 72K   ??       I    Jun 03   0:20.21  -
accepting connections (sendmail)
root     401   0.0 0.2 2.84M 104K  ??       S    Jun 03   0:25.62
/usr/sbin/os_mibs
root     403   0.0 0.1 1.68M 48K   ??       S    Jun 03   3:47.75
/usr/sbin/snmpd
root     420   0.0 0.1 1.62M 64K   ??       I    Jun 03   0:00.58
/usr/sbin/inetd
root     453   0.0 0.2 1.59M 120K  ??       I    Jun 03   0:01.02
/usr/sbin/cron
root     469   0.0 0.0 1.70M 0K    ??       IW   Jun 03   0:00.02
/usr/lbin/lpd
root     536   0.0 0.0 432K  0K    console  IW + Jun 03   0:00.42
/usr/sbin/getty console console vt100
root     7202  0.0 0.4 1.75M 264K  ttyp0    R +  18:49:07 0:00.06  ps auxw
mcheek   28727 0.1 0.4 1.88M 264K  ttyp0    S    17:13:51 0:00.88  -ksh
(ksh)
```

6.3.2. Process Identifiers

Each active process is assigned a *process identifier,* or **PID,** which is a unique positive integer between zero and 32767. A PID is unique, however, only among active processes. PIDs can and are repeated since, obviously, on a busy system with many active users, 32768 processes are not all that many.

The PID is simply a value used by the kernel to report status changes to the user, and by which a user can identify and reference individual processes when, for instance, sending a process a signal. A PID is assigned to a started process in a somewhat random manner and there is no correlation between a process and a PID. Never make any assumptions about which PID is assigned to an active process. Simply use the ps(1) command and search for the command of the desired process in order to obtain the PID of that process. For example:

```
# ps -ef | grep syslogd
root   95   1    0.0   Jun 03 ??   0:16.80      /usr/sbin/syslogd
```

6.3.3. PPID and PGID

In addition to the PID, two other process identifiers are assigned to a process when the process is created, the *parent process identifier* (PPID) and *process group identifier* (PGID). These two IDs are inherited from the process's parent process rather than being generated and, consequently, do not have the uniqueness requirement of the PID.

The *parent process identifier* (PPID) of a particular process is simply the PID of the parent process that started this particular process. All processes are children of some other process and, except for the process scheduler (PID#0), ultimately can trace their "lineage" back to init (PID#1), the great-grandfather of all processes.

The PPID is a default output field in the SYSV flavor of ps(1). The PPID is useful to the system administrator in tracing process ownership, especially when it becomes necessary to terminate processes. Whenever possible, send processes the terminal signal (via the kill(1) command) in the reverse order of creating. This avoids zombie processes and other unpleasant situations where processes can hang. (See section 6.5 for more information on zombie processes.)

The *process group identifier* (PGID) is a number similar to the PID, except that instead of identifying a single process, the PGID is used to identify a set of processes, or a process group. An example of a process group would be a set of commands in a pipeline issued from a shell prompt. For example, the following command,

```
# cat /etc/passwd | grep ksh | cut -d: -f1 | sort
```

which displays a sorted list of userid's whose default shell is /bin/ksh, will consist of four distinct processes (the cat, grep, cut, and sort commands) in a pipeline, each with their own PID. All four processes, however, will have the same PGID. This is especially useful if, for instance, such a pipeline were a long-running job and you wished to terminate the job. Instead of having to search for then specify each process's PID in a kill command, you could specify just the PGID, and the termination signal would be broadcast to each member of the process group. Obviously, this is a trivial example, but process groups are the foundation for the job-control facility in the C shell and Korn shell.

6.3.4. Real and Effective User/Group Identifiers

A process inherits the *user identifer* (UID) and *group identifier* (GID) from that process's parent. The UID and GID of a process are used by the access-control facilities of the file system to determine file and directory access privileges for that process. This is what prevents a nonprivileged user process from writing to the /etc/passwd and changing the root password, for instance. In addition, UIDs are used to define which signals a process may be sent. This protects the system by preventing a regular user from killing important system processes such as init or cron.

The UID and GID are maintained by the system administrator in the /etc/passwd and /etc/group files. When listing processes with the ps(1) command using SYSV -f switch, the UID is translated by ps to the corresponding user name by consulting the system password file. Without this switch, ps displays the numeric value for UIDs.

It is often necessary to allow a regular user process to temporarily assume greater privileges. For example, a user must be able to edit the normally read-only /etc/passwd file in order to change a password. To solved this problem, UNIX allows programs to be configured such that the program assumes additional privileges when run by a nonprivileged user. A program that runs with an additional group privilege are called *set-group-identifier* (SGID) programs; programs which run with an additional user privilege are called *set-user-identifier* (SUID) programs. When a setuid program is run—for example, the passwd(1) program that allows users to change their password—that process has an additional identifier, the *effective user identifier* (EUID), which specifies the additional user privilege that the process possesses during the life of the process. Continuing the example of the passwd(1) program, the EUID of the password-changing process is zero or root, since the passwd program is set to be SUID to root. This allows the passwd process to actually change the password of the executing user in the protected password file. Similarly, the *effective group identifier* (EGID) of a process is set accordingly when running a SGID program.

6.3.5. Process Priority

Digital UNIX processes are scheduled for execution on the CPU based on a value called the process priority parameter. This parameter is a number between 0 and 127, with a lower number indicating a higher priority. The process priority is maintained internally by the kernel, and process priorities are dynamically updated based on a number of variables, such as the nice value of a process.

The concept of nice is the primary way for a system administrator to either start a process with a higher or lower scheduling priority or change an already running process's priority. A process's nice value is a number between -19 and 19 that is added to the process's priority number. Since a lower priority number indicates higher priority, a lower (negative) nice value further reduces the priority number increasing the process's priority. A process with a positive nice value increases the process's priority number, thereby reducing the process's priority, causing that process to be "nicer" to the system, hence the name.

By default, a process starts with a nice value of zero, which neither increases nor decreases the process priority. The nice(1) command is used to start a process with a non-zero nice value:

```
$ nice -n 15 sort bigfile.txt -o sorted.txt
```

This syntax starts and runs the sort command with a nice value of 15, which possibly lowers the process's scheduling priority increasing the execution time. The nice value (-n) is an optional parameter, for example:

```
$ nice cc *.c &
```

This command compiles a group of C programs in the background with a nice value of +10.

Only the superuser can specify nice values less than zero. For example, the following command runs with a nice value of -10, which increases the scheduling priority and prevents regular user processes from delaying execution:

```
# nice -n -10 du -ks /home/*
```

The nice(1) command is used only to start processes with modified nice values. Once a process is already running, its nice value also can be modified via the renice(8) command. The renice command is very flexible for the system administrator in that either a single process or groups of similar processes can be reniced. To change the nice value of a single process, simply specify the *process identifier,* or PID to be reniced:

```
# renice -n -12 -p 783
```

This changes the nice value of process ID 783 to negative 12. Multiple PIDs may be specified on the command line separated by white space.

The renice command can also be used to change groups of similar processes, either by specifying *process group identifiers* (PGIDs) to change all processes in a process group, or by specifying usernames or *user identifiers* (UIDs) to change all processes owned by a particular user. Renice is flexible enough to allow all three types of changes on the command line. For example, the following command changes the nice value of process IDs 2001 and 2005, processes in process group 771, and processes owned by jsmith to -2:

```
# renice -n -2 -p 2001 2005 -g 771 -u jsmith
```

One final restriction of renice is that while the superuser may both increase and decrease the nice value of processes, a non-privileged user may only increase the nice value of processes owned by that user. A user may never decrease the nice value, even if the nice value was previously increased by that user. For instance, if user jsmith increases the nice value of a job from zero to +10, jsmith may not return the nice value to zero; only the system administrator can reduce a nice value.

In addition to the nice value, there are a variety of other factors that influence the value of process priorities. These include the amount of CPU time that a process has used recently, the amount of memory the process is using, and the number of jobs already in the run queue waiting for CPU time.

Both the process priority value and the nice value can be displayed with the ps command by specifying the -l switch for both SYSV and BSD versions. The process priority is displayed in the PRI column, and the nice value is displayed in the NI column of the ps output.

6.3.6. Resource Utilization

As a process executes, the kernel keeps track of the process's utilization of a variety of system resources. These resources include:

- CPU Usage
- Memory Utilization
- Elapsed Time
- Disk I/O and Paging
- Number of Context Switches
- Number of Signals Received

These resource utilization statistics are stored in the proc kernel structure for each process, are updated dynamically by the kernel for all processes, and are available to the system administrator (and regular users as well) via the ps(1) command. This information is useful, for example, in identifying runaway processes by examining CPU utilization or determining the memory usage, both real and virtual, of a particular process.

The most immediately useful process utilization information is the CPU and memory statistics. The CPU utilization of a process is monitored by examining two fields, %CPU and TIME, in the ps(1) output. Memory utilization is tracked in the %MEM, RSS, and VSZ columns. These columns are displayed by using either the SYSV "ps -eo VFMT" options, or the BSD "ps u" option.

%CPU is a dynamically computed value that represents the percentage of CPU resources that a process is consuming. This number is calculated by the kernel as an average of up to a minute of previous time. It is possible for the sum of the %CPU values in a ps listing to exceed 100%. A process that is consistently at or near 100% may possibly indicate a runaway process. It may also, however, be perfectly normal for a process's %CPU to be high, depending on what the process is and what it is doing.

TIME is simply the total time a process has actually been executing on a CPU. This value is cumulative, since the process was started and can be hours or days on a long-running process. This value is not the total elapsed time, just the total time that the process has actually been running on a processor.

%MEM is simply the percentage of real memory used by a process. RSS is the current resident memory size of a process in kilobytes, and VSZ is the total virtual memory size of a process, also in kilobytes. A process's VSZ will always have a value, while the RSS column can vary between the VSZ value and zero. A process's RSS value can be zero, since a process may be entirely swapped out to disk and no longer resident in real memory, either due to the process being idle and moved to swap by the system, or due to a memory shortage when lower priority processes are "swapped out." When confronted with a low- or out-of-memory situation, these three memory utilization fields from the ps output should be examined to determine which processes are consuming both real and virtual memory.

6.3.7. Controlling Terminal

Processes other than system processes that are typically started at system startup time are usually associated with a particular terminal. This controlling terminal is normally the terminal where the user who started or owns the process is logged in. If, however, a user runs a job and places it in the background and then logs out, that process is no longer associated with a terminal, and this is indicated by "??" in the TTY field of the ps(1) output. System processes, or daemons, not associated with a terminal also have a "??" in the TTY field of the ps(1) output.

Knowing the controlling terminal is useful to a system administrator when it becomes necessary to identify all processes associated with a particular logged-in user. Simply run the who(1) command to determine which terminal to query, then specify the terminal of interest to the ps(1) command to display all processes associated with that terminal:

```
# who
mcheek   ttyp1   Jun 4   11:35  <- What are the processes
   associated with the tty?
Styler   ttyp2   Jun 4   13:11
jsmith   ttyp4   Jun 4   15:51
tlee     ttyp5   Jun 4   09:14

# ps -ft ttyp1
mcheek   28727   28801   0.3   11:37:51   ttyp1   0:00.90   -ksh (ksh)
mcheek   29178   28727   0.0   11:52:33   ttyp1   0:01.02   -vi main.c
```

6.3.8. Process State

The kernel maintains the current state of all active processes in the proc structure. This state is simply the status of the process. Even though Digital UNIX is a multitasking operating system, the perception that multiple processes are actually running at the same time is only an illusion. Actually, only one process can run at any one time, except on multiprocessor systems where the number of processors dictates the maximum number of concurrent processes. When a process is not actually running, it can be in several other states, including sleeping, waiting its next turn on the CPU, idle, stopped, or halted.

The state field in a process status list is given by a sequence of letters, for example, RWN. The first letter indicates the status of the process:

R   Runnable process
U   Uninterruptible sleeping process
S   Process sleeping for less than about 20 seconds
I   Process idle (sleeping) longer than about 20 seconds
T   Stopped process
H   Halted process

Additional characters after these, if any, indicate additional state information:

W   Process is swapped out (shows a blank space if the process is loaded (in-core))
>   Process has specified a soft limit on memory requirements and is exceeding that limit; such a process is (necessarily) not swapped

An additional letter may indicate whether a process is running with altered CPU scheduling priority (nice):

N   Process priority is reduced
<   Process priority has been artificially raised
+   Process is a process group leader with a controlling terminal

---

Figure 6.1 ps(1) Output Process State Descriptors

The process state is displayed in the S column of the ps output as a sequence of one or more characters. The first character indicates the status of the process. Additional characters after the first indicate additional state information, including whether the process has been swapped out or if the process's scheduling priority (or nice value) has been altered. See Figure 6.1 for the definition of these state indicator characters.

The ps command shows the state of processes as accurately as possible. However, process states can change quickly and there may be discrepancies between the ps command's snapshot and the actual process state. This does not usually cause problems, but is an issue to be aware of.

The BSD format of ps displays the state information by default. To display the process state when specifying SYSV ps switches, simply add the -l parameter to generate a "long" listing. The process state is displayed in the S column. For example:

```
    # ps -efl
        F   S UID  PID PPID %CPU PRI  NI  RSS  WCHAN  STARTED    TIME            COMMAND
        3   R <  0    0    0  0.0  32 -12 4.6M     *  Jun 03 19:28.34        [kernel idle]
 80048001   I    0    1    0  0.0  44   0  40K  pause  Jun 03  0:35.36        /sbin/init -a
     8001  IW    0    3    1  0.0  44   0   0K sv_msg_ Jun 03  1:30.53        /sbin/kloadsrv
     8001   I    0   22    1  0.0  44   0  56K  pause  Jun 03 14:51.74        /sbin/update
     8001   S    0   95    1  0.0  42   0 120K  event  Jun 03  0:21.45        /usr/sbin/syslogd
     8001  IW    0   97    1  0.0  42   0   0K  event  Jun 03  0:00.13        /usr/sbin/binlogd
     8001   I    0  349    1  0.0  44   0  72K socket  Jun 03  0:29.77 -accepting connections
                                                                               (sendmail)
     8001   I    0  401    1  0.0  42   0 104K  event  Jun 03  0:33.19        /usr/sbin/os_mibs
     8001   I    0  403    1  0.0  42   0  16K  event  Jun 03  4:13.15        /usr/sbin/snmpd
     8001   I    0  420    1  0.0  42   0  64K  event  Jun 03  0:00.90        /usr/sbin/inetd
     8001  IW    0  453    1  0.0  42   0   0K dece94  Jun 03  0:01.46        /usr/sbin/cron
     8001  IW    0  469    1  0.0  44   0   0K  event  Jun 03  0:00.04        /usr/lbin/lpd
 80808001  IW +  0  536    1  0.0  46   0   0K  ttyin  Jun 03  0:00.42/usr/sbin/getty console
                                                                               console vt100
 82808001  R +   0 6739 7095  0.0  47   0 376K     -  18:45:17  0:00.15             ps -efl
 80c08001   S 101 7095 5777  0.1  44   0 264K   wait  18:38:45  0:00.77          -ksh (ksh)
```

6.4. The ps Command

The ps(1) command is the system administrator's window into the state of all the processes running on a Digital UNIX system. Every process statistic collected by the kernel is available for display via the ps command's many options. By default, each version of ps (SYSV or BSD) only displays a few common fields such as the PID, the process owner, the process start time and CPU time, and the process command. To display any of the less common process statistics, such as a process's nice value or the process group identifier (PGID), additional format options must be specified on the ps command line. The ps -o switch also provides the ability to customize the ps output to only display the fields of interest. This can be very useful in generating custom reports of system process activity. For instance, to display the PID, the total elapsed time, the current CPU time, the time processes have spent executing in system and user spaces, and the command—in that order and for all processes on the system—run the following ps command:

```
# ps -A -o pid -o etime -o cputime -o systime -o usertime -o command
  PID     ELAPSED        TIME      SYSTEM      USER          COMMAND
    0  36-09:52:31   22:59.78   22:59.78   0:00.00      [kernel idle]
    1  36-09:52:31    0:35.83    0:34.72   0:01.11      /sbin/init -a
    3  36-09:52:30    1:30.59    0:58.19   0:32.40      /sbin/kloadsrv
   22  36-09:52:20   17:06.41   17:00.09   0:06.32      /sbin/update
   95  36-09:52:14    0:23.17    0:19.73   0:03.44      /usr/sbin/syslogd
   97  36-09:52:14    0:00.13    0:00.11   0:00.02      /usr/sbin/binlogd
  277  36-09:52:07    1:46.42    1:17.01   0:29.41      /usr/sbin/portmap
  349  36-09:52:02    0:39.12    0:38.13   0:01.00      -accepting
connections (sendmail)
  401  36-09:52:00    0:36.32    0:24.92   0:11.40      /usr/sbin/os_mibs
  403  36-09:52:00    4:13.62    3:43.14   0:30.49      /usr/sbin/snmpd
  420  36-09:51:53    0:01.22    0:01.16   0:00.06      /usr/sbin/inetd
  453  36-09:51:52    0:01.95    0:01.81   0:00.14      /usr/sbin/cron
  469  36-09:51:49    0:00.04    0:00.04   0:00.01      /usr/lbin/lpd
  536  36-09:51:38    0:00.42    0:00.40   0:00.03      /usr/sbin/getty
console console vt100
18804     01:42:42    0:00.32    0:00.19   0:00.12      -ksh (ksh)
19570         0:00    0:00.07    0:00.05   0:00.02      ps -A -o pid
-o etime -o cputime -o systime -o usertime -o command
```

Consult the ps(1) man page on your system to see a list of available output specifiers that can be used with the -o option of ps.

6.5. PROCESS PARENT/CHILD RELATIONSHIP

A process is created with the fork system call and is termed a child process of the creating parent process. A child process inherits the privileges of its parent in addition to the parent's priority, signal state, environment, and all other parameters stored in the "proc" structure of the parent process. In fact, except for the PID and PPID, from a user's point of view, a child process is initially a clone of its parent until either the child, the parent, or a privileged user modifies any of the process parameters.

The parent/child relationship is important to keep in mind when managing processes, especially in a problem situation. For instance, if a process begins forking new child processes uncontrollably, you must find and kill the runaway parent process to fix the problem. Killing the child processes in this case would only address the symptom and not the true cause.

The parent/child relationship also comes into play when discussing the "zombie" process. A zombie process is a process that has exited, but whose parent process has not acknowledged that exit. Zombie processes are identified in a ps listing by the string "<defunct>" in place of the process command. Zombies themselves are usually not a problem for system administrators, since the only impact is that the zombie continues to occupy a process table slot. The various conditions that can cause zombie processes, though, may be of concern to a system administrator. These causes can include a hung or blocked parent process, which is unable to catch the exit signal of its child processes, poor programming practices, or system problems.

Zombie processes are so named because, like the zombies of horror movies, they appear alive (in the ps output), but actually are not. This explains why trying to kill a zombie process is futile; the process is already dead. The only way to rid yourself of zombie processes, other than rebooting the system, is to cause the parent to acknowledge that its children have exited. If the parent process is a user shell, such as the Korn shell or C shell, sometimes just having the user press Return at the shell prompt is sufficient to reap its defunct processes. If that fails, or the parent process is not a shell, or the parent process is simply hung, a more drastic measure is to kill the parent process itself. When a process exits, its remaining children are reassigned to process ID #1, init, which will normally acknowledge the exited children and remove the zombies from the process table.

6.6. CONTROLLING RUNNING PROCESSES

Digital UNIX processes are controlled by a mechanism known as signals. A signal is simply that: a message sent by one process to another process. It is equivalent to a hardware interrupt. A signal can originate from a user application program or from an interactive session via the kill(1) command.

There is a defined set of signals for a variety of software and hardware conditions that may arise during the execution of a process. See Table 6.1 for a listing of these signals.

Signal	Number	Default Action	Meaning
SIGHUP	1	Terminate Process	Hang up
SIGINT	2	Terminate Process	Interrupt
SIGQUIT	3	Create core image	Quit
SIGILL	4	Create core image	Invalid instruction (not reset when caught)
SIGTRAP	5	Create core image	Trace trap (not reset when caught)
SIGABRT	6	Create core image	End process (see the abort() function)
SIGEMT	7	Create core image	EMT instruction
SIGFPE	8	Create core image	Arithmetic exception, integer divided by 0 (zero), or floating-point exception
SIGKILL	9	Terminate Process	Kill (cannot be caught or ignored)
SIGBUS	10	Create core image	Specification exception
SIGSEGV	11	Create core image	Segmentation violation
SIGSYS	12	Create core image	Invalid parameter to system call
SIGPIPE	13	Terminate Process	Write on a pipe when there is no process to read it
SIGALRM	14	Terminate Process	Alarm clock
SIGTERM	15	Terminate Process	Software termination signal
SIGURG	16	Discard Signal	Urgent condition on I/O channel
SIGSTOP	17	Stop Process	Stop (cannot be caught or ignored)
SIGTSTP	18	Stop Process	Interactive stop
SIGCONT	19	Discard Signal	Continue if stopped (cannot be caught or ignored)

Table 6.1 Signals Descriptions

Signal	Number	Default Action	Meaning
SIGCHLD	20	Discard Signal	To parent on child stop or exit
SIGTTIN	21	Stop Process	Background read attempted from control terminal
SIGTTOU	22	Stop Process	Background write attempted from control terminal
SIGIO	23	Discard Signal	Input/Output possible or completed
SIGXCPU	24	Terminate Process	CPU time limit exceeded (see the setrlimit() function)
SIGXFSZ	25	Terminate Process	File size limit exceeded (see the setrlimit() function)
SIGVTALRM	26	Terminate Process	Virtual time alarm (see the setitimer() function)
SIGPROF	27	Terminate Process	Profiling time alarm (see the setitimer() function)
SIGWINCH	28	Discard Signal	Window size changed
SIGINFO	29	Discard Signal	Information request
SIGUSR1	30	Terminate Process	User-defined signal 1
SIGUSR2	31	Terminate Process	User-defined signal 2

Table 6.1 Continued

A Digital UNIX system administrator's primary method of controlling processes is by sending them signals with the kill command. The kill command is a misnomer, since issuing a kill command,

```
# kill <PID>
```

does not technically kill the process, but sends a signal to the process or processes specified on the command line, which may or may not cause the process(es) to die. In fact, some signals, including SIGUSR1, do not terminate processes. By default, unless a particular signal is specified, kill sends the SIGTERM signal (signal number 15), which politely asks the process to terminate. Several other common signals are SIGHUP (signal number 1),

SIGKILL (signal number 9), and SIGSTOP (signal number 17). A SIGHUP signal tells the process(es) to hang up and is the signal sent to all processes assigned to a terminal when a user logs out. SIGKILL is the familiar signal for killing a process, and SIGSTOP is a signal that tells a process to stop execution. The SIGKILL and SIGSTOP signals are unique in that they cannot be caught or ignored. This ensures that there exists a method for stopping and killing unruly or runaway processes.

Signals may be specified on the kill(1) command line either as the signal number or the signal name minus the "SIG" prefix. When specifying the signal name, the case is ignored. For example, the following three versions are equivalent:

```
# kill -9 4321
# kill -KILL 4321
# kill -kill 4321
```

In addition, multiple processes may be signaled by listing the PIDs separated by white space, thusly:

```
# kill -HUP 4456 4458
```

The hang-up (HUP) signal is a commonly used signal for the system administrator. Several system daemons, such as inetd(8), syslogd(8), and bootpd(8), will reread their configuration files upon receiving a HUP signal. This allows you to change a daemon's configuration file and cause the change to take effect without stopping and restarting the daemon. For example, the following command,

```
# kill -HUP `cat /var/run/inetd.pid`
```

will cause inetd(8) to reread /etc/inetd.conf, since /var/run/inetd.pid contains the PID of the current running inetd daemon.

Two PIDs have special significance when signaled with the kill command. Specifying zero (0) as a PID sends the signal to all processes having a process group ID (PGID) equal to the (PGID) of the sender, except those with PIDs 0 and 1. Specifying -1 as a PID to signal with a kill command behaves differently depending on the effective user ID (EUID) of the sender. If the EUID is not 0, or root, the signal is sent to all processes with a PGID equal to the EUID of the sender, except those with PIDs 0 and 1. However, if the EUID of the sender is 0, or root, the signal is sent to all processes, excluding numbers 0 and 1.

Finally, the kill command will list the signal names and numbers by specifying the -l command line switch:

```
# kill -1
      1)  HUP    13)  PIPE  25)  XFSZ      37)  RTMIN+4
      2)  INT    14)  ALRM  26)  VTALRM    38)  RTMIN+5
      3)  QUIT   15)  TERM  27)  PROF      39)  RTMIN+6
      4)  ILL    16)  URG   28)  WINCH     40)  RTMIN+7
      5)  TRAP   17)  STOP  29)  PWR       41)  RTMAX-7
      6)  LOST   18)  TSTP  30)  USR1      42)  RTMAX-6
      7)  EMT    19)  CONT  31)  USR2      43)  RTMAX-5
      8)  FPE    20)  CHLD  32)  RESV      44)  RTMAX-4
      9)  KILL   21)  TTIN  33)  RTMIN     45)  RTMAX-3
     10)  BUS    22)  TTOU  34)  RTMIN+1   46)  RTMAX-2
     11)  SEGV   23)  POLL  35)  RTMIN+2   47)  RTMAX-1
     12)  SYS    24)  XCPU  36)  RTMIN+3   48)  RTMAX
```

6.7. FOREGROUND AND BACKGROUND

UNIX is a multiprocessing operating system, and as such, supports the simultaneous execution of many processes. A great many of the processes necessary for the proper operation of a UNIX system are always running. These system processes, or daemons, as they are termed, are typically started as part of the system startup or boot sequence and are not associated with a terminal or user. These processes are thus running in the "background" in a noninteractive fashion. In contrast, when a user is logged onto the system, interactively editing a file or listing the contents of a directory, such tasks are running in the foreground. Foreground processes are processes for which a command interpreter, or shell, is currently waiting.

A process is put into the background by running it with the "&" operator, either from the shell command line or from within a script. Putting a process into the background returns the shell prompt immediately and allows the execution of additional commands. Long-running commands are good candidates for background processing. For example, the following find(1) command will list information on every file on the system and place the output into a file for later review:

```
# find / -ls > /tmp/find.out &
5051
#
```

By appending the "&" character to the end of the command, the shell places the command into the background for processing by the system, the process ID is returned by the shell, and the shell prompt is immediately returned for additional commands. A background process inherits its controlling terminal, in addition to all other process parameters, from the parent process. If the process table entry for this background process is examined, the controlling terminal field (TTY) displays a value:

```
# ps -ef -p 5051
UID    PID   PPID   C      STIME      TTY     TIME      CMD
Root   5051  4988   35.0   14:33:12   ttyp1   0:02.04   find / -ls
```

However, as discussed earlier, if a controlling terminal's primary process terminates, such as when a user logs off the system, all children of that primary process, which is typically a shell, are sent a SIGHUP signal which, by default, causes the remaining child processes to terminate as well. In the find example above, if the user who issued the command were to log off before the find command completed, the find command would be terminated. To avoid this and allow for processes to continue running after the initiating user logs off, UNIX provides the nohup(1) command, which executes a process so it will ignore any hang-up (SIGHUP) or quit (SIGQUIT) signals. To run the example find command making it immune to the hang-up signal, simply prepend nohup to the command:

```
# nohup find / -ls > /tmp/find.out &
5077
#
```

If a process is started in this fashion using nohup, it will continue running even if the issuer logs off intentionally or is inadvertently disconnected, which can occur if the session is a dial-up connection.

The controlling terminal parameter of processes started in the ~~backup~~ *background* with nohup remains the same as the parent process until/unless that parent process terminates, such as when the user who placed the process in the background logs off the system. When this occurs, the controlling terminal field in the process table output is displayed as "??" and, since the parent process has terminated, the init process (PID 1) inherits the background process and the parent process ID (PPID) is displayed as 1:

```
# ps -ef -p 5077
UID    PID   PPID   C      STIME      TTY   TIME      CMD
Root   5077  1      37.9   14:26:52   ??    0:10.97   find / -ls
```

If nohup is used and the output of the command is not redirected to another file, nohup will automatically append any and all output of the process into a file named "nohup.out" in the directory where the command was issued, creating the nohup.out file if necessary, and will remind the user of this with a brief message:

```
# nohup find / -ls &
5194
Sending output to nohup.out
#
```

If the nohup command creates a nohup.out file, the permissions are set to Owner Read and Owner Write (600). If the nohup.out file in the current directory cannot be created or appended to, due to permission problems (if the file is not writable by the user running the nohup command, for instance), nohup attempts to create/append to $HOME/nohup.out. If nohup is still unable to write to $HOME/nohup.out, the execution of the command is aborted with an error message:

```
$ nohup find / -ls &
5211
nohup: cannot open/create nohup.out
$ whoami
mcheek
$ ls -l ./nohup.out $HOME/nohup.out
-rw-----  1 root   system   0 Jun 10 11:17 ./nohup.out
-rw-----  1 root   system   0 Jun 12 14:40
/home/mcheek/nohup.out
$
```

If this occurs, simply remove the nohup.out file(s), change the permissions to allow appending to the file, or change to a different directory when issuing the nohup command. Note that subsequent execution of commands with nohup will not overwrite existing nohup.out files, but will append output to nohup.out. This can result in a nohup.out file containing the output of more than one process. To capture only the output of a single process when using nohup, either explicitly redirect a process's output into a unique file, or remove any existing nohup.out file prior to running the command.

6.8. SCHEDULING PROCESSES FOR FUTURE EXECUTION

UNIX systems are intended to run continuously so as to be available at all times for user activity. This activity can either be of an interactive nature where users are actually logged in doing work, or the activity can be processes running in the background without any user interaction. There are a variety of reasons it is useful to run jobs in an unattended fashion; perhaps the job needs as much of the system's resources as possible and the system is relatively idle during the middle of the night or over a weekend. Another reason is simply to increase the utilization of the system by doing processing overnight and keeping the system busy. A system administrator also needs the ability to run processes unattended. These can include regularly scheduled jobs such as backing up the system, rotating error logs, and scanning file systems. In addition, a system administrator occasionally needs to schedule an ad-hoc job for a future one-time execution. An example of this is scheduling an automatic system shutdown and reboot in the wee hours of the morning.

Digital UNIX provides three tools for scheduling the future execution of processes:

- cron
- at
- batch

Each tool has a similar, but distinctly different purpose: cron(8) is for executing jobs on a repeating regular, periodic schedule; at(1) is for scheduling an ad-hoc job for execution once in the future at a user-specified date/time; batch(1) is also for scheduling the single execution of a job in the future—however, batch runs jobs when the system load level permits. Note that batch is simply a short script to call the at(1) command.

6.8.1. cron and crontabs

The cron facility is probably the most common method in Digital UNIX of scheduling processes for future execution. The cron facility is composed of two main parts: the cron daemon itself, which is always running when the system is in multi-user mode, and the cron tables, or crontabs, which contain the commands to be run and their execution schedules. In addition, there is a mechanism to restrict the ability to submit jobs for execution via cron. By default, all users can submit jobs to cron.

The cron daemon is the primary component of the cron facility and is normally started when the system starts. There should only be one instance of cron running, since cron only exits when explicitly killed or when the system shuts down. The cron daemon logs its startups in the logfile /var/adm/ cron/log. When cron starts and when it is signaled that a crontab has changed, it reads all existing crontab files, which are located in the /var/ spool/cron/crontabs directory. This avoids the overhead of checking the crontab files for changes on a periodic basis.

A crontab file contains both the command for cron to execute and the scheduling information of when to run the command. Each line of a crontab has the following six fields:

- The first field specifies the minute of the hour (0 to 59)
- The second field specifies the hour of the day (0 to 23)
- The third field specifies the day of the month (1 to 31)
- The fourth field specifies the month of the year (1 to 12)
- The fifth field specifies the day of the week (0 to 6 for Sunday to Saturday)
- The sixth field specifies the shell command to be executed

The first five date fields my be an integer, indicating a single value, a comma delimited list of integers for multiple values, two integers separated by a dash to indicate an inclusive range of values, or an asterisk (*) character to indicate all values for a date field. For example, to redirect the output of a ps(1) command into a file every 15 minutes Monday through Friday, the following crontab entry would work:

```
0,15,30,45 * * * 1-5 /usr/bin/ps -ef >> /tmp/ps.out
```

Note that the full pathnames of the ps command and the output file are used. Specifying full pathnames in a crontab is strongly recommended to avoid "command not found" errors or output files in odd places. If the cron-executed command generates errors or output that is not redirected, cron E-mails this output to the crontab owner. To avoid these E-mails, always redirect output or errors to a log file or the bit bucket (/dev/null).

A crontab is named for its owning user. For example, the default Digital UNIX root crontab, (/var/spool/cron/crontab/root), is:

```
#
#     root crontab file
#
15 4 * * * find /var/preserve -mtime +7 -type f -exec rm -f {} \;
20 4 * * * find /tmp -type f -atime +2 -exec rm -f {} \;
30 4 * * * find /var/tmp -type f -atime +7 -exec rm -f {} \;
40 4 * * * find /var/adm/syslog.dated -depth -type d -ctime +5 -
  exec rm -rf {} \
;
#0 3 * * 4 /usr/sbin/acct/dodisk > /var/adm/diskdiag &
```

Note that a line beginning with a pound sign (#) is considered by cron to be a comment and is ignored. Take advantage of this and insert liberal comments into your crontabs for future reference. In addition, a crontab entry can be "commented out" to temporary disable execution of that command by inserting a pound sign at the beginning of the line.

The cron daemon executes the command specified in field six of the crontab from the owner user's $HOME directory with a default environment, defining HOME, LOGNAME, SHELL (/usr/bin/sh), and PATH (/usr/bin). If additional environment variables are necessary, or if a different shell is desired, such as /usr/bin/ksh or /usr/bin/csh, you must explicitly specify them. Except for simple one-line commands, it is recommended that shell scripts be created that contain all necessary environment variables and the script itself be called from the crontab.

The proper way to create or edit a crontab is with the crontab(1) command. The crontab command does two important things: it places the new or edited crontab file into the privileged /var/spool/cron/crontabs directory, and it signals the cron daemon to reread all the crontabs since there has been a change. There are two methods to submit changes to cron using crontab: manually or via the crontab -e command. The manual method is suitable for situations where crontab changes may be scripted, while the crontab -e command is usually appropriate for interactive edits to crontab.

Manually

1. Become the user that corresponds to the appropriate file in the crontabs directory. For instance, if you want to submit commands that will run under adm authority, become user adm.

2. Use the crontab command with the -l flag to copy the appropriate file from the crontabs directory to a temporary file. For example, if you are user adm, you could use the following command:

```
$ crontab -l > /tmp/temp_adm
```

3. Edit the temporary file and add the commands you want to run at a specified time.
4. Use the crontab command and specify the temporary file to submit the commands to the cron daemon:

```
$ crontab /tmp/temp_adm
```

crontab -e

1. Become the user that corresponds to the appropriate file in the crontabs directory.
2. Run crontab specifying the edit command line switch and you will be placed in the editor specified by the EDITOR environment variable, or /usr/bin/vi by default. Simply make the desired changes to the crontab entries and crontab will submit the changes to cron when the edit session is complete:

```
$ crontab -e
```

The system administrator can restrict access to cron services in one of two ways. If there are a small group of users permitted to use cron, simply list their account names, one per line, in /usr/lib/cron/cron.allow. If that file does not exist, the crontab command checks for the existence of /usr/lib/cron/cron.deny to determine which users are denied access to cron services. If neither file exists, only the root account is permitted to submit a job to cron. Note that /usr/lib/cron is a symbolic link to /var/adm/cron.

6.8.2. at

While the cron facility, with its formal crontab scheduling files, is for regularly scheduled jobs, the at(1) command submits a job to be executed only once at a user-specified time in the future. Jobs submitted via the at command are packaged into a script and placed in the /var/spool/cron/atjobs directory for future execution by the cron daemon. The at command provides a more complete environment to the job by including all active environment variables present at the time the job is submitted in the resulting script file. The at command also allows specifying which shell is used to run the job via the [-c | -s | -k] switches for C shell, Bourne shell, and Korn shell, respectively. The default shell is /usr/bin/sh.

The at command's job submission syntax is very flexible, allowing an English-like date/time argument in addition to a more conventional CCYYMMDDhhmm.SS format. For instance, these two commands, each of which schedules a system reboot for the following Saturday at 2:00 A.M., are equivalent:

```
# at 2 am Saturday /sbin/reboot
# at -t 199707190200.00 /sbin/reboot
```

The at command writes the job number and the scheduled time to standard error upon job submission and is similar to this:

```
job root.869299200.a at Sat Jul 19 02:00:00 1997
```

The format of the job name is user.xxxxxxxxx.y, where the user argument identifies the user who submitted the job; xxxxxxxxx is a 9-digit number that is a unique number based on the scheduled date; and y indicates the job type as follows:

```
Argument        Job Type
a               at job
b               batch job
e               ksh job
f               csh job
```

The job name is also the name of the packaged script located in /var/spool/cron/atjobs. The following is the atjob script from the previous reboot example:

```
# ls -l /var/spool/cron/atjobs
total 1
-r-r-Sr-  1 root    daemon    648 Jul 14 18:10 root.869299200.a
# cat /var/spool/cron/atjobs/root.869299200.a
: at job
export EDITOR; EDITOR='/usr/bin/vi'
export HOME; HOME='/'
export LOGNAME; LOGNAME='root'
export MANPATH; MANPATH='/usr/man:/usr/local/man'
```

```
export PATH; PATH='/usr/bin:/sbin:/usr/bin/X11:/usr/tcb/bin'
export PWD; PWD='/usr/bin'
export SHELL; SHELL='/bin/sh'
export TERM; TERM='vt220'
export USER; USER='root'
export VISUAL; VISUAL='/usr/bin/vi'

cd $HOME                          # cd to user's home directory
cd /usr/var/spool/cron/atjobs     # working directory
#ulimit 18014398509481983         # commented out till Sys V shell
umask 22                          # file creation mask
/usr/bin/sh << 'QAZWSXEDCRFVTGBYHNUJMIKOLP'
/sbin/reboot
                                  # shell and jobname
```

The at command also provides arguments to manage atjobs:

```
# at -l               (List all scheduled at jobs)
root.869299200.a      Sat Jul 19 02:00:00 1997
root.869530564.a      Mon Jul 21 18:16:04 1997
root.869098583.a      Wed Jul 16 18:16:23 1997
mcheek.868997800.a    Tue Jul 15 14:16:40 1997

# at -r -u mcheek      (Remove all scheduled jobs owned by mcheek)
at file: mcheek.868997800.a deleted

# at -n root           (List the number of jobs in the queue for the specified user)
3 files in the queue
```

Similarly to cron, the system administrator can enforce access to at services by placing user names in /usr/lib/cron/at.allow or /usr/lib/cron/at.deny. The at command checks these files' authorization when a user attempts to submit a job. By default, all users are permitted to use the at command.

6.8.3. batch

The batch command is simply an interface to the at command that submits a job for execution when the system load level permits. batch(1) is intended to be run interactively with commands to be scheduled to be read from standard input. Depending on how busy the system is at the time of submission, batch jobs may be executed immediately or queued in the /usr/spool/cron/atjobs directory for execution at a later date. The following is an example of the batch submission of a sort job:

```
# batch
/usr/bin/sort /tmp/bigfile.txt -o /tmp/sorted.txt
<Cntrl-D>
job root.868928098.b at Mon Jul 14 18:54:58 1997
#
```

Since jobs submitted with the batch command are actually at jobs, the at(1) command is also used to list and delete batch jobs.

6.9. SUMMARY

Process management on a Digital UNIX system is a broad topic covering starting and stopping processes, viewing process statistics, and controlling processes. A system administrator may be called upon to account for system resource usage; understanding how processes start and are executed by the system and how to display a process's status and state, will help in this type of accountability. In addition, understanding the process signal mechanism and the available signals provides a system administrator with the language of process control; instead of blindly terminating processes, it may only be necessary in certain situations to send a hang-up or stop signal to a process, and this ability is key to the continued availability and stability of your system.

Services

7

7.1. SERVICES

Digital UNIX provides a variety of services that users come to depend on. These services include printing facilities; the ability to read, write, and manipulate files on a diskette, formatted either with an MS-DOS file system or a UNIX File System; and support for both CD-ROMs (data) and audio music CDs. I will detail these services from a system administration viewpoint, especially their initial configuration and use. One or more of these services always seem to find a place in the hearts of users, and you may find yourself spending a fair amount of time supporting and troubleshooting these services.

7.2. PRINTING

Supporting printing from a Digital UNIX system is an important system management function for a system administrator. Digital UNIX supports the ability for users to print both to local printers connected directly to a system's parallel or serial ports and to remote printers via the network. A remote printer can be either another computer's locally connected printer or a stand-alone network printer. In addition, it may be necessary to provide printing services for other remote clients. Digital UNIX supports this print-server ability through the lpd print daemon.

First, the Digital UNIX lpd print daemon's operation and the directory structure that supports this spooling system will be described. The next topic covered will be configuring a Digital UNIX system to print to a locally connected printer. All other print configurations build upon this basic configuration. The configuration to print to a remote printer is similar to that of a local printer and will be detailed. Setting up a Digital UNIX system as a print server for other remote systems requires that local printing be configured. The required configuration to provide these print server services will also be described. Finally, I will list the Digital UNIX utilities and commands available for configuring and managing the print services, and describe the format of the /etc/printcap file, which defines the printers, both local and remote, available to a local user or application on a Digital UNIX system.

7.3. THE DIGITAL UNIX PRINT PROCESS

The print system on a Digital UNIX system is primarily BSD UNIX-based, with the main characteristic being a /etc/printcap configuration file. The BSD UNIX flavor print commands include lpr(1), lprm(1), lpq(1), and lpc(8). In addition, Digital UNIX supports UNIX System V print system commands such as lp(1) and lpstat(1). Either version of print commands are acceptable. For instance, these two commands to submit a print job to the draft print queue are equivalent:

```
# lpr -P draft memo.txt
# lp -d draft memo.txt
```

The Digital UNIX print system is managed by the lpd(8) printer daemon. This daemon is typically started when the system enters multi-user mode (run level 3) and runs continuously. Any queued print jobs that had not been printed when the system was last shutdown are printed when lpd starts up. When a user submits a print job via the lpr or lp command, the following sequence of events occurs:

1. The master lpd printer daemon copies the requested file(s) to the specified printer's spooling directory. If a printer was not specified when the job was submitted, lpd uses the printer specified by the LPDEST[1] or PRINTER environment variable if defined, or else the system default printer is selected. The /etc/printcap file is scanned to determine the spooling directory.

2. The master lpd printer daemon then forks a copy of itself to handle the print job, then returns to silently waiting for another print request submission.

3. The newly forked, or child lpd printer daemon then does the following operations:

   a) The child lpd reads the /etc/printcap file to determine the printer's characteristics.

   b) If the printer is remote, the child lpd contacts the master lpd printer daemon on the remote system, transfers the print job to the remote system, and deletes the local copy from the spool directory.

   c) If the printer is local, the child lpd checks the spool directory for a lock file. The existence of a lock file usually indicates that another child lpd is already processing this print queue. The lock file contains the process ID (PID) of the existing child lpd process and the name of the file currently being printed. If the lock file exists and the PID contained in the lock file is an actively running lpd process, the newly forked lpd printer daemon exits, since the existing lpd process will take care of printing the submitted job. The purpose of the lock file is to prevent more than one child lpd daemon from processing the same print queue.

   d) If, however, the lock file does not exist or the PID in the lock file does not correspond to a running lpd process, the child lpd process creates or overwrites the lock file, inserting its own PID and the name of the first file in the spooling directory, and begins sending the file(s) to the special device supporting the actual printer.

---

[1]Only if the Common Desktop Environment (CDE) is in use.

e) As files are printed, the child lpd daemon updates the status file also contained in the spool directory. This status file describes the current status of the printer.

f) Once the print job has been printed, the child lpd daemon removes the local copy of the file(s) from the spool directory and updates the status file. If additional print jobs have been created, this child lpd will submit them in turn to the printer.

g) This child lpd daemon will exit when there are no longer files to be printed in this spool directory.

7.4. ADDING A LOCAL PRINTER

Configuring local print services on a Digital UNIX system includes the following administrative tasks:

- Ensure the Digital UNIX Local Printer Support subset is installed
- Physically connect a printer to a port on a Digital UNIX system
- Collecting Printer Information
- Adding an entry for the printer to the /etc/printcap file
- Creating the required printer device file and directories in the spooling area
- Starting the lpd printing daemon if it is not already running
- Testing the printer

7.4.1. Required Printing Environment Software

The first step is to confirm that the optional Digital UNIX "Local Printer Support" software subset is loaded. This subset is named OSFPRINTxxx, where the "xxx" specifies the version of the subset, and it contains lpd(8), the line printer daemon, the various configuration and management utilities, and the spooling system directory structure. To determine if this subset is loaded, execute the following command:

```
# /usr/sbin/setld -i | grep -i osfprint
OSFPRINT410   installed   Local Printer Support
  (Printing Environment)
```

Based on this output, the subset is installed. If you do not receive any output, or if the "installed" keyword in the second column is absent, you must install the subset from the master Digital UNIX operating system installation media using the setld command. For assistance in installing Digital UNIX subsets, see Chapter 3, "System Configurations."

7.4.2. Physically Connecting the Printer

Once the required OSFPRINT software subset is installed, the next step to configuring a local printer is to physically connect the printer to the appropriate port. Digital UNIX supports both directly connected serial and parallel printers. Connect such a printer to the system using the appropriate cable, turn the power on to the printer, and ensure that the printer is online and is ready to print as described in the printer owner's documentation.

7.4.3. Collecting Printer Information

Before proceeding to add the printer to the Digital UNIX printing subsystem, it is necessary to gather information about the printer. Most of this information will be added to the /etc/printcap entry for this printer. The /etc/printcap defines a system's printers. The following is a list of the details needed to configure a local printer:

- The Name of the Printer
- Alternative Printer Name(s)
- Printer Type (Manufacturer) and Model
- Connection Type (Serial, Parallel, or LAT)
- Baud Rate (for Serial printers only)
- Special Device File
- Spool Directory
- Error Logfile

The details on how to determine this information follow.

7.4.3.1. Printer Name

The printer name is more accurately the queue name and is the name that you and your users will specify when sending print jobs to this printer. A print queue can have multiple names, or aliases; the only limitation on number and length is that the sum total of characters in all the names be less than 80 characters. The selection of a printer name is almost completely arbitrary, with one exception. The name "lp" is special in that it signifies the system default printer. If a print destination is not specified, the print daemon sends the job to the print queue with the name or alias of "lp". The lprsetup(8) utility, discussed later in this chapter (see section 7.4.4.2.), uses a numbering scheme from 0 to 99 for the primary printer name. The first printer configured will be named printer 0, the second will be printer 1, and so on. This strategy is perhaps a good one to follow, even when not using lprsetup to configure printers. Printer aliases are then used for descriptive printer names.

7.4.3.2. Printer Aliases

It is common to also name a print queue something significant that describes the type, location, or function of the printer. For example, an HP4 laser printer that supports Postscript printing located in room A5 might be named "hp4," "laser," "room-a5," and "postscript." All of these aliases are acceptable and can coexist, all referring to the same print queue and physical printer. To print to this printer, a user must specify one of these printer names, unless this printer also has an alias of "lp," in which case it is also the system default printer and specifying a printer name is unnecessary. Thus, all of these print commands are equivalent:

```
# lpr -Plaser letter.txt
# lpr -Proom-a5 letter.txt
# lpr letter.txt
```

Printer aliases are completely optional. The only requirement for configuring a printer is the initial printer name.

7.4.3.3. Printer Type

The printer type is typically the manufacturer and/or the model number of the printer. Digital UNIX directly supports a variety of common (and not so common) printer types. Refer to the file /etc/lprsetup.dat for the list of supported printers at that specific release. Supported printers already have default values for many of the parameters. Three special printer types are:

- remote
- unknown
- xf

The remote printer type should be specified when configuring a printer that is not directly connected to the system. Two examples of a remote printer are a printer connected to another Digital UNIX system acting as a print server and a network printer directly connected to the network. When configuring a remote printer, two additional pieces of information are required: the host name of the remote system and the printer name on the remote system.

If you are connecting a printer that is not directly supported by Digital UNIX, you can specify a printer type of "unknown." When configuring an unknown printer type, you will be asked a series of printer characteristic questions that should be answerable by consulting the printer's owner's manual. Occasionally, a printer not listed as supported has multiple modes, one of which may be supported. For instance, a printer may have an HP LaserJet-compatible mode or an Epson Fx80-compatible mode, both of which are supported. Simply switch the mode of the printer to one of these compatible modes and specify the printer type as that emulated by the compatibility mode.

Finally, if a printer is unsupported and does not have any supported emulation modes, select "xf" as the type. This configures any printer generically and sends output with no formatting or filtering. This is usually only worthwhile when printing plain text to an ASCII printer. Note that the "xf" printer type is only available on Digital UNIX version 4.0 and higher.

7.4.3.4. Connection Type

The connection type refers to how the printer will be connected to the system. There are three valid connection types: dev, remote, and LAT. Local printers will be connected to the system either through a serial port or parallel port, and since these physical ports are accessed by Digital UNIX through special device files in the /dev directory, a local printer's connection type is "dev." A remote printer's connection type is, not surprisingly, "remote." Finally, for printers accessed via the Local Area Transport (LAT), the connection type is "LAT." The connection type itself is important only in indicating where further information is needed. For instance, when configuring a printer whose connection type is "dev," you will need to know the special device file name for the particular port.

7.4.3.5. Baud Rate

The baud rate is only applicable for locally connected serial printers. Simply determine the baud rate of the printer you are configuring. This value will often be a number such as 4800 or 9600. If the printer is a supported type, a default value will be presented by the set-up program and, unless the setting has been changed on the printer itself, it is often enough to accept this default baud rate.

7.4.3.6. Special Device File

For a locally connected serial or parallel printer, there will be a special device file located in the /dev directory that the system uses to access the port, and thus the printer. The parallel port's special device file is /dev/lpn, and the serial ports are /dev/ttynn, where n and nn specify the number of the port. For instance, the first (or only) parallel port is /dev/lp0; the first serial port /dev/tty00 and the second serial port is /dev/tty01. This device file is specified in the /etc/printcap file by the "lp" option. For example:

```
lp=/dev/lp0
```

7.4.3.7. Spool Directory

The spool directory is where the lpd print daemon temporary places print jobs after submission by the user. In addition, the spool directory is used by the print daemon to store several important files used in managing the print queue. For instance, lpd keeps a file named .seq in the spool directory that contains the sequence number of the next print job. The print daemon also stores a file named status that contains the status of the print queue. Because lpd uses the spool directory for more than just storing submitted print jobs, each print queue should have a unique spool directory. Typically, spool directories are located in /usr/spool and have somewhat arbitrary names. By default, the first printer added will have a spool directory of /usr/spool/lpd, the second printer's spool directory will be /usr/spool/lpd1, and so on. A better name for a spool directory would be the printer's name; for instance, for a printer named "draft," name the spool directory /usr/spool/draft. One point to be aware of is that, by default, the /usr/spool directory is contained in the /usr file system. If a user submits a very large print job, the job will be stored in the specified printer's spool directory, and the potential exists to fill the /usr file system if there is limited free space in the /usr file system. If your /usr file system has limited free space and users frequently print many or large files, you should consider either adding space to your /usr file system or possibly locating printer spool directories on another file system with sufficient free space. This spool directory is specified in the /etc/printcap file by the "sd" option. For example:

```
sd=/usr/spool/lpd
```

7.4.3.8. Error Logfile

The error logfile is simply the location that the lpd print daemon logs printer errors. The type of errors that could be logged include printer errors, such as out-of-paper alerts and printer-offline messages. The error log file is appended to and persists across reboots. For this reason, this error log file grows without bounds and must be manually examined and truncated. The default location for these error log files is in the /usr/adm directory with the name lperr for the first printer, lp1err for the second, and so on. If an error log file is not specified when a printer is configured, any error messages that would have been sent to a log file are instead displayed on the system console. This error log file is specified in the /etc/printcap file by the "lf" option. For example:

```
lf=/usr/adm/lperr
```

7.4.4. The /etc/printcap File

The main configuration file for the print service is /etc/printcap. This file is simply a text file that contains the characteristics about each printer configured on the system. This file is read by the lpd print daemon each time a print job is submitted. This is important to know, since it means that the lpd print daemon does not have to signaled about updates to the /etc/printcap file. The /etc/printcap file consists of options (See Table 7.1) in individual, continuous entries.

Each entry, which describes a single printer, can be broken into multiple lines with a backslash ("\"). Each option is preceded and followed by a colon (":"). If the entry is broken into multiple lines, a colon and a backslash

Name	Type	Default	Description
af	string	NULL	Name of accounting file
br	number	none	For serial printers, sets the baud rate
cd	string	LAT	Remote printing using LAT as the transport
cf	string	NULL	The cifplot data filter
ct	string	dev	The connection type. Only valid when up=psv4.0. The choices are: dev, LAT, and remote. (Required for LAT printers)
df	string	NULL	The tex data filter (DVI format)
fc	number	0	For serial printers, clear flag bits
ff	string	\f	String to send for a form feed
fo	boolean	false	Print a form feed when the device is opened
fs	number	0	Like fc, but set bits
gf	string	NULL	The graph data filter (plot format)
hl	boolean	false	Print the burst header page last
ic	boolean	false	Driver supports (nonstandard) ioctl to indent printout
if	string	NULL	Name of text filter that does accounting
lf	string	/dev/console	Error logging file name
lo	string	lock	Name of lock file
lp	string	/dev/lp	Device name to open for output. (Required for LAT and remote printers)
mx	number	1000	Maximum file size (in BUFSIZ blocks). Zero=unlimited
nf	string	NULL	The ditroff data filter (for device independent troff)
of	string	NULL	Name of output filtering program
pl	number	66	Page length (in lines)
pw	number	132	Page width (in columns)
px	number	0	Page width in pixels (horizontal)
py	number	0	Page length in pixels (vertical)

Table 7.1 /etc/printcap options

Name	Type	Default	Description
rf	string	NULL	Filter for printing FORTRAN style text files
rm	string	NULL	Machine name for remote printer. (Required for remote printers)
rp	string	lp	Remote printer name argument. (Required for remote printers)
rs	boolean	false	Restrict remote users to those with local accounts
rw	boolean	false	Open the printer device for reading and writing
sb	boolean	false	Short banner (one line only)
sc	boolean	false	Suppress multiple copies
sd	string	/usr/spool/lpd	Spool directory. (Required for LAT and remote printers)
sf	boolean	false	Suppress form feeds
sh	boolean	false	Suppress printing of burst page header
st	string	status	Status file name
tf	string	NULL	The troff data filter (for the cat photo-typesetter)
tr	string	NULL	Trailer string to print when queue empties
vf	string	NULL	The raster image filter
xc	number	0	For serial printers, clear local mode bits
xf	string	NULL	Pass-through filter
xs	number	0	Like xc, but set bits
ya	string	NULL	Additional parameters for print filter (I18N)
yd	string	NULL	Secondary device name for font faulting (I18N)
yj	string	NULL	Restart of for every job (I18N)
yp	string	NULL	Printer ID conforming to Wototo standard (I18N)
ys	number	0	Size of SoftODL character cache (I18N)
yt	string	"fifo"	SoftODL character replacement strategy (I18N)

Table 7.1 Continued

are required at the end of each line; each continuation line must begin with a colon, and continuation lines are indented by a tab. Comments can be included on lines beginning with the pound sign (#). The following is an example /etc/printcap entry:

```
laser|lp|lp0|0:\
    :af=/usr/adm/lpacct:\
    :if=/usr/lbin/hplaserof:\
    :lf=/usr/adm/lperr:\
    :lp=/dev/lp0:\
    :mx#0:\
    :of=/usr/lbin/hplaserof:\
    :pl#66:\
    :pw#80:\
    :sd=/usr/spool/lpd:\
    :xf=/usr/lbin/xf:
```

Options can have string, numeric, or boolean values. String options have the format "name=string," where string is zero or more characters. Numeric options have the format "name#num." Boolean options are set true by their presence in the /etc/printcap entry and are set false by their absence. If an option is not explicately included in a printer entry, the option assumes the default value as specified in Table 7.1. Refer to the printcap(4) reference page for a full description of all the options.

7.4.4.1. Adding a Printer Entry to /etc/printcap

There are several methods of creating, updating, or deleting entries in the /etc/printcap file:

- Manually with an editor such as vi(1)
- With the lprsetup(8) utility
- With the Print Configuration application (Digital UNIX version 4.0 and higher)

Of these three methods, the least desirable is manually, since both lprsetup and the Print Configuration application will also automatically create spool directories and/or error log files in addition to updating the /etc/printcap file. However, manually adding or updating entries in /etc/printcap is perfectly acceptable and can be quicker once you are familiar with the format of the file. Since /etc/printcap is a simple text file, it can be edited using the vi or any other editor.

7.4.4.2. lprsetup

The lprsetup utility is an interactive character-based program that prompts you for printer characteristics and updates /etc/printcap. The following is an example of adding a local printer with the lprsetup utility:

```
# lprsetup

Digital UNIX Printer Setup Program

Command < add modify delete exit view quit help >: add

Adding printer entry, type '?' for help.

Enter printer name to add [0] : <Return>

For more information on the specific printer types Enter `printer?'

Enter the FULL name of one of the following printer types:

cp382d       dl1152w      dl5100w      dl510ka      ep1050+    fx1050
fx80         hp4M         hp4Mplus     hp4Mplus_a4  hpIIID     hpIIIP
hpIIP        hpIV         ibmpro       la280        la30n      la30n_a4
la30w        la30w_a4     la324        la380        la380cb    la380k
la424        la50         la70         la75         la84       la86
la88         la88c        la90         lf01r        lg02       lg04plus
lg06         lg08plus     lg12         lg12plus     lg31       lg104plus
lg108plus    lj250        ln03         ln03ja       ln03r      ln03s
ln05         ln05ja       ln05r        ln06         ln06r      ln07
ln07r        ln08         ln08r        ln09         ln10ja     ln14
ln17         ln17_a4      ln17ps       ln17ps_a4    ln82r      nec290
ps_level1    ps_level2    remote       xf           unknown

generic_ansi     generic_ansi_a4      generic_text      generic_text_a4

or press RETURN for [unknown] : hpIIP

Enter printer synonym: laser

Enter printer synonym: <Return>

Set device pathname 'lp' [] ? /dev/lp0

Do you want to capture print job accounting data ([y]|n)? y

Set accounting file 'af' [/usr/adm/lpacct] ? <Return>
```

Set spooler directory 'sd' [/usr/spool/lpd] ? <Return>

Set printer error log file 'lf' [/usr/adm/lperr] ? <Return>

Enter the name of the printcap symbol you wish to modify. Other
valid entries are:
    'q'   to quit (no more changes)
    'p'   to print the symbols you have specified so far
    'l'   to list all of the possible symbols and defaults
The names of the printcap symbols are:

```
af   br   cf   ct   df   dn   du   fc   ff   fo   fs   gf   ic   if   lf   lo
lp   mc   mx   nc   nf   of   op   os   pl   pp   ps   pw   px   py   rf   rm
rp   rs   rw   sb   sc   sd   sf   sh   st   tf   tr   ts   uv   vf   xc   xf
xs   ya   yd   yj   yp   ys   yt   Da   Dl   It   Lf   Lu   Ml   Nu   Or   Ot
Ps   Sd   Si   Ss   Ul   Xf
```

Enter symbol name: mx

Enter a new value for symbol 'mx'? [0] <Return>

Enter symbol name: pl

Enter a new value for symbol 'pl'? [66] <Return>

Enter symbol name: pw

Enter a new value for symbol 'pw'? [80] <Return>

Enter symbol name: q

```
        Printer #0
        ----------

Symbol  type   value
------  ----   -----
af      STR    /usr/adm/lpacct
if      STR    /usr/lbin/hplaserof
lf      STR    /usr/adm/lperr
lp      STR    /dev/lp0
mx      INT    0
of      STR    /usr/lbin/hplaserof
pl      INT    66
pw      INT    80
sd      STR    /usr/spool/lpd
xf      STR    /usr/lbin/xf
```

```
Are these the final values for printer 0 ? [y] <Return>

Adding comments to printcap file for new printer, type '?' for help.
Do you want to add comments to the printcap file [n] ? : y

# 3rd floor laser printer
#

Set up activity is complete for this printer.
Verify that the printer works properly by using
the lpr(1) command to send files to the printer.

Command < add modify delete exit view quit help >: quit

#
```

Digital has indicated that the lprsetup program is to be retired in a future release of Digital UNIX. This utility is primarily for use on Digital UNIX version 3.2 and earlier. When running Digital UNIX version 4.0 and later, the recommended method of managing printers is the Printer Configuration application.

7.4.4.3 The Printer Configuration Application

The Digital UNIX Printer Configuration application, printconfig, is the recommended utility for managing printers on Digital UNIX 4.x and greater systems. The Printer Configuration application has both an X-Windows/ Motif interface and a character-cell interface almost identical to that of the lprsetup utility. This application can be used to add, modify, and delete printers from your system. The Printer Configuration application can be invoked through the CDE Application Manager, which is opened by selecting the Application Manager icon from the CDE Front Panel, followed by selecting System_Admin, then Configuration, and finally the Print application. Once you double-click on the Print application icon, you will be prompted via a Get Password dialog box for the root password. The initial graphical Printer Configuration application window is shown in Figure 7.1.

Optionally, you can start the Printer Configuration application from the command line:

```
/usr/sbin/printconfig [ -ui gui | menu ]
```

Specifying "printconfig" without a command line option causes printconfig to look for the DISPLAY environment variable. If it is defined, the X-Windows user interface starts up. If it is not defined, the character cell

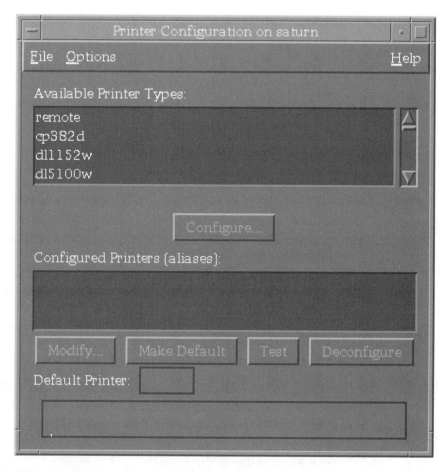

Figure 7.1 The CDE Printer Configuration Application Main Window

user interface starts up (as though you had used printconfig –ui menu).
Since the lprsetup utility will be retired in a future release of Digital UNIX,
if you are running version 4.0 or later of Digital UNIX, I recommend always
using printconfig to manage printers. Doing so will avoid any dependencies
on the lprsetup utility.

7.4.5. Printer Device Files

If either lprsetup or the Printer Configuration application is used to add a
printer, the necessary special device file and/or spooling directories are

automatically created. The device file is the special file in the /dev directory that the lpd printer daemon uses to communicate with a local I/O port. Typically the special devices for the serial ports and parallel port was already created when the system was installed. If, however, these ports are missing or were inadvertently removed, use the following details now to recreate them.

To recreate /dev/tty00 and /dev/tty01 for serial ports one and two:

```
# cd /dev
# ./MAKEDEV ace0
MAKEDEV: special files(0) for ace0:
tty00 tty01
```

To recreate /dev/lp0 for the primary parallel port:

```
# cd /dev
# ./MAKEDEV lp
MAKEDEV: special file(s) for lp:
lp0
```

7.4.5.1. Creating Spooling Directories

The lpd printing daemon manages the printing of multiple print jobs to the same printer by a process commonly known as "spooling." Spooling is saving each submitted print job in an area on disk, typically under the /usr/spool directory hierarchy, and sending each job to the printer in the order in which it was received. This saving, or spooling, of a print job to disk allows the user or application that submitted the print job to resume without waiting for the printer to actually print the output. Each printer has a dedicated spool directory where print jobs destined for that particular printer are saved. This directory is specified in the /etc/printcap file by the "sd" option. For example:

```
sd=/usr/spool/lpd
```

This directory must be created in order for the print daemon to be able to save submitted print jobs.

7.4.6 Starting the lpd Printing Daemon

By default, installing the OSFPRINT subset enables automatic startup of the lpd printer daemon, even if no printers are configured. This subset configures lpd to start when the system is booted. You can determine if the lpd print daemon is currently running by issuing the following command:

```
# ps -ef | grep lpd
root    416   1   0.4    Aug 12   ??   0:41.72    /usr/lbin/lpd
```

If the lpd print daemon is not running and the OSFPRINT subset is installed, start lpd by issuing the following command:

```
# /sbin/init.d/lpd start
```

7.4.7. Testing the Printer

Once a printer has been connected and configured, you should test that the printer was successfully added to the print system. Digital UNIX provides a utility, lptest(8), that writes a test pattern to standard output. This pattern contains all 96 printable ASCII characters, staggered to display each character in each column position of the line. To use this utility, simply pipe its output to the lpr command. For instance:

```
# lptest | lpr -Plaser
```

By default, the lptest command displays 200 lines, each 79 characters wide. To specify a different line width and the number of lines in the output, use lptest's two optional command line arguments. The following command displays 10 lines, each 60 characters wide:

```
# lptest 60 10
!"#$%&'()*+,-./0123456789:;<=>?@ABCDEFGHIJKLMNOPQRSTUVWXYZ[\
"#$%&'()*+,-./0123456789:;<=>?@ABCDEFGHIJKLMNOPQRSTUVWXYZ[\]
#$%&'()*+,-./0123456789:;<=>?@ABCDEFGHIJKLMNOPQRSTUVWXYZ[\]^
$%&'()*+,-./0123456789:;<=>?@ABCDEFGHIJKLMNOPQRSTUVWXYZ[\]^_
%&'()*+,-./0123456789:;<=>?@ABCDEFGHIJKLMNOPQRSTUVWXYZ[\]^_`
&'()*+,-./0123456789:;<=>?@ABCDEFGHIJKLMNOPQRSTUVWXYZ[\]^_`a
'()*+,-./0123456789:;<=>?@ABCDEFGHIJKLMNOPQRSTUVWXYZ[\]^_`ab
()*+,-./0123456789:;<=>?@ABCDEFGHIJKLMNOPQRSTUVWXYZ[\]^_`abc
)*+,-./0123456789:;<=>?@ABCDEFGHIJKLMNOPQRSTUVWXYZ[\]^_`abcd
*+,-./0123456789:;<=>?@ABCDEFGHIJKLMNOPQRSTUVWXYZ[\]^_`abcde
```

Sometimes when troubleshooting printing problems, especially local printers, it is often difficult to isolate the source of a problem. The problem could be with the printer itself, the configuration of the special device of the port the printer is connected to, or the print service configuration. The first step is to ensure that the printer itself is powered on, has sufficient paper, is connected to the appropriate port (parallel or serial) of the Digital UNIX system with the correct cable, and is online. Once these has been checked, send some output directly to the printer via the special device file. For instance, to output a test pattern to a parallel printer use the following command:

```
# lptest > /dev/lp0
```

If this test pattern is successfully printed, you can be reasonably sure that the printer itself is configured and cabled correctly. The next step is to check the error log file, which is specified by the "lf" option in the /etc/ printcap file entry for the printer. If this error file is nonexistent or empty, then it is possible the printer was not added correctly. Delete the printer and re-add it using lprsetup or the Printer Configuration application.

7.5. ADDING A REMOTE PRINTER

Configuring a Digital UNIX system to print to a remote printer is similar to adding a local printer, except that configuring a remote printer requires two additional pieces of information:

- Print Server Host Name
- The Print Queue Name on the Print Server

7.5.1. Print Server Host Name

When configuring a remote printer, it is necessary to know the host name of the print server that is hosting the printer. This host name is usually another computer accessible via the network. This may be another Digital UNIX system, a system running a different implementation of UNIX, or a non-UNIX system altogether. In the case of a stand-alone network printer, this host name may refer to the printer itself. You must be able to resolve the remote system, whether another computer or a network printer, by specifying the host name. This means that the host name and the IP address for the remote system must either be in the local /etc/hosts table or registered with the Domain Name Server (DNS). To test if this is the case, use the ping(1) command. For example, if the remote print server's host name is jupiter, enter the following command:

```
# /sbin/ ping -c 3 jupiter
PING jupiter.company.com (192.128.5.2): 56 data bytes
64 bytes from 192.128.5.2: icmp_seq=0 ttl=62 time=2 ms
64 bytes from 192.128.5.2: icmp_seq=1 ttl=62 time=1 ms
64 bytes from 192.128.5.2: icmp_seq=2 ttl=62 time=1 ms

— jupiter.company.com PING Statistics—
3 packets transmitted, 3 packets received, 0% packet loss
round-trip (ms) min/avg/max = 1/1/2 ms
```

In this example, the host name jupiter resolved to the IP address 192.128.5.2 (this is not an actual IP address) and was able to reach this system via the network.

7.5.2. The Print Queue Name on the Print Server

In addition to the host name of the print server, it is necessary to know the printer, or queue name of the printer you wish to access. Contact the system administrator of the remote system for this information. If you have log-in access to this remote system, simply display the queues on that system with the following command:

```
# lpc status
laser:
        printer is on device '/dev/lp0' speed -1
        queuing is enabled
        printing is enabled
        no entries
        no daemon present
```

In this example, there is a single printer with a print queue name of "laser." In addition, there may be some configuration necessary on the remote print server host to allow remote clients to print to its print queue. These configurations are detailed in a later section of this chapter.

When adding a remote printer, specify a printer type of "remote" in the lprsetup utility or the Printer Configuration application. The remote printer type is special in that it assumes that the true printer type is managed by the remote print server. When configuring a remote printer, you are prompted for two additional pieces of information: the remote system name and the remote system printer name. This information is specified in the /etc/printcap file by the "rm" and "rp" options, respectively. For example:

```
rm=jupiter.company.com
rp=draft
```

Given a printer with these /etc/printcap entries, print jobs submitted to this printer will be sent to the print queue "draft" on the remote system jupier.company.com.

7.6 PROVIDING REMOTE PRINT SERVICES

Once one or more local printers are added to a Digital UNIX system, that system can then be configured to support remote print services. Rather than installing printers on many systems, frequently a single system is selected to act as a print server. This print server system then can configured with sufficient print spool space to support many systems' print activity. There are three requirements in order for a Digital UNIX system to act as a print server:

- The print server and the print clients must be reachable via the network
- The print server and the print clients must each be able to resolve the name of the other
- Authorized print clients' host names must appear in the print server's /etc/hosts.lpd or /etc/hosts.equiv file

7.6.1. Network Access

The first requirement is fairly obvious. The remote print client systems must be able to reach the print server system across the network. The simplest way to validate this requirement is to telnet from the client to the print server. If the print server's log-in prompt is presented, the necessary network connectivity is present. If, however, you are unable to reach the print server from the print client, the network may not be correctly configured on either or both of the systems. See Chapter 8, "Networking," for details on configuring the network.

7.6.2. Name Resolution

Name resolution is a fancy way of saying, "Can one system determine the IP address of another system given only the host name of the remote system?" The most expedient way to ensure successful name resolution is to place an entry for every remote system in the /etc/hosts file. This is a requirement for both the print server and for any remote print clients. For example, in the following /etc/hosts file fragment, jupiter is the print server host name, and saturn and pluto are print client host names:

```
192.128.5.2     jupiter
192.128.5.3     saturn
192.128.5.4     pluto
```

In addition to the local /etc/hosts file, there is also the Domain Name System (DNS) as a way of resolving IP addresses. DNS is also known as the Berkeley Internet Name Domain, or BIND. DNS is a distributed database that contains information used to translate system host names into IP address and vice versa.

7.6.3. Authorizing Remote Print Access

Digital UNIX, by default, disallows remote print access. Allowing users on remote systems to submit print jobs to another system is a capability that you as the system administrator must explicitly enable. When the lpd print daemon on a client system contacts the lpd daemon on a remote system with a print request, the remote lpd daemon determines if remote print access is permitted by searching the /etc/hosts.lpd and the /etc/hosts.equiv files for the name of the system making the print request. If the host name of the requesting system is contained in either of these system files, the remote print request is accepted. Otherwise, the request is rejected and the following message is displayed when querying the status of the queue:

```
# lpq -P draft
saturn:

Warning: saturn.company.com does not have access to
  remote printer draft
```

The format of the /etc/hosts.lpd and /etc/host.equiv are similar. Each line is a single entry of the format [-]host name. To allow a user from another system to print on a local system, that foreign host name must be an entry. Preceding a host name with a dash (-) explicitly denies print access from that system. The lpd print daemon searches first the /etc/hosts.equiv file, then the /etc/hosts.lpd file when determining print access control, so the definitions in /etc/hosts.equiv take precedence over /etc/hosts.lpd. However, since the /etc/hosts.equiv file is also used to specify trusted host relationships for remote command execution, I strongly recommend not using /etc/hosts.equiv to define remote print access. Use /etc/hosts.lpd only to specify this print access. This will avoid confusion and inadvertent trusted host access.

As an example, the following /etc/hosts.lpd file allows remote lpd print access to the system's saturn and pluto and explicitly denies print access to the system neptune. The absence of an entry for neptune would also indicate denial of print access to the lpd print daemon. Note that lines beginning with a pound sign character (#) and blank lines are ignored.

```
#
# /etc/hosts.lpd
#
saturn
-neptune
pluto
```

7.7. MANAGING THE LOCAL PRINTING SYSTEM

Digital UNIX provides a set of commands to manage the print system once printers have been installed and configured. These commands allow submitting print jobs, canceling already submitted print jobs, viewing the status of printers and print queues, enabling and disabling printers, and adjusting the order and priority of individual jobs in the print queue. These commands include:

- lpr(1) and lp(1)
- lpq(1) and lpstat(1)
- lprm(1) and cancel(1)
- lpc(8)

7.7.1. lpr(1) and lp(1)

The lpr and lp commands are the BSD UNIX and System V UNIX commands, respectively, used to submit print jobs to the Digital UNIX print system. The two commands do the same thing, but have different syntax. Deciding which flavor command to use is purely a personal preference. Both lpr and lp can be invoked with just a single argument specifying the file to be printed. For example, each of these commands will print the file "program.c" on the system default printer:

```
# lpr program.c
# lp program.c
```

The most common additional argument to these commands specifies the printer to use. For the lpr command, the flag to use is "-P" for Printer, and for the lp command, use the flag "-d" for Destination:

```
# lpr -P draft program.c
# lp -d draft program.c
```

7.7.2. lpq(1) and lpstat(1)

The lpq and lpstat commands are used to display the status of print queues. Issuing each of these command with no command line arguments displays the status of the system default print queue. For instance, the following example shows that there are three entries in the default printer queue, and one of them (job #91) is actively being printed:

```
# lpq
Sat Sep 20 16:59:20 1997: Attempting to print dfA091saturn
Rank      Pri    Owner    Job    Files                 Total Size
active    0      root     91     /etc/hosts            1107 bytes
1st       0      jsmith   93     /home/jsmith/main.c   21987
bytes
2nd       0      jsmith   94     /home/jsmith/memo     2151 bytes
```

The lpq command has the ability to display the status of an individual print job, a particular printer (the "-P" flag), or print requests from individual users. The lpq command is primarily for displaying the status of print queues. See the lpq man page for more information on its options.

The lpstat command is a more general status utility. In addition to displaying the status of individual print queues, lpstat can display the status of the lpd printer daemon, the name of the system default destination, and which special device files correspond to which printers. A useful switch of the lpstat command is "-t," which displays the status of the entire print system including all defined printers:

```
# lpstat -t
System default destination: lp
Scheduler is running
Output for printer draft is sent to /dev/lp0
draft:
    printer is on device '/dev/lp0' speed -1
    queuing is enabled
    printing is enabled
    3 entries in spool area
    no daemon present
Requests on draft:
Sat Sep 20 16:59:20 1997:
Rank       Pri    Owner     Job    Files                  Total Size
Active     0      root      91     /etc/hosts             1107 bytes
1st        0      jsmith    93     /home/jsmith/main.c    21987
bytes
2nd        0      jsmith    94     /home/jsmith/memo      2151 bytes
```

Refer to the man pages for more information on the various options of the lpq(1) and the lpstat(1) commands.

7.7.3. lprm(1) and cancel(1)

The opposite of the lpr/lp pair, which submit print jobs, is the lprm/cancel utility pair. These programs delete print requests that have already been queued. While the lprm command is a BSD UNIX utility and the cancel command is a System V UNIX utility, each can be used interchangeably on a Digital UNIX system to delete queued print jobs. Both utilities allow deletion of individual print jobs and removal of all jobs from a particular printer; however, the lprm command also supports deleting all print jobs submitted by a particular user.

To remove individual print jobs, simply issue the command specifying the print job request ID on the command line. The request ID for a particular print job can be determined from the output of the lpq or lpstat command. Only users with superuser privilege can remove print jobs of other users. For example, to remove request ID 83, issue either of the following commands:

```
# lprm 83
# cancel 83
```

Removing all print jobs spooled for a particular printer is easily done by specifying the printer name on the lprm and canceling command lines. The lprm command has a similar syntax to the lpr command in that you specify the printer with the "-P" flag. The cancel command, on the other hand, has no special command line flag. As an example, to remove all pending print requests from the draft printer, use either of the following commands:

```
# lprm -P draft
# cancel draft
```

Finally, the lprm command has the ability to remove all print requests submitted by a particular user. Specifying one or more users on the command line removes any requests queued belonging to those users. This works only for a user with superuser authority. For example, the following command removes all queued print jobs submitted by the jsmith account:

```
# lprm jsmith
```

A variation on specifying user accounts to the lprm command is the "-" flag. If a non-root user issues the following command, all requests from the user issuing the command are removed:

```
$ lprm -
```

However, if the root user issues the same command, the entire print spool queue is completely emptied.

7.7.4. lpc(8)

The lpc (Line Printer Control) utility is a tool used to manage printers on a Digital UNIX system. lpc provides a system administrator with the ability to:

- disable and enable printers
- disable and enable print queues
- changing the order of jobs in a print queue
- displaying the status of printers, print queues, and the printer daemon

The lpc utility has two modes of operation, command driven and interactive. The mode is determined by how the utility is invoked. If lpc is run with no arguments, it assumes that the user desires the interactive mode and displays an "lpc>" prompt waiting for input. When arguments are supplied from the command line, lpc executes the command provided as the argument and exits. See Table 7.2 for a list of the lpc commands.

The following is an example of an interactive lpc session:

```
# lpc
lpc> status
draft:
    printer is on device '/dev/lp0' speed -1
    queuing is enabled
    printing is enabled
    no entries
    no daemon present
lpc>
```

Part of a system administrator's role is to manage printers and print queues. If for instance, a particular printer needed repair and would be unavailable for a period of time, you could use the lpc command to mark the printer as "down," which disables printing. The lpc "down" command expects a message that should indicate the cause of the printer unavailability and perhaps an estimated outage duration. For example, the following command will accomplish this:

```
# lpc down draft "Draft printer down for repair until
3pm Monday."
draft:
    printer and queuing disabled

# lpq -P draft
Warning: draft is down:
Warning: draft queue is turned off
Draft printer down for repairs until 3pm Monday.
no entries
```

help [command ...]	Displays a short description of each command specified in the argument list or, when no arguments are supplied, a list of the recognized commands.
abort [all I printer ...]	Terminates an active lpd print daemon running on the local host and then disables printing. This prevents new daemons from being started by lpr or lp for the specified printers.
clean [all I printer ...]	Removes any temporary files, data files, and control files that cannot be printed (files that do not form a complete printer job) from the specified printer queue(s) on the local machine.
disable [all I printer ...]	Turns the specified printer queue(s) off. This prevents new printer jobs from being entered into the queue by lpr or lp.
down [all I printer ...] message ...	Turns the specified printer queue(s) off, disables printing, and puts a message in the printer status file. The message does not need to be quoted because remaining arguments are treated the same as echo. The down command is normally used to take a printer down and let others know why. (The lpq command indicates that the printer is down and prints a status message.)

Table 7.2 Line Printer Control Commands

enable [all	printer ...]	Enables spooling on the local queue(s) for the listed printer(s). This allows lpr or lp to put new jobs in the spool queue.
quit	Exit from lpc.
restart [all	printer ...]	Attempts to start a new printer daemon. This is useful when some abnormal condition causes the daemon to terminate unexpectedly and leave jobs in the queue.
start [all	printer ...]	Enables printing and starts a spooling daemon for the listed printer(s).
status [printer ...]	Displays the status of daemons and queues on the local machine. When printer name parameters are not supplied, information about all printers is provided.
stop [all	printer ...]	Stops a spooling daemon after the current job has completed and disables printing.
topq printer [jobnum ...] [user ...]	Places jobs in the order listed at the top of the printer queue.
up [all	printer ...]	Enables all printing and starts a new printer daemon. Cancels the effect of the down command.

Table 7.2 Continued

Notice that the lpq command reports that the printer is down and the queue is disabled, and the message entered with the "lpc down" command is also displayed. Once the printer is repaired, simply cancel the printer "down" operation with the following command:

```
# lpc up draft
```

7.8. READING AND WRITING 3.5-INCH DISKETTES

Since personal computers running Microsoft operating systems such as MS-DOS, Windows, Windows 95, and Windows NT are so common, the ability to read and write MS-DOS formatted diskettes from a Digital UNIX system can often be useful. Occasionally, it is simply quicker to copy a file or two to a diskette from a system of one type (Digital UNIX or DOS/Windows) for transfer to a system of the other type than across the network. The common denominator in this case is the MS-DOS-formatted 3.5-inch diskette. Obviously the native format of a DOS/Windows PC diskette is MS-DOS; on the Digital UNIX system, the installation of some additional software provides this same ability to manipulate MS-DOS-formatted diskettes. The software that provides this ability is mtools, or Ms-dos TOOLS. The mtools subset is actually a collection of utilities that emulate equivalent MS-DOS utilities. The naming convention for the mtools commands are the same name as the equivalent MS-DOS command prefixed with the letter "m." For instance, the MS-DOS command to display a listing of a directory is "dir"; the mtools counterpart to this command is "mdir." For a list of the mtools commands, see Table 7.3.

The mtools commands work very similarly to their MS-DOS counterparts and, by default, refer to the floppy drive on a Digital UNIX system. For example, on a DOS/Windows PC, consider the following output from the dir command when executed against the primary floppy drive (A:):

```
C:\>dir a:

Volume in drive A has no label
Volume Serial Number is 231F-9201
Directory of A:\

COMMAND     COM       93,812      08-24-96     11:11a    COMMAND.COM
AUTOEXEC    BAT          347      07-23-97     10:56p    AUTOEXEC.BAT
CONFIG      SYS          884      09-22-97      8:06a    CONFIG.SYS
            3 file(s)  95,043     bytes
            0 dir(s)   1,361,920  bytes free
```

If this diskette is moved to the floppy drive of a Digital UNIX system and the mtools mdir command is run, the results are very similar:

```
# mdir

Volume in drive A has no label
Volume Serial Number is 231F-9201
Directory for A:/
```

mattrib	Changes MS-DOS file attribute flags.
mcd	Changes an MS-DOS directory.
mcopy	Copies an MS-DOS file to or from a UNIX machine.
mdel	Deletes an MS-DOS file.
mdir	Displays the contents of an MS-DOS directory.
mformat	Adds an MS-DOS file system to a low-level formatted diskette.
mlabel	Makes an MS-DOS volume label.
mmd	Creates an MS-DOS subdirectory.
mrd	Removes an MS-DOS subdirectory.
mread	Provides a low-level read (copy) of an MS-DOS file to a UNIX system.
mren	Renames an existing MS-DOS file.
mtype	Displays the contents of an MS-DOS file.
mwrite	Provides a low-level write (copy) of a UNIX file to an MS-DOS system.

Table 7.3 mtools Commands

```
COMMAND   COM        93812        08-24-1996   11:11
AUTOEXEC  BAT        347          07-23-1997   22:56
CONFIG    SYS        884          09-22-1997   8:06
          3 file(s)  95 043 bytes
                     1 361 920 bytes free
```

In addition to listing the files contained on an MS-DOS diskette, copying files to and from an MS-DOS diskette is the other common mtools command. As an example of this operation, suppose you wish to copy the /etc/hosts file from a Digital UNIX system to C:\WINDOWS\HOSTS in order to duplicate the hosts file on a Windows95 or Windows NT system. The following sequence of steps/commands would accomplish this operation.

Insert an MS-DOS-formatted diskette in the floppy drive of the source Digital UNIX system and copy the /etc/hosts file to the diskette. (Note that the "-t" flag is used, which specifies that the file being copied is a text file; mcopy then converts the file to MS-DOS format.)

```
# mcopy -t /etc/hosts a:
# mdir
Volume in drive A has no label
Volume Serial Number is 231F-9201
Directory for A:/

hosts      1959 09-24-1997 18:58 hosts
   1 file(s)     1 959 bytes
            1 455 616 bytes free
```

Remove this diskette from the Digital UNIX system floppy drive and insert it into the Windows PC floppy drive and issue the following command from an MS-DOS prompt:

```
C:\>copy a:hosts c:\windows\hosts
```

This is simply the MS-DOS command to copy the file from the diskette to the desired subdirectory on the hard drive. As these two examples demonstrate, the ability to read and write MS-DOS-formatted diskettes can be very useful indeed. The remaining mtools commands function just like their MS-DOS counterparts; just prepend an "m" to the familiar commands.

7.8.1. Installing mtools

There are several ways of getting the mtools package on your Digital UNIX system. If your system is running Digital UNIX 4.0 and above, the simplest way is to load the DOS tools subset provided by Digital, which contains the mtools package. This subset is named OSFDOSTOOLSxxx (the "xxx" stands-in for the version of the subset.) To determine if this subset is loaded, you can check as follows:

```
# /usr/sbin/setld -i | grep -i dos
OSFDOSTOOLS410 installed  DOS tools (General Applications)
```

In this example, the subset is installed. If you do not receive any output, or if the "installed" keyword in the second column is absent, you must install the subset from the master Digital UNIX 4.x operating system install media using the setld command. For assistance in installing Digital UNIX subsets, see Chapter 3, "System Configuration."

If you are running Digital UNIX version 3.2 and earlier, or simply desire the very latest version of mtools, it is necessary to download via anonymous FTP, compile, and install the mtools package manually. Even on systems running Digital UNIX version 4.0 or greater, it may be desirable to obtain the most recent version rather then install the OSFDOSTOOLS subset, which is unlikely to be the very latest version. The following URL specifies the location of the mtools distribution:

> ftp://sunsite.unc.edu/pub/Linux/utils/
>   disk-management/mtools-X.Y.tar.gz

Note that the X.Y notation in the mtools filename specifies the version number. For instance, as of this writing, the current version of mtools is 3.9 (mtools-3.9.tar.gz). After downloading, uncompressing, and unpacking the mtools distribution into a temporary directory (such as /tmp), you will have an mtools-X.Y subdirectory that contains the mtools source. For example:

```
# cd /tmp
# ls mtools*
mtools-3.9.tar.gz
# gunzip mtools-3.9.tar.gz
# tar -xf mtools-3.9.tar
# ls -d mtools*
/tmp/mtools-3.9/      /tmp/mtools-3.9.tar
```

Change to this newly created mtools-X.Y directory and configure, make, and install the mtools package:

```
# cd /tmp/mtools-3.9
# ./configure
# make install
```

This will configure the source for your particular system, compile the mtools package, and install the various mtools utilities onto your system.

By default, the mtools utilities will access the primary diskette drive via the /dev/rfd0c special device. This is the raw floppy disk device that refers to the entire diskette. On the Digital UNIX system, the default ownership and permissions for this special device file are root owner, system group, and read/write only by root. If a non-root user runs an mtools command that attempts to access the floppy drive, these ownership/permissions on this diskette device file cause the following error:

```
$ mdir
Can't open /dev/rfd0c: Permission denied
Cannot initialize 'A:'
```

The work-around to this problem is to change the permissions of the /dev/rfd0c file. This will allow all users on the system to use the mtools commands to access diskettes. All that is necessary is to issue to following command as root:

```
# chmod 666 /dev/rfd0c
```

7.8.2. Formatting and Mounting Floppies

Occasionally, it is useful to create a UNIX File System (UFS) on a floppy disk and mount the diskette as a file system. The resulting mounted file system on a 1.44-megabyte floppy behaves like any other UFS file system and, as such, regular Digital UNIX commands are used to manipulate the floppy file system. For example, files can be copied to the floppy with just the regular cp(1) command. Following are the steps necessary to create a file system on a floppy and mount it:

```
# fddisk -f -fmt /dev/rfd0c
# disklabel -rw /dev/rfd0c RX23
# newfs /dev/rfd0c
# mkdir /floppy
# mount /dev/fd0c /floppy
# df -k /floppy
Filesystem     1024-blocks    Used    Avail    Capacity    Mounted on
/dev/fd0c      1303           1       1171     1%          /floppy
```

Remember that a floppy so mounted has a regular UFS file system on it and should be unmounted before being ejected from the floppy drive to avoid file system corruption. If a floppy containing a mounted file system is ejected, use the fsck(8) command to do a file system check to allow mounting it again. See Chapter 3, "System Configuration," for information on checking UFS file systems with the fsck command.

7.9. CD-ROMS

CD-ROM drives have become nearly universal on Digital systems, no longer an option, but standard equipment. This availability has meant that nearly all Digital UNIX software, including the operating system, layered products, and applications in addition to third-party software, is delivered on CD-ROM. The capacity of a CD-ROM is approximately 650 megabytes of data. Though this is no longer the vast amount of data it was perceived to be in the early 90s, when hard disks greater than a gigabyte were uncommon, 650 megabytes is still sufficient to hold and deliver even large software packages. Newer technologies with the potential to replace the CD-ROM as the software delivery media of choice, such as DVD (Digital Versatile Disc) continue to appear. Though DVD promises capacities from 4.7 gigabytes all the way up to 17 gigabytes, the CD-ROM will be with us for the foreseeable future, primarily because it has reached critical mass and is installed on most modern computers, both UNIX and PCs.

7.9.1. Mounting a CD-ROM

Knowing how to access a CD-ROM on a Digital UNIX system is fairly simple, though not intuitive. On a PC, usually all that is needed is to insert the CD-ROM into the CD-ROM drive, and the disk is automatically accessible as a drive letter or by clicking on an icon. On a Digital UNIX system, the CD-ROM must be mounted like any other disk to make it accessible. However, there are several prerequisites that must be satisfied before a CD-ROM can successfully be mounted. First, the kernel must be built with the CDFS option. The CDFS, or Compact Disc File System option provides the ability to mount CD-ROMs that conform to the ISO9660 standard or the High Sierra Group (HSG) format. If a system's kernel does not have this option, the system does not support mounting CD-ROMs formatted with either of these formats. Note that CD-ROMs that contain Unix File System (UFS) formatting do not require this kernel option to be mounted. An example of a UFS-formatted CD-ROM is the Digital UNIX operating system installation CD-ROM. The easiest way to determine if a particular system has been configured with the CDFS option is to look for the following line in the system configuration file (/sys/conf/UPPERCASE_HOSTNAME):

```
options CDFS
```

If the system configuration file does not contain this line, simply add it to the system configuration file and then rebuild the kernel and reboot. See Chapter 3, "System Configuration," for guidelines in building and reconfiguring a Digital UNIX kernel.

After confirming the Digital UNIX kernel support CDFS, the next piece of information necessary before being able to mount a CD-ROM is what is the CD-ROM drive's device name. If you do not know this device name, use the file(1) command to determine the correct device. The file command displays a file's type; when a file is used on raw disk device files, useful information about the disk, such as type and SCSI ID, are displayed. Since CD-ROM device types in Digital UNIX have the prefix "RRD," it becomes easy to determine the CD-ROM device with a command similar to the following:

```
# file /dev/rrz*c | grep RRD
/dev/rrz5c:   character special (8/5122) SCSI #0
  RRD45 disk #40 (SCSI ID #5)
```

In this example, the CD-ROM device is RRD45 on device /dev/rz5c. Note that the file command requires you to specify the raw, or character, device, but you must specify the cooked, or block, device when mounting a CD-ROM. Also, the "c" partition must be specified, which refers to the entire CD-ROM disk.

Finally, create a directory that will be the mount point for the CD-ROM. A recommended mount point is /cdrom. Create the selected directory with the mkdir command:

```
# mkdir /cdrom
```

Once the running kernel has the CDFS option, you know the CD-ROM device file, and a mount point has been chosen (and created, if necessary), you are ready to mount a CD-ROM. Insert the CD-ROM into the CD-ROM drive. If the CD-ROM drive requires a caddy, insert the CD-ROM into the caddy, then insert the caddy into the CD-ROM drive. Ensure that the labeled side of the CD-ROM is up. Then mount the CD-ROM using the following mount command syntax, substituting the appropriate CD-ROM device file determined earlier and the selected mount point:

```
# mount -r /dev/rzXc /mount_point
```

For example, to mount the CD-ROM in the CD-ROM drive identified by /dev/rz5c on the mount point /cdrom, use the following command:

```
# mount -r /dev/rz5c /cdrom
```

The "-r" mount flag specifies to mount the CD-ROM with read-only access. Since CD-ROMs are read only, this ensures that the system does not attempt to update file access times. This mount command will work only with Digital CD-ROMs created with UFS formatting; this includes the Digital UNIX operating system and layered product CD-ROMs. Most CD-ROMs, however, require additional mount flags to be successfully mounted. If, for example, you attempt to mount a CD-ROM and receive the following error message:

```
/dev/rz5c on /cdrom: No valid filesystem exists on
   this partition
```

this indicates that the CD-ROM you are trying to mount is not UFS-formatted. Simply add an additional flag to the mount command to specify that the CD-ROM is CDFS-formatted:

```
# mount -r -t cdfs /dev/rz5c /cdrom
```

Another occasional difficulty arising from mounting CD-ROMs occurs when a ISO 9660 or High Sierra Group formatted CD-ROM contains version numbers. Version numbers are a characteristic of operating system such as Digital's OpenVMS. UNIX, however, does not have a provision for multiple versions of a file; therefore, UNIX does not include version numbers as part of a file name. The following listing of the contents of a CDFS-formatted CD-ROM is an example of version strings:

```
# ls /cdrom
ALPHA_FR.PS;1   BINMX        DOC              INCLUDE   MAN
APP_DEFA        CD_LINK.;1   FREEWARE.OSF;1   KITS      README.1ST;1
BIN             DEC_DOC      IMAGES           LIB       UID
```

Note also that the file and directory names are uppercase. In order resolve this, simply unmount the CD-ROM, and remount it, adding another mount option, the "noversion" flag:

```
# umount /cdrom
# mount -r -t cdfs -o noversion /dev/rz5c /cdrom
# ls /cdrom
alpha_fr.ps  binmx    doc            include   man
app_defa     cd_link  freeware.osf   kits      readme.1st
bin          dec_doc  images         lib       uid
```

7.9.2. Unmounting a CD-ROM

This last example used the umount(8) command. Before a CD-ROM can be removed from the CD-ROM drive, the CD-ROM must be unmounted. Even if the eject button on the front panel of the CD-ROM drive is physically pressed, the CD-ROM will not be ejected as long as the CD-ROM remains mounted. Simply issue the umount command, specifying either the mount point or the CD-ROM drive device to unmount the CD-ROM. For example, to unmount the CD-ROM in the CD-ROM drive identified by /dev/rz5c on the mount point /cdrom, the two following commands are equivalent:

```
# umount /cdrom
# umount /dev/rz5c
```

One caveat: If any user has changed a directory into the CD-ROM mount point or below and you try to unmount the CD-ROM, you will receive the following error message and the CD-ROM will not be unmounted:

```
/cdrom: Device busy
```

If this occurs, it will be necessary to identify which users are on the CD-ROM. This could also occur if a locally mounted CD-ROM is exported via NFS (the Network File System) and other systems have mounted the CD-ROM across the network. Before you can unmount the CD-ROM locally, the remote systems will have to also umount it.

Finally, in Digital UNIX, only the root user can mount and unmount CD-ROMs. This is a limitation that can cause additional work for the system administrator, but prevents regular users from mounting and unmounting file systems.

7.9.2. Automatically Mounting CD-ROMs

It may be desirable for the system at bootup to attempt to mount any CD-ROM inserted in the CD-ROM drive. This can be accomplished by inserting an entry for the CD-ROM in the /etc/fstab, which is a table of known file systems and swap partitions. This file is consulted when the system boots up and an attempt is made to mount all listed file systems. Insert a line similar to the following to mount any UFS-formatted CD-ROM in the drive when the system starts:

```
/dev/rz5c /cdromufs   ro 0 0
```

Substitute the appropriate CD-ROM drive device for /dev/rz5c and your selected mount point for /cdrom. If the CD-ROM you wish to have mounted at startup is a CDFS and you wish to specify the "noversion" option, this /etc/fstab entry will work:

```
/dev/rz5c /cdromcdfs  ro,noversion 0 0
```

7.10. PLAYING AUDIO CDS

Besides being about to mount and access CD-ROMs containing file system data, the CD-ROM drive on a Digital UNIX system has the ability to play audio CDs containing music. Most CD-ROM drives have a headphone jack on the front panel of the drive. Unfortunately Digital does not supply an audio CD player with Digital UNIX. Fortunately, however, someone has written a utility that allows the playing of audio CDs. This utility, xmcd, is authored by Ti Tan. Xmcd is a CD Player package that is composed of two utilities: xmcd, a CD Player for the X window system with a Motif graphical interface, and cda, a command-line driven, text mode CD player that also features a character-based, screen-oriented mode. Both utilities allow your CD-ROM drive to play music CDs. The xmcd package has a rich feature set including shuffle play and support for CD databases. See the Xmcd web page for more information and the link to download a Digital UNIX binary distribution at:

http://sunsite.unc.edu/~cddb/xmcd/

Networking

8

8.1. NETWORKING

A network is a collection of computers connected by hardware and software to allow the sharing of data and resources. In order for the computers on a network to communicate, they must all speak the same language, or protocol. Today, it is a rare Digital UNIX system that is not a member of a network of some sort. Digital UNIX, like all other flavors of UNIX, supports Transmission Control Protocol/Internet Protocol (TCP/IP) networking natively, which is the networking protocol of the Internet. In addition, Digital UNIX also supports Digital's DECnet, the native networking protocol of Digital's OpenVMS operating system, though only as an extra cost option. Due to the almost universal acceptance of TCP/IP, that is the only networking protocol that will be covered. This chapter is intended as a guide to configuring and managing basic TCP/IP networking on Digital UNIX systems. The first part of the chapter is an introduction to the requirements of TCP/IP networking on a Digital UNIX system. This includes Internet Protocol (IP) addresses, subnets and subnet masks, and gateways and routing.

I will then cover the configuration process and provide examples of both the character-based setup sequence and the graphical configuration utility available on Digital UNIX version 4.0 and above. Following this, the different network interfaces available on a Digital UNIX system will be outlined, along with any special requirements or considerations. Next, some basic network troubleshooting tips will be demonstrated. Finally, several common network services for sharing resources across a network, such as the Domain Name Service (DNS) and File Transfer Protocol (FTP), will be covered.

8.2. NETWORK CONFIGURATION

There are several prerequisites to configuring TCP/IP networking on a Digital UNIX system. The first, of course, is that the system has a network interface and is connected to a network. Digital UNIX supports several different network interfaces, including Ethernet, Token Ring, Fiber Distributed Data Interface (FDDI), Asynchronous Transfer Mode (ATM), and both Serial Line Internet Protocol (SLIP) and Point-to-Point Protocol (PPP) for TCP/IP networking across serial lines, particularly dial-up modems. Since most, if not all, Digital UNIX systems have at least an Ethernet interface, I will use Ethernet as an example.

There are two different network layouts, or topologies, and the determining factor in which topology is used is the way a computer is physically connected to the network. The first, and by far the most common, is a star topology (Figure 8.1) in which each host is connected to a central hub via a direct cable. A star network is termed that because of the use of a central hub with each host radiating out on an individual spoke. This type of network is commonly referred to as a 10BaseT, a UTP (Unshielded Twisted-Pair), or simply a Twisted-Pair network and is readily identified by the distinctive RJ-45 connector on the host network interface. This RJ-45 connector looks like a jumbo U.S.-style phone jack and snaps into the jack with an audible click. The identifier "10BaseT" is an IEEE designator that includes three pieces of information. The first part, "10," indicates the media speed—in this case, 10 Megabits per second (Mbps). The word "Base" stands for "Baseband," a type of network signaling where Ethernet signals are the sole signals carried across the wire. The last piece, "T," stands for "Twisted-Pair" and simply designates the cable type. A Fast Ethernet network or interface using twisted-pair cabling would be termed "100BaseT" to indicate a media speed of 100-Mbps, and a dual regular and Fast Ethernet network interface is frequently referred to as a "10/100BaseT" card. One big advantage of a star topology network is that a cable break or cut effects only one host; the remaining hosts are not impacted. Troubleshooting a star network can be simpler since each segment, or spoke, supports only a single host. A disadvantage is the additional requirement for a hub. Ethernet hubs are available in sizes ranging from very small five-port units to large rack-mounted units with hundreds of ports.

The second type of network topology is a bus layout (Figure 8.2) in which each host is attached to a single cable, or bus, via tee connectors. This type of network is commonly referred to as a 10Base2, Thinnet, or Thin Coax network, and is characterized by the coaxial connector on the host network interface. This connector is typically termed a BNC (Bayonet Nut Coupling) and requires a tee connector for insertion into the main bus cable. The identifier "10Base2" indicates that the media speed is 10-Mbps and uses Baseband signaling. The "2" is an indicator of segment length and is rounded up from the 185 meter maximum length for individual thin coaxial segments. The main disadvantage to a bus topology network is that a single cable cut or break can disable the entire network if it occurs on the main bus cable. In addition, a bus network requires tee connectors for each host and 50Ω terminators to be attached to each end of the coaxial segment. However, if the network is small, consisting of just a few hosts physically close to one another, a bus network may be the simplest type of network to configure.

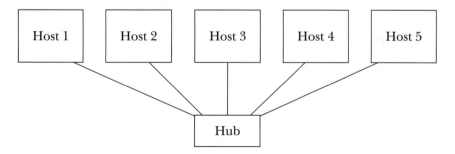

Figure 8.1 A Star Topology Network (10BaseT or Twisted-Pair)

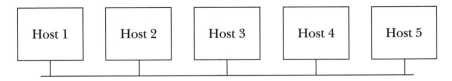

Figure 8.2 A Bus Topology Network (10Base2 or Thin Coax)

Once a system is properly connected to a network, the next step is to configure and enable TCP/IP networking on the system. This requires at least two and possibly three pieces of Address information:

- An IP address
- A Subnet Mask, and possibly
- A Gateway Address (or Default Route)

8.3. ADDRESSING

Every host on a network must have a unique address. This uniqueness is necessary to allow one host to contact and communicate with any other host on the network. There are actually three layers of addressing, each serving a specific purpose, and each referring to the layer below it and ultimately to a distinct network interface:

- Host name
- Internet Protocol (IP) Address
- Hardware Address

8.3.1. Host Name

A system's host name is simply a convenient name for use by people and programs. It is much easier to remember and use a name such as "saturn" rather then referring to a system by its IP address. A system's host name is configured at system installation time and is fairly arbitrary. Obviously, though, the networking software cannot directly use a host name when attempting to communicate with another host on the network and must translate a host name into the next lower type of address—an IP address.

The mechanism that does this translation is called the Resolver, and in the simplest configuration, it consults the /etc/hosts file for the corresponding IP address for a given host name. More complex configurations use the Internet Domain Name Server (DNS), which is a distributed database of host names and their associated IP addresses. Later in this chapter, the DNS implementation supported by Digital UNIX are discussed (see section 8.10).

8.3.2. IP Address

An IP address is a 32-bit number that is assigned to uniquely identify a particular network interface. This number is normally written as four numbers separated by periods: for example, 192.168.4.100. Each of the four period-delimited numbers, or octets, represents 8 bits of the IP address. An IP address is not arbitrary and must be selected carefully based on the network the computer will reside on. An IP address is actually composed of two pieces: a Network number and a Host number. The Network number must be identical for all hosts on the same network. An analogy to the Network number is the area code of a telephone number. All phone numbers in the same geographic region have the same area code. The Host number must be unique within a network. Continuing the telephone number example, all telephone numbers must be unique within a given area code.

The designers of TCP/IP networking anticipated differing sized networks and partitioned the network space defined by an IP address into three main categories:

- Class A—For this type of network, the first octet of the IP address specifies the network number and the remaining three octets define the host number. There are 126 Class A networks, each able to have up to 16,777,214 hosts. Class A networks are in the range 1.0.0.0 through 126.0.0.0 (the 0.0.0.0 and 127.0.0.0 ranges are reserved). Only very large organizations or companies can justify a Class A network, and in fact, there are no longer any available Class A addresses. As an example, Digital Equipment Corporation has a Class A network.
- Class B—A Class B network uses the first two octets of the IP address to specify the network number and the remaining two octets to

define the host number. There are 16,384 Class B networks, each able to have up to 65,534 hosts. Class B networks are in the range 128.1.0.0 through 191.254.0.0. Class B networks are frequently used in medium-sized companies and universities.

- Class C—A Class C network uses the first three octets of the IP address to specify the network number and the remaining octet to define the host number. There are 2,097,151 Class C networks, each able to have up to 254 hosts. Class C networks are in the range 192.0.1.0 through 223.255.254.0. Class C networks are the most common and, in some ways, the most versatile networks because they are the smallest grouping of hosts available and there are so many Class C addresses available. Organizations unable to justify the larger Class B networks will frequently obtain multiple Class C addresses in order to meet their needs.

Table 8.1 shows some example IP addresses and their logical division based on which Class they are. Note that these sample addresses assume no subnetting, a topic that is covered below (see section 8.4).

Additionally, there are also Class D and Class E networks. Class D networks are numbered starting at 224.0.0.0 and are used for multicasting. Class E networks start at 240.0.0.0 and are currently only used for experimental and research purposes.

If a network is either currently connected to the Internet or is anticipated to be connected to the Internet, contact the Internet Network Information Center (InterNIC) Registration Service (or equivalent) to apply for a block of IP addresses for your network from the IP address space. See below for contact information of IP address registration organizations.

IP Address	Class	Network Number	Host Number
18.131.55.75	A	18	131.55.75
138.12.70.190	B	138.12	70.190
216.196.23.17	C	216.196.23	17

Table 8.1 Example IP Addresses

In the United States, contact:
Network Solutions Inc.
InterNIC Registration Service
505 Huntmar Park Drive
Herndon, VA 22070
Voice: (703) 742-4777
FAX: (703) 742-4811
E-mail: hostmaster@internic.net
Website: http://rs.internic.net/rs-internic.html

In Europe, contact:

RIPE Network Coordination Center
Kruislaan 409
NL-1098 SJ Amsterdam
The Netherlands
Voice: +31 20 592 5065
FAX: +31 20 592 5090
E-mail: Hostmaster@ripe.net
Website: http://ripe.net

In Asia and the Pacific region, contact:

AP-NIC
c/o United Nations University
3-70 Jingumae 5-chome
Shibuya-ku
Shibuya-ku, Tokyo, 150, Japan
Voice: +81 3 5276 3973
FAX: +81 3 5276 6239
E-mail: hostmaster@apnic.net
Website: http://www.apnic.net

This block of IP addresses could be one or more Class C addresses or simply a subset of a Class C block depending on the size of the network. For a private network, one completely isolated from the Internet, it is not necessary to register addresses with the InterNIC. However, it is still recommended that IP addresses be applied for to avoid having to renumber the network in the event a connection to the Internet is added later. As an alternative, three blocks of IP addresses have been reserved for private networks:

> 10.0.0.0 - 10.255.255.255
> 172.16.0.0 - 172.31.255.255
> 192.168.0.0 - 192.168.255.255

The advantages of using IP addresses from these ranges are that no coordination with the InterNIC is necessary to use these addresses; in the event that a network that is numbered in this range is connected to the Internet, there will be no conflict with registered hosts.

8.3.3. /etc/hosts File

The /etc/hosts file is a network configuration file that can contain a list of host names, their IP addresses, and, optionally, one or more host name aliases for systems reachable via the network. At a minimum, an individual system's /etc/hosts file should contain an entry (host name and IP address pair) for the system itself and for the system's loopback or localhost interface, which always has the IP address "127.0.0.1." For small networks or on systems that communicate with only a few remote hosts, it is probably reasonable to keep all host information in local /etc/hosts files on all the systems. However, as the number of systems increases, the process of managing this large list of host names and associated IP addresses and aliases quickly becomes impractical. For anything more than just a handful of hosts, a distributed host name database such as the Domain Name Service (DNS) is almost a necessity. When using DNS, the /etc/hosts file becomes a backup for when the name server is not running. In this case, it is suggested that only a few hosts be included in this file. These should include addresses for the local interfaces that ifconfig(8) needs at boot time.

The format of the /etc/hosts file is one entry per host, each entry on a single line. Each host's record should have the following information:

```
IP_Address Canonical_Host name [Alias_1,...,Alias_n] [# Comments]
```

Any number of spaces and/or tab characters separates items. A pound sign (#) indicates the beginning of a comment, and any characters between the pound sign and the end of the line are ignored. The following is a fragment of an /etc/hosts file:

```
# /etc/hosts
127.0.0.1 localhost
192.168.171.78 saturn prod # Production Server
192.168.171.80 jupiter
```

8.4. THE SUBNET MASK

Frequently, a network is subdivided into smaller segments. For instance, while a Class A network can support over 16 million hosts, it simply is not practical and definitely not recommended to have that many hosts on one segment. Dividing or subnetting a network into smaller sections is done for a variety of reasons, including network performance efficiency; ease of management, such as decentralization of network administration; and overcoming physical cable distance limitations. The mechanism for subnetting is the Subnet Mask, a modifier that is used to determine how the network is subdivided. Every network configuration requires a subnet mask in addition to the IP address. The subnet mask is a 32-bit number specified in the same dotted decimal format as an IP address and, together with the IP address, is used to specify which part of the address is the network and which is the host. One minor disadvantage of subnetting is that in each subnet, the first number and last subnet number is reserved. Additionally, the first and last host number of each subnet is also reserved and cannot be used as a host address.

For networks that are not subnetted, the default subnet mask is specified:

    Class A—255.0.0.0
    Class B—255.255.0.0
    Class C—255.255.255.0

For a subnetted network, the subnet mask specifies a further logical subdivision of the host part of the IP address into a subnet number and a smaller host number. When the subnet mask is represented in binary, each bit that is a one indicates that the corresponding bit in the IP address is the network number and the subnet number; each zero bit in the subnet mask indicates the host number in the in the IP address. For instance, consider the following Class B IP address:

```
172.30.12.75
```

Converting each octet of this address to binary results in the following representation:

```
10101100    00011110    00001100    01001011
```

If this IP address were part of a network that is not subnetted, the following subnet mask, and its binary representation, would be used:

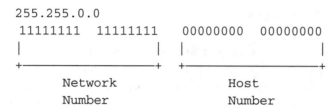

```
255.255.0.0
11111111  11111111    00000000  00000000
|                  |  |                  |
+------------------+  +------------------+
       Network              Host
       Number              Number
```

This would result in the first two octets (172.30) representing the network number and the second two octets (12.75) representing the host number.

If this IP address is part of a network that is subnetted with the following subnet mask, the resulting division would be:

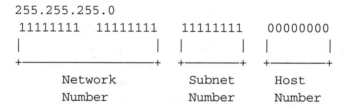

```
255.255.255.0
11111111  11111111    11111111    00000000
|                  |  |        |  |        |
+------------------+  +--------+  +--------+
       Network          Subnet      Host
       Number           Number     Number
```

This would result in the first two octets (172.30) representing the network number, the third octet (12) representing the subnet number, and the fourth octet (75) representing the host number. This subnets the Class B network into 254 (256-2 reserved) subnets, each capable of supporting 254 hosts.

Finally, if the Class B network needed to be logically divided into more subnets, each with few hosts, the following subnet mask might be used:

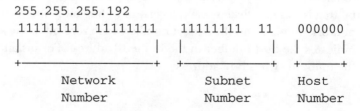

```
255.255.255.192
11111111  11111111    11111111  11    000000
|                  |  |            |  |      |
+------------------+  +------------+  +------+
       Network          Subnet          Host
       Number           Number         Number
```

As this example shows, the subnet does not necessarily have to be on a byte boundary and can be at any bit position in the host part of the IP address. This subnet mask would result in the first two octets (172.30) representing the network number; the third octet (12) and two bits of the fourth octet representing the subnet number; and the last six bits of the fourth octet representing the host number. This subnets the Class B network into 1022 (1024-2 reserved) subnets, each capable of supporting 62 hosts.

See Table 8.2 for the results of different subnet masks on Class B and Class C networks. Note that two has already been subtracted from the resulting subnet and host quantities to take into account the reserved subnet and host numbers.

Class B Subnetting

Subnet Mask	Number of Subnets	Number of Hosts
255.255.192.0	2	16382
255.255.224.0	6	8190
255.255.240.0	14	4094
255.255.248.0	30	2046
255.255.252.0	62	1022
255.255.254.0	126	510
255.255.255.0	254	254
255.255.255.128	510	126
255.255.255.192	1022	62
255.255.255.224	2046	30
255.255.255.240	4094	14
255.255.255.248	8190	6
255.255.255.252	16382	2
		(continued)

Table 8.2 The Results of Subnetting on Class B and C Networks

Class C Subnetting

Subnet Mask	Number of Subnets	Number of Hosts
255.255.255.192	2	62
255.255.255.224	6	30
255.255.255.240	14	14
255.255.255.248	30	6
255.255.255.252	62	2

Table 8.2 Continued

8.5. HARDWARE ADDRESS

Once a host name has been translated into an IP address, the next step for the networking subsystem to do is identify which physical computer on the network is assigned that IP address. The third and final address is the hardware or Media Access Control (MAC) address. Every network interface (Ethernet, Token Ring, FDDI, etc.) has a unique hardware address, and this address is typically burned into a read-only memory (ROM) chip and is unchangeable. A system's MAC address is displayed from the SRM console prompt with the "show device" command:

```
>>> show device
dka0.0.0.6.0          DKA0       RZ26N 0568
dka100.0.0.6.0        DKA100     RZ26N 0568
dka300.3.0.6.0        DKA300     RRD45 0436
dva0.0.0.1000.0       DVA0
ewa0.0.0.11.0         EWA0       00-00-F8-01-42-5F
pka0.7.0.6.0          PKA0       SCSI Bus ID 7
```

In this example, the Ethernet interface (EWA0) has a hardware address of "00-00-F8-01-42-5F". The TCP/IP networking software must know the hardware address of a destination host in order to communicate with that host. Translating an IP address into a hardware address is accomplished with the Address Resolution Protocol or ARP. This basically broadcasts a request across the network asking if any other host knows the location of the system with the target IP address. Once the hardware address of the destination host has been identified, network communication can commence.

8.6. ROUTING

Routing is the process where network packets are routed or directed to and from different networks. The TCP/IP networking subsystem on a system is able to accomplish the routing of information by consulting a list that contains instructions on where to send any particular packet based on the packet's destination address. This list, the routing table, is basically a list of destination networks or hosts, the corresponding network interface, and the next stop on the way to the final destination. For instance, consider the following routing table:

```
# /usr/sbin/netstat -nr
Routing tables
Destination       Gateway            Flags  Refs  Use   Interface
default           192.168.171.254    UGS    0     44    tu0
127.0.0.1         127.0.0.1          UH     3     4294  lo0
192.168.171/24    192.168.171.78     U      4     1166  tu0
```

Note that there are three records in this table, each providing routing instructions for a different destination. Every network packet has coded within it a destination address, and the networking software takes that destination address and compares it with the destination value of each routing table entry, starting at the bottom, looking for a match. For example, a packet destined for IP address 172.31.12.75 does not match the third destination, which is for hosts in the range of 192.168.171.0 to 192.168.171.254. This route is for systems on the local network, and packets for this destination are sent out the local Ethernet interface (192.168.171.78). The second destination (127.0.0.1) matches packets intended for services on the local system, and this route is to keep internal packets from ever getting out onto the network. The route is the loopback interface that "loops" the packets right back into the system. The first and final destination is labeled "default." Since our imaginary packet destination (172.31.12.75) does not match any other destination in the routing table, this final default route is

applied. This instructs the networking software to pass the packet onto the
gateway at 192.168.171.254, which will accept the packet and then repeat
the process, comparing the packet's destination address to its own routing
table. See the next section for information on Gateways. This simple example shows how network packets are routed from host to host until they arrive
at their final destination. Each step, or hop, gets the packet a little closer to
its destination.

There are three ways of managing the routing table on a Digital UNIX
system: minimal, static, and dynamic. Determining which routing configuration to use depends on the size and type of the network a system is connected to. The three types of routing configuration are explained as follows.

8.6.1. Minimal

A minimal routing configuration is one which contains only the routes created when the ifconfig(8) command activated the networking system. Typically, this means only a single route that corresponds to each network
interface in use, plus the loopback route. This configuration is sufficient for
small networks that are not connected to any other networks or are subnetted. For this configuration, no additional steps are necessary to manage the
routing table. Here is an example of a minimal routing table:

```
Destination       Gateway          Flags  Refs   Use    Interface
127.0.0.1         127.0.0.1        UH     3      4294   lo0
192.168.171/24    192.168.171.78   U      4      1166   tu0
```

8.6.2. Static

A static routing configuration is characterized by a routing table that contains, in addition to the routes present in a minimal configuration, one or
more routes added manually by the system administrator. The simplest static routing table has one additional route: a Default route that points to a
gateway where all nonlocal network traffic should be directed. Additionally,
there may be other, special static routes added in order to route certain packets to specific hosts or networks. These static routes are managed manually
with the route(8) command. The following example demonstrates adding
a static route to a network to the routing table:

```
# /usr/sbin/netstat -nr
Routing tables
Destination        Gateway            Flags   Refs   Use    Interface
default            192.168.171.254    UGS     0      44     tu0
127.0.0.1          127.0.0.1          UH      3      4294   lo0
192.168.171/24     192.168.171.78     U       4      1166   tu0
# /usr/sbin/route add -net 192.168.159 192.168.171.101
# /usr/sbin/netstat -nr
Routing tables
Destination        Gateway            Flags   Refs   Use    Interface
default            192.168.171.254    UGS     0      44     tu0
127.0.0.1          127.0.0.1          UH      3      4294   lo0
192.168.159/24     192.168.171.101    UGS     0      0      tu0
192.168.171/24     192.168.171.78     U       4      1166   tu0
```

The first netstat command displays the routing table showing a default route, a loopback route to the local host, and a route to network 192.168.171 through interface tu0. The route add command adds a static route to another network (192.168.159) through interface tu0, with the next destination being the host at IP address 192.168.171.101. The second netstat command again displays the routing table, and the newly added static route is now displayed immediately after the loopback route.

8.6.3. Dynamic

A dynamic routing configuration is one where the routing table is dynamically updated by a program using one or more routing protocols to determine the "best" route to a destination. The program is able to dynamically react and reroute around temporary or permanent network outages. Dynamic routing should be used on a network, which has more than one possible route to a destination. Digital UNIX provides two routing daemons, routed (pronounced "route d") and gated ("gate d"). The routed routing daemon is the older of the two daemons and also the least flexible, for it only understands one routing protocol, RIP (Routing Information Protocol). RIP is well suited for small local area networks and is probably the most commonly used routing protocol. The gated routing daemon is a more modern program and understands RIP as well as several other routing protocols. The gated daemon is normally considered a replacement for routed.

You can run either gated or routed on a system but not both. If the only routing protocol in use is or will be RIP, it is generally recommended to run routed, though gated will also do RIP. If, however, the network is running a routing protocol different from RIP, you must run gated. It is beyond the scope of this text to explore IP routing and routing protocols. Refer to one of the recommended references on TCP/IP networking in Appendix B for further information on configuring routing daemons and routing protocols.

8.7. GATEWAY

A system is able to communicate directly with other systems located on the same network or subnet. In order to reach a system on a different network, however, a system must go through a gateway. A gateway is typically a dedicated piece of hardware, either a repeater, a bridge, or a router, but a computer system may also function as a gateway if it has more than one network interface.

The simplest types of gateways are repeaters and bridges, which are used to connect distinct network cable sections to overcome network cable distance limitations. Repeaters and bridges extend a single network rather than connecting different networks together. A repeater simply passes all network traffic transparently between the two network segments without any type of filtering or modification. A bridge is an intelligent repeater and has the ability to filter traffic based on various criteria.

The most common type of gateway is known as a router, so named because it "routes" network traffic between different networks. A router has connections simultaneously on multiple networks. All network traffic originating on a specific network and destined for systems on remote networks must travel through this router, which is also called a default route. A router is usually a stand-alone device with sophisticated software that has the ability to examine individual network packets and make a determination, based on source, destination, or type, whether to forward the packet on to another network.

When configuration TCP/IP networking on a Digital UNIX system, it is usually not necessary to know what type your gateway is. Simply knowing the IP address of the gateway is sufficient. For example, Figure 8.3 shows two networks connected by a Gateway. Host 1 is able to communicate to Host 2 directly without traveling through the gateway, but in order for Host 1 to

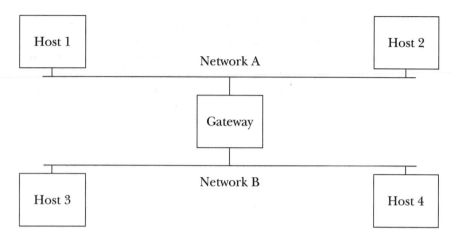

Figure 8.3 A Gateway Connecting Two Networks

communicate with Host 3, the network traffic must be routed through the
gateway between the two networks. Providing the gateway's address instructs
the TCP/IP software where to send network packets destined for hosts not
on the local network.

8.8. ACTIVATING NETWORKING

Once a system's network parameters are in hand, the next step is to actually
configure and start the Digital UNIX TCP/IP networking subsystem. Digital provides a character cell utility for configuring networking at all levels of
Digital UNIX. This utility, netsetup(8), works in the same way, regardless of
the version of Digital UNIX, and provides a text-only menu-driven interface
for configuring individual network interfaces, starting and stopping certain
network daemons, entering gateway information, and adding and deleting
remote host information. Starting at Digital UNIX version 4.0, Digital
added a new TCP/IP network configuration tool with three modes of operation providing more flexibility then the netsetup utility. This tool, netcon-
fig(8X), defaults to an X-Windows graphical user interface, but can also be
run from a character-cell menu interface, or from the command line specifying configuration options. This last mode, the command line interface, is
useful for automating network configuration tasks with shell scripts.

This section will only cover the use of the netsetup(8) utility and the graphical netconfig(8X) tool for basic TCP/IP network configuration. For information on the menu and command line interfaces of the netconfig tool, refer to the man page for netconfig(8X). For the following examples, consider a Digital UNIX system on an Ethernet network with these settings:

```
IP Address:        192.168.171.78
Subnet Mask:       255.255.255.0
Gateway Address:   192.168.171.254
```

8.8.1. netsetup

The netsetup(8) utility provides a simple, menu-driven method of configuring or reconfiguring the TCP/IP network subsystem on Digital UNIX. Run the netsetup utility as root,

```
# /usr/sbin/netsetup
```

and the main menu (Figure 8.4) will be presented. The user interface is straightforward: type the desired menu choice number and press <Return>. Within each menu choice, default answers are shown in square brackets ([]). To use a default answer, press <Return>. The five menu choices follow.

8.8.1.1. Configure Network Interfaces

This menu choice walks the user through configuring or deleting (unconfiguring) a system's network interface(s). The following information is prompted for:

- The network interface to be configured. See Table 8.3 for a list of the common network interface device names.
- The system's host name
- The IP Address for the chosen network interface
- For a Serial Line Internet Protocol (SLIP) interface, the IP Address for the remote SLIP interface
- The Subnet Mask. The presented default subnet mask should be chosen unless the local network is subnetted.
- For a Token Ring interface, the speed of the adapter (4Mb/s or 16Mb/s)

- Optional ifconfig(8) flags. Refer to the ifconfig(8) reference page for the available flags. Typically no additional flags are needed.
- For a SLIP interface, optional slattach(8) command flags, command terminal name, and baud rate. Refer to the slattach(8) reference page for information on the available command flags and the terminal name and baud rate.

Once the information is successfully entered and confirmed, netsetup displays the newly entered network configuration and prompts for final confirmation before updating various system configuration files. See Figure 8.5 for an example of a network configuration session.

Note that the network interface is only configured at this point. For the network modifications to take effect, the TCP/IP network services must be restarted. You will be prompted to restart the network services when you leave netsetup utility via the main menu "Exit" choice.

In addition to configuring a network interface for the first time or reconfiguring a previously configured interface, the "Configure Network Interfaces" menu choice also allows the system administrator to delete a previously configured network interface. This option actually unconfigures a

```
                       **** MAIN MENU ****

        1 Configure Network Interfaces

        2 Enable/Disable Network Daemons and Add Static Routes

        3 Add/Delete Host Information

        4 Display Network Configuration

        5 Exit

    Enter the number for your choice:
```

Figure 8.4 Netsetup Main Menu

Network Interface Type	Network Interface Device Name
Loopback	lo
Ethernet	tu, le, ln, xna
Token Ring	tra
FDDI	fta, faa, fza
ATM	lta
Serial Line Interface	sl

Note: The Network Interface Device Name will be followed with a number designating a particular device (for example, tu0, fta1).

Table 8.3 Network Interface Types and Device Names

```
                    **** MAIN MENU ****

        1 Configure Network Interfaces

        2 Enable/Disable Network Daemons and Add Static Routes

        3 Add/Delete Host Information

        4 Display Network Configuration

        5 Exit

    Enter the number for your choice: 1

        ***** CONFIGURE/DELETE NETWORK INTERFACES *****
```

Figure 8.5 Example Configure Network Interface Session in netsetup(8)

```
You can configure or delete network interfaces.
Configuration information is updated in /etc/rc.config
and /etc/hosts.  Choose "configure" or "delete" at the
prompt.

Enter whether you want to "(c)onfigure" or "(d)elete"
network interfaces.
If you are finished, press the RETURN key: c
You want to "configure" interfaces.  Is this correct
[yes]? yes

You will now be asked a series of questions about the
system.
Default answers are shown in square brackets ([]).  To
use a default answer, press the RETURN key.

This machine contains the following network interfaces:
    tu0
    sl0

Which interface do you want to configure [tu0]: tu0
You want to configure "tu0".  Is this correct [yes]? yes

The hostname for the system is "saturn".
Is this correct [yes]? yes

Enter the Internet Protocol (IP) address for interface
"tu0" in dot notation []: 192.168.171.78
The IP address for interface "tu0" is "192.168.171.78".
Is this correct [yes]? yes

Subnetworks allow the systems on a local area network
to be on different physical networks.  For the
following question, use the default answer unless the
existing local area network is using subnet routing.
If the local area network is using subnet routing, you
need to know the subnet mask.

Enter the subnet mask in dot notation [255.255.0.0]:
255.255.255.0
The subnet mask for "tu0" is "255.255.255.0".
Is this correct [yes]? yes
                                              (continued)
```

Figure 8.5 Continued

```
Is this correct [yes]? yes

For the following question USE THE DEFAULT ANSWER
unless you would like to add additional flags (found in
the ifconfig reference page) to the ifconfig command.
Normally, you will USE THE DEFAULT ANSWER.

Do you want to use additional ifconfig flags for this
interface [no]? no

The configuration looks like:

    system hostname: "saturn"
    ifconfig tu0 192.168.171.78 netmask 255.255.255.0

Is this correct [yes]? yes

***** UPDATING /etc/rc.config *****

"tu0" is configured in /etc/rc.config

***** UPDATING /etc/hosts *****

"192.168.171.78 saturn" is configured in /etc/hosts

Do you want to configure another network interface
[yes]? no

Enter whether you want to "(c)onfigure" or "(d)elete"
network interfaces.
If you are finished, press the RETURN key: <Return>
```

Figure 8.5 Continued

network interface and deletes all references to it from the system configuration. If an interface configuration is to be deleted, ensure that the configuration information is recorded if it will be necessary to reconfigure the interface at a later time.

8.8.1.2. Enable/Disable Network Daemons and Add Static Routes

This option allows a system administrator to enable and configure or disable several network daemons. By default, none of these processes are enabled, and they must be explicitly activated. These daemons are:

- rwhod (rwho Daemon)
- routed (Routing Daemon)
- gated (Gateway Routing Daemon)

8.8.1.2.1. rwhod

The rwho daemon is a network server that maintains a database of information used by the rwho(1) and ruptime(1) commands. The rwhod(8) server broadcasts a status message across the network every three minutes, which is received by any other rwhod servers on the network. This information includes the status of the system (up time, load averages, who is logged on, when they logged on, and how long each connection has been idle). The rwho daemon can provide valuable system status for a system administrator responsible for a number of machines on the network. Conversely, the rwho information can also provide useful system information, such as account names to an unscrupulous user intent on compromising a system or network. Unless there is an overriding need for the facility provided by the rwho daemon, I recommend that it be left disabled.

8.8.1.2.2. routed

The routing daemon routed supports the Routing Information Protocol (RIP) and should be started if you will be using dynamic routing based on this routing protocol. See section 8.6.3. in this chapter for information on routed.

8.8.1.2.3. gated

The gateway routing daemon gated supports several routing protocols including RIP, BGP, EGP, HELLO, and OSPF. The gated daemon should be enabled if the network is running one or more of these protocols for dynamic routing. See section 8.6.3. for information on gated. Note that in Digital UNIX version 4.0 and greater, the netsetup utility enables an older version of gated, called ogated(8), that does not support either the BGP or OSPF routing protocols. In order to run the latest version of gated, gated(8), the netconfig utility must be run to set up the gateway routing daemon.

8.8.1.2.4. Static Routes

Finally, the "Enable/Disable Network Daemons and Add Static Routes" menu choice allows the system administrator to add static routes. Creating a static route via netsetup actually updates the /etc/routes file, which identifies static routes that are automatically added to the network routing table when the networking subsystem is started or restarted. There are three possible types of static routes:

- Default
- Network
- Host

A default route is the route to which all network packets that do not match any other route are sent. A network route is a route to a specific network, and a host route is, of course, a route to a specific host.

8.8.1.3. Add/Delete Host Information

This options allows the system administrator to add or delete host entries to or from the following files:

- /etc/hosts
- /etc/hosts.equiv
- /etc/networks

The process of modifying these network configuration files is simply a series of questions, prompting the user for host names, IP addresses, host or network aliases, or account names of trusted users, depending on the operation and file selected. Once the necessary information is collected, the netsetup utility edits the appropriate configuration file and either adds or deletes the entry.

The /etc/hosts file contains information regarding known systems on the network. The /etc/hosts file was discussed earlier in section 8.3., "Addressing." The /etc/hosts.equiv file is a configuration file specifying "Trusted Host" relationships. This file is covered in Chapter 5, "Security." The /etc/networks file lists the known networks in the Internet and is used by the route daemon, routed(8), and other networking utilities.

8.8.1.4. Display Network Configuration

Selecting this choice displays the current network configuration, including all available network interfaces on the system. This display will show any network interface changes made during the current netsetup session, and may not accurately reflect the active state of the network interfaces. See Figure

8.6 for a sample output from this menu choice. Note that this choice will not indicate any additions or deletions of host information.

8.8.1.5. Exit

Any updates made to the networking configuration are not enabled until either the system's networking services are restarted or the system is rebooted. Upon exiting from netsetup, the user is given the opportunity to restart the network services. Typically, if modifications were made to the network configuration, especially if the initial configuration was just done, it is a good idea to proceed with the networking restart. For a system whose network is already up, warn any users currently using the system that the network will be stopped and restarted, and there may be a momentary interruption, or possibly a disconnect, depending on the nature of the network

```
Current network adapters on this system:

    tu0
    sl0

Current software configuration in /etc/rc.config:

HOSTNAME = saturn
NUM_NETCONFIG = 1
NETDEV_0 = tu0
IFCONFIG_0 = 192.168.171.78 netmask 255.255.255.0
RWHOD = no
ROUTED = no
ROUTED_FLAGS =
GATED = no
GATED_FLAGS =
GATED_OLD = no
ROUTER = no
MAX_NETDEVS = 24
```

Figure 8.6 Example netsetup(8) Display Network Configuration Output

configurations. If the network services are not restarted when exiting net-setup, the network can be restarted from the command line with the following command,

```
# /usr/sbin/rcinet restart
```

or by simply rebooting the system:

```
# /usr/sbin/shutdown -r now "Rebooting to restart networking..."
```

Be aware that any NFS mounted file system that is not listed in the /etc/fstab or mounted by the automounter facility will no longer be mounted after restarting the networking services. Any such file system will have to be manually remounted; or, if the file system should be automatically mounted, add it to the /etc/fstab file or configure the automount(8) utility.

Finally, note that the netsetup(8) utility does not track whether or not modifications to the networking configuration were made, and always prompts to restart the networking services upon exiting. Obviously, if no changes were made, there is likely no need to restart networking. Keep in mind which modifications are made during a netsetup session, and assess whether a network restart is necessary. For instance, if a network interface is reconfigured, a restart is necessary for the change to take effect. However, if, for example, host information added to the /etc/hosts file is the only update, a network restart is not required since host information updates take effect immediately.

8.8.2. netconfig

The Network Configuration Manager, netconfig, is an X-Windows/Motif application on Digital UNIX version 4.0 and greater systems that can be used to initially configure and modify the TCP/IP network configuration. The Network Configuration Manager is invoked through the CDE Application Manager, which is opened by selecting the Application Manager icon from the CDE Front Panel, followed by selecting the System_Admin application group icon, then the Configuration application group icon, and finally the Network icon. Once you double-click on the Network icon, if you are not logged in as root, you will be prompted via a Get Password dialog box for the root password. The initial Network Configuration Manager window is shown in Figure 8.7.

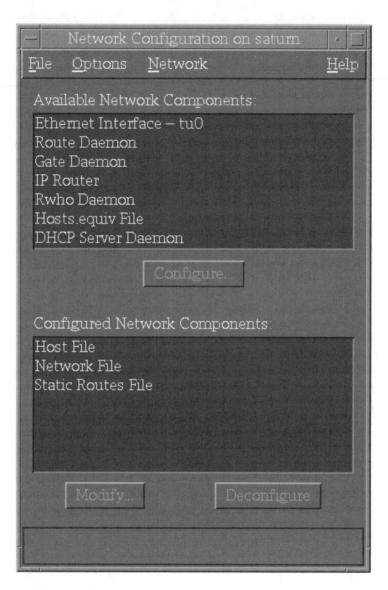

Figure 8.7 netconfig(8X) Main Window

Optionally, you can start the Network Configuration Manager from the command line:

```
# /usr/sbin/netconfig
```

This application provides all the configuration options that the netsetup(8) utility does, plus a configuration window for the Dynamic Host Configuration Protocol (DHCP), which is new in Digital UNIX version 4.0. The netconfig main window is divided into two panes, Available Network Components and Configured Network Components. The list of Available Network Components displays the network components that are available to be configured. These components are not yet configured in any way. The Configured Network Components pane lists the network components that are currently configured.

To initially configure or modify an already configured network component, either select the component by clicking on the component's name, then clicking the Configure... or Modify... button, or by simply double-clicking on the component desired. This will display the configuration window for the selected network component. Fill in the necessary fields with the desired values, or select options by clicking on the check boxes. For example, Figure 8.8 shows the Configuring Ethernet Interface window with the host name, IP address, and subnet mask entered. Clicking on the Commit button at this point will save this configuration. To close this dialog box and return to the main netconfig window, click on the Close button either before making or after committing any changes. To discard any modifications without committing them, simply click the Cancel button.

Clicking on the Help pull-down menu and selecting the Overview menu choice accesses the online help facility for the netconfig utility. For help on a specific network component configuration window, open that window and click the Help button for context-sensitive help on the current window. To dismiss the Help window, pull down the File menu and select the Close menu choice. For a hint on a particular field, check box, or button, simply place the cursor over the object of interest to display a brief description of the object in the box above the row of buttons.

As in the netsetup utility, once all the desired network components are configured and their values are committed, the final step is to start or restart the networking services. This can be accomplished from within the netconfig application by selecting the Network pull-down menu and selecting the appropriate menu choice. The Restart Services selection is equivalent to running the "rcinet restart" command from the command line. Be

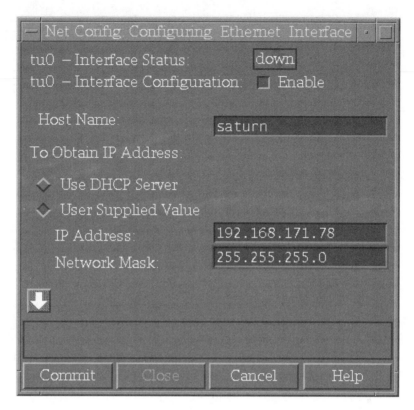

Figure 8.8 netconfig(8X) Configuring Ethernet Interface Window

aware that if the netconfig application is being run across the network on an X display that is not the system console, restarting the network services will almost certainly cause the X connection to be lost and, in certain instances, could cause the restart process to abort. To ensure that connectivity to a system is not lost, always restart the networking services from the console.

8.9. NETWORK TROUBLESHOOTING TOOLS

When a problem arises on a network of systems, it can initially be overwhelming due to the range of possible sources of trouble. Trying to determine whether the problem is hardware (a computer, hub, or router, or cables or connectors, etc.) or software (an improperly configured network interface, incomplete or incorrect routing table information, or invalid or missing host information) can be difficult to isolate. The best approach is to understand the symptoms of the issue and then methodically try to isolate the actual problem. Digital UNIX (and all other UNIX implementations) provides several troubleshooting utilities, each with a special purpose or focus. Knowing each tool's specialty and what can be learned from their output is important in knowing where to start troubleshooting.

A network problem will probably manifest itself in a connectivity loss between systems. Typically, an individual system or group of systems is unable to communicate with some other system or group of systems. The very first thing that should be done is to attempt to define the problem. Initially this may be something as vague as a user reporting that he or she cannot connect to the company web site using the browser on his or her workstation. Using this example, the system administrator should be able to refine and bound the problem by asking questions or trying variations of the problem. For instance:

- "Are you able to connect to other web sites?"
- "Do any of your co-workers have the same problem?"
- "Are any other network services (telnet, FTP, printing) also not working?"
- "Have there been any recent hardware or software configuration changes?"

After collecting further information, the system administrator is able to determine the following:

- The user who raised the issue appears to be the only one impacted.
- The user is experiencing network time-outs regardless of which web site is attempted.
- All other network services are also failing.
- The networking configuration of the user's workstation was recently changed, but the user does not know what was done.

From this description, it appears that the user's system is no longer a part of the network. More than likely, the recent network reconfiguration has introduced a problem preventing the system from communicating with the rest of the network. The following is an example of a plan of attack and introduces the UNIX network troubleshooting utilities.

The first thing that should be checked is the basic connectivity. Ensure that the system is physically still connected to the network. For a thin-net or coax cable Ethernet network, check that the tee connector is firmly attached to the coax connector of the system's network interface card. For a 10BaseT Ethernet, token ring, or FDDI network, make sure that the connectors on each end of the system's cable run are properly attached to the system and to the network hub or concentrator. Some network interface cards provide a "link" light, frequently green in color, that glows when there is solid network connectivity.

Assuming that the physical connectivity is fine, the next place to investigate is the network configuration on the affected system. The four utilities described below are listed in a recommended order of use. Each has a specific purpose and is used in a troubleshooting situation to either confirm or deny that a particular process or system is part of the problem.

8.9.1. ifconfig

Normally, the ifconfig(8) utility is used by the system at startup to configure and activate network interfaces. However, ifconfig is handy for quickly displaying a system's interface configuration. The three most pertinent pieces of information for each network interface are:

- Interface State (Up or Down)
- IP Address
- Subnet Mask

Simply run the following command to display the information about all the network interfaces on a system:

```
# /usr/sbin/ifconfig -a
tu0:
  flags=c63<UP,BROADCAST,NOTRAILERS,RUNNING,MULTICAST,SIMPLEX>
  inet 192.168.171.78 netmask ffffff00 broadcast 192.168.171.255
  ipmtu 1500

lo0:
  flags=100c89<UP,LOOPBACK,NOARP,MULTICAST,SIMPLEX,NOCHECKSUM>
  inet 127.0.0.1 netmask ff000000 ipmtu 4096
```

In this example, there are two interfaces, an Ethernet interface (tu0) and the loopback interface (lo0). Each interface's status is listed as the first field in the "flags=" string. In both of these cases, the status is "UP." The absence of the string "UP" indicates that the interface is down. An interface must be up, otherwise the system does not transmit messages through that interface. If the interface is not up, the following command (using tu0 as an example) will activate the interface:

```
# ifconfig tu0 up
```

The second line of each interface's ifconfig output lists the IP address (inet), the subnet mask (netmask) and the maximum transfer unit value (ipmtu). While the IP address is displayed in a dotted decimal format, the subnet mask is displayed as a hexadecimal value that must be converted to decimal. Ensure that the IP address and subnet mask displayed reflect the correct address information for each interface. If the incorrect IP address and/or subnet mask are shown, reconfigure the interface via the netstat(8) or netconfig(8X) command and restart the networking services.

8.9.2. netstat

Once the network interface(s) have been confirmed as correctly configured, the next item to examine is the routing table. The netstat command is primarily a tool to display network statistics; however, it also can be used to display a system's routing table:

```
# /usr/sbin/netstat -nr
Routing tables
Destination    Gateway    Flags    Refs    Use    Interface
Netmasks:
Inet          255.255.255.0

Route Tree for Protocol Family 2:
default        192.168.171.254   UGS   0   32551   tu0
127.0.0.1      127.0.0.1         UH    3   955     lo0
192.168.171/24 192.168.171.78    U     4   19110   tu0
```

If the system is on a network that requires a gateway to reach other networks, ensure that the proper gateway(s) are listed in the routing table.

Also make sure that there is an entry for the loopback route and any specific static routes that should exist. If the system is using dynamic routing (routed or gated), check that the routes listed are correct. If the routing table is incomplete or has incorrect entries, check that the /etc/routes file contains the correct static routes or, if using dynamic routing, verify the configuration of the routing daemon in use. The following describes the route flags displayed in the netstat output:

- U Up, or available.
- G This route is to a gateway
- H This route is to a host
- S This is a static route that was created by the route command

8.9.3. ping

The next step is to check some network connectivity. The tool for this purpose is ping(1). The ping command is used to send one or more ICMP (Internet Control Message Protocol) ECHO_REQUEST packets to a specific host, which should respond back to the pinging host with a matching ICMP ECHO_RESPONSE packet.

To use the ping command, specify the host target name or IP address as a command line argument. Another common flag is "-c" for "count" to specify the number of ICMP packets to send before terminating. If the "-c" argument is omitted, the ping command continuously sends packets until interrupted with Ctrl-C. For example, the following example sends five ICMP packets to the host jupiter and displays the results of each ping, followed by a summary of the entire sequence:

```
# /usr/sbin/ping -c 5 jupiter
PING jupiter (192.168.171.80): 56 data bytes
64 bytes from 192.168.171.80: icmp_seq=0 ttl=128 time=2 ms
64 bytes from 192.168.171.80: icmp_seq=1 ttl=128 time=0 ms
64 bytes from 192.168.171.80: icmp_seq=2 ttl=128 time=0 ms
64 bytes from 192.168.171.80: icmp_seq=3 ttl=128 time=0 ms
64 bytes from 192.168.171.80: icmp_seq=4 ttl=128 time=0 ms

—jupiter PING Statistics—
5 packets transmitted, 5 packets received, 0% packet loss
round-trip (ms) min/avg/max = 0/0/2 ms
```

In this example, connectivity between the pinging host and jupiter is fine. This can be determined both by the low round-trip times of each ping (<=2ms) and that there was 0% packet loss, that is, all five packets successfully reached the destination (jupiter) and returned.

To show the results of a ping where there is a connectivity problem, consider this similar example to a different host:

```
# /usr/sbin/ping -c 5 192.168.171.81
PING 192.168.171.81 (192.168.171.81): 56 data bytes

—192.168.171.81 PING Statistics—
5 packets transmitted, 0 packets received, 100% packet loss
```

This ping demonstrates the outcome when the pinging system does not receive the ECHO_RESPONSE packets from the remote host. One thing to be aware of is that a ping resulting in 100% packet loss could mean one of several things. The ECHO_REQUEST packets may never have reached their destination, or possibly the ECHO_REQUEST packets did reach the destination, but the ECHO_RESPONSE packets were not able to successfully return. Another possibility is that the network between the source and destination are fine, and the destination host is simply down or unavailable.

Note that this example used an IP address rather than a host name on the ping command line. One recommendation is to always use specific IP addresses rather than host names when troubleshooting using the ping command, to ensure that there is no ambiguity about which host is the target of the ping. However, even if a host name is specified, the ping output displays the resolved IP address.

The best strategy to use when attempting to isolate a network connectivity problem is to ping first the local interface on the system to ensure that a system's own interface is up and running. Next, attempt to ping hosts and gateways further away to try to identify where the fault lies. The most complete picture of a network fault is best drawn through a combination of pings and the output of the next utility, traceroute.

8.9.4. traceroute

While the ping command will indicate a loss of basic connectivity between two systems, its output cannot identify where the connectivity may be breaking down. For this, the traceroute(8) is used. Except for very simple connections, the route between two systems may be through a variety of routers, gateways, or hosts. Any one of the nodes along the path may in fact be the issue. The traceroute command displays the route that network packets travel to reach a remote system. If one of the intermediate stops along the way is down or otherwise not forwarding packets further downstream, it is immediately obvious from the traceroute output.

The traceroute command is run specifying the target destination on the command line. For example, the following is a successful traceroute to the Digital Website:

```
# /usr/sbin/traceroute www.digital.com
traceroute to www.digital.com (192.208.46.158), 30 hops max, 40
byte packets
 1 903.Hssi9-0-0.GW1.DEN1.ALTER.NET (157.130.162.57) 6.3 ms 6.9
ms ˮ.4 ms
 2 125.Hssi4-0.CR2.KCY1.Alter.Net (137.39.59.214) 30.8 ms 37.5
ms 31.8 ms
 3 126.ATM10-0-0.CR2.EWR1.Alter.Net (137.39.59.89) 68.5 ms 168.3
ms 66.1 ms
 4 112.ATM10-0-0.XR2.EWR1.ALTER.NET (146.188.176.22) 70.9 ms
70.7 ms 66.9 ms
 5 192.ATM11-0-0.XR2.BOS1.ALTER.NET (146.188.176.158) 109.5 ms
111.3 ms 82.8 ms
 6 190.ATM5-0-0.SR1.BOS1.ALTER.NET (146.188.177.13) 73.0 ms 73.3
ms 74.6 ms
 7 boston1-br2.bbnplanet.net (4.0.2.73) 74.1 ms 77.7 ms 77.8 ms
 8 cambridge2-br1.bbnplanet.net (4.0.1.186) 82.1 ms 84.4 ms 81.1
ms
 9 cambridge2-cr3.bbnplanet.net (192.233.33.10) 73.7 ms 76.2 ms
73.8 ms
10 dec.bbnplanet.net (131.192.95.2) 107.0 ms 79.0 ms 78.5 ms
11 199.93.199.4 (199.93.199.4) 78.5 ms 77.0 ms 78.8 ms
12 www.digital.com (192.208.46.158) 87.1 ms 82.6 ms 88.9 ms
```

This example indicates that the distance from the source to the destination is twelve steps or hops. For each gateway, the traceroute command launches three small probe packets and listens for a specific response from the gateway. Each line in the traceroute output shows the gateway's IP address (and host name, if the name can be resolved) and the round-trip time for each of the three probe packets.

Below is an example of a traceroute sequence to a host that the ping command indicates is unreachable. As this output shows, the packets do not even reach the destination system, which may be working perfectly fine. If the traceroute command does not receive a response from the next gateway within a three-second time-out interval, an asterisk (*) is printed for that probe.

```
$ /usr/sbin/traceroute jupiter.somedomain.com
traceroute to jupiter.somedomain.com (192.168.171.80), 30 hops
max, 40 byte packets
 1 903.Hssi9-0-0.GW1.DEN1.ALTER.NET (157.130.162.57) 6.3 ms 6.9
ms 7.4 ms
 2 125.Hssi4-0.CR2.KCY1.Alter.Net (137.39.59.214) 30.8 ms 37.5
ms 31.8 ms
 3 126.ATM10-0-0.CR2.EWR1.Alter.Net (137.39.59.89) 68.5 ms 168.3
ms 66.1 ms
 4 112.ATM10-0-0.XR2.EWR1.ALTER.NET (146.188.176.22) 70.9 ms
70.7 ms 66.9 ms
 5 192.ATM11-0-0.XR2.BOS1.ALTER.NET (146.188.176.158) 109.5 ms
111.3 ms 82.8 ms
 6 190.ATM5-0-0.SR1.BOS1.ALTER.NET (146.188.177.13) 73.0 ms 73.3
ms 74.6 ms
 7 * * *
 8 * * *
 .
 .
 .
30 * * *
```

By default, traceroute shows a maximum of only thirty hops and so, unless interrupted with Ctrl-C, traceroute will stop after thirty probes. The number of hops can be adjusted by specifying a value with the "-m" command line flag. In the preceding example, the problem appears to actually be between the source and destination hosts. If you have control over the entire network path, the next step is to identity which gateway is not responding and why. If, as in this case, the nonresponsive gateway is somewhere out on the Internet, the next course of action is to attempt to locate the responsible party and notify them of an apparent issue.

As you may well understand, being familiar with the "normal" output of these tools on a system properly connected and configured can be helpful in identifying problems. Experiment and explore these troubleshooting tools to become comfortable with their switches, options, and output. Refer to their man pages for more information.

8.10. DOMAIN NAME SYSTEM (DNS)

The main reason UNIX systems have host names is to provide a convenient name for use by people. An IP address is simply not an easily remembered identifier, and the future of IP promises even longer IP addresses. However, the TCP/IP software cannot use a host name directly. As discussed earlier, the networking software must convert, or resolve, a host name to an IP address to initiate communication. The simplest mechanism for providing this host name to IP address correlation is the /etc/hosts file, which is a text file listing IP addresses and their corresponding host name(s). The sole use of hosts files may be appropriate for small networks with a limited number of systems. However, as the size of a network grows, or even more pertinent, if a network is connected to the Internet, it becomes unfeasible to include every possible host in the /etc/hosts file. Considering that the Internet is many millions of systems, the lack of scalability of the /etc/hosts file is apparent. The answer to this need is the Domain Name System or DNS.

DNS is a distributed host-name-to-IP and vice versa database that is used as the primary host name resolution environment by most networked systems. The Digital UNIX stock DNS is an implementation of the Berkeley Internet Name Domain (BIND). Knowing this is probably not relevant, since most DNS implementations on the Internet are also based on BIND. A system running BIND can be configured to be a primary server, a secondary server, a slave server, a caching server, or simply as a client.

It is beyond the scope of this text to detail the configuration of the different types of DNS servers. Refer to one of the recommended references on TCP/IP networking and DNS in Appendix B for further information on configuring this complex network facility.

8.11. FILE TRANSFER PROTOCOL

The File Transfer Protocol (FTP) is a mechanism for transferring files between computers across a network. FTP was designed to support straightforward file transfers between different computer system types. For instance, there are FTP clients available for MS-DOS, Microsoft Windows, Digital's OpenVMS, IBM mainframes, and just about any other type of computer in addition to every flavor of UNIX. When transferring files, FTP can also do translations between different types of systems. For example, FTP can convert a text file to the appropriate format while transferring it between a Digital UNIX system and an MS-DOS system.

In this section, I will cover the configuration of FTP on Digital UNIX, including the FTP client and server. By default, FTP is enabled on a Digital UNIX system, but understanding what configuration options are available is important to managing this facility. In addition, a special variant of FTP, Anonymous FTP, will be discussed. Anonymous FTP, which allows FTP access to a system without user authentication, will be covered.

The ftp(1) command is the Digital UNIX interface to the File Transfer Protocol. This command is a character-cell utility for connecting to remote systems and transferring files. For its simplest form, specify the remote system's name on the FTP command line. An FTP log-in to the remote system will be attempted and, if successful, you will be prompted for a user name and password on the remote system. For example:

```
# ftp saturn
Connected to saturn.
220 saturn FTP server (Digital UNIX Version 5.60)
ready.
Name (saturn:root): jsmith
331 Password required for jsmith.
Password:
230 User jsmith logged in.
Remote system type is UNIX.
Using binary mode to transfer files.
ftp>
```

This example demonstrates a successful log-in to the remote system saturn. The ftp> prompt is then displayed indicating that FTP commands may now be entered. These commands include moving around the remote and local directory hierarchy, listing the contents of subdirectories, and getting and putting files to and from the remote system. For example, the following example resumes where the previous example left off, and it demonstrates changing to a particular directory on the remote system and downloading a specific file:

```
ftp> pwd
257 "/" is current directory.
ftp> cd /pub/data
250 CWD command successful.
ftp> ls -l
150 Opening ASCII mode data connection for /bin/ls
(10.0.0.1,1030).
total 3
-rw-r-r-  1 root    system    1019 Jan 6 12:08 file1
-rw-r-r-  1 root    system    1201 Jan 6 13:54 file2
-rw-r-r-  1 root    system    3772 Jan 6 13:58 file3
226 Transfer complete.
ftp> get file1
200 PORT command successful.
150 Opening BINARY mode data connection for file1
(10.0.0.1,1031) (1019 bytes).
226 Transfer complete.
1019 bytes received in 0.0029 seconds (3.4e+02
Kbytes/s)
ftp> bye
221 Goodbye.
#
```

Such an FTP dialog is actually carried out by two pieces, the client ftp(1) utility on the local system and an FTP server daemon on the remote system. This FTP server, ftpd(8), is only invoked when an incoming FTP connection is detected by inetd(8), the system's network server. One ftpd process is started for each inbound FTP connection and exists only for the duration of that particular FTP session.

The ftpd program has two types of configuration options available to the system administrator:

- Debugging and logging switches
- Security and authentication options

The default values of these options, which will be outlined, are usually sufficient for most situations and configurations. However, when troubleshooting problems or looking to increase security, the FTP server does provide this additional configurability. These options are specified and maintained in several configuration files.

8.11.1. FTP Debugging and Logging

By default, the Digital UNIX FTP server, ftpd(8), does not do any logging of
FTP connections or file transfers. If additional information about incoming
FTP connections is needed, either for the purpose of debugging problems
or as a historical record of connections and file transfers, there are two ftpd
command line switches that each instruct ftpd to log additional information
via the system logger facility (syslog).

The first of these switches is –d, which provides debugging and output
detailing inbound FTP connections. The information logged by ftpd
includes the date and time of the FTP connection, which user account was
used to log in, whether the log-in was successful or not, and an indication of
which commands were issued during the session. Here is an example log of
a simple FTP log-in and file transfer session:

```
Jan 14 12:33:47 saturn ftpd[824]: <-- 220 saturn FTP server (Digital
UNIX Version 5.60) ready.
Jan 14 12:33:48 saturn ftpd[824]: command: USER root
Jan 14 12:33:48 saturn ftpd[824]: <-- 331 Password required for root.
Jan 14 12:33:52 saturn ftpd[824]: command: PASS XXXX
Jan 14 12:33:52 saturn ftpd[824]: <-- 230 User root logged in.
Jan 14 12:33:52 saturn ftpd[824]: command: SYST
Jan 14 12:33:52 saturn ftpd[824]: <-- 215 UNIX Type: L8 Version:
Digital UNIX V4.0 (Rev.  878)
Jan 14 12:33:54 saturn ftpd[824]: command: CWD /pub/data
Jan 14 12:33:54 saturn ftpd[824]: <-- 250 CWD command successful.
Jan 14 12:33:57 saturn ftpd[824]: command: TYPE I
Jan 14 12:33:57 saturn ftpd[824]: <-- 200 Type set to I.
Jan 14 12:33:57 saturn ftpd[824]: command: PORT 10,0,0,1,4,13
Jan 14 12:33:57 saturn ftpd[824]: <-- 200 PORT command successful.
Jan 14 12:33:57 saturn ftpd[824]: command: RETR file1
Jan 14 12:33:57 saturn ftpd[824]: <-- 150 Opening BINARY mode data
connection for file1 (10.0.0.1,1037) (1019 bytes).
Jan 14 12:33:57 saturn ftpd[824]: <-- 226 Transfer complete.
Jan 14 12:33:59 saturn ftpd[824]: command: QUIT
Jan 14 12:33:59 saturn ftpd[824]: <-- 221 Goodbye.
```

Note that the actual commands the user typed at the ftp> prompt are
not listed; instead, the FTP requests themselves are displayed. For instance,
while the user typed "get file1", the log displays "command: RETR file1".

This may require some amount of interpretation in order to determine what exactly the user did during the FTP session. Refer to the man page for ftpd(8) for a list of FTP server requests supported by the Digital UNIX FTP server.

The second FTP server command line switch is –l, which simply logs each FTP session's log-in success and failures along with file transfer operations. The output of the –l log is fairly sparse, but may be sufficient if all that is desired is a record of log-ins and file transfers. For example, this log is a record of the exact same operation logged in the previous example:

```
Jan 14 12:34:53 saturn ftpd[833]: connection from saturn at Wed Jan
14 12:34:531998
Jan 14 12:34:57 saturn ftpd[833]: FTP LOGIN FROM saturn, root
Jan 14 12:35:04 saturn ftpd[833]: retrieve /pub/data/file1
succeeded, 1019 bytes.
Jan 14 12:35:05 saturn ftpd[833]: FTP LOGOUT, root
```

Finally, each of these two FTP server switches can be specified together (-dl) to generate the absolute maximum amount of log output. If both switches are used, the log generated is simply the combination of the output produced by each of the individual switches; that is, no additional information is generated. As this produces the greatest volume of log data, use the –dl switch combination sparingly on a system with high FTP activity to avoid filling the file system where the log resides, typically /var. Below is an example of an FTP connection and file transfer logged with the –dl switch combination:

```
Jan 14 12:35:38 saturn ftpd[841]: connection from saturn at Wed Jan
14 12:35:381998
Jan 14 12:35:38 saturn ftpd[841]: <-- 220 saturn FTP server
(Digital UNIX Version 5.60) ready.
Jan 14 12:35:39 saturn ftpd[841]: command: USER root
Jan 14 12:35:39 saturn ftpd[841]: <-- 331 Password required for root.
Jan 14 12:35:42 saturn ftpd[841]: command: PASS XXXX
Jan 14 12:35:42 saturn ftpd[841]: <-- 230 User root logged in.
Jan 14 12:35:42 saturn ftpd[841]: FTP LOGIN FROM saturn, root
Jan 14 12:35:42 saturn ftpd[841]: command: SYST
Jan 14 12:35:42 saturn ftpd[841]: <-- 215 UNIX Type: L8 Version:
Digital UNIX V4.0 (Rev. 878)
Jan 14 12:35:47 saturn ftpd[841]: command: CWD /pub/data
```

```
Jan 14 12:35:47 saturn ftpd[841]: <-- 250 CWD command successful.
Jan 14 12:35:51 saturn ftpd[841]: command: TYPE I
Jan 14 12:35:51 saturn ftpd[841]: <-- 200 Type set to I.
Jan 14 12:35:51 saturn ftpd[841]: command: PORT 10,0,0,1,4,21
Jan 14 12:35:51 saturn ftpd[841]: <-- 200 PORT command successful.
Jan 14 12:35:51 saturn ftpd[841]: command: RETR file1
Jan 14 12:35:51 saturn ftpd[841]: <-- 150 Opening BINARY mode data
connection for file1 (10.0.0.1,1045) (1019 bytes).
Jan 14 12:35:51 saturn ftpd[841]: <-- 226 Transfer complete.
Jan 14 12:35:51 saturn ftpd[841]: retrieve /pub/data/file1
succeeded, 1019 bytes.
Jan 14 12:35:52 saturn ftpd[841]: command: QUIT
Jan 14 12:35:52 saturn ftpd[841]: <-- 221 Goodbye.
Jan 14 12:35:52 saturn ftpd[841]: FTP LOGOUT, root
```

By default, this FTP server log information is placed in the file daemon.
log in a date-stamped directory under the /var/adm/syslog.dated directory.
For instance the previous ftpd log output was copied from the following file:

```
/var/adm/syslog.dated/14-Jan-04:02/daemon.log
```

See the section on the syslog daemon in Chapter 11 for details on the
/var/adm/syslog.dated facility.

Since the FTP server is actually started by the inetd(8) process, it is
necessary to edit the inetd configuration file, /etc/inetd.conf, to specify
command line switches to ftpd(8). After any changes to /etc/inetd.conf,
simply send the inetd process a hang-up signal to force the inetd to reread
its configuration file. For example, to run ftpd with the –dl switch combination, follow these steps:

1. Edit /etc/inetd.conf
2. Locate the entry in /etc/inetd.conf for ftpd. By default, the line is
   similar to:

```
ftp stream tcp  nowait root  /usr/sbin/ftpd    ftpd
```

3. Add the desired command line argument(s) to the end of the line.
   For example:

```
ftp stream tcp  nowait root  /usr/sbin/ftpd    ftpd -dl
```

4. Save the file and exit the editor.

5. Signal inetd(8) to reread the /etc/inetd.conf file to cause the updates to take effect:

```
# kill -HUP `cat /var/run/inetd.pid`
```

All future FTP connections will then be logged as specified by the ftpd command line arguments in the /etc/inetd.conf file. To change the logging or stop FTP logging altogether, edit /etc/inetd.conf and modify or remove any ftpd command line arguments and signal inetd(8) to reread the configuration file.

8.11.2. FTP Security Configuration

The Digital UNIX FTP server, ftpd(8), has the ability to deny access to particular user accounts based on the contents of two configuration files. The first, /etc/ftpusers, is checked by the FTP server when a user attempts to log in via FTP. If the account name is listed in /etc/ftpusers, that user is not permitted to log in. In addition, the FTP server verifies that the log-in shell specified in the seventh field of the /etc/passwd file is listed in the /etc/shells file. When troubleshooting a problem where a user is unable to log in to a system via FTP, ensure that the user's account name is not listed in /etc/ftpusers and the user account's log-in shell is contained in /etc/shells. See section 5.4., "Log-in Controls" in Chapter 5, "Security," for details on the format of these two ftpd configuration files.

8.11.3. Anonymous FTP Configuration

A special FTP server configuration that is commonly used on the Internet as a means of allowing the public to download and upload files is called Anonymous FTP. This configuration does not require an individual account, but rather allows anyone to log in via FTP using a commonly known user account, typically "anonymous" or "ftp." A password is prompted for, but the convention is for the user logging in to specify his or her E-mail address, though this convention is not enforced with the Digital UNIX FTP server. Because Anonymous FTP allows FTP connections without any authentication, it is critical that Anonymous FTP is configured properly to avoid compromising the security of your system, especially if the system is accessible via the Internet. Following are the minimal steps necessary to securely configure Anonymous FTP on a Digital UNIX system.

1. Create an "ftp" user account specifying an appropriate home directory, such as /var/ftp. Note that the remaining steps assume /var/ftp. If another location was selected, substitute that home directory in the following commands.

2. Create several subdirectories in the ftp home directory:

```
# mkdir /var/ftp/bin
# mkdir /var/ftp/etc
# mkdir /var/ftp/pub
```

3. Change the ownership and permissions of the ftp home and subdirectories:

```
# chown root:system /var/ftp
# chown root:system /var/ftp/bin
# chown root:system /var/ftp/etc
# chown ftp /var/ftp/pub
# chmod 755 /var/ftp
# chmod 755 /var/ftp/bin
# chmod 755 /var/ftp/etc
# chmod 777 /var/ftp/pub
```

4. Copy the statically linked ls(1) executable from /sbin into the ftp $HOME/bin subdirectory:

```
# cp /sbin/ls /var/ftp/bin
# chown bin:bin /var/ftp/bin/ls
# chmod 111 /var/ftp/bin/ls
```

This step is necessary to provide the ls(1) command to anonymous FTP users. Ensure that you copy /sbin/ls, which is statically linked, rather than the dynamically linked /usr/bin/ls executable.

5. Create minimal passwd(4) and group(4) files in the ftp $HOME/ etc subdirectory:

```
# cp /etc/passwd /var/ftp/etc
# cp /etc/group /var/ftp/etc
# chmod 444 /var/ftp/etc/passwd
# chmod 444 /var/ftp/etc/group
```

```
root:*:0:1:system PRIVILEGED account:/:/bin/sh
bin:*:3:4:system librarian account:/bin:
ftp:*:1001:15:ftp Account:/var/ftp:/bin/sh
```

Figure 8.9 Example of an anonymous FTP passwd(4) file

```
system:*:0:root
bin:*:4:bin
users:*:15:bin
```

Figure 8.10 Example of an anonymous FTP group(4) file

Edit these new files to remove all unnecessary entries. The password field in the passwd file is not used and should not contain real encrypted passwords. Replace any encrypted password strings with an asterisk (*). See Figures 8.9 and 8.10 for sample passwd(4) and group(4) files suitable for anonymous FTP.

6. Copy the Digital UNIX SIA (Security Integration Architecture) subdirectory into the ftp $HOME/etc subdirectory:

```
# cp -R /etc/sia /var/ftp/etc/sia
```

Steps 5 and 6 are necessary to allow the ls(1) command to be able to display file owner and group names rather than user and group ID numbers.

Once Anonymous FTP has been set up, test the configuration by attempting to log in to the system anonymously. Specify either anonymous or ftp as the log-in name. The following example demonstrates a successful anonymous FTP log-in:

```
# ftp saturn
Connected to saturn.
220 saturn FTP server (Digital UNIX Version 5.60) ready.
```

```
Name (saturn:root): ftp
331 Guest login ok, send ident as password.
Password:
230 Guest login ok, access restrictions apply.
Remote system type is UNIX.
Using binary mode to transfer files.
ftp> dir
200 PORT command successful.
150 Opening ASCII mode data connection for /bin/ls
(10.0.0.1,1046).
total 24
drwxr-xr-x  2 root    system    8192 Mar 15 14:21 bin
drwxr-xr-x  3 root    system    8192 Mar 25 18:53 etc
drwxrwxrwx  2 ftp     users     8192 Mar 15 14:22 pub
226 Transfer complete.
ftp>
```

Performance Monitoring and Tuning

9

9.1. OVERVIEW

The performance of a UNIX system is best defined as the ability of the system to accomplish a given task or set of tasks. Good performance is a slippery target that depends on a great many variables, including user perception, performance indexes, and available system resources. A system administrator is frequently called upon to evaluate and improve the performance of a system; the ability to do so to the satisfaction of the user community can be a challenging task. In this chapter, I will discuss the performance indexes available to you in quantifying system performance, define the four primary system resource categories that effect UNIX system performance and the tools to measure the performance indexes of these categories, and provide strategies for translating user complaints into basic and objective information useful for evaluating performance problems.

Once the performance of a system has been quantified and performance problems have been identified, the next step is tuning. Tuning is the process of adjusting the system configuration to compensate for an identified performance bottleneck. Following the discussion of performance indexes and system monitoring, I will outline a tuning methodology that aims for the best average performance over time.

9.2. PERFORMANCE MANAGEMENT

Performance management is an ongoing process of continued system monitoring and configuration adjustments to maintain an acceptable level of performance. In order to successfully manage performance, a system administrator must understand:

- Performance Indexes
- System Resources and their Performance Characteristics
- Performance Management Strategies

9.3. PERFORMANCE INDEXES

There are a variety of factors that affect the performance of a Digital UNIX system, and frequently these factors are nontechnical and beyond the ability of a system administrator to change. Understanding the nature of these indexes is the first step in being able to effectively manager the performance of a UNIX system.

Perhaps the most important factor is understanding your system environment and workload. Simply put, it is difficult to identify abnormalities without knowing what is normal. This understanding is gained over time by monitoring a system to determine its average throughput and behavior. Knowing a system's typical workload also allows an administrator to see trends in system activity over time and to predict the effects of changes to the system, applications, or usage patterns.

Regardless of whether a system administrator has been involved with a particular system from its inception, was part of a system's design, system installation and configuration, and early use, or simply inherited an existing system that has been running for months or years, an administrator should spend some time with the system in order to be able to answer system characterization questions such as:

- What is(are) the type of application(s) running on the system?
  - Database
  - Development

- Graphics
- World Wide Web (WWW) or other network service
- What is the average number of users on the system at each time of day?
- What are the busiest times of operation?
- Which jobs run at which times of the day?
- What are the known resource-intensive jobs?
- What is the average response time for various times of the day?

(Note: Response Time is defined as the time interval between entering a command to an interactive system and the appearance of the response.)

The answers to some of these questions are learned by being logged onto the system and monitoring its behavior. Digital UNIX provides tools and utilities that provide a way to view the usage of the various system resources. In the next section (9.4.), "System Resources," I cover the usage of these tools and the interpretation of their output. Over time, a system administrator will come to understand what is "normal" for a given system. Normal, of course, is a relative term and assumes that the workload does not change. For example, a system that supports an organization's financial activity may seem quite speedy during the month, but around the end of the month, may become nearly unusable as the system is under stress to complete the month-end close-out. In this case, both situations are normal as long as it is understood what the system is being asked to do and when. If, however, the system's response time were to increase dramatically in the middle of a month, this behavior would probably be abnormal and worthy of investigation.

Other of the above characterization questions are best answered by working closely with the user community and understanding their needs and perceptions. Users tend to accept an average response time as normal, and jobs are expected to complete in the same amount of time every time they are run. These expectations are sometimes invalid, but exist nevertheless. In addition, you may discover that a user's perception of reduced response times or increased execution times may be factors outside of your control. For example, a user may be connected to the system via a slower connection resulting in a slower response just to that user's terminal. The system may be running well in the range of acceptability but may "seem" slower to that user. Keep in mind that the purpose of the system is for the completion of productive work regardless of system irregularities, and you will be called upon to evaluate the inevitable user complaints.

A Digital UNIX system administrator has to develop the skills to interpret user complaints. One of the most important of such skills is patience. You will occasionally receive feedback that "the system seems slow." Work with the user(s) to quantify their perceptions by enlisting their help in collecting the basic information you will need:

- What is the user's measured response/execution time versus normal?
- Determine if reported "hung" processes are truly hung.
- Did the problem occur suddenly or did it degrade over time?
- Is this the first time this behavior has been experienced?
- Can the problem be duplicated?
- How many and which users were on the system at the time of the problem?
- Is the problem program on the local system or a remote system?

Going through this process with users will help educate them and hopefully impress upon them the importance of collecting useful data rather then just yelling that the system seems slow.

9.4. SYSTEM RESOURCES

A Digital UNIX system can seem like a complex environment with many variables that impact performance. A system administrator may initially feel overwhelmed when first presented with a performance problem. In reality, though, there are only four categories of system resources, and all performance issues are related to the availability—or lack—of:

- CPU
- Memory
- Input/Output (I/O)
- Network

Once an administrator understands these four resources and how to view their usage, it is often an easy task to identify which resource is insufficient and is a bottleneck to the timely completion of work. After describing the particulars of each resource, I will list the utilities available for characterizing the usage of the resource, and strategies for translating this usage information into conclusions on any performance issues.

9.4.1. The CPU Resource

The CPU capacity of a UNIX system is defined by the quantity, type, and speed of the processor. All Digital UNIX systems have one or more Alpha processors. The CPU is the resource that actually executes instructions and is frequently perceived by users to be the primary factor in specifying overall system speed. The speed of a given machine is a function of that system's CPU cycle time; the greater the clock speed of the process, the faster the CPU. However, doubling the clock speed of the Alpha chip in a system does not automatically double the overall speed of a system. There are a number of other factors that influence the speed with which individual instructions are executed on a given system, such as:

- Number of CPUs in the system
- Complexity of the instructions being executed
- Effectiveness of memory caches (see section 9.4.2., "The Memory Resource")

In addition, there is the issue of process scheduling and priority. A process with a higher priority will typically impact a process with a lower priority. Digital UNIX does favor interactive processes over compute-intensive processes by maintaining or raising the priorities of the interactive process. A system administrator must be able to monitor the CPU utilization and process scheduling status in order to understand and identify performance problems.

The CPU is always running in one of two modes, kernel mode or user mode, at any one time. Kernel mode (sometimes referred to as System Mode) is a privileged processor access mode that handles most operating system functions. For instance, handling hardware and software interrupts and processing system calls are done in kernel mode. User application processes, on the other hand, run in user mode, which is less privileged than kernel mode. If a user process makes a system call, however, the CPU mode switches to kernel mode to process the system call.

There is no rule of thumb regarding an acceptable ratio of CPU time spent in Kernel mode verses User mode. The distribution depends on a variety of factors including the type of application(s) running (database, graphics, development, networking, etc.), the number of system calls the application(s) make, and the state of the system (system health, number of users, etc.). It is, then, crucial that a system administrator have the experience to know what is "normal" for a given system.

9.4.1.1. Tuning CPU

CPU performance issues usually fall into one of the following three categories, each of which prevents user processes from being executed and completed in an acceptable time frame:

- The CPU is at capacity
- The CPU is busy doing things other than the desired task(s)
- The CPU is idle, waiting for other resources

9.4.1.1.1. CPU at Capacity

If the amount of work being demanded of the CPU in a given system exceeds the capacity of that CPU, the system's response time will increase as jobs queue up waiting for the CPU, which is working at 100% trying to keep up. In this instance, there are only two things to be done: purchase more CPU capacity, or demand less of the existing CPU resource. Assuming that buying more hardware is often not feasible, a system administrator must look at either reducing the priority of jobs or shifting the execution of computer-intensive jobs to other times when the CPU is not in such demand; the middle of the night or during the weekend, for instance.

9.4.1.1.2. CPU is Busy

The CPU may have high utilization and yet users may still see unacceptable response times. In this case, the CPU may be busy doing something other than the work the users are asking of it. Remember that the CPU's kernel mode is a higher priority mode then user mode, and certain events will pre-empt the execution of user processes, forcing the CPU to stop executing user code in favor of other work. One such event of particular interest to a system administrator is a hardware interrupt. If there exists a hardware problem on the system, the CPU will be notified via such an interrupt and be required to deal with the error. If repeated errors, such as disk or memory errors, are present, the CPU may be constantly interrupted and user work will suffer. If you suspect such a situation, examine the system error logs. Perhaps a perceived performance problem is actually a hardware problem.

9.4.1.1.3. CPU idle

Today's high-speed processors such as the Alpha in Digital UNIX systems are as speedy as ever and continue to get faster still. Memory and disk performance, though also always improving, continue to lag behind. If the jobs being run on a system require large amounts of memory or disk I/O, you may find the CPU sitting around doing nothing waiting for the I/O systems to catch up. Since the CPU is so much faster than the I/O on any UNIX system, there will always be some amount of CPU wait time. If, however, the CPU is idle 100% of the time during busy periods, there may a severe I/O bottleneck that needs to be examined. When investigating a high CPU idle percentage, always examine the disk load before assuming that the entire system is simply idle. In addition, the vmstat(1) command has an undocumented switch, -w, which displays the percentage of time the CPU is in an I/O wait condition.

9.4.2. The Memory Resource

There are several types of memory on a Digital UNIX system that differ in purpose, speed, capacity, and cost. A system administrator must understand the characteristics of each to identify and fix memory resource problems. The three types are:

- Real Memory (RAM)
- Virtual Memory
- Cache Memory

9.4.2.1. Real Memory

The primary and most familiar type of memory in a Digital UNIX system is composed of Random Access Memory chips, or RAM. This memory is typically what is meant when referring to the memory size of an individual system. For example, an Alphastation with 64 Megabytes of memory has 67,108,864 characters of storage. The total or Physical memory on a running Digital UNIX system will always contain the Digital console code, the Digital UNIX kernel, and the kernel's associated data structures. The memory remaining after system initialization loads these system resources is termed the Available Memory and is what is used when running user processes.

To determine the physical memory configuration on a Digital UNIX system, use the uerf(8) command to view the most recent boot message. See Figure 9.1 for a representative boot message and the fields of interest. Note that a fairly significant amount of real memory is occupied by the Digital

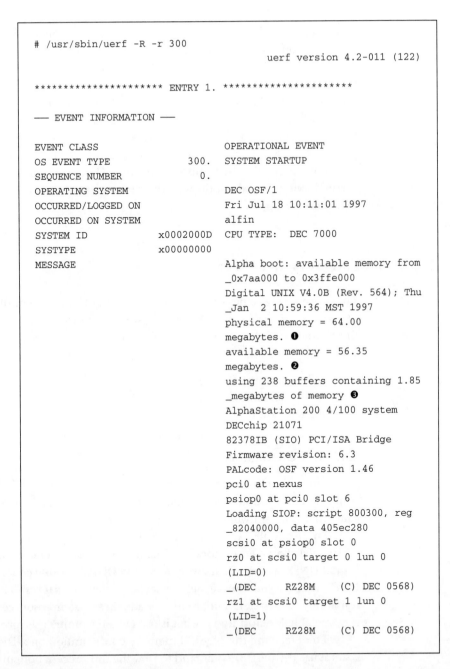

```
# /usr/sbin/uerf -R -r 300
                                              uerf version 4.2-011 (122)


********************** ENTRY 1. **********************

—— EVENT INFORMATION ——


EVENT CLASS                       OPERATIONAL EVENT
OS EVENT TYPE             300.    SYSTEM STARTUP
SEQUENCE NUMBER             0.
OPERATING SYSTEM                  DEC OSF/1
OCCURRED/LOGGED ON                Fri Jul 18 10:11:01 1997
OCCURRED ON SYSTEM                alfin
SYSTEM ID         x0002000D       CPU TYPE:  DEC 7000
SYSTYPE           x00000000
MESSAGE                           Alpha boot: available memory from
                                  _0x7aa000 to 0x3ffe000
                                  Digital UNIX V4.0B (Rev. 564); Thu
                                  _Jan  2 10:59:36 MST 1997
                                  physical memory = 64.00
                                  megabytes. ❶
                                  available memory = 56.35
                                  megabytes. ❷
                                  using 238 buffers containing 1.85
                                  _megabytes of memory ❸
                                  AlphaStation 200 4/100 system
                                  DECchip 21071
                                  82378IB (SIO) PCI/ISA Bridge
                                  Firmware revision: 6.3
                                  PALcode: OSF version 1.46
                                  pci0 at nexus
                                  psiop0 at pci0 slot 6
                                  Loading SIOP: script 800300, reg
                                  _82040000, data 405ec280
                                  scsi0 at psiop0 slot 0
                                  rz0 at scsi0 target 0 lun 0
                                  (LID=0)
                                  _(DEC      RZ28M     (C) DEC 0568)
                                  rz1 at scsi0 target 1 lun 0
                                  (LID=1)
                                  _(DEC      RZ28M     (C) DEC 0568)
```

Figure 9.1 Determining the Memory Configuration

```
                              rz4 at scsi0 target 4 lun 0 (LID=2)
                              _(DEC      RRD45    (C) DEC  1645)
                              isa0 at pci0
                              gpc0 at isa0
                              ace0 at isa0
                              ace1 at isa0
                              lp0 at isa0
                              fdi0 at isa0
                              fd0 at fdi0 unit 0
                              tu0: DECchip 21040-AA: Revision: 2.3
                              tu0 at pci0 slot 11
                              tu0: DEC TULIP Ethernet Interface,
                              _hardware address: 08-00-2B-E7-76-B2
                              tu0: console mode: selecting 10BaseT
                              _(UTP) port: half duplex
                              tga0 at pci0 slot 13
                              tga0: depth 8, map size 4MB, 1280x1024
                              tga0: ZLXp-E
                              kernel console: tga0
                              dli: configured

  ❶ Total physical memory installed in system
  ❷ Total available after loading kernel and associated data
    structures
  ❸ Size of the File System Cache (Traditional Buffer Cache)
```

Figure 9.1 Continued

UNIX kernel and associated data structures. The size of the kernel and these data structures are determined by which kernel options are selected when the kernel is built. To minimize the size of the kernel and, hence, the amount of physical memory occupied, only select the kernel options that are necessary or appropriate for a Digital UNIX system. See Chapter 3, "System Configuration," for guidelines in building a Digital UNIX kernel.

9.4.2.2. Virtual Memory

Digital UNIX supports a facility where the total addressable memory size is independent of the physical memory size. This ability, called virtual memory, allows a system to appear to have more physical memory than is actually installed. The basic unit of memory, virtual and physical, is the page. The virtual memory facility is managed by the Digital UNIX kernel by transparently moving pages between physical memory, where instructions can be run, and temporary holding areas on disks, known as swap files. The kernel basically plays a shell game with processes and data, moving idle objects to disk and recalling objects from disk back into physical memory when needed. There are two types of virtual memory operations that the operating system performs: paging and swapping.

9.4.2.2.1. Paging

Paging is moving a single page or a small group of pages of virtual memory between disk and physical memory. It is conceivable that a process's memory image is too large to fit into available physical memory and only part of the process can be resident at any one time. UNIX has the ability to execute such a process through the mechanism of paging. If the process references a location in virtual memory that is not currently resident, the process generates a *page fault,* which is a hardware interrupt that instructs the Digital UNIX memory manager to move the required page from disk to physical memory. In doing so, the memory manager may be required to move another page from physical memory to disk to make room. Some paging is a normal activity on a UNIX system, and the amount of pageins and pageouts is monitored via the vmstat(1) command. If pageins or pageouts are constant or excessive, this could indicate a physical memory shortage.

9.4.2.2.2. Swapping

The process of swapping is similar to paging in that virtual memory pages are moved between disk and physical memory. The primary difference is that instead of moving a single page as paging does, swapping moves all pages associated with a particular process between disk and memory. This operation on a process is known as a swapout and is initiated by the Digital UNIX memory manager for one of the following three reasons:

- A memory shortage so severe that the paging process cannot free memory fast enough
- The memory space becomes too fragmented to allow new or growing processes to allocate space
- Processes have been inactive for more than 20 seconds

Swapping is usually the result of insufficient physical memory on the system. Swapping is usually bad and should be avoided at all costs, due to the high performance cost of moving entire processes to and from disk. In extreme cases of memory shortages, a condition known as *thrashing* can occur. Thrashing is when the requested memory resources far exceeds the availability of physical memory, and the system spends more time performing memory related tasks such as paging and swapping than executing user application code. The name thrashing is derived from how the disks behave in this situation.

9.4.2.3. Cache Memory

Cache memory is a type of memory that typically resides between a slow resource, such as disks or network, and a fast resource, such as our speedy Alpha processor, and acts as a buffer. There are several types of caches that, though important and desirable, are not directly under the system administrator's control; that is, the sizing of these caches is not configurable. An example of these caches are the CPUs on-chip cache and disk controller hardware caches, such as those provided by the Digital StorageWorks Hierarchical Storage family of controllers (HSZ50, HSZ70, etc). The two cache memories that are configurable are:

- Traditional Buffer Cache (File System Metadata Cache)
- Unified Buffer Cache (UBC)

Each of these caches are composed of some percentage of physical memory that is configurable by the system administrator.

9.4.2.3.1. *Traditional Buffer Cache*

As users and processes access a Digital UNIX system's file systems, the file system metadata (directories, symbolic links, inodes, and blocks) is cached in the Traditional Buffer Cache. If every implied disk transfer really had to occur, a UNIX system would spend a great deal of time waiting for the completion of I/O. However, through the use of this traditional buffer cache, which contains recently used disk blocks, typically over 80% of all disk transfers will be satisfied from the contents of this cache, dramatically reducing necessary disk I/O.

By default, the size of the traditional buffer cache is 3% of physical memory. This is a reasonably sane default, except in special situations where such a value may incur unacceptably high physical memory usage. For example, an Alphastation workstation with 64 megabytes of memory will have a traditional buffer cache size of approximately 1.9 megabytes. However, on a system whose physical memory is 4 gigabytes, the cache size would be almost 123 megabytes, which is possibly excessive. Reducing the size of the cache on such a system to 2% (82 megabytes), or even 1% (41 megabytes) of physical memory is probably sufficient, plus the total available memory for user processes is increased.

Another variable to keep in mind when sizing the traditional buffer cache is that its purpose is caching file system metadata. If there are a small number of file systems on a system, for example, on a database server where the bulk of the disk space is accessed by the database management system in character (raw) mode, a smaller traditional buffer cache may be warranted, since the raw mode access bypasses all Digital UNIX I/O buffering.

The traditional buffer cache size is specified in the kernel configuration file by the bufcache keyword. For example, placing the following entry in the kernel configuration file, rebuilding the kernel, and booting from that new kernel would set the traditional buffer cache size to 2%:

```
bufcache   2
```

See Chapter 3, "System Configuration," for instructions on building a new kernel.

To determine if the traditional buffer cache is sized appropriately, examine the hit rate. The hit rate is the percentage of time the requested data is in the cache preventing a physical disk I/O. Use the dbx(8) debugger to examine the cache statistics (see Figure 9.2). A good hit rate is 97% or better. If the hit rate is below 97%, you may consider increasing the bufcache attribute to increase the size of the traditional buffer cache, thereby increasing its effectiveness.

9.4.2.3.2. *Unified Buffer Cache*

Digital UNIX utilizes a second type of cache called the Unified Buffer Cache (UBC), which is different in two ways from the Traditional Buffer Cache. Whereas the Traditional Buffer Cache caches file system metadata (for example, directories, symbolic links, inodes, and blocks), the UBC buffers file contents. In addition, the size of the UBC is dynamic, whereas the Traditional Buffer Cache is fixed at a certain percentage of physical memory. The UBC grows and shrinks in response to changing system demands and can potentially grow to utilize all physical memory. Heavy

```
# dbx -k /vmunix /dev/mem
dbx version 3.11.8
Type 'help' for help.

thread 0xfffffc00ffdce000 stopped at   [thread_run:2302
,0xfffffc0000432f04]
Source not available

warning: Files compiled -g3: parameter values probably wrong
(dbx) p bio_stats
struct {
  getblk_hits = 43847707 ❶
  getblk_misses = 104437 ❷
  getblk_research = 0
  getblk_dupbuf = 122
  getnewbuf_calls = 105800
  getnewbuf_buflocked = 0
  vflushbuf_lockskips = 7
  mntflushbuf_misses = 0
  mntinvalbuf_misses = 0
  vinvalbuf_misses = 0
  allocbuf_buflocked = 0
  ufssync_misses = 0
}
(dbx) quit
# bc
scale = 5
( 1 - ( 104437 / (104437 + 43848279) ) ) * 100 ❸
99.76300 ❹
#

❶ Total number of block misses
❷ Total number of block hits
❸ Subtract one from the number of block misses divided by the sum
of block misses and block hits to get hit percentage
❹ The Traditional Buffer Cache hit rate percentage
```

Figure 9.2 Calculating the Traditional Buffer Cache Hit Rate

file system activity will increase the number of physical memory pages reserved for the UBC, and heavy virtual memory demands, such as requirements to run large executable files, will reduce the number of pages reserved for the UBC, thereby reclaiming those pages back into the user memory space.

The upper and lower bounds of the UBC can be specified by the system administrator by setting two kernel attributes in the vm subsystem. These attributes are set in the kernel subsystem database (/etc/sysconfigtab). By default, the maximum percentage of physical memory that the UBC can grow to is 100%. The ubc-maxpercent attribute can be set to specify a different maximum value. Similarly, the ubc-minpercent attribute, which defaults to 10%, specifies the minimum percentage of physical memory that the UBC will shrink to when page reclamation occurs. Note that the ubc-minpercent value is not the minimum value that the UBC can be. Often, the UBC starts below the ubc-minpercent value, and it is possible for the UBC to never grow above this minimum value.

To determine the effectiveness of the Unified Buffer Cache, monitor the cache hit rate. This is the percentage of times the requested data was found in the buffer preventing a physical I/O to retrieve the data. This value can be calculated with the dbx(8) debugger (see Figure 9.3). A good hit rate is 95% or better. If the hit rate is below 90%, you may consider increasing the ubc-minpercent attribute to increase the minimum size of the UBC, thereby increasing its effectiveness.

9.4.2.4. Tuning Memory

Memory performance issues are typically either caused by an insufficiency in one or more of the three types of memory resources, or an inefficient use of existing memory resources. The former situation is addressed by either adding more of the required resource (RAM, cache, or swap space), or demanding less of the existing memory resource by shifting usage to off hours, and so on. The latter problem is where a system administrator can make adjustments. Several suggestions to focus on are:

- Kernel Configuration
- Traditional/Unified Buffer Cache Sizing
- Swap Space Configuration

9.4.2.4.1. Kernel Configuration

When a Digital UNIX kernel is built with the doconfig(8) command, the resulting /vmunix file size is determined by the kernel options selected from the doconfig (see Figure 9.4), or by specifying values for certain kernel parameters in the kernel configuration file. If the kernel contains inappropriate options, the resulting vmunix file could be unnecessarily large, con-

```
# dbx -k /vmunix /dev/mem
dbx version 3.11.8
Type 'help' for help.

thread 0xfffffc00ffdce000 stopped at   [thread_run:2302
,0xfffffc0000432f04]
Source not available

warning: Files compiled -g3: parameter values probably wrong
(dbx) p ufs_getapage_stats
struct {
  read_looks = 49678827 ❶
  read_hits = 48551227 ❷
  read_miss = 1128369
  alloc_error = 0
  alloc_in_cache = 0
}
(dbx) quit
# bc
scale = 5
( 48551227 / 49678827 ) * 100 ❸
97.73000 ❹
#

❶ Total number of read attempts
❷ Total number of read hits
❸ Divide total number of hits by total number of attempts to get
hit percentage
❹ The UBC cache hit rate percentage
```

Figure 9.3 Calculating the Unified Buffer Cache Hit Rate

suming valuable physical memory. To conserve RAM, only select the kernel options that apply for a particular system. Additionally, specifying unused or nonexistent devices or pseudo-devices such as network or disk interfaces, disks, or tapes, also increases the size of the kernel by linking additional code into the kernel. Remove any such extraneous devices from the kernel configuration file as well, and rebuild the kernel.

```
Selection   Kernel Option

    1       Asynchronous Transfer Mode (ATM)
    2       System V Devices
    3       Logical Volume Manager (LVM)
    4       Kernel Breakpoint Debugger (KDEBUG)
    5       Packetfilter driver (PACKETFILTER)
    6       Point-to-Point Protocol (PPP)
    7       STREAMS pckt module (PCKT)
    8       X/Open Transport Interface (XTISO, TIMOD, TIRDWR)
    9       File on File File System (FFM)
   10       ISO 9660 Compact Disc File System (CDFS)
   11       Audit Subsystem
   12       Logical Storage Manager (LSM)
   13       All of the above
   14       None of the above
   15       Help
```

Figure 9.4 doconfig(8) Kernel Options

In addition, certain kernel configuration file parameters, such as maxusers, which is used to size a variety of kernel tables and structures, should be set appropriately for a given system. The maxusers parameter is, by definition, the number of simultaneous users that your system can support without straining system resources. Setting maxusers higher than necessary also wastes physical memory. Determining an optimal value for maxusers can sometimes be difficult, but making an assessment of the projected use of the system can point you in the right direction. For instance, on a large server that will have several hundred interactive users, each running a large number of processes, it may make sense to set maxusers to 512 or higher. On the other hand, a small desktop workstation that will have only a single user running a handful of windows probably will be fine with a maxuser value of 32. Trying several values on a busy system may be necessary in order to select an appropriate setting.

9.4.2.4.2. Traditional/Unified Buffer Cache Sizing

The sizing of both the Traditional Buffer Cache and the Unified Buffer Cache on a Digital UNIX system is important in order to provide as much available memory to the user space while having adequate buffers to prevent I/O performance degradation. The Traditional Buffer Cache's default size of 3% of physical memory is sufficient for all but extreme situations, such as a system whose physical memory is greater than two gigabytes, in which case I recommend reducing the size to 2% of physical memory.

The Unified Buffer Cache (UBC), on the other hand, is dynamically sized and is controlled by specifying a high-water value (ubc-maxpercent) that is 100% of physical memory by default, and a low-water value (ubc-minpercent) that is 10% by default. If more real memory is needed to execute a system's processes and the system is not doing a great deal of I/O, you can reduce the amount of memory made available to the UBC by setting the ubc-maxpercent parameter to 50%. This prevents that UBC from growing beyond half of physical memory rather than taking the entire 100% if necessary. On systems doing a great deal of I/O, such as an NFS server or a development system, you may wish to increase the initial size of the UBC, thereby, one hopes, reducing I/O by providing a larger cache by raising the ubc-minpercent parameter above the default of 10% of physical memory. To determine if the ubc-minpercent value is set too high, causing a real memory shortage and resulting in higher paging activity, monitor the page-out rate using the vmstat(1) command.

9.4.2.4.3. Swap Space Configuration

There are several swap space configuration issues to focus on that impact virtual memory performance on a Digital UNIX system. The first of these is swap space size and layout. The total size of the swap area should be at least one times the size of a system's physical memory and two or more times physical memory if the system is running many large jobs simultaneously. Though there is no performance penalty for having more swap space than necessary, there will definitely be problems if there is not enough swap space. Large programs will be prevented from running if insufficient swap space is available.

For best performance, spread your swap space across multiple disk devices and, if possible, multiple disk controllers as well. Use the fastest disks available in a system when placing swap space. By having multiple smaller swap partitions, each on its own disk, rather than one large swap partition on a single disk, the system is able to stripe swap activity across multiple disks, thereby increasing performance. In order to provide the best swap space interleaving, as this striping is termed, activate all swap partitions at system bootup by placing them in the /etc/fstab file, as detailed in Chapter 3, "System Configuration." The swapon –s command displays the current swap space configuration and status. See section 9.7.4. for a usage example of the swapon(8) command.

The second swap space consideration is the Swap Space Allocation Mode. The swap space on a Digital UNIX system usage is determined by two allocated modes: *immediate mode* or *deferred mode.* These two modes differ in when swap space is allocated and result in different swap space requirements.

- Immediate mode causes a chunk of swap space to be allocated immediately after a process starts and is reserved for that process.
- Deferred mode delays the allocation of swap space until the system needs to write a memory page to swap space.

Digital UNIX's default swap allocation mode is immediate mode. This causes the operating system to reserve swap space for every process, which allocates memory via the malloc command. Immediate mode typically forces the system administrator to configure more swap space than is probably required.

Deferred mode, or Over-Commitment mode, on the other hand, delays the reservation of swap space to be postponed until the swap space is actually required for a pageout. Deferred mode requires less configured swap space and may cause the system to perform better, since less swap space overhead is required. However, since the swap space is not reserved until needed, the swap space may be unavailable when it is required and the operating system may terminate the process. Unfortunately, in deferred mode, the system will occasionally kill processes other than the one needing the swap space, and the system does not discriminate between system processes and user processes. You should ensure that you have configured sufficient swap space if you are going to run in deferred mode.

Immediate swap mode is used if the file /sbin/swapdefault exists. This file should be a symbolic link to the first defined swap device. If this file does not exist, the system is running in deferred mode. To change from one mode to the other, either remove or create the /sbin/swapdefault file and reboot the system. For example, the following sequence will convert a system running immediate swap mode to deferred mode:

```
# ls -l /sbin/swapdefault
lrwxr-xr-x  1 root    system    11 Apr 17 15:15
  /sbin/swapdefault -> ../dev/rz0b
# rm /sbin/swapdefault
# shutdown -r now
```

After running this system in deferred mode, the following commands will change back to immediate mode:

```
# ls -l /sbin/swapdefault
/sbin/swapdefault not found
# ln -s /dev/rz0b /sbin/swapdefault
# shutdown -r now
```

Generally, adding real memory to a system is the best way to increase performance of that system. However, a system administrator frequently does not have that luxury and has to work with what is available to increase memory performance.

9.4.3. I/O Resource

The I/O resource on a Digital UNIX system typically is related to the disk subsystem. Disk performance on a system is usually the greatest determining factor in that system's perceived overall performance. Modern CPUs, memory, and networks all have greater throughput than disks and, therefore, understanding disk I/O problems is key to configuring and tuning disk subsystems.

Systems with disk performance problems usually fall into one of two categories:

- Disk-bound systems
- Swap-bound systems

9.4.3.1. Disk-Bound System

A system is disk-bound if there is a large amount of disk traffic on one or more disk drives and the CPU is spending a great deal of time idle, waiting for disk I/Os to complete. If a system is disk-bound, there are two things to focus one's attention on: the physical disk layout, and the file system type and configuration on those disks. Both are important and go hand-in-hand, but, depending on a particular system, one may weigh more heavily than the other.

Since most disk performance problems are related to the physical disk configuration, it makes sense to start with the disk subsystem. There are a variety of strategies to investigate in order to increase disk throughput, and most attempt to avoid saturation of an individual disk, which should be avoided if at all possible.

- Use the fastest disks possible
- Spread disks across as many SCSI channels as possible
- Where possible, use many small disks rather than a few large disks
- Use disk controllers with hardware cache, such as Digital's HSZ family of controllers
- Use disk mirroring, either software such as the Logical Storage Manager (LSM), or hardware such as an HSZ controller.
- Balance disk load by distributing file systems across multiple disks/ controllers

The iostat(1) command is invaluable for determining if one or more disks on a system are saturated, or "hot." At a typical time during the workday, if one disk's transfer rate is significantly higher than that of the other disks, or worse, if one disk is supporting all I/O while the remaining disks are idle, this is indicative of an unbalanced disk subsystem. In this situation, the only remedy is to distribute the disk usage more evenly among all the disks or controllers. This may involve physically relocating disks between disk controllers, or moving file systems between disks to balance the usage.

This type of physical layout is especially crucial for a database system that uses raw space, rather then file systems, for data storage. A database server using raw devices bypasses the entire operating system buffering and caching system and, thus, depends more heavily on the efficiency of the distribution of disks.

Once the disk subsystem has been examined, the next area of focus is the file system configuration and layout. The two primary types of file systems supported by Digital UNIX are UFS and AdvFS, and each has its own unique tuning issues and strategies.

9.4.3.2. UFS

The UNIX File System (UFS) is the default file system on a Digital UNIX system, and this file system type is very common. There are a number of options and techniques available to a system administrator to tune a UFS file system. One or more of the following tips may suit your environment:

- Mirror file systems with Digital's Logical Storage Manager (LSM). Mirroring a file system can improve disk reads and increase availability, by the way. However, mirroring typically slows down write operations.
- Defragment file systems if necessary. Using the dbx(8) debugger, examine the ufs_clusterstats, ufs_clusterstats_read, and ufs_clusterstat_write structure, to determine whether a disk is fragmented. See Figure 9.3 for an example of examining a kernel structure. If the values in these UFS clustering structures show that clustering is not being effective, the disk may be fragmented.

  Digital UNIX does not currently provide an automated mechanism for defragmenting a UFS file system. However, it is possible to defragment a file system following this procedure:

  1. Back up the file system data to tape or another partition
  2. Unmount the fragmented file system
  3. Recreate the file system, using newfs(8)
  4. Mount the file system
  5. Restore the file system data to the newly recreated file system

- Adjust the number of inodes to match the file system usage. If the file system has fewer, larger files, reduce the density of inodes with the newfs −i command when creating the file system.
- Adjust the fragment size to match the file system usage. By default, the fragment size on UFS is 1KB. This is appropriate on a file system containing many small files of 1KB or less. However, a larger fragment size (8KB) is less wasteful of disk space and provides better performance for a file system that contains larger (greater than 16KB) files. The fragment size is specified with the newfs command when the file system is created.
- Adjust the maximum number of blocks per cylinder group. This value, the maxbpg parameter, is set either when a UFS file system is created or changed on an existing file system via the tunefs(8) command. The default value for maxbpg is approximately one fourth of the total blocks in a cylinder group, and this default is designed to benefit file systems containing average file size. Accessing performance on large files is degraded by the restriction of the parameter.

The maxbpg parameter should be set higher than the default only on a file system that contains only large files. If maxbpg is changed for an existing file system, the files must be laid out on the disk again, similarly to a defragmentation procedure to gain the benefit.

9.4.3.3. AdvFS

The Advanced File System (AdvFS) is an optional file system on Digital UNIX systems. AdvFS provides significant performance and tuning advantages over UFS to the system administrator. Whereas certain tuning operations, such as defragmentation, on a UFS file system can only be done manually, Digital's POLYCENTER AdvFS Utilities provides multiple volume capacity, online reconfiguration, performance tuning, and online backups. The POLYCENTER AdvFS Utilities are an optional, layered product, that are included in Digital's NAS packages.

Some strategies for improving AdvFS performance include:

- Dedicate an entire disk to a single AdvFS file domain, rather than multiple file domains on a single disk, to avoid disk contention.
- Defragment AdvFS filesets frequently. If you have the optional POLYCENTER AdvFS Utilities, use the defragment utility, which allows online defragmenting without reducing file system availability. If you do not have the AdvFS utilities, you can, similarly to UFS, back up, recreate, and restore filesets to defragment them. This, however, forces filesets to be unavailable during the operation.
- Use AdvFS fileset quotas to limit the amount of space an individual fileset may consume of the file domain. Frequently it makes sense for an AdvFS file domain to contain multiple filesets, and quotas prevent a single fileset from using all available space.
- Stripe individual files across multiple physical disks (or volumes) to increase performance. The optional POLYCENTER AdvFS Utilities contains a utility to allow distributing distinct operating system files across specific disks in one file domain. This can provide better file access throughput and some degree of load balancing across disks and/or controllers.

9.4.4. Network Resource

The network resource is technically an I/O-type resource, but since so many modern Digital UNIX applications are no longer isolated on a single system but are dependent on many systems on the network (e.g., Web servers), I felt it necessary to discuss network performance issues separately. In any case, good network performance is, by its nature, a hard thing to pin down. The state of the network is dependent on a variety of factors, many of which may be out of a system administrator's control. For example, network performance is affected by:

- Applications, both local and remote
- Network Controllers (Ethernet, SLIP/PPP, Token Ring, FDDI, ATM, etc.), again, both local and remote
- The Communications Channels themselves
- The local and remote hosts

Just like the other three performance resources (CPU, Memory, and I/O), Network performance is impacted when the demand for resources exceeds the supply of resources. This is usually manifested in network congestion caused by one of two issues:

- A physical problem with either network hardware or software somewhere in the network
- Network traffic that simply outstrips the capacity of the existing network resource

Neither of these problems are fixable by tuning. In the first case, something is broken and needs to be fixed, and in the second case, the solution is either to reduce the demand on the resource or add more resources.

Identifying where network throughput bottlenecks are is the first step when investigating perceived network issues. By finding such bottlenecks, you can quickly rule out problems with systems under local control. As an example, if the performance of a link between two systems suddenly degrades, the strategy might be to first measure the throughput rate by transferring several large files via ftp(1) and recording the transfer rate. (Here is where knowing the performance characteristics of a "normal" network connection becomes invaluable. If you know what a typical transfer rate is, it becomes an easy step to compare the two transfer times and quickly ascertain if there is, in fact, a problem.) Once it is determined that the transfer rate has degraded, the next step is to trace the network path, capturing the hops and times and looking for abnormal hops and/or times. Use the traceroute(1) utility for this data collection. Hopefully, this will point you in the right direction to a solution. Obviously, this is just an example, but it shows how a step-by-step troubleshooting process is essential in troubleshooting network performance problems.

There is, however, one Digital UNIX-specific network parameter to be aware of and possibly adjust. This parameter, netisrthreads, specifies the number of network threads configured on a Digital UNIX system. The only issue with the parameter is to avoid having it set needlessly high. You can check the status of netisrthreads by examining the output of the netstat –m command. If the number of network threads configured exceeds the peak number of currently active threads, your system may be configured with too many threads. If this is the case, reducing the value for netisrthreads will free up memory for use by user processes. To change this value, specify the following lines in /etc/sysconfigtab:

```
net:
        netisrthreads = n
```

where n equals the number of network threads to configure. After making this change in /etc/sysconfigtab, reboot the system.

9.5. FINDING PERFORMANCE BOTTLENECKS

Finding a performance problem is the first step in fixing such a problem. The following is a simple four-step approach to identifying Digital UNIX bottlenecks:

1) Examine the system load average. Hint: Use uptime(1) command.
   - Load average higher than normal: There may be a performance bottleneck. Continue to Step 2.
2) Determine how the CPU is spending the majority of its time. Hint: Use the vmstat(1) and iostat(1) commands.
   - User mode abnormally high: CPU resource may be at capacity.
   - System mode abnormally high: If system interrupts are exceptionally high, there may be hardware problems. Examine binary errorlog for issues. (See Chapter 11 for details on troubleshooting hardware issues.)
   - Idle mode higher than normal: Memory resource may be reaching capacity, causing increased paging/swapping. Continue to Step 3.
   - Idle mode abnormally high: Disk (I/O) resource may be at capacity. Continue to Step 4.

3) Monitor the available memory and the paging rate. Hint: Use the vmstat(1) command.
   - If total number of available pages (vmstat(1) free field) is less than the value of the sysconfig parameter vm_page_free_target (128 by default), the system may be paging. Investigate paging/ swapping subsystem.
4) Determine if the disk usage is balanced evenly across the disks/controllers. Hint: Use the iostat(1) command.
   - If one or more disks have higher activity (tps and/or bps) than the other disks, balance the disk load across all disks/ controllers.

9.6. RESOLVING PERFORMANCE BOTTLENECKS

Such performance bottlenecks, once identified, are nearly always related to insufficiencies in one or more of the four performance resources (CPU, memory, I/O, or network). A system administrator has three strategies for compensating for such resource bottlenecks:

- Increase the capacity of the limiting resource:
  By adjusting system configuration (kernel parameters, etc.)
  By purchasing additional hardware
- Reduce the demand on the limiting resource:
  By running fewer simultaneous jobs
  By redesigning the application(s) on the system
- Shift the demand from the limiting resource to another resource:
  By running application(s) remotely on other, less busy systems
  Distributing files and file systems across multiple disks/controllers
  Increase system buffer cache size to reduce disk I/O, thereby reducing memory available to users

9.7. PERFORMANCE MONITORING UTILITIES

Digital UNIX provides several native tools to monitor resource utilization. These include:

- uptime(1)
- iostat(1)

- vmstat(1)
- swapon(8)
- netstat(1)

9.7.1. uptime

The uptime(1) command's primary purpose is to report how long a system has been running. In addition, uptime indicates how many users are logged in and displays three load-average values. The load-average numbers give the number of jobs in the run queue for the last 5 seconds, the last 30 seconds, and the last 60 seconds, and can be a rough indicator of how "busy" a system is. For example:

```
$ uptime
16:59 up 26 days, 21:12, 10 users, load average: 2.81, 2.80, 2.65
```

These three load-average number tell us that, on average, there were less than three jobs waiting for CPU time over the last 60 seconds. This particular system is a large database server with eight CPUs and a modest load. Load-average numbers of zero usually indicate an idle system:

```
15:40 up 6 days, 17 mins, 9 users, load average: 0.00, 0.00, 0.00
```

Extremely high load averages (> 10), on the other hand, may indicate a CPU bottleneck as jobs are queued waiting for CPU resources. Since the load-average numbers are only one parameter, however, do additional investigations to determine the performance issue, if any.

One way to understand a system's activity is to periodically run the uptime command over several days and review the output. To run uptime every 15 minutes and place the output in a logfile, put the following line in your crontab:

```
0,15,30,45 * * * * /usr/bin/uptime >> /tmp/uptime.log
```

Be sure to monitor the size of the uptime.log and truncate or remove as necessary, for the log will grow by approximately 70 bytes every 15 minutes. After running uptime in this manner for several days, review the logfile and determine what the busiest times of the day are, both in log-in activity and load averages.

9.7.2. iostat

The iostat(1) command is primarily a tool for displaying terminal and disk I/O statistics. However, iostat also displays useful information about CPU utilization. The iostat command's syntax is:

```
iostat [drive ...] [interval [count]]
```

Table 9.1 describes the arguments of the iostat command. For example:

```
$ iostat
        tty         rz1         rz2         rz3         rz4         cpu
tin  tout  bps  tps  bps  tps  bps  tps  bps  tps  us  ni  sy  id
0    39    5    0    5    0    2    0    6    0    5   0   23  72
$ iostat 5 5
        tty         rz1         rz2         rz3         rz4         cpu
tin  tout  bps  tps  bps  tps  bps  tps  bps  tps  us  ni  sy  id
0    39    5    0    5    0    2    0    6    0    5   0   23  72
0    59    0    0    0    0    0    0    0    7   12  43  38
0    59    0    0    0    0    0    0    0    7   12  45  36
0    58    0    0    0    0    0    0    0    7   12  41  40
0    58    0    0    0    0    0    0    0    7   12  48  33
$
```

See Table 9.2 for a description of the output fields from the iostat command. The first invocation of iostat displays a summary of activity since the system was last started. This summary line is always displayed as the first output line when running iostat. The CPU fields (us, ni, sy, and id) indicate that, on average, the CPU has been idle 72% of the time and busy running system and user instructions the remaining 28% of the time. The second iostat session also displays the summary line first, followed by four "snapshots" of current system activity at five-second intervals. At this time, the CPU is busier than average, and each time the CPU utilization is approximately 63% (the average of the sum of the us, ni, and sy field). Note that the CPU fields, in addition to the other fields, are displayed as rounded integers, so it is possible for the sum of the four CPU values to equal less than 100%.

The iostat output is useful in identifying CPU resource limitations. While the system is running a typical or representative workload, run iostat

Argument	Meaning
drive...	Forces iostat to display information on specific drives. If drive is not specified iostat displays the first four drives (even if more than four disk drives are configured in the system).
interval	Causes iostat to report once each interval second. The first report is for all time since a reboot, and each subsequent report is for the last interval only.
count	Specifies the number of reports.
For example, iostat 1 10 would produce 10 reports at 1-second intervals. You cannot specify count without interval, because the first numeric argument to iostat is assumed to be interval.	

Table 9.1 iostat(1) Arguments

with an interval of five seconds and no count and monitor how the CPU is spending its time.

9.7.3. vmstat

The vmstat(1) command is used to display virtual memory statistics such as free memory, pageins and pageouts, and page faults. Additionally, vmstat shows the number of running processes categorized into running or runnable, waiting interruptably, or waiting uninterruptably. The type and quantity of interrupts, systems calls, and context switches per second is also displayed, along with CPU usage statistics. The CPU information is displayed by vmstat similarly to the iostat command. The vmstat command's syntax is:

```
vmstat [interval [count]]
```

Table 9.3 describes the arguments of the vmstat command.

Field	Meaning
tin	The number of characters read per second from terminals (collectively)
tout	The number of characters written per second to terminals (collectively)
bps	For the specified disk, the amount of data (in kilobytes) transferred per second
tps	For the specified disk, the number of disk transfers per second
us*	The percentage of time the CPU has spent in user mode
ni*	The percentage of time the CPU has spent in user mode running low priority (niced) processes
sy*	The percentage of time the CPU has spent in system mode
id*	The percentage of time the CPU has spend idling
*Note: If the system has multiple CPUs, these values are calculated across all CPUs.	

Table 9.2 iostat(1) Output

Argument	Meaning
interval	Causes vmstat to report once each interval seconds. The first report is a summary since the last reboot, and each subsequent report is for the last interval only.
count	Specifies the number of reports.
For example, vmstat 2 5 would produce 5 reports at 2-second intervals. You cannot specify count without interval, because the first numeric argument to vmstat is assumed to be interval.	

Table 9.3 vmstat(1) Arguments

For example:

```
$ vmstat 5 5
procs       memory           page              disk         faults      cpu
r b w    swap   free  re mf pi po fr de  sr s6 sd sd sd   in  sy   cs us sy id
0 0 38   7032   9952   0 13 51 30 62  0  11  0  0  0   0 143 234  126 0 1  99
0 0 82 1734848 16568 0  0  0  0  0  0   0  0  0  0   0 137 148  101 0 0 100
0 0 82 1734848 16568 0  0  0  0  0  0   0  0  0  0   0 138 177  127 0 0 100
0 0 82 1734848 16568 0  0  1  1  0  0   0  0  0  0   0 133 155   98 0 0 100
0 0 82 1734848 16568 0  0  0  0  0  0   0  0  0  0   0 140 189  127 0 0 100
$
```

See Table 9.4 for a description of the output fields from the vmstat command. Each invocation of vmstat displays a summary of activity, since the system was last booted as the first line of output. The example vmstat session displays the summary line first, followed by four "snapshots" of current system activity at five-second intervals. At this time, for instance, the pageins and pageouts are effectively zero, indicating minimal paging. Also, the number of free memory pages is 27K, or approximately 219 megabytes available.

The vmstat output is helpful in identifying memory resource limitations. While the system is running a typical or representative workload, run vmstat with an interval of five seconds and no count, and monitor the memory free value, plus the number of pageins and pageouts and page faults.

9.7.4. swapon

The swapon(8) command is primarily used to activate swap areas and is either called at system startup for this purpose or to add additional swap space without rebooting the system. In addition, the swapon command –s command line argument displays the status of the swap space on a Digital UNIX system. For example:

```
# swapon -s
Swap partition /dev/vol/swapvol (default swap):
    Allocated space:        131005 pages (1023MB)
    In-use space:           4865 pages (3%)
    Free space:             126140 pages (96%)
```

Field	Meaning
r	Number of threads that are running or are runable
w	Number of threads waiting interruptably
u	Number of threads waiting uninterruptably
act	Total number of pages on the active list, the inactive list, and the Unified Buffer Cache (UBC) least-recently-used (LRU) list
free	Total number of pages that are clean and available for use
wire	Total number of pages that are currently in use and cannot be used for paging
fault	Number of address translation faults that have occurred.
cow	Number of copy-on-write page faults
zero	Number of zero-filled-on-demand page faults
react	Number of pages that have been faulted while on the inactive list
pin	Number of requests for pages from a pager
pout	Number of pages that have been paged out
in	Number of nonclock-device interrupts per second
sy	Number of system calls called per second
cs	Number of task and thread context switches per second
us*	Percentage of user time for normal and priority processes
sy*	Percentage of system time
id*	Percentage of idle time
*Note: If the system has multiple CPUs, these values are calculated across all CPUs.	

Table 9.4 vmstat(1) Output

```
Swap partition /dev/vol/swap01:
    Allocated space:        131072 pages (1024MB)
    In-use space:           4658 pages (3%)
    Free space:             126414 pages (96%)

Total swap allocation:
    Allocated space:        262077 pages (2047MB)
    Reserved space:         22233 pages (8%)
    In-use space:           9523 pages (3%)
    Available space:        239844 pages (91%)
```

This status display lists information for each individual swap area and summarizes the total swap space for the system. The important value to monitor is Total Available space. If the amount of available space is constantly around—or worse, below—10%, more swap space is urgently required. In this event, allocate additional swap space immediately and add it using the swapon command.

9.7.5. netstat

The netstat(1) command is a multipurpose tool that provides a variety of information about the state of the network and network interfaces. From a performance monitoring standpoint, the netstat –m command is very useful. Specifying the –m switch causes netstat to Display information about memory allocated to data structures associated with network operations. This information is useful when trying to determine where and how memory is configured on a Digital UNIX system. For example:

```
# netstat -m
  55 Kbytes for small mbufs (peak usage 114 Kbytes)
  66 Kbytes for mbuf clusters (peak usage 526 Kbytes)
  131 Kbytes for sockets (peak usage 215 Kbytes)
  170 Kbytes for protocol control blocks (peak usage 326 Kbytes)
  7 Kbytes for routing table (peak usage 11 Kbytes)
  3 Kbytes for interface addresses (peak usage 3 Kbytes)
  < 1 Kbyte for ip multicast addresses (peak usage < 1 Kbyte)
  < 1 Kbyte for interface multicast addresses (peak usage < 1 Kbyte)
```

```
   0 requests for mbufs denied
   0 calls to protocol drain routines
 431 Kbytes allocated to network

  Network threads:  1 netisrthreads configured (peak active  1)
```

9.8. SUMMARY

I have barely scratched the surface on monitoring and managing performance on a Digital UNIX system, but hope I have impressed upon you the importance of being familiar with a system and understanding what is "normal" before attempting to make adjustments. Performance problems are usually just resource deficiencies, and the first step is identifying which resource is constrained. Once the resource limitation is isolated, the system administrator's next step is to adjust either the workload or the resource, if possible, or collect justification for increasing the resource, such as purchasing more hardware.

Backups

10

10.1. SYSTEM BACKUPS

System backups are often a neglected or completely overlooked function on all too many UNIX systems. The reasons for this are many and varied. Many novice system administrators are simply unfamiliar with the variety of backup utilities available, while more experienced administrators may consider backups to be "grunt" work. In other cases, backups are not a priority with management or users . . . until, of course, the inevitable occurs and data or files are lost. Statistics have shown that most companies that are unable to recover quickly from a data loss often never recover. The key to preventing this situation is developing and implementing a backup strategy. In this chapter I will present guidelines for developing your own backup strategy. Following that, the various backup tools and utilities provided on Digital UNIX systems will be discussed. I will focus on those utilities that are part of the base Digital UNIX product, but I will briefly mention several alternative backup solutions.

10.2. BACKUP STRATEGY

Backups on a Digital UNIX system must be more than an occasional file system dump off to a tape. Developing an effective backup strategy is an important responsibility for a Digital UNIX system administrator. Such a backup plan must take into account the type of data to be backed up, how frequently the data should be saved, or more importantly, how much data can afford to be lost, the amount of time available for the backup operation itself, and the tools available. Finally, backing up the system is only half of a complete backup strategy. Being able to restore from the system backups, whether the entire system or just a file or two, is equally important. A complete backup strategy must backup the entire system. This may not mean, of course, copying every file to tape every night. It may mean backing up key file systems nightly, or even more frequently if necessary, while only backing up some of the more static system areas, such as the root and /usr file systems, on a weekly basic. The key is having an understanding of your system's data and use.

An effective backup strategy should address at least the following issues:

- What will be backed up?
- When will the backups occur?
- How will the backups be done?
- Selection of Backup Device and Media
- Backup and Restore Documentation
- Restore Dress Rehearsal

Additionally, planning for the following items will make a good backup strategy into a great one:

- Offsite Storage
- Disaster Recovery Plan

10.2.1. What Will Be Backed Up?

Determining what to backup is the first step in developing a backup strategy. Of course the answer is "everything," right? Given unlimited resources and time, backing up everything would be ideal. However, the requirement for systems to be available around the clock, and the ever-increasing amount of disk space on today's modern UNIX systems, probably precludes backing up every file each night. Of course, if time and resources permit, doing a daily complete backup is certainly an option. If this is the case, by all means do so and avoid the added complexity of managing incremental backups. If this is not a feasible option, however, you as the system administrator must decide the frequency in which to copy your data to the backup media. The answer to this question requires some thought into the nature of your users' data, the amount of data your users can afford to lose, and the restore strategy.

The two categories of data on a Digital UNIX system are system data, which is primarily located in the root, /usr, and /var file systems, and user data, which can be anywhere, including in the previously listed system file systems. Obviously, to be able to restore the entire system, it is necessary to have a backup copy of the entire system. This usually means copying all files to a backup media such as tape. However, if resources such as time or tape capacity are limited, an option to consider is to identify parts of the system that exist on the vendor's distribution media. This can include third-party applications, static sections of the operating system such as the man pages, or even the entire base operating system itself. In the event of a system problem requiring a full system restoration, it would be necessary to reload these subsystems from the manufacturer's media. Obviously, this is a drastic measure requiring careful consideration. Perhaps a better strategy would be to make separate backups of these static subsystems outside of the normal backup schedule and archive these backups. This certainly is a more sound strategy for the base operating system as it avoids having to reload the base system from scratch.

10.2.2. When Will the Backups Occur?

There are three factors to consider when deciding the scheduling of system backups: how frequently to run the backups, what time of the day to start the backups, and will the system be in single- or multi-user mode during the backup window. Each of these questions must be answered before an appropriate backup strategy can be defined. Also, all three of these questions are usually best answered by the end-users themselves. The actual owners of the data should have an idea of how often to run backups and at what time during the day would cause the least impact.

How often to run regularly scheduled backups is directly related to how dynamic your user's data is. If the data to be backed up is fairly static, it may make sense to only back up once a week. However, if a system is actively updated around the clock, perhaps a single nightly backup is insufficient and several backups a day are necessary. The basic question to pose is, "What is the minimum amount of data that can be lost?" If the answer to this question is 24 hours of updates, then a single daily backup would suffice. If, however, no more than four hours of updates can be lost, for example, then the backup strategy must take into account this requirement and ensure that changes are safeguarded. This may seem like a drastic example, but as systems become more mission critical, the requirement for no data loss whatsoever is becoming normal.

If, or more likely when, you are faced with such a requirement of no data loss, your backup strategy must be more than simply copying files off to tape. Modern database systems, such as Oracle, provide a facility where database transactions are logged, thus providing the ability to restore the database to any point in time. Normal tape backups still must be done, of course, but the database itself effectively continues to back itself up between tape backups. The database facility does not protect your data from accidental or intentional deletions, of course, and this is the reason that regularly scheduled backups are still vital. In the event a critical table is dropped in error, the database will happily log the table as dropped. The tape backups from the previous evening will be required to restore data lost in this manner.

Another type of system backup is to use clusters, thereby having completely redundant systems. Digital's DECsafe Available Server Environment (ASE) is such a configuration. ASE supports a redundant environment that prevents system or component failures from taking an application or service down. Similarly, using either mirroring or RAID can protect your data from individual disk failures. Just like databases, though, neither ASE nor disk mirroring will protect your data from human error, such as an important file accidentally being deleted or modified. I cannot stress this point enough: The use of redundant hardware, whether duplicating entire systems using ASE, or redundant disks/controllers and mirroring or RAID, does not preclude regularly scheduled backups. Do not rely on such system configurations as a backup method. When a user mistypes a command and deletes an important file, the fact that the file system is mirrored does not in any way prevent that file from being deleted. The use of clusters and disk mirroring are primarily to increase system availability, and as such, are important tools.

The second aspect of when a backup will occur is deciding what time of the day the backup process itself should be executed. The answer to this question may at first glance be easy: the middle of the night; and, depending on your environment, it's likely this may be the case. However, there are situations in which the middle of the night may be the worst time to do backups. If your organization is global and a system is used by international users, perhaps the best time would be early morning, U.S. time; 4:00 A.M., for instance. Another possibility is that the system's busiest time may be the middle of the night, and a backup starting at 1:00 A.M. would further load the system. I have worked with a system that supported interactive users from 7:00 A.M. to 4:00 P.M., and processed nightly downloads from 8:00 P.M. to 7:00 A.M. This schedule left only four hours between 4:00 P.M. and 8:00 P.M. in which to do backups, so the backup process was started each day at 4:00 P.M. in the afternoon. This example points out the necessity of knowing your system's workload when scheduling system backups.

Finally, the question of whether the backup will be done while the system is running in multi-user mode or single-user mode must be considered. Given the opportunity, having the system in single-user mode would ensure the most reliable backups, since no users will be actively using the system and all files will be closed. However, it is unlikely that many systems can afford to be unavailable to users to do regular off-line backups. Additionally, the risk of on-line, or hot backups, is fairly low. My recommendation is to do off-line backups only when it makes sense and the system is unavailable to users anyway, for instance, after an initial system install or major upgrade, and to do on-line backups the rest of the time to minimize system downtime.

The primary exception to this may involve systems that run database systems such as Oracle and Informix, since the database files themselves are typically large and are, while the database engine itself is running, rarely static, even if there are no interactive users. For this reason, the database vendors provide methods and utilities for either doing hot backups directly or check-pointing the database to allow traditional backup tools to safely backup the data files. In these cases, the additional requirements of such applications must be taken into consideration when planning a backup strategy. Perhaps it may be that in order to accomplish backups on a system running a large database, it may be necessary to use both the database vendor's backup tool and a tradition UNIX backup utility. Work closely with the database administrator (DBA) to coordinate system backups.

10.2.3. How Will the Backups Be Done?

The method of actually copying system files to backup media is frequently thought of as the meat of the backup process. Actually, the process of copying data off to tape is fairly straightforward. There are several utilities provided with the Digital UNIX operating system that provide sufficient functionality for most systems. These tools are all command line programs that are each suited for a different type of backup and generate backups that are fairly portable, allowing them to be read by equivalent tools on other vendors' UNIX implementations. The four utilities are:

- tar
- vdump/vrestore
- dd
- cpio

In addition, Digital has bundled a single-user version of Legato's Networker backup program with Digital UNIX. This program, renamed POLY-CENTER Network Save and Restore (NSR) by Digital, provides both a command line and a graphical user interface to system backups. The bundled version of NSR supports backups of a single system to a local tape drive. Digital sells upgrades to this product to allow backing up multiple clients across a network to an NSR server, which supports multiple tapes drives, including tape jukeboxes and changers. NSR is a richer backup tool than any of the three native Digital UNIX backup utilities, supporting multiple backup sets and schedules, E-mail notification of backup success and failure, indexing of backed up files allowing quick restoration, and flexible user interfaces for both backup and restore.

10.2.3.1. tar(1)

The tar utility is a simple tool that can be used to save multiple files and directories quickly and easily. tar, which stands for Tape ARchiver, can write either directly to tape, floppy disk or other magnetic media, or can create a single archive file on disk, usually identified by a filename with a .tar suffix. The tar utility has become a defacto standard on the Internet for packaging and distribution of files. Understanding the use of tar, both for creating and unpacking archives, is a must-have skill for a UNIX system administrator.

The syntax of the Digital UNIX tar utility may at first glance appear complex, but there are actually only five main command line switches that specify tar's function (see Table 10.1).

The remaining switches are modifiers that define how tar behaves. See Table 10.2 for a list of the most common modifiers.

Argument	Meaning
c	Create a new archive; if the destination is a tape, the archive is written to the beginning of the tape instead of after the last file. Directories are recursively copied to the archive.
t	List the contents of the specified archive.
x	Extract the named files from the archive. If no file argument is given, the entire archive is extracted. Directories are recursively extracted.
r	Write the named files to the tape after the last file.
u	Add the named files to the tape archive if the files are not already in the archive or if the files have been modified since they were last copied to the tape.
Note: These five flags are all mutually exclusive. Only one of these flags may be specified at a time.	

Table 10.1 tar(1) Required Arguments

Typically, only a handful of switches are used with tar in normal operation. For instance, to copy a directory to tape, the following minimal tar command will do the job:

```
# tar -c /data
```

Since a specific tape drive or archive file is not specified (via the –f switch), this command copies the contents of the /data directory to /dev/rmt0h. If /dev/rmt0h does not correspond to a tape drive on the system, tar will dutifully create a archive named rmt0h in the /dev directory. Since the /dev directory is a subdirectory of the root file system, it is easy to fill up the root file system with an error of this type. For this reason, I recommend always using the –f switch and explicitly specifying the archive destination. For example:

```
# tar -c -f /dev/rmt1h /data
```

One confusing aspect of the tar command is whether to specify a minus sign (-) at the beginning of a flag set or not. In some UNIX vendor's

Argument	Meaning
v	Verbose mode. Normally tar is silent as it performs its work. If the v switch is specified with the t argument, additional information about each file in an archive is displayed.
f	The next argument is the name of the archive instead of the default value of /dev/rmt0h. If the name of the file is a - (dash), tar writes to standard output or reads from standard input, whichever is appropriate.
b	The next argument is the blocking factor for tape records. The default is 20 (larger values can be specified at the risk of creating a tape archive that some systems' tape drives might not be able to restore). Use this flag only with raw magnetic tape archives. This flag is only appropriate when writing archives to tape, as the block size is determined automatically when reading tapes.
p	This switch tells tar to restores files to their original modes, ignoring the present umask. Set-user-ID and sticky information will also be restored if the user is root.
P	The next argument specifies the prefix that is to be stripped off of the file names copied to or extracted from archives.
s	This switch tells tar to strip off any leading slashes from pathnames during extraction. This is useful when restoring an archive that was created on a system with a different file system structure, or when the archive was created with absolute pathnames.

Note: These flags are modifiers to the required flag (Table 10.1). This is not an exhaustive list of modifiers. See the man page for tar(1) for the entire set of modifiers.

Table 10.2 Common tar(1) Argument Modifiers

implementations of the tar command, the minus sign is optional. In Digital UNIX version 3.2 and above, however, the minus sign is not optional. If a minus sign is specified in front of a flag that requires an argument, the argument must follow immediately after the flag. If no minus sign is specified in front of a set of flags, the arguments, if any, must follow the entire flag set in the order of the specifying flags. For example, the following two tar commands are equivalent:

```
# tar -c -f /dev/rmt1h -b 20 /data
# tar cfb /dev/rmt1h 20 /data
```

Both these commands create an archive on /dev/rmt1h with a blocking factor of 20, which contains the contents of the /data directory.

The opposite of creating archives is, of course, extracting archives. An example of this operation is:

```
# tar xf /dev/rmt1h
```

This will extract the entire contents of the archive residing on a tape. Similarly, an archive can be a single file. For example:

```
# tar xf /tmp/data.tar
```

Where files extracted from an archive are restored is determined by the manner in which the files were copied to the archive in the first place. If, when creating an archive, the files are specified with an absolute pathname, for example,

```
# tar cf /dev/rmt0h /etc
```

the files will be restored to their original location when the archive is extracted—in this case, the /etc directory. However, if a relative pathname is specified when creating an archive:

```
# cd /etc
# tar cf /dev/rmt0h .
```

the files will be restored relative to the current directory where the archive is extracted from. In this example, extracting this archive from the root directory will also restore the files back into the /etc directory. However, if the archive is extracted from, say the /tmp directory, the files will be restored into /tmp/etc, possibly a new directory.

If an archive has been created containing files with absolute pathnames, such as those beginning with a slash (/), and it is inappropriate to

extract these files as they could overwrite existing files, simply add the –s
switch to the tar command line to strip the leading slash from the files in the
archive and restore the files relative to a location other than the root file system. For example:

```
# tar tf /dev/rmt1h
/etc/passwd
/etc/passwd.dir
/etc/passwd.pag
# cd /tmp
# tar xfs /dev/rmt1h
# ls /tmp/etc
passwd      passwd.dir      passwd.pag
```

Another common tar argument is –t for Table of Contents. The –t flag
displays the contents of a tar archive. Specified without the –v modifier, only
the file names are listed. The –v modifier tells tar to list the file names in a
format similar to that produced by an "ls –l" command. For example:

```
# tar tf /dev/rmt1h
/etc/passwd
/etc/passwd.dir
/etc/passwd.pag

# tar tvf /dev/rmt1h
-rw-r-r—   0/0   1074 Jul 13 13:57:29 1997 /etc/passwd
-rw-r-r—   0/0   4096 Jul 11 10:46:41 1997 /etc/passwd.dir
-rw-r-r—   0/0   4096 Jul 13 13:57:29 1997 /etc/passwd.pag
```

One handy use of the tar command is to copy directory hierarchies
between disks while maintaining file permissions and ownerships. It would
be a simple matter to create an archive of a directory hierarchy, then extract
that archive to another place on the system. Since the tar command provides
the ability to write to standard output and to read from standard input, the
following command pipeline copies a directory structure without having to
create an intermediate archive:

```
# cd fromdir; tar cf - . | (cd todir; tar xfBp -)
```

By specifying a minus sign (-) as the argument to the –f switch, the tar
on the left side of the pipe (|) writes the archive to standard output, which
is then read by the tar command on the right side of the pipe, which reads

standard input. For example, to copy the contents of the /usr/data hierarchy to the /home/data subdirectory, use the following command:

```
# cd /usr/data; tar cf - . | (cd /home/data; tar xfBp -)
```

Remember that this operation is only a copy; the original hierarchy is not removed. If a move-type operation is desired, simply follow this pipeline with an "rm –r /usr/data" command.

The tar utility is best for ad-hoc backups and for packaging files for transport. Tar archives are fairly portable among other vendor implementations of UNIX. In addition, there are tar utilities for non-UNIX systems, such as Windows NT. However, since the tar utility lacks robust error checking and correction and the ability to do incremental backups, it is not an ideal choice for regular system backups. It is handy, though, for quickly backing up a file or directory or two, either to magnetic media, such as tape or floppy, or to a .tar archive on disk.

10.2.3.2. vdump/vrestore

The vdump utility (and corresponding vrestore utility) is the most flexible and robust backup utility in the base Digital UNIX operating system. The vdump/vrestore utility pair support backing up and restoring AdvFS filesets, UFS file systems, and MFS or memory file systems. The similar dump/restore utility pair only support backing up and restoring UFS file systems. For this reason, I recommend using vdump/vrestore for all dump/restore operations. Additionally, there is a third derivative of this command pair: rdump/ rrestore, for Remote dump and Remote restore. The rdump/rrestore are for backing up UFS file systems to and restoring from remote backup devices, such as a tape drive on another system. Unfortunately, vdump/ vrestore do not directly support this remote facility; in section 10.2.3.4., "Incremental vdumps," I will detail a method of accomplishing remote vdumps/vrestores. In this section, references to vdump and vrestore will apply to vdump/vrestore, dump/restore, and rdump/rrestore, except where noted. The vdump and vrestore utilities are designed to backup and restore entire filesets (or UFS file systems, in the case of dump/restore). However, the vdump utility provides the ability to backup individual directories, though not individual files, and the vrestore utility allows recovery of individual directories or files. Incremental backups are supported, which makes rdump an acceptable method of doing regular system backups.

10.2.3.3. vdump(8)

Since the vdump utility only does backups, as opposed to the tar command that is used for both backup and restore operations, its syntax is fairly straightforward. The command line switches of the vdump command are listed in Table 10.3.

Argument	Meaning
-0-9	Specifies the dump level. A level 0 dump backs up the entire fileset to the backup device. The default dump level is 9.
-C	Causes vdump to compress the data as it is backed up. This minimizes the size of the resulting dump file at the expense of the time needed to do the compression.
-D	Dumps only the specified subdirectory of a fileset to the backup device. When the flag is used, the dump level specification is ignored and a level-0 backup is run regardless of the dump level that is specified. Without the -D flag, the vdump command backs up the entire fileset that contains the subdirectory. Only a single subdirectory may be backed up.
-F #_of_buffers	Specifies the number of in-memory buffers to use. The valid range is 1 through 64 buffers; the default is 8 buffers. Specifying more buffers may increase the performance of the vdump.
-N	Disables the rewinding of the tape and placing the tape offline after completing the vdump session. By default, when the dump command finishes backing up a file system, it rewinds the tape and takes it offline. The -N flag is the default when the -f parameter is a no-rewind tape device; e.g., /dev/nrmt*.
-V	Displays the version of vdump.

Table 10.3 vdump(8) Arguments

Argument	Meaning
-b #_of_blocks	Specifies the number of blocks (1024-bytes each) for writes. The valid range is 1 to 64 blocks; the default is 60 blocks.
-f device	The next argument is the destination of the saveset, which can be a device, file, or a - (dash). If the name of the file is - , vdump writes the saveset to standard output.
-h	Displays usage instructions for vdump.
-q	Quiet mode. Only error messages are displayed.
-u	Updates the /etc/vdumpdates file with a time-stamp entry from the beginning of the backup.
-v	Verbose mode. Displays the names of files as they are backed up.
-w	Displays the filesets that have not been backed up within one week.

Table 10.3 Continued

To backup a single file system, the following vdump command is sufficient:

```
# vdump -0 -f /dev/rmt0h /
path    : /
dev/fset : root_domain#root
type    : advfs
advfs id : 0x342ab78e.000c3270.1
vdump: Dumping directories
vdump: Dumping 63516207 bytes, 131 directories, 1151 files
vdump: Dumping regular files

vdump: Status at Fri Jul 25 21:32:05 1997
vdump: Dumped 63516295 of 63516207 bytes; 100.0% completed
vdump: Dumped 131 of 131 directories; 100.0% completed
vdump: Dumped 1151 of 1151 files; 100.0% completed
vdump: Dump completed at Fri Jul 25 21:32:05 1997
#
```

In this example, vdump performs a level-0 dump, or all files/ directories, of the root file system to the primary tape drive. Since the –q switch was not specified on the command line, vdump outputs a informational messages as the vdump progresses.

A recommended switch to use with vdump is –u, which updates the /etc/vdumpdates file. The /etc/vdumpdates file is a text file that vdump uses to keep track of when file systems were last backed up and at which dump level. If incremental backups are instituted with vdump, it is imperative that the –u switch be used. An example /etc/vdumpdates file includes entries like the following, defining the fileset name, dump level, and date:

```
usr_domain#home 0 Mon Jul 21 02:00:22 1997
/dev/rz1c 0 Thu Jul 24 02:00:13 1997
usr_domain#home 5 Thu Jul 24 06:30:07 1997
usr_domain#home 9 Fri Jul 25 06:45:51 1997
```

In this example, usr_domain#home represents an AdvFS fileset mounted on /home, and /dev/rz1c represents a UNIX file system mounted elsewhere. If you perform a level-8 backup of the usr_domain#home, for example,

```
# vdump -8 -u -f /dev/rmt0h /home
```

using this /etc/vdumpdates file, the following occurs:

- The vdump command ignores the /dev/rz1c entry, since it does not match the specified fileset, usr_domain#home.
- The vdump command ignores the level-9 entry, since this entry is equal to or higher than the level-8 backup you requested. This leaves only the level-0 and level-5 entries.
- Of the two remaining entries, the vdump command chooses the entry with the most recent dump date, which is the level-5 entry.
- The vdump command backs up all files that were created or modified after the dump date of the level-5 entry.

When a vdump operation is started, if a file system entry with that specific dump level does not already exist in the /etc/vdumpdates file, the vdump command appends a new record to the file for the dump level; otherwise, the vdump command overwrites the existing record for that dump level, changing the backup date to reflect the most current backup session. This occurs after all files in the named file system are successfully backed up.

10.2.3.4. Incremental vdumps

Incremental backups are a way of reducing the amount of time and backup media a backup consumes by only backing up the files that have changed since the last backup. By consulting the /etc/vdumpdates file, the vdump utility is able to manage incremental backups and determine which files have changed. The main drawback to incremental backup strategies is that the system administrator must manage the multiple tapes between level-0 dumps in order to completely restore a system. Consider the following 28-day incremental backup schedule:

S	M	T	W	T	F	S
0	5	4	7	6	9	8
0	5	4	7	6	9	8
0	5	4	7	6	9	8
0	5	4	7	6	9	8

A full (level-0) dump is performed once a week, with incrementals the remaining days of the week. The number of dump files to perform a full restore can vary from 1 to 4, depending when during the week a restore becomes necessary. Following this schedule would mean a minimum of 7 tapes in the backup rotation; a better idea would be to have the full 28 tapes in a rotation, especially since tapes are relatively inexpensive compared to lost data. In any case, if this type of schedule is adopted, it is important to safeguard all tapes between level-0 dumps to complete a full restore. For instance, if the system required a full recovery on a Wednesday morning before that day's backup, it would be necessary to first apply the level-0 dump from Sunday, then apply the level-5 dump from Monday, followed by the level-4 dump from Tuesday, to restore the system to the state it was immediately after Tuesday's dump. In this example, any changes after the Tuesday backup would be lost.

This 28-day incremental vdump schedule can be run by inserting the following entries in root's crontab. This example only backs up the /home file system:

```
0 2 * * 0 /sbin/vdump -0 -u -f /dev/rmt0h /home
0 2 * * 1 /sbin/vdump -5 -u -f /dev/rmt0h /home
0 2 * * 2 /sbin/vdump -4 -u -f /dev/rmt0h /home
0 2 * * 3 /sbin/vdump -7 -u -f /dev/rmt0h /home
0 2 * * 4 /sbin/vdump -6 -u -f /dev/rmt0h /home
0 2 * * 5 /sbin/vdump -9 -u -f /dev/rmt0h /home
0 2 * * 6 /sbin/vdump -8 -u -f /dev/rmt0h /home
```

Obviously, if a system has many file systems, this method of individual crontab entries would be very unmanageable. A better solution is a single script that is run each night, which backs up all desired file systems at the appropriate dump level that is determined by the current day of the week.

One capability the vdump utility does not directly provide is the ability to send the backup across the network to a tape drive on a remote system. The rdump utility does support this functionality by requiring the specification of a remote system name and a tape device on that system via the –f command line parameter. The format of the rdump's –f option is "machine: device" as in the following example:

```
# rdump -0 -u -f saturn:/dev/rmt0h /
```

This command does a level-0 dump of the root file system to the /dev/rmt0h tape drive on the remote system saturn. This command also updates the /etc/dumpdates, which is functionally identical to the /etc /vdumpdates file for the vdump command. Additionally, the remote system's /.rhosts file must contain the name of the local, or client, machine. This requirement is necessary to provide the necessary trusted host relationship between the two systems (remote and local).

The main drawback to the rdump command is rdump's inability to backup AdvFS filesets. This remote backup functionality is achievable using the vdump command by the use of a workaround. The workaround is to run the vdump command on the local system with the output of the vdump sent to standard output by specifying a dash (-) to the –f parameter. The standard output is then piped to a remote shell on the remote system running a dd command to its local tape drive. (See section 10.2.3.6. in this chapter for information on the dd command.) The following example backs up the root file system to the /dev/rmt0h tape drive on the remote system saturn:

```
# vdump -0 -u -b 64 -f - / | rsh saturn dd of=/dev/rmt0h bs=64k
```

This example command is equivalent to the previous rdump command. Note that the block size must be specified to both the rdump command (-b 64) and the dd command (bs = 64k). This workaround has the same requirement as the remote system's /.rhosts file, which must contain the name of the local, or client, machine. See the vrestore section for information on the reverse of this workaround—restoring from a remote system's tape drive with the vrestore command.

10.2.3.5. vrestore(8)

The vrestore utility restores files from archives written by the vdump utility. Similarly to vdump, the vrestore utility is like its restore/rrestore counterparts. The vrestore command line parameters are listed in Table 10.4.

Argument	Meaning	
-D	Restores the file(s) to the directory specified by this parameter. By default files are restored to the directory where the vrestore command was invoked.	
-V	Displays the version of vrestore.	
-f *device*	The next argument is the destination of the saveset, which can be a device, file, or a - (dash). If the name of the file is - , vrestore reads the saveset from standard input.	
-h	Displays usage instructions for vrestore.	
-i	Invokes vrestore in interactive mode. After reading directory information from the archive, a shell-like interface is displayed that allows files to be selected interactively. See Figure 10.5 for a listing of the interactive vrestore commands.	
-l	Displays the vdump archive structure.	
-m	Do not preserve the ownership or permissions of restored files.	
-o *opt*	Specifies the action to take when a file being restored already exists. Note that only the file name is checked for collision. The following options are recognized:	
	yes	Overwrite existing files without asking. The default option is yes.
	no	Do not overwrite existing files. Conflicting files are not restored.
		(*continued*)

Table 10.4 vrestore(8) Arguments

Argument	Meaning	
	ask	Query where to overwrite an existing file.
-q	Quiet mode. Only error messages are displayed.	
-t	Displays the names and sizes of all files contained in the vdump archive.	
-v	Verbose mode. Displays the names of files as they are restored.	
-x	Extract files from a vdump archive. If the last command line option is a file specification, vrestore extracts only the file(s) that match, or no file list is specified, all files in the archive are restored.	

Table 10.4 Continued

Restoring a single file or an entire system is easily accomplished with the vrestore command. For example, to restore the password file from a vdump of the root file system, use the following vrestore command:

```
# vrestore -x -f /dev/rmt0h ./etc/passwd
```

Note that the backed up files in a vdump are stored using a relative pathname. In a vrestore, this means that by default, the files are restored in the directory where the vrestore command was invoked. In this example, if the vrestore was run from the root file system, the password file would have been restored to /etc/passwd, overwriting any existing /etc/passwd file. The final parameter in this command specifies the file(s) to be restored. This parameter can be a single file or a directory, which restores the directory and its contents, including any subdirectories. Multiple files and/or directories separated by spaces can be specified to be restored. This parameter, however, cannot be a wildcard. For instance, the following vrestore commands are all legal:

```
# vrestore -x -f /dev/rmt0h ./etc
# vrestore -x -f /dev/rmt0h ./.profile ./.rhosts
# vrestore -x -f /dev/rmt0h ./etc/passwd ./etc/group ./sbin
```

add *arg*	Adds the files in the saveset specified by arg to the list of files to be restored from the device. Files on the list of files to be restored are prepended with the * (asterisk) character when they are listed with the ls interactive command.
cd *[arg]*	Changes the current saveset directory to the directory specified with the arg parameter.
delete *arg*	Deletes all files and their subdirectories specified by the arg parameter from the list of files to be restored from the device. An expedient way to select wanted files from any directory whose files are stored on the device is to add the directory to the list of files to be restored and then delete the ones that are not wanted.
extract or restore	Restores all files added to the list of files to be restored to the previously specified destination.
help or ?	Displays help information for the interactive commands.
ls *[arg]*	Lists files in the current saveset directory or the directory specified with the arg parameter. Directory entries are appended with a / (slash) character. Entries that have been marked to be restored are prepended with an * (asterisk) character.
pwd	Prints the pathname of the current saveset directory to the standard output device.
quit or exit	Exits immediately, even when the files on the list of files to restored have not been read.
verbose	Toggles the -v modifier (see the -v flag of the vrestore command). The name of each file restored from the device is written to the standard output device.

Table 10.5 vrestore(8) interactive mode commands

This vrestore example, on the other hand, is not legal:

```
# vrestore -x -f /dev/rmt0h ./etc/pass*
```

A useful vrestore flag is –t, or Table of Contents. This flag displays the date the save-set was created, the filenames of the save-set, and the size in bytes. For example:

```
# vrestore -t -f /dev/rmt0h | head
vrestore: Date of the vdump save-set: Wed Oct 1 01:00:05 1997
./etc/
./etc/sia/
./etc/sia/matrix.conf @-> /etc/sia/bsd_matrix.conf
./etc/sia/OSFC2_matrix.conf, 2387
./etc/sia/bsd_matrix.conf, 2191
./etc/disktab, 30278
./etc/group, 480
./etc/passwd, 1074
./etc/profile, 402
./etc/rc.config, 4835
```

The vrestore command supports an interactive mode that allows quick selection and recovery of files and directories, especially when the files to be recovered are spread around a directory hierarchy. This interactive mode is specified by the –i command line switch. Once the interactive mode is entered, the save-set is accessed from a shell-like interface that allows selection of files to be restored. This interface has a set of interactive commands for navigating within the save-set directory structure and selecting and extracting files. See Table 10.5 for a list of these commands.

The following is an example of an interactive vrestore session in a save-set of a root file system:

```
# vrestore -i -f /dev/rmt0h
vrestore: Date of the vdump save-set: Wed Oct 1 01:00:05 1997
(/) ls
.:
  #.mrg..DXsession      .cshrc      .login    .new...cshrc
   .new...login   .new..DXsession    .profile  .proto...cshrc
   .proto...login  .proto..DXsession    .rhosts        .tags
    bin       dev/       etc/    genvmunix
    ome/       lib      mdec/       mnt/
```

```
    opt/          osf_boot           proc/       real.profile
    sbin/         subsys/             sys            tcb/
    tmp/          usr/               var/          vmunix
(/) add .profile
(/) add .rhosts
(/) ls
.:
  #.mrg..DXsession          .cshrc          .login      .new...cshrc
   .new...login   .new..DXsession        *.profile    .proto...cshrc
   .proto...login  .proto..DXsession         *.rhosts            .tags
    bin          dev/         etc/       genvmunix
    home/         lib         mdec/          mnt/
    opt/          osf_boot           proc/       real.profile
    sbin/         subsys/             sys            tcb/
    tmp/          usr/               var/          vmunix
(/) cd /etc
(/etc/) ls
.:
      acucap            atm.conf            atmhosts
      auth/            autopush.conf        binlog.conf
      csh.login           disktab              dt/
       eca/             exports             fdmns/
      fstab             ftpusers            gettydefs
      group             hosts            hosts.equiv
      ifconfig          inetd.conf         inetd.conf.sav1
       inittab         latautopush.conf        lprsetup.dat
       magic             motd            namedb/
      networks            nls/              ntp.conf
      ntp.drift           passwd           passwd.dir
      passwd.pag          phones               ppp/
      profile           protocols          rc.config
      remote              rmt               routes
       rpc              sec/            securettys
      services         services.sav1        setup.conf
      shells             sia/                sm/
      sm.bak/          snmpd.conf           srconf/
      state           strsetup.conf          sudoers
      svc.conf         svid2_login          svid2_path
     svid2_profile       svid3_login           svid3_path
```

```
     svid3_profile          svid3_tz          sysconfigtab
  sysconfigtab.PreUPD      sysconfigtab.lite          syslog.conf
     termcap             ttysrch       ultrix_logi
     ultrix_path       ultrix_profile            uucp/
     uugettydefs        vdumpdates            visudo
          vol/            yp        zoneinfo/
(/etc/) add passwd
(/etc/) extract
#
```

This example adds /.profile, /.rhosts, and /etc/passwd to the list of files to be restored, then recovers those files from the save-set with the extract command.

Finally, since the vrestore command lacks the remote restore capability of the rrestore command, the workaround to accomplish a restore from a remote system's tape drive is presented. This workaround only supports noninteractive vrestores via the –x flag as remote interactive vrestores are not possible, since the shell-like interface that the interactive option of vrestore invokes will not work with an rsh. For instance, the following command restores the /etc/passwd file from a vdump save-set that resides on the remote system saturn's tape drive:

```
# rsh saturn dd if=/dev/rmt0h bs=64k | vrestore -x
  -f - ./etc/passwd
```

This workaround has the same requirement as the remote vdump workaround, that is, that the remote system's /.rhosts file contain the name of the local, or client, machine.

10.2.3.6. dd(1)

The dd command is a specialized utility for copying data from one place to another. See the dd man page for dd's options. The three most common options are if, of, and conv, which refer to Input File, Output File, and CONVersion, respectively. As part of a dd copy operation, dd can also perform certain conversions to the data. For instance, dd can be used to convert an ASCII file to EBCDIC, or all alphabetic characters in a file can be converted to uppercase:

```
# dd if=text.ascii of=text.ebcdic conv=ebcdic
# dd if=text.lower of=text.upper conv=ucase
```

As such, the dd command is not a general purpose backup utility. However, dd is a useful tool when confronted with special situations. Since dd's input and output is specified to be a file, dd can read from and write to special device files just as handily as to normal operating system files. For example, suppose it became necessary to duplicate a disk drive—one possible motivation for doing this could be to clone a system for deployment. The dd command is perfect for this type of task. The following commands will copy the contents of disk rz0 to disk rz1:

```
# disklabel -z rz1
# dd if=/dev/rrz0c of=/dev/rrz1c conv=noerror,sync
```

For this operation to succeed, the two disk drives should be identical in size and ideally should be the same model. The initial disklabel command removes any existing disk label from disk rz1. This is necessary as the dd command will not proceed if the target disk has a disk label. Note that both the input file (if) and the output file (of) are specified as the raw or character device. Finally, the two conversion options (noerror and sync) are specified to ensure that dd stays synchronized in the event that either disk has bad sectors. Upon completion of this dd command, the contents of disk rz0 and rz1 will be identical. This type of disk-to-disk copy operation can take a tremendous amount of time (hours or days) to complete, depending on the size of the disks and the type and number of I/O channels.

Another situation where the dd command is useful is as a method for copying a data stream off to tape. You have already seen the dd command used in the following workaround:

```
# vdump -0 -u -b 64 -f - / | rsh remotesystem dd
    of=/dev/rmt0h bs=64k
```

The vdump command writes the save-set to standard output, which is piped to a dd process on a remote system via the rsh command. This dd command reads from the standard input (since an "if" parameter is not specified to dd) and writes the data directly to the raw tape drive. In this example, the dd command is simply a method to write to the tape drive.

10.2.3.7. cpio(1)

The cpio utility is a tool for copying files to and from cpio archives. The cpio utility, which stands for CoPy Input Output, can write archives either directly to tape or other magnetic media, or can create a single archive file on disk.

As a general purpose backup tool, cpio is of limited use for two primary reasons: cpio does not support backing up special files, such as device files located in the /dev directory, and cpio cannot back up files with pathnames that exceed 128 bytes. However, as a system administrator, you will occasionally be called upon to restore a cpio archive. This most often occurs when a software is delivered in a cpio archive, which is sometimes seen as a "least common denominator" format. This is probably because cpio is a "legacy" UNIX command, at least compared to relative newcomer utilities such as vdump. For this reason, an understanding of cpio's somewhat arcane syntax can be quite useful in certain situations.

The cpio command is used both to create archives and to restore files from archives; not surprisingly, there are two main cpio command line switches to accomplish these two functions:

- cpio –o   This command reads filenames from standard input and copies these files to a specified archive (either tape or a operating system file).
- cpio –i   This command reads a cpio archive from standard input and copies from it the specified files.

These descriptions identify one unique characteristic of cpio: cpio expects to get its input, whether this is a list of files to back up or an existing archive to restore, from standard input. For example, to back up all the files in the /home subdirectory to a tape drive with cpio, use the following command:

```
# find /home -print | cpio -o -O/dev/rmt0h
```

The find(1) command is used to generate a list of all the files and directories under /home. This list is then piped to cpio, which copies the files specified in the list to the tape device specified by the –O flag.

The restoration of files from a cpio archive is somewhat more straight-forward:

```
# cpio -idm -I/dev/rmt0h
```

This command restores the files previously saved onto /dev/rmt0h by cpio. The "d" flag specifies that any directories saved in the archive should be recreated by cpio if necessary, and the "m" flag tells cpio to maintain the last modification time when the files were archived.

Finally, it is often useful to be able to display the contents of a cpio archive. A variation of the "cpio –i" command displays the filenames contained in an archive. This command is:

```
# cpio -it -I/dev/rmt0h
```

The cpio command is not quite obsolete, for it continues to be used by some people to generate "portable" archives that can be read by many different flavors of UNIX. Knowing how to list and extract the contents of a cpio archive is still useful. See the cpio man page for the other flags that further modify cpio's functionality.

10.2.4. Selection of Backup Device and Media

Selecting which backup media to trust your regular system backups to is often a decision already made for you. Whichever model tape drive that ships with your system is often your only choice. If, however, you are able to be involved in the selection of a backup device, there are several issues to consider:

- The capacity of a tape drive
- The speed of a tape drive
- Media availability, cost, and size

The first and foremost issue is the capacity of the tape drive as compared to the amount of data to be regularly backed up. It makes no sense to purchase a single, small 4-gigabyte tape drive when the system has hundreds of gigabytes of disk storage. Conversely, a 280-gigabyte multi-tape jukebox is probably overkill for a desktop workstation with just two gigabytes of disk space. There is no quick and easy formula for determining what is a good ratio of tape capacity compared to disk capacity, but a rule of thumb I recommend is to have enough tape capacity to be able to back up the entire system unattended. This requirement for an unattended backup can be accomplished either by a single tape with sufficient capacity, or a multi-tape changer with the backup spanning multiple tapes. Note that this does not mean having equal amounts of tape space and disk space, only being able to copy all the data to tape.

Another consideration in selecting a tape is tape speed. You must be able to complete the backup procedure in the amount of time allotted. This is not as important an issue as it has been in the past, now that backup technology has progressed beyond paper tape and 9-track tapes. Most modern tape technology is fairly quick, supporting high-speed interfaces and cache buffers to increase tape throughput. If a system is constrained by either tape drive capacity or speed, an option to consider is multiple tape drives.

If tape drive speed is the concern, connecting multiple tape drives to the system on individual interfaces (e.g., SCSI channels) is recommended.

The final issue in selecting a backup device concerns the media. Choose a tape drive whose media is convenient. The convenience factors include cost, availability, and ease of storage. If all the existing systems in an organization are using 4mm DAT media, it may be wise to consider a 4mm DAT drive for a new system, rather then selecting an 8mm tape drive. Choosing a common format could considerably reduce the administrative hassles presented by a "foreign" media format. This media factor is likely to be have the least weight in your decision, but it should still be considered.

The most common tape drive on a Digital system is the 4mm DAT drive (TLZ09), which has a capacity of 4-gigabytes uncompressed (up to 8-gigabytes compressed). This tape drive is usually shipped as the default drive on most Digital systems. The advantages of this drive are a good size capacity, fair backup speed (up to 775 KB/s), and widely available and inexpensive media. The next step up in Digital's tape lineup is DLT, or Digital Linear Tape. Digital's TZ89 DLT tape drive provides 35-gigabytes uncompressed (up to 70-gigabytes compressed). DLT's biggest advantages are high capacity and very high data transfer rate (up to 5 GB/s). Both the media cost and physical size for DLT are greater than for 4mm DAT. Though DLT and 4mm DAT are currently Digital's main backup architectures, Digital's backup technology includes other tape formats such as Quarter-Inch Cartridge (QIC) and optical drives.

10.2.5. Backup and Restore Documentation

The final requirement of a backup strategy is sufficient documentation of the backup and restore process. Ideally this should include written procedures and examples of how the backups were done, where the backup media is stored, and how to recover from these backups in the event of a file or system loss. This documentation should be printed out and located in a place where any staff member who would be called upon to perform a restore has access to it. These procedures can certainly be online, but having hard copies of the instructions to restore a file or system may prove invaluable in a crisis.

At a minimum, this documentation should document the schedule of the backups, the level of the backups if incremental dumps are being done, the location of the backup media, both the backup rotation tapes and blank media for any ad hoc backups, the exact commands that generated the backups, and the restoration procedures and commands. The restore instructions should provide procedures for restoring individual files or directories and for recovering the entire system, both the operating system and the user applications and data. As the system administrator, it is in your best interest to create this backup and restore documentation so that even a user with limited system administration skills can at least restore files.

Another requirement of backup and restore documentation is that the information be updated if and when the backup or restore process changes. For instance, if new disks are installed on a system and the backup process is amended to back up newly created file systems, it is imperative that the backup and restore documentation is updated to reflect this change. Other changes that should be propagated for this documentation could include new backup hardware or software, changes in the backup strategy, and staffing reorganizations.

10.2.6. Restore Dress Rehearsal

Developing and implementing a backup strategy is well and good. However, if there is a flaw in the backup procedure, or the recover documentation is incorrect, or there is a hardware issue preventing valid backups, the wrong time to find out is in a recovery situation. For this reason, it is imperative that the backup and restore procedure be tested as often as is feasible. This rehearsal is simply to validate the backups themselves and to ensure that the restore instructions in the Backup and Restore documentation are accurate.

The least that should be done is to restore several files or directories from a recent regular system backup using the documented recovery procedures. For instance, assuming a recent vdump of the root file system were inserted into the primary tape drive, the following commands would recover a fairly large file (/vmunix) and compare the restored file with the original file:

```
# vrestore -x -v -f /dev/rmt0h -D /tmp ./vmunix
vrestore: Date of the vdump save-set: Wed Oct 1 02:45:44 1997
r /tmp/./vmunix, 11323768

# cksum /vmunix /tmp/vmunix
1731969811 11323768 /vmunix
1731969811 11323768 /tmp/vmunix
```

The cksum(1) command displays the checksum and byte count for the files specified on the command line. If the checksum value and the byte count are the same for the two files, you can assume that the file was successfully backed up.

The second phase of a restore rehearsal is to shutdown a system and restore it from a regular system backup. Ideally, a second test system would be the best place to test a full system recovery. However, it may not be practical to simulate a system failure and completely restore a system from tape. This may be because there is only one system and you cannot afford the system to be down. If this is the case, an alternative strategy could be to test restoring key user file systems to a spare disk partition. If this is successful, your restore strategy may have to be:

1. Rebuild the system from the Digital UNIX Installation Media.
2. Recreate the necessary user file systems.
3. Restore the user applications and data from backups.

Obviously such a strategy would be more time consuming as the system would have to be reinstalled from scratch, and some amount of system configuration would be necessary before the system could be considered successfully restored. This configuration activity would include recreating user accounts, reconfiguring the network, and possibly loading optional Digital layered products. The best recovery solution would be to restore the entire system from the last full backup.

10.3. OPTIONAL BACKUP STRATEGY COMPONENTS

Once a backup strategy is developed and the necessary components detailed in the previous section are in place, several other items may be considered that will further enhance such a backup strategy. These optional components are typically not necessary for most organizations, but completing some or all will greatly enhance your ability to withstand even the most severe data or system loss.

10.3.1. Offsite Storage of Backups

The purpose of regular system backups is to be able to recover from a system or user error that causes a file loss. At a minimum, such a loss could be the accidental deletion of a file or directory by a user, or the failure of a single hardware component that causes the loss of many files, or even the entire operating system, such as a disk crash. Given adequate backups, these losses can quickly be recovered from tape. The next severe system problem is a catastrophic hardware failure that causes the loss of some or all of the computer system itself. Such a failure could entail replacing some or all of the computer system in its entirety and being forced to restore the system from backups. A system failure of this scope would require a full system recovery; but if the backup strategy is sound, such a recovery is straightforward in approach.

One aspect of a backup strategy that has not been covered is the storage of the media from regular system backups. All too frequently, the entire rotation of nightly backup tapes are simply stored in the same room the computer resides in, often stacked on or near the system cabinet itself. Even if the tapes are not kept in the computer room, they are still stored in the same building as the computer, which is somewhat safer, but still not ideal. Both of the previously described types of data loss are recoverable from backup tapes that are stored on-site. However, there is a final failure, a loss of a facility or building, that would destroy the computer and the backup tapes. Such a loss would include a fire, flood, or other natural disaster, not to mention man-made catastrophes. An important piece of a good backup strategy is the storage of backups at an off-site location. A common practice is not to send every backup off-site, only a representative snapshot that would allow recovery to a known state, perhaps a monthly full backup. Ideally, an acceptable off-site location would be secure, geographically distant enough not to be vulnerable to natural disasters common to the location of the computer, and close enough to facilitate a relatively quick (within 24 hours) recovery of the tapes. There are companies that provide such vaulting services, including pickup and delivery, secure and climate-controlled vaults, and even tape-labeling services. Of course, such services cost money and may or may not be feasible. If, however, a computer system supports mission-critical applications, and the organization must ensure that the computer and data can be recovered from any failure, no matter how catastrophic, off-site storage of backups is a must.

10.3.2. Disaster Recovery Plan

In addition to off-site storage of backups, the development of a Disaster Recovery Plan (DRP) can reduce the risk that a catastrophic failure could prevent the restoration of a system. A DRP complements the Backup and Recovery Document discussed earlier in this chapter. Where the Backup and Recover document details how a backup was done and how to recover from that backup, a DRP has a larger scope. A DRP should outline the process to follow in the event of the total loss of the computer system, the computer room, or the entire facility. Some of the issues to explore when developing a DRP are what system functionality is critical to the continued operation of the organization, where can replacement systems and facilities be obtained, even on a temporary basis, and which personnel will need to be involved in carrying out a DRP in the unlikely event of a disaster.

Developing a DRP should be a joint effort between the operations staff such as the system administrator, the user community, and possibly facilities staff. In addition, a DRP, once created, must be revisited periodically to ensure that the information contained within is still accurate. Certain data tends to be volatile, for example, contact information for company personnel, such as telephone numbers, pager numbers, and responsibilities. Other fundamentals that may change over time are the assumptions made during development of the DRS, such as the minimum time to recovery, the order of system recovery, and the strategy for system or facility restoration.

10.4. SUMMARY

System backups are a critical responsibility for a UNIX system administrator. Developing and implementing a robust backup strategy is a requirement for being able to quickly and accurately restore data that will eventually be lost. The ability to restore an accidentally deleted file will demonstrate to your users that the system is in good hands.

Digital provides several different utilities for backing up a Digital UNIX system. Of these, the vdump/vrestore pair is the most versatile. Whichever backup tool you select, whether one provided with the base Digital UNIX product, the POLYCENTER Network Save and Restore tool, or a third-party backup application, spend sufficient time with it to understand its ability and options. Do not wait until a crisis to discover that the backups you have been dutifully making every night are invalid. Test your backup procedure frequently by doing test restores. Finally, the backups process should not require massive amounts of resources to manage if sufficient system administration time and energy have been devoted to developing the process up front.

Troubleshooting and Recovery

11

11.1. OVERVIEW

When something goes wrong and a Digital UNIX system crashes, the first
person to be called is the system administrator. Unfortunately, these events
seem to happen at the most inopportune time. Whether it is in the middle
of an important demonstration, crunch time at month's end, or simply in
the middle of the night, it is up to you to quickly diagnose the problem,
identify a solution, and get the system back up. This skill is probably best
defined as problem management. Problem management is a broad topic
that includes dealing with hardware and software errors, handling system
crashes, and administering the system logging facility. Digital UNIX is a
complex system, and often a system administrator's only recourse when
confronted with a system problem is to provide as much diagnostic information as possible to your support organization, whether that be Digital's
Customer Support Center or another organization. This information can
include system crash dumps or hardware, software, or system error log
entries. In this chapter I will provide some insight into the output of these
problem-reporting facilities and how to correlate system problems with their
resulting crash dump output or error-log events. Then, as an administrator's

knowledge and experience increases, these same Digital UNIX problem management facilities can allow for more proactive problem resolution.

At your disposal in this effort are several Digital UNIX facilities to assist you in this problem management effort. These are:

- The System Log
- The Binary Error Log
- The Crash Dump Process

These facilities are simply mechanisms used by the system to capture information when something goes wrong. In the following sections I will cover the issues of administering these tools. This includes determining what information is to be collected by these facilities, ensuring that there are adequate system resources to capture the desired information, configuring the tools appropriately, and strategies to follow when examining the collected information either before or after a system problem arises. In addition, the utilities provided by Digital for examining this information will be detailed. Understanding the information these facilities can provide is an important factor in being able to quickly diagnose and recover from system problems.

11.2. THE SYSTEM LOG

Modern UNIX implementations, Digital UNIX included, provide a centralized facility for collecting and recording messages. This facility, commonly referred to as the syslog function, is the primary logging mechanism used by many system processes and utilities. In addition, due to syslog's architecture, nonsystem applications, including user and administrative scripts, are able to send messages to syslog for disposition. Because syslog is typically the destination for error messages from system processes, understanding how syslog works and how to interpret and manage the entries in syslog's configuration file is important to effective system administration. The syslog facility has two components, the syslog daemon, /usr/sbin/syslogd, and the syslog configuration file, /etc/syslog.conf.

11.2.1. syslogd

The syslog daemon is an executable system utility normally started at system startup and always running while the system is in multi-user mode. The syslogd utility reads messages sent to it from system processes, the kernel itself, and user applications. These messages can be informational only, warnings, or errors that need attention. The messages themselves are single lines, optionally containing a priority value indicating the severity of the message. These priorities are defined in the /usr/include/sys/syslog.h header file. Messages are received by syslogd from three sources:

- The special device file /dev/log, the domain socket
- The special device file /dev/klog, which reads kernel messages.
- Other systems across the network, via a socket specified in /etc /services

Most system processes and utilities, and all user applications, submit messages to syslog using the syslog(3) function call or the logger(1) command. These messages are relayed to syslog via the special device file /dev /log. Kernel messages are similarly sent to syslog through the special device file /dev/klog. Finally, syslog may receive messages from other systems via the network using a network socket specified in the /etc/services file. The only point in mentioning these syslog message sources is to identify these files when troubleshooting syslog problems. For instance, if kernel messages are not being received and logged by syslog, ensure that the /dev/klog file exists:

```
# ls -l /dev/klog
crw------  1 root    system   3, 0 Jul 19 1996 klog
```

If the file is missing or not correct, simply recreate the klog file:

```
# cd /dev
# ./MAKEDEV klog
```

Similarly, if syslog messages are not being received from other systems via the network, as part of your troubleshooting effort, ensure that the /etc /services file exists and contains the following entry:

```
syslog    514/udp
```

Note that the /dev/log file is a socket that is created and maintained by the syslogd itself and exists only while syslogd is running. If the /dev/log file is absent, it is likely that the syslog daemon is not running. Simply restart syslogd and the /dev/log socket will be created:

```
# /usr/sbin/syslogd
```

11.2.2. Starting and Stopping syslogd

The syslog daemon, syslogd, is usually started when the system starts from the syslog startup script, /sbin/rc3.d/S10syslog, which is actually a symbolic link to the /sbin/init.d/syslog script. Syslog is started fairly early in the boot process due to its importance in the error-logging process. Syslog reads its configuration file when it starts up and rereads the configuration file when it receives a hangup signal. The configuration file is simply a set of rules that instruct the syslog daemon what messages to log and where to log those messages.

When syslogd starts, it creates the file /var/run/syslog.pid if possible. This file contains a single line with the process ID (PID) of the syslogd process. This file can then be consulted to obtain syslogd's PID when it is necessary to stop or restart syslogd. For example, to terminate syslogd, use the following command:

```
# kill `cat /var/run/syslog.pid`
```

A common destination for syslog messages is the system console. Depending on the amount of activity or the health of the system, the volume of messages printed on the console may be very low. Occasionally, however, the system administrator needs to diagnose one or more ongoing system problems from the console. If the syslog daemon is sending frequent messages to the console in this situation, it may be difficult to troubleshoot problems. Beginning with Digital UNIX version 4.0, there is a new command, /usr/sbin/syslog, that allows enabling and disabling syslog-generated console messages. When you are working from the console and find syslog informational messages hampering your effectiveness, simply issue this command,

```
# /usr/sbin/syslog console_off
```

to disable future syslog messages. Remember to turn syslog messages to the console back on with this command when the console work is complete:

```
# /usr/sbin/syslog console_on
```

If console messages are disabled and the system is rebooted, the default behavior of enabled syslog console messages is restored.

11.2.3. The Syslog Configuration File

The syslog facility has a single configuration file, /etc/syslog.conf. This file is simply a text file that contains entries that specify the facility (see Table

11.1), which is the part of the system that produced the message, the message severity level (see Table 11.2), and the destination to which the syslogd daemon should send the message.

Each line of the syslog configuration file contains a single entry. See Figure 11.1 for an example of an /etc/syslog.conf file.

Name(s)	Description
kern	Kernel messages
user	User-level messages
mail	Mail system messages
daemon	System daemon messages
auth, security	Security/authorization messages
syslog	Messages generated by syslogd itself
lpr	Printer subsystem messages
news	Network news subsystem messages
uucp	UUCP subsystem messages
cron	Clock daemon messages
megasafe	Polycenter AdvFS
local0	Reserved for local use
local1	Reserved for local use
local2	Reserved for local use
local3	Reserved for local use
local4	Reserved for local use
local5	Reserved for local use
local6	Reserved for local use
local7	Reserved for local use

Table 11.1 Available syslog Facilities

Name(s)	Number	Description
emerg, panic	0	System is unusable
alert	1	Action must be taken immediately
crit	2	Critical conditions
err, error	3	Error conditions
warn, warning	4	Warning conditions
notice	5	Normal but significant condition
info	6	Informational
debug	7	Debug messages

Table 11.2 Available syslog Priorities

The syntax and format of the /etc/syslog.conf file must be followed exactly, as the syslog daemon will stop reading the syslog.conf file if an error or format violation is encountered. This means that a simple typographical error in the middle of the syslog.conf file will prevent syslogd from seeing any entries after the error. The most common error is using spaces to delimit the facility and severity levels from the destination. The only permitted delimiter is one or more tab characters—spaces are not allowed in a syslog.conf entry.

The first half of a syslog.conf entry specifies the source and severity of messages that syslog should watch for. The facility and its severity level must be separated by a period (.); more than one facility can be specified on a line by separating the multiple facilities with commas (,). Additionally, more than one facility and severity level can be specified on a line by separating them with semicolons (;). Finally, an asterisk (*) may be specified in place of a facility, indicating that messages generated by all parts of the system are to be logged. All messages of the specified severity and greater will be logged.

A Digital UNIX-unique facility.severity pair is "msgbuf.err." This facility.severity pair is crucial for recovering any messages that may be pending in the kernel syslog buffer in the event of a system crash. When a Digital UNIX system recovers from a system crash, any such messages recovered are placed in the file specified as the "msgbuf.err" destination in the syslog.conf

```
#
# syslogd config file
#
# facilities: kern user mail daemon auth syslog
lpr binary
# priorities: emerg alert crit err warning notice
info debug
kern.debug           /var/adm/syslog.dated/kern.log
user.debug           /var/adm/syslog.dated/user.log
mail.debug           /var/adm/syslog.dated/mail.log
daemon.debug         /var/adm/syslog.dated/daemon.log
auth.debug           /var/adm/syslog.dated/auth.log
syslog.debug         /var/adm/syslog.dated/syslog.log
lpr.debug            /var/adm/syslog.dated/lpr.log

msgbuf.err           /var/adm/crash/msgbuf.savecore

kern.debug           /var/adm/messages
kern.debug           /dev/console
*.emerg              *
```

Figure 11.1 An Example /etc/syslog.conf

file. When syslog starts, it looks for this file and, if it exists, processes any messages contained within and deletes the file. The default syslog.conf entry to provide this functionality is:

```
msgbuf.err              /var/adm/crash/msgbuf.savecore
```

The second half of a syslog.conf entry specifies the destination where syslog will log the messages that match the "facility.severity" criteria defined by the first half of the syslog.conf entry. There are four possible destinations for messages:

- A file name that begins with a leading slash (/)—The syslog daemon will append messages to this file. Note that this can be an ordinary file or a special device file such as /dev/console, which will cause all messages sent to this destination to appear on the system console.

- A host name preceded by an "at" sign (@)—Appropriate messages are forwarded to the syslog daemon on the named host.
- A comma-separated list of users—Appropriate messages are written to those users if they are logged-in.
- An asterisk (*)—Appropriate messages are written to all users who are logged-in.

A variation of the file name syslog.conf destination that is unique to Digital UNIX is when the file name destination begins with the pathname /var/adm/syslog.dated. When the syslog.dated syntax is specified, the syslog daemon creates a date subdirectory under /var/adm/syslog.dated, and thus produces a day-by-day account of the messages received. For example, the following /etc/syslog.conf entry,

```
kern.debug              /var/adm/syslog.dated/kern.log
```

will cause syslog to log kernel debug messages in the following file if the syslog were to be started or restarted on August 17 at 8 P.M.:

```
/var/adm/syslog.dated/17-Aug-20:00/kern.log
```

Be aware that if a syslog destination is a normal file (e.g., begins with a leading slash in /etc/syslog.conf), syslog always appends to that file and the file will grow indefinitely. Monitor such log files and trim them when necessary to avoid filling your file system(s). The following is an example of trimming /var/adm/messages:

```
# cp /var/adm/messages /var/adm/messages.1
# cp /dev/null /var/adm/messages
```

Note that the existing messages file is copied to a backup, then the original messages file is emptied by copying the /dev/null file to it. This file-emptying technique is used here rather than simply deleting the original messages file because if a syslog log file is removed, the log file will not be recreated until the next time syslogd is restarted.

As mentioned before, the facility.severity level pair(s) must be separated from the destination by one or more tabs. Blank lines and lines beginning with a pound sign (#) are considered comments and are ignored. Finally, the /etc/syslog.conf file should not be world-writable. The appropriate permissions on this file are 644, or readable by everyone and writable only by the owner, which is bin.

As an example of some of syslog's configuration rules, consider the following sample syslog.conf entries:

```
kern.*                      /dev/console
*.notice;mail.info          /var/adm/mail.log
kern.err                    @saturn
*                           /var/adm/messages
*.emerg                     *
*.alert;auth.warning        root
```

These example configuration file entries log messages as follows:

- Log all kernel messages onto the system console.
- Log all notice (or higher) level messages and all mail system messages except debug messages into the file /var/adm/syslog/mail.
- Forward kernel messages of error severity or higher to the syslogd on saturn.
- Log all messages into the /var/adm/messages file.
- Inform all logged-in users of any emergency messages and inform the root user, if logged-in, of any alert message or any warning message (or higher) from the authorization system.

11.2.4. Default syslog.conf

When the syslog daemon starts, it looks for /etc/syslog.conf by default. An alternate configuration file may be specified on the syslogd command line when starting syslog. For example, to start syslog and use /var/adm/syslog.txt, use the following syntax:

```
# /usr/sbin/syslogd -f /var/adm/syslog.txt
```

If the syslog configuration file is absent, syslog defaults to these message rules:

```
*.err        /dev/console
*.panic      *
```

These defaults instruct syslog to send all error messages to the console and all kernel panic messages to all logged-in users. No files are written.

11.2.5. Sending Messages to Syslog from Scripts

Since syslog is the primary logging mechanism for the operating system, it occasionally may make sense to use syslog for logging in custom system administration or user scripts. The way to send messages to syslog from a script, or the command line, for that matter, is the logger(1) command. The logger command provides an interface to the syslog() routine. The syntax of the logger command allows specification of the facility and severity, plus provides the ability to either specify the text of the message to be logged on the command line, or indicate a file whose contents will be the text of the message. For example:

```
# logger -p user.debug "Program error"
```

will cause syslog to log the following message:

```
Aug 17 20:28:58 saturn root: Program error
```

in the destination specified in /etc/syslog.conf for the "user.debug" facility.severity pair.

11.3. THE BINARY ERROR LOG

While syslog exists on all modern implementations of UNIX, the Binary Error Log facility is unique to Digital UNIX. This facility, normally referred to as the binlog, from the name of the system daemon responsible, binlogd, generates the binary error log. The binlog is a mechanism, similar in functionality to syslog, that collects and logs messages from the kernel. The types of messages that the binlog daemon logs are hardware and software errors and operational events, such as system startups and shutdowns. Obviously, these messages are of great interest to a system administrator, and understanding how to examine and interpret the binary error log is the key to successfully troubleshooting system problems. The binlog facility has two components, the binlog daemon, /usr/sbin/binlogd, and the binlog configuration file, /etc/binlog.conf. In addition, since the resulting binary error log is, as its name implies, in a binary format, there are two utilities provided by Digital to view and manipulate this log, uerf(8) and DECevent.

11.3.1. binlogd

The binlog daemon is an executable system utility normally started at system startup and always running while the system is in multi-user mode. The binlogd utility reads messages sent to it from the system kernel. These messages can be informational only, warnings, or errors that need attention. The messages themselves are single lines, optionally containing a priority value indicating the severity of the message. Messages are received by binlogd from two sources:

- The special device file /dev/kbinlog
- Other systems across the network, via a socket specified in /etc /services

The system kernel itself submits messages to binlog via the special device file /dev/kbinlog. Additionally, binlog may receive messages from other systems via the network using a network socket specified in the /etc /services file. The only reason I mention these two sources for messages is to identify places to check when troubleshooting binlog problems. For instance, if kernel messages are not being received into the binary error log, ensure that the /dev/kbinlog file exists:

```
# ls -l /dev/klog
crw------  1 root    system  31, 0 Jul 19 1996 kbinlog
```

If the file is missing or not correct, simply recreate the kbinlog file:

```
# cd /dev
# ./MAKEDEV kbinlog
```

Similarly, if other Digital UNIX systems are sending binary error log messages to a particular system but the messages are not being logged, ensure that the /etc/services file exists and contains the following entry:

```
binlogd     706/udp
```

11.3.2. Starting and Stopping binlogd

The binary error log daemon, binlogd, is usually started when the system starts from the syslog startup script, /sbin/rc3.d/S10syslog, which is actually a symbolic link to the /sbin/init.d/syslog script. The binlog daemon is started fairly early in the boot process due to its importance in the error-logging process. Note that both the syslog daemon and the binlog daemon are started from the same startup script, /sbin/init.d/syslog. More importantly, be aware that the same script, /sbin/init.d/syslog will stop the syslog daemon when the system shuts down, but the binlog daemon is not shut down. I mention this because if you use the syslog startup script to manually stop and start syslog, only syslogd will be stopped by the first invocation, but both syslogd and binlogd will be started by the second invocation, resulting in two binlogd daemons running. For example:

```
# /sbin/init.d/syslog/stop
# /sbin/init.d/syslog/start
System error logger started
Binary error logger started
# ps -ef | egrep 'binlog|syslog'
root    4754    1 0.0 13:40:41 ??       0:00.03
/usr/sbin/syslogd
root    4763    1 0.0 13:40:41 ??       0:00.01
/usr/sbin/binlogd
root     225    1 0.0  Aug 19 ??       0:00.06
/usr/sbin/binlogd
```

This situation is to be avoided at all costs, for having multiple binlog daemons running can corrupt the binary error log, preventing access to error log entries. The solution to this is to not use the /sbin/init.d/syslog start/stop script to manually start or stop either syslogd or binlogd. If it becomes necessary to start or stop either daemon, simply send the daemon a terminate signal via the kill command.

When binlogd starts, it creates the file /var/run/binlogd.pid, if possible. This file contains a single line with the process ID (PID) of the binlogd process. This file can then be consulted to obtain binlogd's PID when it is necessary to stop or restart binlogd.

11.3.3. The Binlog Configuration File

The binlog facility has a single configuration file, /etc/binlog.conf, that is read when binlogd starts up, and reread when it receives a hang-up signal. This file is simply a text file containing entries that specify the event code (Table 11.3), which is the source of the message; the message priority level, which can be severe, high, or low; and the destination to which the binlogd daemon should send the message.

Each line of the binlog configuration file contains a single entry. See Figure 11.2 for an example of the default /etc/binlog.conf file.

Number	Description	Category
100	CPU machine checks and exceptions	Hardware
101	Memory	Hardware
102	Disks	Hardware
103	Tapes	Hardware
104	Device controllers	Hardware
105	Adapters	Hardware
106	Buses	Hardware
107	Stray interrupts	Hardware
108	Console events	Hardware
109	Stack dumps	Hardware
199	SCSI CAM events	Hardware
201	CI port-to-port driver events	Software
202	System communications services events	Software
250	Generic ASCII informational messages	Informational
300	ASCII startup messages	Operational
301	ASCII shutdown messages	Operational
302	Panic messages	Operational
310	Timestamp	Operational
350	Diagnostic status messages	Operational
351	Repair and maintenance messages	Operational

Table 11.3 Available binlog Events

```
#
# binlogd configuration file
#
# format of a line:  event_code.priority        destination
#
# where: event_code - see codes in binlog.h and man page, * = all
events
#        priority   - severe, high, low, * = all priorities
#        destination - local file pathname or remote system
hostname
#

*.*
/usr/adm/binary.errlog

dumpfile
/usr/adm/crash/binlogdumpfile
```

Figure 11.2 An Example /etc/binlog.conf

The syntax and format of the /etc/binlog.conf file must be followed exactly, as the binlog daemon is as unforgiving of configuration file errors as the syslog daemon.

The first half of a binlog.conf entry specifies the event code and priority of messages that the binlog daemon should watch for. The event code and priority level must be separated by a period (.). In addition, an asterisk (*) may be specified in place of both an event code and a priority, indicating that all event codes and all priorities, respectively, are to be logged.

The second half of a binlog.conf entry specifies the destination where the binlog daemon will log the messages that match the "event_code. priority" criteria defined by the first half of the binlog.conf entry. There are two possible destinations for binlog messages:

- A file name that begins with a leading slash (/)—The binlog daemon will append messages to this file. Note that this file should be an ordinary file, since the resulting messages are logged in a binary format.
- A host name preceded by an at sign (@)—Appropriate messages are forwarded to the binlog daemon on the named host. Obviously,

since the binlog is a Digital UNIX facility, it is only reasonable to forward binlog messages to other Digital UNIX systems.

A special binlog.conf entry is necessary for recovering any error messages that may be pending in the kernel binary event-log buffer in the event of a system crash. When a Digital UNIX system recovers from a system crash, the savecore(8) command recovers any such pending messages from a system dump and places them in /usr/adm/crash/binlogdumpfile. When binlog starts, it looks for this file and, if it exists, processes any messages contained within and deletes the file. The default binlog.conf entry to provide this functionality is:

```
dumpfile        /usr/adm/crash/binlogdumpfile
```

The primary binary error-log destination specified by the *.* eventcode.priority pair is always appended to by binlogd. This binary.errlog file should be monitored and trimmed when necessary to avoid running out of disk space. Another reason to trim the binary.errlog is to keep the log to a manageable size to reduce the time queries against the file takes. To trim the binary.errlog, do the following:

```
# cp /var/adm/binary.errlog /var/adm/binary.errlog.1
# cp /dev/null /var/adm/binary.errlog
```

This copies the current binary.errlog to a backup, then empties the active binary.errlog by copying /dev/null to it.

Within the binlog.conf file, event code and priority pair(s) must be separated from the destination by one or more tabs. Spaces are not allowed. Blank lines and lines beginning with a pound sign (#) are considered comments and are ignored. Finally, the /etc/binlog.conf file should not be world writable. The appropriate permissions on this file are 755, or readable and executable by everyone and writable only by the owner, which is bin.

11.3.4. Default binlog.conf

When the syslog daemon starts, it looks for /etc/binlogd.conf by default. An alternate configuration file may be specified on the binlogd command line when starting binlog. The default /etc/binlogd.conf delivered by Digital (Figure 11.2) is usually sufficient for more systems—all event classes and severity levels are logged to /usr/adm/binary.errlog.

11.3.5. Examining the Binary Error Log

As mentioned previously, the log file generated by the binlog daemon is a binary file not directly human-readable. The format of the binary error log is such that the binlog daemon can quickly process and append events it receives. An advantage of the binary error log not being ASCII is that events can be extracted and sorted quickly by the Digital-supplied tools. Two utilities are available for examining and manipulating the messages contained in the binary error log:

- uerf(8), the Ultrix Event Report Formatter
- dia(8), the DECevent event report formatter

11.3.5.1. uerf

The uerf utility is part of the base Digital UNIX operating system and is a tool to translate the binary error log produced by the binlog daemon into human-readable output. Run with no options, the uerf command simply reads the file specified as the destination for the *.* entry in the /etc/binlog. conf file, typically /var/adm/binary.errlog, and prints on standard output each entry in chronological order, oldest events first. This default ordering is not tremendously useful, for the most recent events are usually the ones of immediate interest, especially when investigating a problem. A commonly specified command line option, -R, outputs the records in reverse chronological order, showing the most recent events first. See Figure 11.3 for the uerf output of several different types of events.

Note that the binary.error log file is owned by root and belongs to the adm group, and that the default permissions are 640. If you want to use the uerf command to translate the default binary.errlog, you must belong to the adm group or be root. Optionally, you can change the ownership or permissions to allow others to access this file via the uerf command. For instance, to allow all users to read the file:

```
# ls -l /var/adm/binary.errlog
-rw-r——  1 root    adm      692400 Aug 25 12:46
   /var/adm/binary.errlog
# chmod 644 /var/adm/binary.errlog
-rw-r—r—  1 root    adm      692400 Aug 25 12:46
   /var/adm/binary.errlog
```

```
# uerf -R ❶
                                                     uerf version 4.2-011 (122)

******************************** ENTRY    1. ********************************
— EVENT INFORMATION —
EVENT CLASS                             OPERATIONAL EVENT
OS EVENT TYPE              300.         SYSTEM STARTUP ❷
SEQUENCE NUMBER             0.
OPERATING SYSTEM                        DEC OSF/1
OCCURRED/LOGGED ON                      Tue Aug 26 17:36:46 1997
OCCURRED ON SYSTEM                      saturn
SYSTEM ID             x00060011
SYSTYPE               x00000000
MESSAGE                                 Alpha boot: available memory from
                                         _0x76e000 to 0x3fee000
                                        Digital UNIX V4.0B  (Rev. 564); Sat
                                         _Aug 23 11:34:06 MDT 1997
                                        physical memory = 64.00 megabytes.
                                        available memory = 56.64 megabytes.
                                        using 238 buffers containing 1.85
                                        _megabytes of memory
                                        AlphaServer 1000 4/266
                                        Firmware revision: 4.8
                                        PALcode: OSF version 1.45
                                        pci0 at nexus
                                        psiop0 at pci0 slot 6
                                        Loading SIOP: script 800000, reg
                                         _82040000, data 80dff0
                                        scsi0 at psiop0 slot 0
                                        rz0 at scsi0 target 0 lun 0 (LID=0)
                                         _(DEC       RZ28      (C) DEC D41C)
                                        rz1 at scsi0 target 1 lun 0 (LID=1)
                                         _(DEC       RZ28      (C) DEC D41C)
                                        rz4 at scsi0 target 4 lun 0 (LID=2)
                                         _(DEC       RRD43     (C) DEC 1084)
                                        eisa0 at pci0
                                        ace0 at eisa0
                                        ace1 at eisa0
                                        lp0 at eisa0
                                        fdi0 at eisa0
                                        fd0 at fdi0 unit 0
                                        cirrus0 at eisa0
                                        cirrus0: Cirrus Logic CL-GD5424 (SVGA)
                                         _512 Kbytes
                                        tu0: DECchip 21041-AA: Revision: 1.1
                                        tu0 at pci0 slot 11
                                                            (continued)
```

Figure 11.3 An Example uerf(8) Output

```
                                        tu0: DEC TULIP Ethernet Interface,
                                        _hardware address: 00-00-F8-01-42-5F
                                        tu0: console mode: selecting 10BaseT
                                        _(UTP) port: half duplex: no link
                                        gpc0 at eisa0
                                        kernel console: cirrus0
                                        dli: configured
******************************* ENTRY    2. *******************************
   —— EVENT INFORMATION ——

EVENT CLASS                             OPERATIONAL EVENT
OS EVENT TYPE              301.         SYSTEM SHUTDOWN ❸
SEQUENCE NUMBER            3.
OPERATING SYSTEM                        DEC OSF/1
OCCURRED/LOGGED ON                      Sun Aug 24 17:42:57 1997
OCCURRED ON SYSTEM                      saturn
SYSTEM ID          x00060011
SYSTYPE            x00000000
MESSAGE                                 System halted by root:

******************************* ENTRY    3. *******************************
   —— EVENT INFORMATION ——

EVENT CLASS                             ERROR EVENT
OS EVENT TYPE              199.         CAM SCSI ❹
SEQUENCE NUMBER           2.
OPERATING SYSTEM                        DEC OSF/1
OCCURRED/LOGGED ON                      Sun Aug 24 07:26:15 1997
OCCURRED ON SYSTEM                      saturn
SYSTEM ID          x00060011
SYSTYPE            x00000000
   —— UNIT INFORMATION ——

CLASS                     x0005         RODIRECT
SUBSYSTEM                 x0000         DISK
BUS #                     x0000
                          x0018         LUN x0
                                        TARGET x3
```

❶ The uerf(8) command to display binary.errlog events in reverse chronological
order, i.e. Most recent events first
❷ An operational event for a system startup showing some very descriptive
system configuration information
❸ A operational event indicating that the system was manually halted by the
superuser
❹ A hardware event indicating a SCSI disk error; in this case a problem with
the CD-ROM drive at SCSI address 3

Figure 11.3 Continued

This change will persist across reboots as long as the file is not removed or renamed, in which case the binlogd will recreate the file with the original default permissions. Unless there is an overriding reason for allowing world access to the binary.errlog, however, I recommend against changing the defaults specified by Digital to avoid problems in future releases of Digital UNIX.

Obviously, since the binary.errlog contains all binlog events since the binary.errlog was started, one after another, sorting out useful information would seem at first glance difficult. However, by using several of uerf's command line parameters, you can request to see only certain types of events, events related just to particular disks, events in a specified time range, or summaries of the events categorized by quantity. Additionally, as uerf's output can be many pages, piping this output to a favorite pager, such as more(1) or pg(1) is recommended. Some commonly used uerf commands are:

- Display the most recent system startup events, including the system configuration information:

```
# uerf -R -r 300 | more
```

- Show a summary report of all events in the binary.errlog:

```
# uerf -S
```

- Show all events between 6:30 p.m. on July 15, 1997 and 6:30 p.m. on August 15, 1997:

```
# uerf -t s:15-jul-1997,18:30:00 e:15-aug-1997,18:30:00
```

- Show all events from a backup binary.errlog:

```
# uerf -R -f /var/adm/binary.errlog.old
```

- Show all memory-related events, such as single-bit corrected read data and double-bit uncorrectable errors, in reverse chronological order with the most detailed output:

```
# uerf -R -M mem -o full
```

These and the many other uerf command line parameters detailed in the uerf reference page can be combined, as in the last example above, to further narrow the search query. All specified parameters are "AND'ed" together by uerf when determining matching events. Basically, the uerf command allows the system administrator to query the binary.errlog for the records of interest. For example, if you suspect a particular disk is beginning to fail, keep a watch on the binary error log for events from that disk. Perhaps run the following uerf command each night before midnight via cron(8) to E-mail you the disk-related events since the last midnight:

```
uerf -R -D rz9 -t s:00:00      (Assuming the suspect disk is rz9)
```

Useful though it may be, the uerf command does not provide absolutely every useful piece of information that exists in the binary errorlog, though specifying the "-o full" command line switch does provide more detailed output. The uerf command's main advantage is that it will exist on all Digital UNIX systems. To address uerf's translation shortcomings, Digital created a more advanced tool to complement uerf: DECevent.

11.3.5.2. DECevent

DECevent is an optional product available directly from Digital's customer support organizations, or downloadable from the Digital Equipment DECevent web page:

> http://www.service.digital.com/decevent/

Per the web page, "DECevent is a rules-based hardware fault management diagnostic tool that provides error event translation. During translation, the binary portion of an event log is transformed into human-readable text. These events can then be displayed on the screen or printed." DECevent is simply a better uerf(8). DECevent, or dia(8) as the DECevent executable is called, mostly has the same syntax as uerf and reads the same binary.errlog as uerf. See the man page for dia for the differences. As an example, compare the uerf output in Figure 11.3 to the DECevent output in Figure 11.4 for the same events.

It is immediately apparent that the DECevent output is more detailed than the equivalent uerf output, and although much of the DECevent output is unintelligible to the average person, this is exactly the level of detail that the Digital field engineers need to quickly identify and resolve problems.

The DECevent product is actually two components, the Translation module and the Analysis/Notification module. The Translation piece of DECevent is the uerf-like functionality and is available to all Digital UNIX users. I strongly recommend getting DECevent, if only for this Translation piece. The Analysis/Notification module is only available to those Digital UNIX users having a support contract with Digital Equipment and requires

```
# dia -R ❶

DECevent V2.5

******************************* ENTRY   1 *******************************
Logging OS                        2. Digital UNIX
System Architecture               2. Alpha
Event sequence number             0.
Timestamp of occurrence              26-AUG-1997 17:36:46
Host name                            saturn
System type register     x00000011  AlphaServer 1000
Number of CPUs (mpnum)   x00000001
CPU logging event (mperr) x00000000


Event validity                   1. O/S claims event is valid
Event severity                   5. Low Priority
Entry type                     300. Start-Up ASCII Message Type


SWI Minor class                  9. ASCII Message
SWI Minor sub class              3. Startup

ASCII Message
    Alpha boot: available memory from 0x76e000 to 0x3fee000
    Digital UNIX V4.0B  (Rev. 564); Sat Aug 23 11:34:06 MDT 1997
    physical memory = 64.00 megabytes.
    available memory = 56.64 megabytes.
    using 238 buffers containing 1.85 megabytes of memory
    AlphaServer 1000 4/266
    Firmware revision: 4.8
    PALcode: OSF version 1.45
    pci0 at nexus
    psiop0 at pci0 slot 6
    Loading SIOP: script 800000, reg 82040000, data 80dff0
    scsi0 at psiop0 slot 0
    rz0 at scsi0 target 0 lun 0 (LID=0) (DEC     RZ28     (C) DEC D41C)
    rz1 at scsi0 target 1 lun 0 (LID=1) (DEC     RZ28     (C) DEC D41C)
    rz4 at scsi0 target 4 lun 0 (LID=2) (DEC     RRD43    (C) DEC 1084)
    eisa0 at pci0     ace0 at eisa0
    ace1 at eisa0
    lp0 at eisa0
    fdi0 at eisa0

                                                          (continued)
```

Figure 11.4 An Example DECevent Output

```
        fd0 at fdi0 unit 0
        cirrus0 at eisa0
        cirrus0: Cirrus Logic CL-GD5424 (SVGA) 512 Kbytes
        tu0: DECchip 21041-AA: Revision: 1.1
        tu0 at pci0 slot 11
        tu0: DEC TULIP Ethernet Interface, hardware address: 00-00-F8-01-42-5F
        tu0: console mode: selecting 10BaseT (UTP) port: half duplex: no link
        gpc0 at eisa0
        kernel console: cirrus0
        dli: configured


******************************* ENTRY    2 *******************************
Logging OS                      2. Digital UNIX
System Architecture             2. Alpha
Event sequence number           3.
Timestamp of occurrence            24-AUG-1997 17:42:57
Host name                          saturn


System type register      x00000011  AlphaServer 1000
Number of CPUs (mpnum)     x00000001
CPU logging event (mperr)  x00000000


Event validity                  1. O/S claims event is valid
Event severity                  5. Low Priority
Entry type                    301. Shutdown ASCII Message Type


SWI Minor class                 9. ASCII Message
SWI Minor sub class             2. Shutdown


ASCII Message                      System halted by root:


******************************* ENTRY    3 *******************************
Logging OS                      2. Digital UNIX
System Architecture             2. Alpha
Event sequence number           2.
Timestamp of occurrence            24-AUG-1997 07:26:15
Host name                          saturn


System type register      x00000011  AlphaServer 1000
Number of CPUs (mpnum)     x00000001
CPU logging event (mperr)  x00000000
```

Figure 11.4 Continued

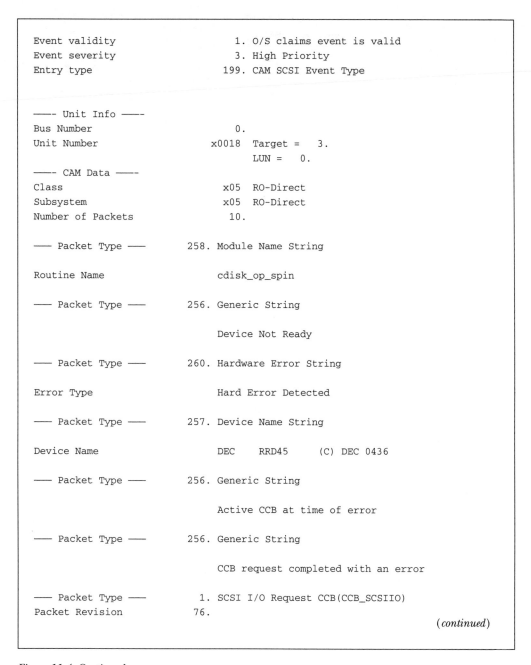

```
Event validity                    1. O/S claims event is valid
Event severity                    3. High Priority
Entry type                      199. CAM SCSI Event Type


—--- Unit Info —--
Bus Number                        0.
Unit Number                   x0018  Target =   3.
                                     LUN =    0.
—--- CAM Data —--
Class                         x05  RO-Direct
Subsystem                     x05  RO-Direct
Number of Packets              10.

—— Packet Type ——          258. Module Name String

Routine Name                     cdisk_op_spin

—— Packet Type ——          256. Generic String

                                 Device Not Ready

—— Packet Type ——          260. Hardware Error String

Error Type                       Hard Error Detected

—— Packet Type ——          257. Device Name String

Device Name                      DEC    RRD45     (C) DEC 0436

—— Packet Type ——          256. Generic String

                                 Active CCB at time of error

—— Packet Type ——          256. Generic String

                                 CCB request completed with an error

—— Packet Type ——            1. SCSI I/O Request CCB(CCB_SCSIIO)
Packet Revision               76.
                                                     (continued)
```

Figure 11.4 Continued

```
CCB Address              xFFFFFC0003F89580
CCB Length                  x00C0
XPT Function Code            x01  Execute requested SCSI I/O
Cam Status                   x84  CCB Request Completed WITH Error
                                  Autosense Data Valid for Target
Path ID                      0.
Target ID                    3.
Target LUN                   0.
Cam Flags                x000000C0  Data Direction (11: no data)
*pdrv_ptr                xFFFFFC0003F89228
*next_ccb                x0000000000000000
*req_map                 x0000000000000000
void (*cam_cbfcnp)()     xFFFFFC0000481600
*data_ptr                x0000000000000000
Data Transfer Length         0.
*sense_ptr               xFFFFFC0003F89250
Auotsense Byte Length       64.
CDB Length                   6.
Scatter/Gather Entry Cnt     0.
SCSI Status                  x02  Check Condition
Autosense Residue Length    x33
Transfer Residue Length  x00000000
(CDB) Command & Data Buf


       15—<-12  11—<-08  07—<-04  03—<-00    :Byte Order
  0000:           00000000  00000000  00000000   *   ............*


Timeout Value            x0000000A
*msg_ptr                 x0000000000000000
Message Length               0.
Vendor Unique Flags        x0000
Tag Queue Actions          x00


—— Packet Type ——       256. Generic String

                              Error, exception, or abnormal condition


—— Packet Type ——       256. Generic String

                              NOT READY - Logical unit is NOT ready


—— Packet Type ——       768. SCSI Sense Data
Packet Revision              0.
```

Figure 11.4 Continued

```
Error Code                        x70   Current Error
Segment #                         x00
Information Byte 3                x00
             Byte 2               x00
             Byte 1               x00
             Byte 0               x00
Sense Key                         x02   Not Ready
Additional Sense Length           x05
CMD Specific Info Byte 3          x00
                  Byte 2          x00
                  Byte 1          x00
                  Byte 0          x00
ASC & ASCQ                        x3A00  ASC  =   x003A
                                         ASCQ =   x0000
                                         Medium Not Present
FRU Code                          x00
Sense Key Specific Byte 0         x00   Sense Key Data NOT Valid
                  Byte 1          x00
                  Byte 2          x00

Addition Sense Data Size                Allocated by Driver

Count of valid bytes:             46.


        15—<-12  11—<-08  07—<-04  03—<-00   :Byte Order
 0000:   00000000 00000000 00000000 00000000   *...............*
 0010:   00000000 00000000 00000000 00000000   *...............*
 0020:   00000000 00000000 00000000 00000000   *...............*


❶ The dia(8) command to display binary.errlog events in reverse chronological
order, i.e. Most recent events first
```

Figure 11.4 Continued

a Product Authorization Key (PAK) license to activate. Basically, the DECevent Analysis/Notification functionality provides automatic proactive monitoring of a system's binary error log for identified error conditions and notification when such errors are detected. This notification can take several forms, including E-mail notification either directly to Digital field engineers or to the system administrator. If you do have a support agreement with Digital Equipment, contact your support representative for information on getting and configuring DECevent's Analysis/Notification module.

11.4. THE CRASH DUMP PROCESS

When a Digital UNIX system encounters a problem so severe, whether a software issue in the kernel or an unexpected hardware fault, that further operation is impossible or just unwise, the operating system will halt operation. This immediate halt typically results in a panic and, if the auto_action console prompt is set to boot, a system reboot. Usually when a system crashes in this manner, the operating system copies an image of the contents of all or part of the physical memory to disk. As part of the reboot process, the operating system checks if a memory image from a system crash exists, and if so, moves that image from disk to an operating system file and creates several other ancillary files that, together, are called the Crash Dump Files. The system administrator and/or an experienced Digital support engineer can then use these Crash Dump Files to determine the cause of the crash.

In order to ensure that these Crash Dump Files are created, it is important to understand the sequence of events in a crash dump recovery so that sufficient system resources, primarily disk space, are preallocated. The following topics will be covered:

- The Crash Dump sequence
- Guidelines for deciding how much disk space to allocate
- Forcing a hung system to generate a crash dump

11.4.1. The Crash Dump Sequence

When a Digital UNIX system crashes, an image of the memory is copied to disk, specifically to the swap area(s). Which swap areas are copied to is determined by the size of the memory image to be saved, and the number and size of the available swap areas:

- If the memory image fits in the primary swap area (identified as swap1 in the /etc/fstab file), the memory image is written into this primary swap area, starting at the end of the partition. The image is placed as far from the front of the primary swap partition to avoid being overwritten when the system is next rebooted.

- If the memory image does not fit into the primary swap area, the memory image is written into the secondary swap areas (identified as swap2 in the /etc/fstab file).
- If the memory image is too large to fit into the secondary swap areas, the memory image is written to the secondary swap partitions until those partitions are full. The remaining part is then written to the end of the primary swap partition.
- If the memory image is too large to fit into all swap areas, combined, no crash dump is created.

After the memory image is copied to the swap area(s), the system reboots. During the reboot process, the /sbin/init.d/savecore startup script runs the savecore(8) program, determines if a crash dump has been made and if sufficient file system space exists in which to save the crash dump. If a crash has occurred and a crash dump was successfully saved, and there is enough file system space, savecore begins to copy the memory image from the swap area(s) into a file system, /var/adm/crash, by default.

After the savecore command has successfully saved a crash dump, at least three files are produced, where n specifies the number of the crash:

- vmcore.n—The physical memory image at the time of the crash
- vmunix.n—The running kernel at the time of the crash
- crash-data.n—A human-readable crash summary file

The value of n is maintained by savecore in the bounds file in the crash directory. This value is simply a sequence number that is incremented after each crash, with the first crash being number 0. As crash dump files can be quite large, especially the vmcore.n files, ensure that crash dump files that are no longer needed are removed to avoid running out of disk space.

When diagnosing a system crash, an experienced crash dump analyst will need all three files in order to troubleshoot what caused the crash and how to prevent future crashes. You may be required to transfer the crash dump files for a particular crash to a Digital customer service center for analysis. While such crash dump troubleshooting is beyond the scope of this text, it is at least interesting to examine the crash-data.n file, for this file contains a summary of the system at the time of the crash. It is sometimes possible to determine from the contents of the crash-data.n file if a particular process, or possibly a hardware problem, may have caused the crash.

11.4.2. Crash Dump Disk Space Guidelines

There are two types of disk space to consider when planning for Crash Dump disk space: swap space and the crash file system. Both types must be sufficient to hold at least one crash dump. Since the crash dump is an image of physical memory, the absolute minimum space required for each type of disk space is one-time physical memory. For instance, if a system has 512 megabytes of memory, I would recommend starting at that size.

The first place a crash dump is saved to is the swap partition(s). The swap partitions should be at least 1X physical memory, if only to hold a crash dump. A possible exception to this rule-of-thumb is on Very Large Memory (VLM) systems with physical memory sizes over one gigabyte. On these types of systems, it may simply be unfeasible or undesirable to allocate 1X physical memory for swap space. If this is the case, I would recommend having the ability to temporarily add additional swap space to capture a crash dump if such a system were to begin crashing. Once a crash dump is captured and the reason for the crashes is identified, reassign that extra swap space.

The second place a crash dump is saved is to the crash file system, which is /var/adm/crash by default. Again, the file system where the crash dump files will be saved must be sufficiently sized to hold at least one crash dump; that is, 1X physical memory. If /var/adm/crash is not appropriate, set the run-time configuration variable SAVECORE_DIR to another location. For example, to set /usr/crash as the crash directory, issue this command:

```
# rcmgr set SAVECORE_DIR /usr/crash
```

Again, if it is unreasonable on a VLM system to keep a large amount of disk space available in a file system on a permanent basis, simply be prepared to point the SAVECORE_DIR to a temporary location in the event of system crash problems, at least until a crash dump is captured.

11.4.3. Forcing a Crash Dump

It is possible for a Digital UNIX system to stop responding in any way as the result of a software or hardware problem. When this occurs, a crash dump is not generated, due to the system being in a hung state. In order to force a crash when a system is hung, and generate a crash dump that may indicate the cause of the system hang, do the following:

- If the system has a HALT button on the operator control panel:

  1. Press the HALT button to bring the system to the "triple chevron" console prompt (>>>).
     (Note: If the system has a switch for enabling and disabling the HALT button, set that switch to the ENABLE position.)
  2. At the console prompt, type crash and press return.

- If the system does not have a HALT button:

  1. Press the Ctrl/P key sequence at the system console.
  2. At the console prompt, type crash and press return.

These steps will halt the system and initiate the generation of a crash dump, saving a memory image at the time of the halt, and, one hopes, containing information about the original system hang. After the crash dump save is complete, reboot the system to complete the generation of the crash dump.

11.5. SUMMARY

As this chapter outlined, Digital UNIX provides several tools and facilities to assist in identifying, diagnosing, and preventing system problems. Between syslog and binlog, Digital UNIX's logging is very complete, giving you, the system administrator, a great deal of useful information about software and hardware errors. Finally, once a problem is so severe that the system cannot continue, the crash dump facility is available to provide a dump of core memory for faster analysis.

Electronic Resources

A

A.1. MAILING LISTS

There are a couple of mailing lists that are of direct interest to a Digital UNIX system administrator. These mailing lists contain a great deal of useful information and can be an invaluable resource. Be aware, though, that mailing lists can easily overwhelm you with their volume. An active mailing list can and will generate hundreds of E-mails a day. One useful strategy when subscribing to mailing lists is to use an E-mail client with filtering capabilities and to transfer incoming mailing list traffic into another folder for later perusal. In addition, many mailing lists provide the ability to receive "digests" where you are periodically sent a summary of list activity. Such digests typically are sent weekly or monthly depending on the list volume. Some mailing lists are also archived, allowing easy keyword searching through months or years of list activity.

   Note: Always regard information read in a mailing list with caution, especially if the list is unmoderated. While there will always be expert individuals who happily share their experience and knowledge, there are also less experienced folks who, either through error or malice, provide incorrect information to the list. Never blindly believe a single person's contribution.

Always substantiate any piece of information if you are unsure of either its source or validity. Remember as well that even the experts can make an error. Mailing lists are frequently valuable sources of useful and pertinent information, simply tread carefully.

A.1.1. Alpha-OSF-Managers List

The Alpha-OSF-Managers list is a quick-turnaround troubleshooting aid for people who administer and manage Alpha systems running Digital UNIX. Its primary purpose is to provide a Digital UNIX system administrator with a quick source of information for system management problems that are of a time-critical nature. This list allows any subscriber to pose a question to the entire list or contribute to another individual's question.

To subscribe to the list, send an E-mail to *majordomo@ornl.gov* containing the command "subscribe alpha-osf-managers".

The Alpha-OSF-Managers list is archived at:

http://www.ornl.gov/its/archives/mailing-lists/

Additionally, the following URL provides the ability to keyword search the entire Alpha-OSF-Managers list archive:

http://www-archive.ornl.gov:8000/

A.1.2. Digital UNIX Patch List

The Digital UNIX Patch list is a nondiscussion list provided by Digital Equipment Corporation that announces the latest patches on the Digital UNIX operating system and layered software products. These notices cover both Public and Entitled patches. While the Entitled patches are available only to contract customers, the Public patches are readily available via anonymous FTP from:

ftp://ftp.service.digital.com

To subscribe to the list and receive individual patch notices, send an E-mail to *majordomo@data.service.digital.com* containing the command "subscribe dunix-patches".

To subscribe to the list and only receive weekly digests, send an E-mail to *majordomo@data.service.digital.com* containing the "subscribe dunix-patches-digest".

A.2. USENET NEWSGROUPS

There are several USENET newsgroups that may be of interest to a Digital UNIX system administrator. These newsgroups typically have an even higher "noise ratio" than mailing lists, and the recommendation is to be cautious with information presented in a mailing list.

- comp.unix.osf.osf1—The primary Digital UNIX discussion group
- comp.unix.osf.misc—Miscellaneous Digital UNIX discussions
- comp.unix.admin—General UNIX system administration topics
- comp.admin.policy—General UNIX system administration policy issues
- comp.security.unix—UNIX Security
- comp.security.misc—Miscellaneous system and network security
- comp.unix.questions—A forum for general UNIX user questions
- comp.unix.wizards—Advanced UNIX topics

A.3. WEB RESOURCES

The World Wide Web (WWW) has grown tremendously since its inception and is now a valuable resource. Some Web pages are extremely broad in content, while others are narrowly focused or address single topics. The pages listed below are a good starting point for a Digital UNIX system administrator. Many of these pages provide links to other, associated pages. Over time, you will build a personal set of favorite pages.

Note that online resources do change and these addresses may not apply in the future. For example, the acquisition of Digital Equipment Corporation by Compaq may result in some web pages addresses becoming Compaq addresses. Readers may always use a web search engine to identify the new location if an address is not found.

A.3.1. The Digital UNIX Homepage

Digital Equipment Corporation has created a comprehensive Digital UNIX Website with many useful and informative links to other WWW pages related to Digital UNIX at:

http://www.unix.digital.com/

A.3.2. Digital UNIX Frequently Asked Questions (FAQs)

The Digital UNIX FAQ page provides links to various lists of Frequently Asked Questions about Digital UNIX. These FAQ resources are a common resource that should be consulted before contacting Digital for support on an issue.

http://www.unix.digital.com/faqs/faqs.html

A.3.3. Digital UNIX Technical Documentation

Digital Equipment has created a Web resource containing the entire documentation set for Digital UNIX. This includes online versions of the Release Notes, Installation Guide, and System Administration Guide. This online library is an invaluable reference and may be found at:

http://www.unix.digital.com/unix/techncl.htm

A.3.4. The Digital Services Online

The Digital Services Division homepage provides a variety of online services, including access directly to the Digital Mission Critical Services call-logging systems and problem-diagnosis systems, the Digital UNIX patch repositories, and miscellaneous product support information.

http://www.service.digital.com/

A.3.5. Digital UNIX Patch Services

The Patch Services page provides easy access to Digital UNIX patch kits, including publicly available and contract-only patches. Users are permitted to search for individual patches either through a Search and Download utility or via traditional FTP access:

http://www.service.digital.com/html/patch_service.html

A.3.6. The Alpha Systems Firmware Update Page

The firmware update page provides online access to current and past versions of the Alpha system firmware images. In addition, this Web page is also the place to check for interim firmware versions released between regular firmware CD-ROM distributions:

http://ftp.digital.com/pub/Digital/Alpha/firmware/index.html

A.3.7. Digital UNIX Freely Available Software

This page contains a dynamic list of pointers that have been sent in from customers around the world who have made software for DIGITAL UNIX freely available over the Internet for other users of Digital UNIX.

http://www.digital.com/info/misc/pub-domain-osf1.txt.html

A.3.8. Digital DECevent Homepage

The DECevent utility, an optional product that can be used in place of the uerf(8) program, is a highly recommended addition to a Digital UNIX system. The latest version may be downloaded from:

http://www.service.digital.com/decevent/

A.3.9. Tuning DIGITAL UNIX for Internet Servers

This document describes how to tune DIGITAL UNIX to improve the performance of Internet servers, which include Web servers, proxy servers, ftp servers, mail servers and relays, gateway systems, and firewall systems. The recommendations result from testing DIGITAL UNIX systems that run Internet server software such as altavista.digital.com.

Some of the information in this document applies only to systems running the latest version of DIGITAL UNIX or systems that have the latest patches installed. DIGITAL recommends that you install any patches that are recommended for your operating system version. See the DIGITAL UNIX Operating System Patches section for more information.

This document is periodically updated as new information becomes available. For document revisions and information about changes since the last revision, see the Revision History section. You can access the latest version of this document at:

http://www.digital.com/internet/document/ias/tuning.html

A.3.10. The Global Knowledge Network Homepage

The Global Knowledge Network is the company that provides Digital UNIX training for Digital Equipment Corporation. For class summaries and training schedules, see:

http://www.globalknowledge.com/

Recommended Supplemental Reading

B

Some of the Digital UNIX topics mentioned in this book are so broad that they would require an entire book to cover them completely. Happily, there already exist excellent texts on many of these standard UNIX subsystems. Rather than attempting to address these topics, I encourage the reader to refer to one or more of the following titles when working with these topics, some of which are considered the "Bible" of their subject.

B.1. TCP/IP NETWORKING, DNS, NFS, AND NIS

Albitz, Paul, and Liu, Cricket. *DNS and BIND, Second Edition.* O'Reilly & Associates, 1996.

Hunt, Craig. *TCP/IP Network Administration, Second Edition.* O'Reilly & Associates, 1997.

Stern, Hal. *Managing NFS and NIS.* O'Reilly & Associates, 1991.

B.2. SENDMAIL

Costales, Bryan, and Allman, Eric. *sendmail, Second Edition.* O'Reilly & Associates, 1997.

B.3. UNIX INTERNALS

McKusick, Marshall Kirk, Bostic, Keith, and Karels, Michael J. *The Design and Implementation of the 4.4BSD Operating System.* Addison-Wesley, 1996.

Index

Other Books from Digital Press

Alpha Architecture Reference Manual, Third Edition by The Alpha Architecture Committee
1998   1000pp   pb   1-55558-202-8

DCOM Explained by Rosemary Rock-Evans
1998   256pp   pb   1-55558-216-8

OpenVMS Operating System Concepts, Second Edition by David Miller
1997   550pp   pb   1-55558-157-9

Reengineering Legacy Software Systems by Howard Miller
1997   250pp   pb   1-55558-195-1

UNIX for OpenVMS Users, Second Edition by Philip Bourne, Richard Holstein and Joseph McMullen
1998   450pp   pb   1-55558-155-2

Windows NT Infrastructure Design by Mike Collins
1998   450pp   pb   1-55558-170-6

Writing Device Drivers: Tutorial and Reference (Digital UNIX) by Tim Burke, Mark A. Parenti and Al Wojtas
1995   1140pp   pb   1-55558-141-2

Feel free to visit our web site at: http://www.bh.com/digitalpress

These books are available from all good bookstores or in case of difficulty call:
1-800-366-2665 in the U.S. or +44-1865-310366 in Europe.

E-MAIL MAILING LIST
An e-mail mailing list giving information on latest releases, special promotions, offers and other news relating to Digital Press titles is available. To subscribe, send an e-mail message to majordomo@world.std.com.
Include in message body (not in subject line): subscribe digital-press